The Consultant's Handbook

by Flo DiBona

The Consultant's Handbook – KDP Paperback Edition

Copyright 2019 by Flo DiBona

Table of Contents

Acknowledgments

First and foremost, I thank God for giving me the opportunity to write this book. I thank my family for their support, especially Danny Willis for the hours he spent proofreading and providing invaluable feedback. I thank Pastor Sandra Jones for her spiritual guidance, her unwavering belief in me and all I do, and her uplifting words whenever I need them.

Thank you to Ken Pomeroy, Esquire and Colin Grose who, separately, I have worked side-by-side with throughout the years delivering various complex projects. We have shared the good, the bad, and the ugly of consulting, in a profession that often leaves you feeling like a lone island. Your camaraderie during those times made some of the more challenging experiences we shared much easier. Ken, our shared experiences, especially the last, made us stronger and thank God we can look back now and laugh. Colin, we made a great team who at times had to take turns peeling each other off the ceiling with the astounding things we dealt with and faced, but we were always able to work together to solve them. Thank you both for taking the time to review the draft manuscript and lend your valuable time, expertise, insights, observations, and suggestions to make it a much better book.

I thank Barb Munro, co-founder, and Kari Cipriani, Director of IT Talent Management at the Carrera Agency for carving time out of their very busy schedules to review the draft manuscript. Your insights, feedback, and suggestions helped me see the material from a completely different perspective and were extremely helpful.

Many consulting companies are job shops, caring little for the consultant or the appropriateness of their fit with a client or project. Their primary and seemingly only goal is making money and there is little regard or respect for the people making the money for them by delivering products and services to their clients. I want to acknowledge and thank The Carrera Agency for being the first consulting company I have encountered that treats their consultants with respect and views them as talent needing to be placed in the right situation and environment to succeed. They are genuinely interested in the success of both their consultants and their clients, and they always operate with integrity and respect. Thank you to Barb Munro, Morgen Richmond, and Team Carrera for the opportunity you provided me, the tools you gave me to be successful, the unwavering interest in my success, and your continued friendship.

Thank you to the many places where I had the space and environment to work on this book. Thank you to the Extended Stay America in Birmingham, AL, and the Lawndale, CA and Malibu, CA branches of the Los Angeles County CA public library system. Thank you to all the Starbucks outlets and staffs who know me and were so kind to let me spend hours sitting and working. Special thanks to Chris Hatanelas and his wonderful staff at Sacks on the Beach, Redondo Beach, CA where I found an incredible sanctuary to complete this book along with delicious organic foods, and always a welcome, friendly, warm vibe.

Finally, I would like to acknowledge all those who may work in different industries but share common ground in the field of consulting with similar challenges, experiences, and successes. You have brought credibility and professionalism to this field and made it viable for me and others to grow and thrive within it.

Flo DiBona, Redondo Beach, CA, Feb 2014, Revised Apr 2019

Foreword

This book is intended for those individuals interested in becoming a consultant, those curious about the world of a consultant, and those consultants who might be looking for some tips and tricks to make their lives easier.

Consulting is more than a career choice it is a way of life. When starting out it can feel like you must figure everything on your own and that you are the only one on the planet having to figure it out.

Being a consultant affects everyone around you, especially your family. While it can be a very rewarding career, it is also one that can require one-hundred percent of your focus, time, and energy during both business and non-business hours. It can be very hectic at times and requires a very strong worth ethic, a can-do whatever-it-takes attitude, and the tenacity to successfully deliver a product or service within sometimes impossible time constraints.

There is a Catch-22 in the workplace today that didn't exist previously. For most of the twentieth century the workforce went to school, often without higher education, and then went off to work. They apprenticed or started their careers at the lowest levels of a company's career path ladders and worked their way up that ladder by building on-the-job experience. Workers learned new skills and developed their careers through on-the-job training and being partnered with someone who taught them how to do a job. Much of the workforce tended to stay with one company their entire careers and would ultimately retire from the same company they started out in. The children of workers would often join the same company and follow the same career path as their parents.

Higher education was generally reserved for professionals such as doctors, lawyers, nurses, engineers, educators, and accountants. Highly educated people who did not pursue these professions filled upper management positions in companies but at the same time there was plenty of room and opportunity for less educated workers to work their way up the ladder and into these management positions through hard work and experience.

In the late part of the twentieth century as new technologies began to emerge this model began to change. The introduction of new technologies brought with it both opportunities and challenges. Opportunities were everywhere for people to become early adopters and help create, expand, and support new technologies as they emerged. At first there was no school curriculum to support these advances because they were so new, continuously changing, evolving, and expanding. Some of the old workplace model held up as early technology adopters learned about the technologies, how to expand on them, use them, support them, and train others on them. Higher education, while always attractive, was not necessarily essential or prerequisite to advancing a career. At that point in the evolution of the workplace and technology, innovation, imagination, and how well someone grasped the concepts of technology and put them to practical use could often outweigh experience and education in the workforce and in hiring decisions.

As institutional education and the workplace began to catch up and adopt technology, teach it, support it, and use it, the workforce continued to evolve in kind. Many of the jobs and tasks that workers previously performed were replaced by technology solutions. A divide began to occur in the workforce as blue-collar jobs began to disappear. Companies began to require a more educated workforce.

New technology curriculums emerged, and standardized teaching methods, testing, and certifications were developed around them. Widespread use of apprenticeship, mentoring, and on-the-job training models were slowly being displaced by baseline skill sets proven through college degrees programs. Advertisements for help wanted went from "no experience required," and "will train," to "degree required," and/or "experience required." This change created a gap in the potentials of the workforce versus the requirements of the workplace.

By the beginning of the twenty-first century the model changed even further. The world was entering a global market and with it a global workplace. Positions that had previously been filled by middle America's laborers and blue-collar workforce were now being outsourced and shipped overseas to countries who provided cheaper factory labor and cheaper, more educated blue-collar workers.

At the same time, employment practices were becoming much more sophisticated than ever before as formal resource management methodologies emerged. Employment requirements began to refocus on higher education requirements and more experience as the supply of existing workforce resources and newly graduated resources increased and open positions decreased.

Today, competition for jobs is at an all-time high. It has allowed companies to offer less and demand more. Yet another new workplace model has emerged. This one is defined by two distinct workforces; an uneducated, lower-educated, and unskilled workforce; and a higher, highly educated, highly skilled workforce.

This new model offers smaller, narrower opportunities for the workforce. Most positions for the uneducated, lower-education, and unskilled labor force today are part-time offering low wages with no benefits. This practice seems to give hiring companies an advantage by avoiding higher overheads for benefits coverage for non-mission critical positions. For the more educated and skilled workforce the same model exists. While available positions tend to be full-time in nature, they are often temporary, again avoiding higher overhead costs.

Within these two emergent workforce sectors, the demands of employment are more competitive than ever before. "Experience a must," and "advanced degree plus experience," are typical in employment ads today and therein lies the Catch-22. How does someone gain experience when experience is prerequisite to employment and how does someone earn an advanced degree without the means to pay for it?

Temporary positions or consulting positions can be the stop-gap to this dilemma. Staffing or consulting companies have emerged on the employment scene to do the ground work of finding open positions and establishing relationships with hiring companies. The terms "staffing company" and "consulting firm," for the purposes of this book, includes consulting and other agencies who play the role of middleman in pairing clients and resources. For example, in the Information Technology field, the term also includes system integrators and service providers.

Some positions are never advertised publicly and are only available through partner staffing companies. Many larger companies today will only hire resources through a partner staffing company and will not consider outside applicants.

Staffing companies pre-screen and pre-qualify applicants for their clients. They verify work history, references, certifications, education, and run background checks. Their pool of resources is available to clients with little risk to the client. If a position is filled by a staffing company and the resource does not work out for one reason or another the staffing company will often absorb the cost of the resource's salary for their limited time in the position and not pass the cost to the client.

Consulting, contracting, or temporary employment are ideal ways to gain employment, experience, and a foot in the door of a company. Consultant or contract positions are a way to build experience while being gainfully employed. These positions can also open the door of opportunity in other ways. The client gets to observe the consultant's capabilities and value with little or no risk. Quality consultants are sometimes offered full time employment by staffing company clients as permanent positions become available, an opportunity that might not otherwise arise. When a client company can see someone's capabilities and not just read about them on a resume or hear about them during an interview, they are more likely to take a chance on someone who may not meet all their usual prerequisite requirements.

What may start out as a means of gaining employment and experience just might turn out to become a career choice. While full-time employment may be perceived as the holy grail for some, others sometimes find that the career choice of being a consultant provides many rewards a full-time position never will.

Consultant

A consultant (from Latin: consultare, "to discuss") is a professional who provides professional or expert advice in a particular area such as management, accountancy, the environment, entertainment, technology, law (tax law, in particular), human resources, marketing, emergency management, food production, medicine, finance, life management, economics, public affairs, communication, engineering, sound system design, graphic design, or waste management.

A consultant is usually an expert or a professional in a specific field and has a wide knowledge of the subject matter. A consultant usually works for a consultancy firm or is self-employed and engages with multiple and changing clients. Thus, clients have access to deeper levels of expertise than would be feasible for them to retain in-house and may purchase only as much service from the outside consultant as desired.

'Consultant' is also the term used to denote the most senior medical position in the United Kingdom, Australia and Ireland (e.g., a consultant surgeon).

Some consultants are employed by a consult staffing company, a company that provides consultants to clients. This is particularly common in the technology sector. Consultants are often called contractors in the technology sector in reference to their employment contract.

Strategy consultants are common in upper management in many industries. There are also independent consultants who act as interim executives with decision-making power under corporate policies or statutes. They may sit on specially constituted boards or committees.

Consultants work at client places [sites] on behalf of a consultancy or billing company. Some consultants are individuals hired by companies to do work for them on a contractual basis. They are not employees of the company hired to do a specific work. They are expected to do their job ethically and responsibly with minimum supervision.

Source: Wikipedia, the free encyclopedia

con·sul·tant

noun \kən-ˈsəl-tənt\

Definition of CONSULTANT

1. One who consults another

2. One who gives professional advice or services: expert

Source: Thefreedictionary.com

Consulting

There are thousands of consulting firms in the United States and across the world ranging from large global firms to medium and small-sized firms who are sometimes considered specialized boutique firms. Most larger consulting firms offer their consultants extensive training programs and boot camps teaching them the art and business of consulting. Most large firms actively recruit many of their junior consultants from universities prior to, or just after, graduation and usually offer attractive internship programs to promising candidates.

Larger consulting firm client lists usually consist of very large, recognizable companies. It is difficult for most smaller firms to compete with the larger firms for large corporate client contracts due to the expensive process required to qualify for, and participate in, their proposal and selection processes.

Smaller boutique firms often specialize in a very niche piece of the consulting market. Some of the smaller firms are partnered with vendors and offer their consultants reduced rates or free certification programs for their partners' products. To attract qualified talent some of the mid to small-sized companies will also offer limited benefits such as paid holidays and 401K plans to their consultants.

Some of the larger firms and smaller boutique "talent" agencies will only work with deeply experienced consultants having 7 to 10 years or more of relevant industry experience. Most of these consultants are expected to be subject matter experts (SMEs) in their given areas of expertise. These companies charge premium rates for their consultants and cannot afford to deal with junior consultants or those in the process of building their experience and expertise.

In the Information Technology field, the largest four operations consulting firms today are Deloitte Touche, Price Waterhouse (PWC), Accenture, and IBM (not necessarily in that order). KPMG and Ernst and Young (EY) are very large organizations who specialize in the field of accounting. Each industry has field-specific firms that cater to their particular needs.

So, You Want to Be a Consultant ...
So, you want to be a consultant. People who have not consulted for a living or lived the life of a consultant often envy the consultant's lifestyle. Consultants have such a glamorous job and live such an exciting life. They get to travel and see new places, make good money, and are not trapped in a cubicle or behind a desk doing the same thing every day. Free travel, paid expenses, alternate work hours – who could ask for more! Yes, consultants are a lucky bunch…

But Seriously…
So, you want to be a consultant? Consulting can be a very rewarding career choice; but it is not a life conducive to normalcy. It has its rewards and its shortcomings. The biggest shortcoming is the affect it has on the people around you and your relationships with them. It takes strong and often unique bonds to survive this career choice. If you have a spouse, significant other, and/or children make no mistake, they will suffer most from your career choice second only to you. Don't feel too guilty though. At the same time, they will have unique opportunities and experiences that only come from the perks of having a consultant in the family.

Consulting can be exhausting and at the same time invigorating. It is much like an actor and their performance. When you arrive at a client site for the first time, you are the person the client is anxiously anticipating will help resolve an issue or educate them through your presence and experience. Consultants are typically paid very well and with that pay comes a high level of expectation. It is not unusual for an experienced, well reputed consultant to meet a new team for the first time only to hear how much they have heard about them. That type of professional reputation does not come by chance or from a personal Facebook page.

A successful consultant will always strive to meet or exceed expectations while knowing that in some cases success may come by trying to reset those expectations. A successful consultant will also realize that there will be situations and clients that put them in a no-win situation. Learning how to deal best with all situations is an important part of the consultant's value.

Travel is a major part of a consultant's life. This can sound very attractive to someone who is not a consultant. Free travel and reward points! Exotic locations! Many consultants travel most of the time. They follow fairly set patterns of travel and for some, traveling becomes part of their social interaction. Some consulting teams routinely meet at airports to travel to their destinations together. Other consultants travel in the same patterns even though they work for different companies and different industries. When a project is a long-distance commute, consultants typically travel Sunday through Friday or Saturday; Sunday through Thursday; or, when they are really lucky, Tuesday through Thursday.

As a new consultant, the first week of travel can be exhausting but exciting with new surroundings, new people, and new patterns. It isn't so bad and the end of the week comes quickly. By the second week, the bright shine and novelty of this new lifestyle can begin to lose a little luster as home seems just a little further away and more attractive. By the end of three to six months or longer, for most consultants those frequent flier miles do not make up for the time away from home or the wear and tear on your body and your life.

The Good, the Bad, and the Ugly of a Consultant's Life
Consulting can provide a good life for the consultant and their family. The pay is normally significantly higher than someone who is an employee of a company and there can be many perks and freedoms to living the life of a consultant. However, if you are a consultant you will likely take the perks of the position for granted. That's because they quickly become non-perks when you constantly live with them.

For many consultants the biggest perk is travel. Travel is often a requirement and can consume a great deal of a consultant's time. Airline frequent flier miles and hotel loyalty points accumulate quickly when a consultant is on a long-term project or in a field that requires constant travel. Many consultant families enjoy incredible vacations to destinations they could never normally afford due to free hotels and airfares through loyalty programs. However, getting a consultant to travel for vacation is another matter.

When required to travel many or most weeks a year the disruption to home life and the stress of traveling can make a consultant dread the thought of a vacation that includes travel. It can be difficult to get a consultant to take a vacation at all. Often a vacation for a consultant is several days in a row spent at home. This can be frustrating for the rest of the family.

Taking a break for a vacation can be very difficult for a consultant. When they are employed it is often difficult for them to justify the loss of income. For consultants who travel it can be difficult to return to the regime of traveling after a vacation. When a consultant is unemployed it can be difficult for them to justify the expense of the vacation when they have no income and the time taken out of chasing the next project or assignment.

Consultants rarely work doing the same thing day-in and day-out and rarely work in the same environment for long periods of time. This can be very attractive to those sitting in their cubicle day-in and day-out, year-in, and year-out. However, the stability of knowing that cubicle is waiting for them every Monday morning can be a strong argument for an employee to remain an employee and not seek the life of a consultant.

Employment can be a challenge for a consultant and can be very hit-and-miss. Each time a project or assignment ends there is no guarantee there will be another project or assignment waiting. Economic downturns can cause long periods of unemployment for a consultant and along with them the stresses, uncertainty, and instability of joblessness. A consultant is subjected to the constant stress of self-marketing and promotion when seeking out a new project or assignment.

Consultants tend to get employed for what they know and not their potential. Evaluating and weighing the cost of maintaining experience, familiarity with new technology, and qualifications is important. It can be easy for a consultant to get involved in a long-term project and at the end of it find that their skill-set is has become out-of-date and obsolete. It is quite common for a consultant to fulfill the same job role today as they did a decade ago.

Consulting is not necessarily a good fit for someone who has a planned career path in mind.

Consulting can be good, bad, and ugly, all at the same time. It is not a profession for the weak. It requires great self-motivation, self-confidence, stamina, flexibility, and dedication.

Direct Employment versus Consulting

There is an invisible fence that exists in the corporate workplace. It is the fence between full-time employees (or FTEs, as they are referred to) and consultants. There is typically one set of rules for FTEs and another for consultants.

FTEs work full time directly for a company. They have opted for the perceived stability of a permanent position replete with all the trappings. However, the perception and reality of FTEs has changed as the loyalty between employers and employees has lessened over the past several decades. Today, many FTEs job-hop to gain experience in different corporate environments, industries, and technical platforms. They also seek career advancement and increased compensation by changing jobs. On the flip side, some consultants remain on client projects longer than some FTEs remain with a company.

Full-time Employees
FTEs typically have full healthcare benefits, money market funds, paid holidays and vacations, retirement, and other perks to keep them as employees. For consultants, this is known as benefit blackmail. The better the compensation package the more difficult it is to imagine a non-FTE life. As long as you follow the rules and a company does not decide to down-size you may continue to enjoy the generous benefits package.

18

In the past century, most workers were FTEs. The typical career path was to join a company as an hourly low-level employee with little compensation or benefits. Then, through the years, the employee climbed the corporate ladder, gaining more company experience, compensation, and benefits along the way until they reached retirement. While they were on this ladder, it was not unusual for their sons to join the company and start their climbs as well. During this period, most women stayed at home and did not have careers. In today's economy and corporate climate, many companies are laying off FTEs only to turn around and rehire them as consultants thus saving the company expensive compensation packages, taxes, and insurance. In many companies only key positions are now filled by FTEs.

FTEs have very set patterns from the time they arrive at work to the time they leave. They spend years honing these patterns based on reactions, rewards, and promotions. There is a hierarchy to FTEs, a pecking order, one outside the formal organizational structure. Many workplaces are very similar in behavior to an elementary schoolyard or hen house.

Consultants
Consultants are a unique breed. They are temporary, contract employees. At many companies, temporary employees and contract employees have a separate classification from consultants. Most consultants work on a contract or project basis. They contract for the piece of work within a project that they will perform whereas temporary or contract employees typically work purely on an hourly basis and are hired to perform a specific task. Most temporary or contract employees work for an agency who contracts with a client company to provide personnel to perform specific tasks.

There are three types of consultant: Self-employed, W-2

contract consultants, and full-time consultants.

Self-Employed and Independent Consultants
A self-employed consultant works under a contract they make directly with a client company at either an agreed upon hourly rate or an agreed fixed price for a deliverable or agreed piece of work. The work or product to be delivered is usually specified in a Statement of Work (SOW) attached to the contract between them. For example, a technical writing consultant may contract to write a manual or training guide at an hourly rate of $75 per hour for a maximum of 80 hours. They could also contract to deliver the manual or guide for a fixed price of $5000 regardless of the hours it takes to complete the task. The contract describes the agreement between the company and consultant and includes specifics of how much the consultant will be paid, how they will be paid, whether expenses will be reimbursed, and other details agreed to between the two parties. In our example, the SOW will provide the guidelines for how the manual or guide will be written, what the content should include, and may include specifics on how the content needs to be presented based on a company's policies, procedures, and guidelines.

Self-employed consultants are also sometimes known as independent consultants. They are paid the full amount of a contract and are responsible for all income tax withholding and insurance required. Any business expenses related to the work they perform may or may not be reimbursable depending on what is agreed to between the consultant and client company.

All money paid to the consultant is reported on an Internal Revenue Services (IRS) form 1099 and all relevant expenses are deductible. However, if expenses are not a part of the client company contract, the self-employed consultant must absorb all relevant expenses until filing their taxes. Then they can deduct the expenses from the earnings they made from the client contract.

Independent consultants create their own businesses and LLC or S-Corp corporations. In these cases, fees for any consulting they perform are paid directly to the corporation and not to the individual consultant. Taxes are handled at the corporate level based on the type of corporation the consultant operates under.

Self-employed and independent consultants can also contract and work for a staffing company or agency who matches them up with their clients' needs, but they are still treated and paid as an independent, self-employed consultant. Self-employed or independent consultants are typically paid the highest hourly rates available to offset some costs such as taxes and insurance that a company or client does not have to pay.

Companies require self-employed consultants to provide a valid IRS Form W-4. Independent consultants may be required to provide a valid business license, proof of business insurance, and applicable certifications. When a project is complete, self-employed and independent consultants are not eligible for unemployment compensation. Self-employed and independent consultants typically pay quarterly tax payments to the IRS based on their earnings for a previous calendar quarter. Self-employed consultants receive IRS Form 1099 statements of income at the beginning of each year from all clients or staffing companies or agencies they have worked for in the previous year.

Self-employed and independent consultants now account for most consultants because the client company or staffing company or agency assumes no liability for them and is required to provide no benefits. All self-employed and independent consultants are required to file an IRS Form W-9 with their clients whether the client is a direct client or a staffing company. IRS Form W-9 is used to report the consultant's Social Security Number (SSN) or Employee Identification Number (EIN) to the client or staffing company for tax purposes.

W-2 Contract Employee Consultants

The second type of consultant is a W-2 contract employee. These consultants typically work for a staffing company or agency who specializes in supplying client companies with short-term help to fill out or add expertise to a client's existing teams. These consultants usually sign an employment contract with a staffing company or agency for a set hourly rate and are direct employees, or FTEs of the staffing company who screens and hires them. They are paid by the staffing company, not the client, and receive regular paychecks or direct deposits for their work. The staffing company is responsible for deducting required federal, social security, state, and local taxes as well as disability and unemployment insurance contributions. They contribute to social security tax deductions and provide required disability and unemployment insurance for the employee. Staffing companies find clients and projects and match them with the skill sets of their pool of consultants. Staffing companies make their money by adding a premium percentage to the consultants' base hourly rates. Consultants do not get paid for any hours they do not work and do not get paid for holidays or accrue vacation time but they are eligible for unemployment when they roll off a six month or longer project if the staffing company cannot place them on another project or with another client. Some staffing companies the ability to participate in 401K plans and other minimal benefits such as group insurance plan participation usually at 100% out-of-pocket cost. W-2 contract consultants receive an IRS

Form W-2 income statement at the beginning of each year that lists their earnings and deductions.

Full-Time Staff Consultants

The third type of consultant is a full-time employee (FTE) staff consultant. This is often perceived as the holy grail of consulting positions and is becoming more difficult to find. These consultants are typically senior consultants who require an advanced degree and substantial experience. Staff consultants usually work for a staffing company or agency that provides very specific gap resources to clients when they need resources to temporarily back-fill open positions; supplemental resources to add to their existing teams; or temporarily provide project-specific expertise. Staff consultants come at a premium to clients. Their value is in their ability to quickly and easily partner with a client and be highly productive. They offer their client immediate access to their experience, expertise, and knowledge. Staff consultants are often known in their respective industries by their reputation and they can sometimes have a more loyal client base then the staffing company or agency they work for.

Staff consultants are expected to have the highest degree of expertise, integrity, self-motivation, flexibility, and dedication in the industry and set the bar for other consultants. They are usually subject matter experts (SMEs) in their given field based on years of actual experience. Staff consultants are often mentors to more junior consultants, partnering with them to further develop the junior consultant's skills.

Staff consultants receive a regular paycheck where all usual employee tax and insurance deductions are withheld. The staffing company contributes to social security taxes as well as disability and unemployment insurance. Staff consultants also receive all the benefits of an FTE including health insurance, paid vacation time, and sick leave. They may also receive many other benefits and perks such as 401K (retirement) contributions, bonuses, and stock options. Staff consultants are paid whether they are assigned to a client or not.

When a staff consultant is working with a client or on a client project they are considered "billable." Billable means the staffing company or agency bills their client for any hours the staff consultant works. The agency makes its money by adding a premium to the staff consultant's salary. Depending on the contract with the client the rate that the company or agency is paid can be a straight hourly rate equivalent to the staff consultant's base hourly rate or a "loaded" rate where the client pays for the consultant's hourly rate plus all their benefits and overhead. The staffing company or agency pays all reasonable expenses the staff consultant incurs during the course of working for a client. These expense costs may or may not be passed on to the client depending on the contract between the client and the staffing company or agency.

When a staff consultant is not working on a billable project, they are are still paid their regular salary but are considered "non-billable." When a staff consultant is non-billable, they are said to be working on "the bench." When a staff consultant is on the bench, they are typically expected to report to the staffing company or agency offices and support in-house projects and sales efforts, mentor or train other consultants, work on special projects, or attend specialized training to increase their skill set and add value to the pool of consultants the staffing company or agency has to offer its clients. Staff consultants receive an IRS W2 income statement at the beginning of each year listing their earnings, deductions, and contributions.

While staff consultants are perceived as the holy grail of

consulting, the position comes with some challenges. In addition to being a highly competitive position, billable and non-billable hours are very closely scrutinized and if a staff consultant logs too many non-billable hours over a given period of time they run the risk of being reclassified as a self-employed consultant, W-2 contract consultant, or worse, being laid off due to the high rate of overhead costs to support them.

Staff consultants are often subjected to constant travel that leads to burnout, especially when they work for larger consulting firms. Their role becomes one of firefighters, going wherever they are needed to put out client fires.

The Consultant Tool Bag

Consultants bring a virtual set of tools to the table with them when they join a staffing company or directly approach a client. The more tools in a consultant's tool bag, the more likely they are to get hired and the more prepared they are to contribute to a successful engagement. At a minimum, there are a core set of tools every consultant should possess.

Degree
In the highly competitive world of consulting, an advanced degree from a prestigious school can certainly help get a foot in the door. In fact, it has become nearly impossible to enter the consulting field today without a degree. Many consulting positions require a minimum of a bachelor's degree to submit a resume and an advanced degree is often preferred. But it is not the only prerequisite to consulting, experience is equally as important. A degree may get a foot in the door, but a consultant's integrity, reputation, references, and past successes will get them through the door.

If the consultant is in a professional or technical field, they may require proper accreditation, licensing, and/or certification, as applicable. For example, for technical consultants, certifications are a way to distinguish and measure specific skill levels. Once a consultant gains a certification, it is very important to keep the certification current. When companies look at a consultant's qualifications, they want to see the most current certifications and technologies to ensure the consultant provides cutting edge expertise.

Is the cost of a first or advanced degree, or certification worth the payoff? This is a question anyone considering a career in consulting must ask themselves. While the majority of consulting positions require a degree there are still many consulting positions that state "degree preferred," "some college required," or "equivalent experience." In these cases a company or client is willing to consider candidates without a degree if the candidate shows strengths in other areas such as extensive or specific experience.

Experience
What makes a consultant valuable to a client is the experience or expertise they bring to a company, position, or project. Consultants are brought into companies to solve challenges and issues. The challenge or issue can be anything from lack of internal resources to lack of expertise among internal resources. Often consultants are expected to mentor internal resources, working side-by-side with them so when the consultant completes their contract internal resources have learned enough to do what the consultant did or support the end product the consultant leaves behind. Consulting is about experience. The more experience a consultant has, the better equipped they are to recognize, identify, and deal successfully with potential

issues during the engagement. More successful high-profile client engagement experience equates to better credentials, credibility, and value to future clients.

Experience is a Catch 22. It is a double-edged sword because new consultants or recent college graduates do not typically have experience to show for what they know or have learned. The tradeoff for experience is lower salary rates to compete with the higher rates of more experienced consultants as a less experienced consultant builds their experience. Without experience, how do you gain it when everyone requires it? There are a couple of ways to get your feet wet. The first is to consider engagements based on what you can gain in knowledge and experience versus how much you will make. This may seem difficult after the investment of schooling and preparation to become a consultant. However, it will usually pay off in the long run and a lower initial salary base can be an investment in the future. The lower salary will not last forever. The beauty of consulting is that it is usually client to client and project to project. This means that each client and each project provide a unique experience and basis for negotiating salary compensation.

Current experience is very important. The expected technology lifecycle today is eighteen months. That means that the technology being introduced today will be considered obsolete and will be superseded by the next best technologies within an eighteen-month period. This does not only affect technology consultants but almost every consulting field. Consultants almost always use some form of technology in the course of their work from highly complex technologies to more common desktop applications to perform routine day-to-day tasks such as word processing.

For consultants it is key to be exposed to new technologies as they are introduced and emerging. Companies are not always willing to make long-term investments training their resources in the shiniest new technology. Instead, they will often hire short-term expertise to provide technical assistance and resource mentoring to circumvent longer learning curves and slower adaptation of a new technology.

A second way to gain experience is to sell your capabilities. This requires a realistic assessment of your skills, strengths, and weaknesses regardless of professional experience. Market your skill set and strengths and be aware of your weaknesses and work on them. Soft skills such as personality, attitude, and work ethics can sometimes overcome a lack of experience during an interview. Most importantly, be honest. If you don't have the experience, be honest about it. Often, an interviewer will appreciate the honesty and work with you. Always remember the most important asset of a consultant is their integrity. Do not try to sell a client your services to install components on the payload shelf of a satellite if you've never done it before!

Curriculum Vitae, Resumes, and Qualifications
Curriculum Vitae
A Curriculum Vitae (CV) is primarily used in academic circles, medical careers, and technology fields as a replacement for a resume and is far more comprehensive than a resume. A CV typically begins with a brief overview of accomplishments but then includes an individual's comprehensive detailed listing of professional history including every term of employment and technologies used, academic history and credentials, publications, contributions, and significant achievements. In certain professions a CV may also include samples of a person's work. A CV typically consists of many pages. Depending on the industry, some executives and

professionals choose to use short CVs that highlight the focus of their lives and not necessarily their employment or education.

Resumes
In contrast to a CV, a resume is a summary of professional experience and education. Resumes are typically one to two-page condensed summaries of an individual's work history, education, and expertise. Resumes contain short, clear, one to two-line descriptions of experience and a simple listing of education and educational credentials. Consultants may be required to maintain both a CV and resume so either can be used based on the requirements of a specific client and/or project.

Qualifications
Qualifications vary wildly by a consultant's industry focus. For example, consultants in the healthcare and educational fields often have periodic certifications and licensing that are required in order to be considered for a position. In the technology field, certain baseline qualifications such as technology or vendor certifications may be required before being considered. When working in project management, Project Management Institute (PMI) certification may be required by the client. Qualifications can also include such things as security clearances and classifications when a certain security level is required and must be maintained to be considered for a project.

References
References, to an extent, go hand-in-hand with experience. When a consultant has delivered a successful product, service, project, or assignment, it can be an opportunity to build references for future engagements. Note that some organizations have policies that prohibit this practice for legal reasons. But for others, if a manager or supervisor has a positive, successful experience with a consultant they

may be willing to share their positive experience with others in the future.

A consultant should first ensure that a potential reference did indeed have a positive experience before asking whether they would be willing to provide a future reference. This is easily accomplished by a simple conversation discussing the other person's experience, impressions, and satisfaction with the outcome of work the consultant did. There are times when a consultant may think they did an incredible job but when they ask for a reference, the person they ask may share with them a less than satisfactory experience from their perspective. If this is the case, a good consultant will never take it personally but look at the input as an opportunity to use the information as a learning tool to examine the gap between their perspective and the potential reference's, and use the input to improve those areas in the future. Whenever a consultant asks for a reference, they should always thank the other person whether they give the reference or not.

Some people are not comfortable being used as a reference whether their company policy allows it or not. If a potential reference declines the request the consultant should always thank them anyway, not take it personally, and respect the person's position. The last thing a consultant wants to do is leave an uncomfortable impression on someone who has otherwise had a positive experience with them.

Letters of reference are always great tools to have in hand when being considered for new positions but hiring decision makers are usually more likely to want to interact with a consultant's references directly through either email, a telephone conversation, or both. It is common courtesy to warn someone prior to using them as a reference so they can be prepared should someone contact them. Always check with potential references before offering them as references, sharing their email address, or offering their telephone number to others.

A consultant can have a variety of references depending on the type of consulting work they do. References can include previous managers or supervisors; colleagues; students; software end-users; or in some instances, personal references. A pool and variety of references to choose from is a good tool for a consultant to have.

Publications
Publications are a powerful tool for building credibility, reputation, and a following. As a consultant gains experience, they often grow into the position of Subject Matter Expert (SMEs). Whether a consultant becomes a SME or not their experience can provide an opportunity to write about their field of expertise. Published works can be impressive and can influence hiring decision makers.

Publications such as White Papers (reports based on experience, research, or both) provide concise, pertinent information on a given subject. They are usually technical in nature or take the form of specific business challenges with recommended solutions. Other forms of publications can include new product reviews, product or vendor comparisons, and opinion papers on pertinent subjects.

Whether a consultant creates material that is published via their staffing company or independently it is a great way to familiarize clients with their name, area of expertise, and work.

Homework

A successful consultant always does their homework. Homework is just that, work that is typically accomplished on the consultant's own time at their convenience.

Consultant homework can take many forms and varies based on the field or industry a consultant is in.

Administrative
Administrative homework can take many forms. If a consultant travels for a client or project, it can include doing research to find the best deals on airfare, hotels, and car rentals. It can include cost comparisons of multiple airline ticket pricing choices, multiple seat class costs, and in some cases the cost of different close-proximity airport destinations. It can also include comparisons of car rental costs versus taxis or public transportation at the destination, and hotel room rate comparisons.

Administrative homework can also include analysis of recurring monthly business expenses such as cell phone plans; home office equipment rentals versus ownership; and regular transportation alternatives such as automobile rentals and automobile lease options versus ownership comparisons.

Client
A consultant's client homework can be key in being awarded a contract, securing a position or contract, or creating a positive impression with a client.

Client homework may include learning as much as possible about the client. Most information can be easily obtained through a simple Internet search. At times a client will offer up documentation pertaining to their company for a consultant to review. Doing the homework of thoroughly reading any available information before engaging with the client can result in a lasting positive impression with the client.

Information such as a company's history, mission, and goals give a consultant the tools to converse with the client about their company and shows the client that the consultant has a genuine interest in them. When bidding on a contract, thoroughly reading and understanding a Request for Proposal (RFP) or Statement of Work (SOW) to understand the challenges a company faces and the solutions they are looking for can make the difference in submitting a winning bid or proposal. If the company is a publicly traded company (selling stock and recognized by a public stock exchange) a read-through of their latest annual report can provide insight into a company's health, challenges, and bottom line as well as their current and future activities and goals.

Self-Improvement
Self-improvement homework will vary depending on the field a consultant is in. Generally, it includes reading the latest information published in a given field through publications, articles, Internet blogs, and vendor documentation such as user manuals and release notes. The more information in a given field a consultant can obtain, study, and retain, the higher the value and greater the asset to a company and/or client.

Self-improvement homework can also include self-directed and self-study programs to improve existing skills and expertise. Based on the specific field of a consultant there are often free courses and seminars available, many of them available online and on-demand. Others are often available for a nominal fee that can be well worth the investment of time and money to gain the knowledge they offer.

Health

Health is an important part of a consultant's tool bag whether a consultant travels or works from home. A good consultant will do everything in their power to stay healthy even when they are at greater risk of becoming ill due to the nature of their profession. Regular doctor checkups can help keep a consultant on track in remaining healthy.

It can sometimes help for a consultant to take a daily multi-vitamin to help keep the immune system healthy. During the cold and flu season it can also sometimes help to take Vitamin C to give the immune system an additional boost. When a consultant eats right, exercises regularly, and takes precautions not to contract the illnesses they are continuously exposed to it can help keep them healthy when those around them find themselves constantly sick. Whether traveling or at home diet, exercise, and regular check-ups are three important things to remaining healthy.

Traveling Consultants
Traveling consultants can run a higher risk of contracting illnesses due to their constant exposure to other people, new environments, different geographic locations, weather patterns, and higher potential exposure to unfamiliar allergens and pollutants.

Unfortunately, consultants have no control over others who go to work sick and expose those around them to their illnesses. As a consultant travels it is not unusual for people to be coughing and sneezing next to them on airplanes. Healthy consultants have good hygiene habits like washing their hands often, especially when they are exposed to others who are ill or coming down with a cold or the flu. They also take extra Vitamin C during peak seasons when colds and flues are spreading to help keep their immune systems healthy and strong.

Traveling consultants can find it difficult to eat healthy while on the road. Most of the time the only food choice a consultant on the road has is eating out and that choice seldom includes healthy foods. Many consultants have eaten every take out and restaurant offering there is because they have been on the road for so long. While some hotels offer free breakfast grab-and-go service or buffets, to keep costs down these offerings often consist of non-organic options laden with high fructose corn syrup and Genetically Modified Organisms (GMOs). To save time many consultants each lunch at fast food restaurants where, again, the options are usually high fructose corn syrup and GMO heavy.

Diet is a very important part of remaining healthy and although it can be challenging to eat healthy on the road, it can be done. Looking for restaurants that offer organic options and substituting some fast food meals with fruits or salads can help. Many consultants will seek out a local health food store when they arrive at a new location and buy healthy snacks and organic fruits. Consultants who stay at hotels with kitchenettes will often buy and prepare their own healthy meals and avoid the pitfalls of constantly eating out.

Keeping snacking to a minimum will help a consultant's overall diet and health. Consultants often snack mindlessly due to loneliness and stress. Being mindful of snacking habits can help a consultant keep the habit under control and improve their overall health.

When a consultant does snack, substituting traditional unhealthy snacks with an organic or healthy alternative is a good practice. An example of this is substituting organic trail mix or fruit for a bag of greasy, high salt content chips. Eating healthy can be difficult but a smart consultant will look at it as a challenge and seek out creative ways to overcome it.

Regular exercise is another element in remaining healthy. Exercise can be an excellent way to reduce stress. It can be very difficult to find a place or the time to exercise regularly when on the road. However, many hotels offer fully equipped workout rooms and pools to their guests. A consultant interested in staying healthy will seek these services and facilities out and use them regularly while on the road. When there are no exercise facilities where a consultant is staying, taking brisk walks or runs can be an easy, no-cost alternative that can help keep the consultant in shape and healthy.

Work-at-Home Consultants

Work-at-home consultants must also be sure they remain in good health. Their health can affect their availability and can affect their effectiveness in performing tasks. A work-at-home consultant can have health challenges that differ from a traveling consultant.

When consultants have children, they are constantly exposed to, and bombarded by, colds, flues, viruses, and other germs. Children can be walking germ incubators as they share common toys and other items that have been exposed to many other children. A smart consultant keeps their immune system in good health by taking extra vitamin C during peak illness seasons and by washing their hands after interacting with children and items exposed to others.

For consultants who work from home it is very easy to get from their work space to the kitchen – many consultants say it is too easy. Their favorite foods and snacks are always just a short walk away. Some consultants say that their refrigerator knows them by name and calls to them constantly. Another pitfall for a consultant working at home is stopping often to reward themselves with treats for work well done. It may take a consultant some effort to overcome these bad habits and it can be difficult. Keeping the kitchen stocked with healthy, low-fat snacks and fruits to substitute for more unhealthy choices can help counter these pitfalls. It can also help to establish a regular schedule during the day for snack breaks and lunch.

A consultant who normally travels and is at home between trips or projects can have the additional challenge of having eaten most every take out and restaurant chain offering available while on the road and then finding themselves craving these unhealthy foods when they are at home. The family of a consultant may also look at eating out as a special occasion and press the consultant to enjoy eating out together with them. Making eating out an occasional and special event can help counter this tendency and at the same time allow the family to enjoy a special night out with their consultant family member.

Establishing a regular exercise routine can be difficult. Getting back to a routine can be even more difficult when a consultant is away from home so much of the time. There are many excuses a consultant can come up with not to exercise when they are at home. When a consultant establishes a regular exercise routine for when they are home it helps them find their way back to it easier when they return. Finding activities that a consultant can participate in with family members or friends can also help make it easier to get back to regular exercise without it feeling like another task or chore.

Hardware

Certain hardware, while in most cases not a hard requirement to be a consultant, are highly recommended and often expected and essential for a professional consultant. While the following hardware is part of a typical consultant's tool bag, remember that it is the consultant, their experience, knowledge, integrity, reputation, and expertise - not the material things loaded with all the latest bells and whistles - that make a consultant attractive and an asset to a staffing company or client.

Cell Phone

A cell phone is a lifeline to clients, colleagues, team members, and a consultant's family members. The more accessible a consultant is to their client, team, and colleagues, the more comfortable they feel that the consultant is there for them if and when they need them. During business hours accessibility to a consultant can be very important for a client. However, some clients prefer a consultant only use a hard line provided to them at an assigned desk on site at a client's facility. This is often the case for monitoring and security purposes. A consultant should always be aware of, and respect, a client's policy for cell phone use.

During non-business hours, a consultant should be flexible based on the engagement or project to determine whether client contact is necessary. For example, when working with international teams in multiple time zones, although it may not be normal business hours for a consultant, they may need to be available during non-business hours to distant team members due to time zone differences.

Although a cell phone can be a direct link to mobile applications such as YouTube, Facebook, Twitter, and other social network platforms that can keep you entertained for hours, it is a piece of business equipment during business hours and should never be used for those purposes during such times. Sitting in a cubicle playing Angry Birds is never acceptable use of a cell phone during business hours. Imagine a client, paying premium rates for a consultant's services, seeing that consultant's postings and comments to virtual friends on a social network when they are suppose to be working on client tasks.

Although a cell phone can be a lifeline to family away from home it should only be used for personal use during breaks, lunch, or during non-business hours. The only acceptable use of a phone for personal use during business hours is in the case of an emergency. This is an essential factor in a consultant's professionalism, credibility and reputation with a client and in the consultant community.

When evaluating cell phone service plans a consultant must look at a service provider and plan that will work for their anticipated use and within their anticipated travel zone. It does no good if a consultant selects a local service provider and plan with a low monthly charge if they cannot call outside a local area, cannot get service, or are charged a premium when traveling.

A cell phone equipped with conferencing, speaker phone, and network/Internet capabilities for such things as email will allow the consultant to function and be accessible while mobile. Smart Phones with these multiple capabilities are becoming more and more affordable as new technologies and competition between service providers continues to emerge. Whether a staffing company or client reimburses for cell phone service or not, unless they have a preferred carrier they work with, shop for the most cost-effective plans available. Many service providers now offer all-inclusive plans at reasonable monthly rates. If monthly expenses are not reimbursed, the business use of a cell phone is tax deductible.

Laptop, Tablet, or Desktop Computer
A laptop can be one of the most essential pieces of equipment (along with a cell phone) that a consultant has, especially if working off-site or from home. This is particularly true for technology consultants and consultants who are routinely required to write reports, work with spreadsheets, or those who rely heavily on email as their main means of business communication. Traveling consultants can spend many hours in airports and hotel rooms working on projects.

A consultant may need to consider weight, size, and battery life when selecting a laptop, based on their anticipated need. Carrying a heavy laptop around for extended periods of time can cause painful back, neck, and shoulder issues. Consultants often find themselves in places with no electrical outlet and may need to work off a battery for extended periods of time. If a consultant plans to work during airline flights, they will need their laptop to fully open even when a passenger in front of them reclines their seat.

Tablets can be a handy tool for more lightweight duty than a laptop. For those consultants who only need a device for accessing their calendars, email, and taking notes on the fly a tablet device may work as a substitute for a laptop and be all they need. However, if heavy keyboard input and data files such as documents and spreadsheets are required, there is currently no substitute for a laptop.

Desktop computers may sometimes be necessary for consultants who work in more technology-demanding fields such as software developers, engineering, music production, graphic arts, and gaming. Often in these consultant fields the additional computing, memory, and graphics capabilities of a desktop computer are essential for carrying out assigned tasks. If a consultant in these fields is not working at a client site, they may need to invest in a powerful desktop computer for remote work.

There are times when a company and/or client will supply a desktop computer or laptop because they prohibit the use of personal computers on their networks for security reasons. In those cases, the consultant should always treat the equipment with respect as if it were their own. Never use client equipment for any personal use. This includes a client's network and Internet connection. Even when a client offers, it is never recommended to use their network for personal use. For one thing, the consultant relinquishes all rights to privacy. More importantly, the consultant is there to do a job and deliver a product. The client is paying a premium rate for their services and/or product and even the perception that a consultant is focused on personal tasks instead of client/company tasks can leave a permanent negative impression whether something is said or not. This negative perception can carry through to affect future or follow-on work with that client and in some cases can even affect the ability to secure work with other clients because of word-of-mouth.

When computer equipment is supplied by a client or company, at the end of an assignment, contract, or project, the consultant should always ensure all client/company owned equipment is returned in the same or better condition than when it was received. The consultant should also have the client/company issue a receipt for any returned equipment so there is no question later whether it was turned in or not. Receipts should, at a minimum, include make and model numbers along with associated serial numbers.

Software

Microsoft or Open Office
The Microsoft Office® (MS) suite is essential software for almost any consultant. While it can be relatively costly to purchase, there are free equivalents such as Open Office by Apache or Oracle that have the same basic capabilities and can produce a compatible output file that MS products can interact with. At a minimum, the suite includes word processing, spreadsheet, and presentation applications.

Adobe Acrobat
Another software essential is Adobe Acrobat Reader. This software enables the user to read Portable Document Files

(PDFs) that are used universally throughout the business world. Depending on the ongoing needs of a consultant, the full Adobe Acrobat product versus the Reader version may be needed. The full version of Acrobat includes, among other things, the capability to create PDFs and digitally sign them.

Microsoft Visio and Project
A consultant may also require MS Visio and MS Project depending on the type of consulting they are involved in. Visio is used for diagramming organizational charts, flow charts, process flows, hardware and software layouts, room layouts, and includes industry-specific tools and icons to represent objects. It is usually a required software application for project managers and software analysts.

MS Project is used to plan and track all aspects of a project including project phases, tasks, resources, timelines, and budgets. It is typically needed if the consultant is assuming a project management role.

In most cases, the company or client will provide any equipment and software needed to complete a task. However, it is strongly recommended to at least be familiar with these software applications.

Email, Calendar, and Contact Management
A good application for managing calendars and contacts is crucial to maintain a schedule and a professional network of colleagues and business acquaintances. There are many free calendars and contact applications available and many, such as MS Outlook or Google's Gmail, are available online.

The MS Professional Office suite includes MS Outlook which can be set up to manage email, contacts and calendars. Most companies use Outlook for their corporate mail system, so it is best, at a minimum, to at least be familiar with it and how it works.

Other Tools

Professional Email Account
A professional email account can be as simple as a free web-based account such as Google's Gmail – (user name)@gmail.com or MS Outlook – (user name)@outlook.com. A professional email account is distinguished from a personal one by using it only for business purposes and assigning it a professional sounding user name. Examples of professional email addresses would be John.Smith@, JSmith@, or SmithJ@.

Professional consultants do not use addresses that would likely be more appropriate with family, friends, or casual acquaintances. Examples of user names that would not be appropriate to use professionally would be Rockmyworld@, Avengingwarrior@, or Weed4U@.

A professional email account should be one that easily and quickly identifies your professional name to others. The exception to this would be if everyone knows you professionally by a specific online user name as, for example, can be the case for a gaming consultant. In this case, if a consultant has a recognized online user name of Avenging Warrior, for example, Avengingwarrior@ might work. Otherwise, consultants use their professional (usually proper name) on email accounts.

Credit Card
A consultant cannot survive for long without a major credit card. Credit cards are needed to secure airline flights, hotel rooms, and car rentals. They are also required to secure payment for incidentals during hotel stays. It is strongly recommended consultants use a separate credit card for

business expenses only. This will make the consultant's life a great deal less complicated when filing their income taxes and if they use an accountant, it will make their work a lot easier. Whenever possible it is a good practice to pay off credit cards in full each month to avoid interest and higher balances on the account.

Some credit cards offer travel and rental car insurance. These offerings can be beneficial and offset some annual premium costs.

Debit cards are not credit cards. While most things can be reserved and paid for with a debit card, some things like car rentals require a credit card. If obtaining a credit card is a challenge a consultant may consider a secured credit card. Secured credit cards are issued by banks who require the cardholder to deposit funds into an account. The money deposited in the bank account cannot be withdrawn or used but remains held there as security to guarantee payment for any future charges to the credit card. Secured credit cards can be easier to obtain for those with challenging past credit histories, no credit history, or low credit scores.

In some cases, a company will arrange travel for a consultant and arrange direct payment for airfare and hotel costs. However, when renting a car, the individual must present a valid credit card in their name when picking up the car.

When a company does reimburse travel expenses they typically do so after the fact, based on actual receipts. That means a consultant may potentially float (pay up front) travel expenses on their credit card for as long as it takes to submit an itemized expense report for payment and actually get reimbursed. During this period, the consultant will be required to continue making payments on their credit card and can accrue non-reimbursable interest on any unpaid balances.

Global Positioning System

Global Positioning System (GPS) access is often very useful for a traveling consultant. It can be an essential when a consultant is trying to find their way around a new city, especially when the consultant flies into a new city and has a very small window of time to find their way from an airport to a client site.

In the past, GPS devices were very costly and often very unreliable at mapping out where you needed to go. However, with technological advances, today's GPS devices are becoming more and more reliable and affordable and often can be rented at the car rental counter right along with a car rental. There are now many GPS mobile applications available for smart phones. Providers such as Google offer free GPS mobile applications that can be downloaded onto a smart phone, are very reliable, and work well.

The Starbucks Club

Like it or not Starbucks is a way of life for most consultants. While not a hard requirement, for many consultants the office away from home is the nearest Starbucks.

Starbucks is perfectly geared for the non-conventional existence of a consultant. Whether meeting clients, colleagues, applicants, or management, Starbucks provides an easily accessible common public place to meet. They provide a free wireless Internet connection along with their coffee and tea products. Located in almost all major airports, near most major business centers, on almost every street corner in urban areas, open early, late closing, they are often the easiest place logistically for meeting up with others and for holding impromptu meetings. Starbucks provides instantaneous common ground for business professionals and are found in almost every area of the country.

Starbucks has become such an accepted way of business life there are some companies that actually list the local Starbucks as a meeting destination on their internal available conference room lists for scheduling meetings.

Patronizing Starbucks can easily become a costly business (and personal) expense. Joining the free Starbucks membership program can help offset a small amount of those costs with perks such as free drinks, discounts, special offers, and a quick, easy way to pay for Starbucks products using a smart phone and the Starbucks' free mobile application. Quick payment can be especially useful when running to catch a flight at an airport or getting back to your table when conducting a meeting.

Consultant Skill Sets

There is a core set of foundation skills that every consultant should possess. Based on the consultant's focus, field, and industry, additional skills may be required. This core set of skills has been broken down here into Hard Skills and Soft Skills. They are a combination of learned skills and people, or common-sense skills.

Hard Skills

Hard skills are defined as skills that can typically be measured and quantified in some way. Even new consultants are almost always expected to have some basic hard skills.

Typing

Typing is an essential skill needed for all aspects of consulting. No matter what field a consultant is in typing is necessary for creating reports, correspondence, documentation, and often for taking notes and meeting minutes.

The more proficient a consultant is with typing the less time they spend hunting and pecking around a keyboard. One-finger and hunt-and-peck typing is often perceived by others as inefficient and as a sign that a consultant is less than professional. Although the wave of the future for data input is voice recognition, typing is still a basic skill that will be required for several years to come.

Writing

Writing is a basic skill that anyone can master. The secret to mastering good writing skills and habits is simple: READ WHAT YOU WRITE. It is absolutely amazing the mistakes authors make because they do not read what they write. Reading aloud can quickly help identify any issues with what was written. If it doesn't sound right, chances are pretty good it is not right. Always listen to how it sounds to determine if it sounds correct. The more a consultant writes the more proficient they will become through practice.

The style of writing a consultant uses is a very specific style and generally follows the style of technical writing where sentences are clear, concise, to the point, and avoid unnecessary words or sentences. Clichés, gobbledygook, and slang are not used in technical writing.

Consultants are always writers. A consultant begins writing with their resume or Curriculum Vitae. A consultant must be able to concisely describe their experience in short, clear, concise descriptions that include company, title/role, description of responsibilities, goals/accomplishments, and technologies used (if applicable).

During a consulting engagement a consultant may be required to write reports, marketing or legal draft documents, policies and procedures, instruction or technical documents, guides, plans, test scripts, or training material, depending on their role and area of consulting. High quality writing is a fundamental skill of a good consultant.

In most consulting engagements a product is created and/or a service is delivered. Part or all of the delivered product or service is documentation. That documentation is as much a part of the product or service as any widget created or line of code. It is the artifact the consultant leaves behind when they leave a client and that artifact is part of their reputation. It is the impression left with a client long after the consultant is gone. It can also be part of the word-of-mouth, good or bad, that follows a consultant.

Analysis

No matter the field of expertise, consultants are required to be analysts on the run. When a consultant steps into a new assignment, they need to quickly learn all aspects of the client environment. The client's expectation is that the consultant will hit the ground running. The result is that a consultant must be able to quickly assess the environment or situation and understand the client's needs, expectations, options, and solutions in context with that environment. They must quickly provide a viable, attainable, reasonable solution to meet the client's needs.

A simple, successful formula for analysis is: A) Assess what assets and resources are available for use; B) Assess any constraints; C) Articulate the issue, problem or pain point being addressed by the effort; and D) Based on the given environment, available resources, and constraints define options that can address and resolve the issue, problem and/or pain point.

To determine the recommended option, the merits and risks (pros and cons) of each option need to be identified. Each pro and con is then weighted and scored to determine the best option to recommend.

Analysis paralysis is worth mentioning here because it occurs so frequently in the consulting world. Analysis paralysis is a term used within the consulting world when the analysis becomes more involved and complex than the solution. When this phenomenon occurs it is typically circular, unproductive and never-ending.

Analysis paralysis can cause timelines to slip and budgets to overrun on a regular basis in projects. It can become especially costly during technology projects when it happens during the development phase of the project at a time when all analysis should have been completed. During development, a design has already been created and a solution is being built. If the solution is second-guessed at that point or a critical element has been omitted, it can halt or even kill a project.

To avoid analysis paralysis, good planning is essential. Setting limits on data collection, time for analysis, and development of recommendations is key to avoiding this condition. It is also important to have a process in place for reporting, recording, tracking, and implementing additional changes to a solution so that if changes are required they are managed with minimal or no impact to existing budgets and timelines.

Presentations
Creating presentations is a necessary and essential skill for many consultants. The exception are highly technical consultants such as programmers and laboratory resources; task-specific consultants such as software testers, technical writers, and healthcare professionals; and those who work

in fields where reports are more often used as the primary communications tool.

In many fields, presentations are a common tool for effectively communicating ideas and concepts, and are often also used as a means of reporting progress. Presentations consist of a collection of individual slides, referred to as a slide deck, that are projected for a group to see. They are also often distributed to an audience electronically or in hard copy. Presentations are used to market products and services, provide management updates, and they are frequently used as the backbone of training material.

Building a presentation or slide deck is easier to tackle when it begins with an outline. This provides a rough storyboard of the flow of the presentation. When drilling down to individual slides within it, the focus of each slide should be kept on the message that the slide is conveying in context to the overall message of the presentation. If there is no message in a slide, it should not be in the deck. If the message is not clear, concise, and easily identified it should be reworked because the audience will not receive the message.

Presentation layout and writing are skills requiring a unique style of writing. The layout must be simple and easy for the audience to consume while the text must be short, clear and concise. Bullets are often used to list items in a slide. These bullet points are used as visual cues during a presentation for emphasizing key points that the presenter can elaborate on verbally. Written notes can also be included in presentations to elaborate further on a point or concept, or to direct members of the audience to additional information or reference material. Presentation notes can be published along with the slide deck for distribution to the audience, or they can be used only by the presenter.

Many consultants have a library of slides to choose from that they go to when creating a new slide deck. This catalog of slides is a collection of slides that have been proven successful in past presentations and can easily be modified based on need. This library is built over time and allows the consultant to hone and sharpen their base set of slides. A good consultant never needs to create a slide presentation from scratch, but instead begins with their library.

Presentation software such as Microsoft PowerPoint or Open Office Presentation have a wide breadth of capabilities including embedded audio, video, animation, and special effects such as transitioning between slides. It is fine to use the full capabilities of the software and build a massively sophisticated, dazzling, spectacular presentation but if the message is not clear and simple the time was wasted because the message will likely be lost. Always keep the audience in mind and keep the message simple.

If a consultant does not possess the skills necessary to put together a set of slides with the standard software available it is highly recommended they look into a class to learn these skills. A presentation can make or break a consultant. It is often a primary communication tool for articulating and sharing information with clients and management.

Soft Skills

Soft skills (sometimes referred to as "people" skills) are essential to the success of a consultant. They are the skills we learn to use and hone when dealing with people and situations. Soft skills are often as important, or more important, than hard or trade skills learned in school. Consultants need a bagful of soft skills to deal with the diverse array of people and situations they often face daily.

Soft or people skills are used to collaborate and communicate with people. Often consultants are expected to blend with, or create, teams of people to complete a task, project, or deliverables. Within these teams are multiple personalities, skill sets, egos, agendas, and moods. Managing all of them is essential to the success of the consultant, the team, the deliverable, the company, and the client.

Attitude

Attitude is like possession as the old saying goes – it is nine-tenths of the law of a successful consultant. A positive attitude will always attract. Conversely, a negative attitude will always repel.

A consultant's attitude sets the stage for the ultimate success or failure of themselves, a project, task, client experience, and the staffing company they may represent. The overall attitude of a consultant tends to precede them wherever they go. A consultant's attitude, positive or negative, leaves a lasting impression on the client, the consultant themselves, the staffing company they may represent, the teams they work with, and everyone they meet.

A positive, cooperative, enthusiastic attitude helps make each experience positive for everyone involved and sets an example for others. It becomes a part of the consultant's overall reputation as they build more and more experience.

A positive attitude includes a can-do outlook, even when others seem to think something cannot be done or will not be successful. Part of a consultant's unspoken job is to be a cheerleader of sorts. Often, they are brought into a situation or onto a project because a client is experiencing issues or pain points. While a can-do attitude may sometimes be resented or resisted at first, the more the consultant's attitude conveys confidence and remains positive, the more likely they are to promote enthusiasm, convert naysayers, and turn a situation around to a successful outcome.

When dealing directly with clients, attitude is not only a reflection of the consultant, but it is also a reflection of the organization they may represent. A consultant is always wearing the hat of an ambassador whether they are advocating and promoting themselves as an independent consultant or as a representative of a bigger staffing company team of consultants.

Patience

Patience is always a virtue, but it is especially so for a consultant in many aspects of their careers and home lives. Patience is particularly important when dealing with clients, client team members, and other consultants. There are likely going to be times when a consultant finds themselves working with someone who may not have the level of expertise they have, do not grasp concepts as quickly as they do, or learn at the pace required to receive the information a consultant needs to transfer to them.

In these instances, a consultant needs to have the patience to understand the other person's challenge so they can find the most effective way to overcome it. Sometimes that may mean spending extra time with a team member to bring them up to speed, sometimes it may mean changing an approach to something, and sometimes it may mean resetting expectations of what an outcome will be. In any case, a consultant is expected to find a solution to the challenge, not by throwing up their hands in frustration or throwing a temper tantrum. Frustration and tantrums can be the death knell of a consultant.

Flexibility

Flexibility is a very desirable trait of a good consultant.

Very seldom is there only one way to do something. There are clients and times when an alternative route may be desired and a consultant's flexibility, cooperation, and attitude will play an important role in how smoothly and quickly an approach or course is changed.

There may be times when a change in direction will seem ill-conceived or illogical. It will still require that a consultant be flexible with the change because often a consultant is not privy to all the factors involved in a decision. Sometimes, while it may seem to be detrimental to a successful outcome, a change or decision may be what a client wants (right or wrong) and ultimately the saying, "the customer is always right," is indeed true. The customer is the one paying the premium for a consultant's time. While it is the responsibility of a consultant to point out any risks an ill-conceived decision might involve, it is also the responsibility of the consultant to remain flexible and proceed the way a client wants them to.

Cooperation

Cooperation will often be required at some point during an engagement depending on the field a consultant is in, the client, and/or the team they are assigned to,. The more willing a consultant is to cooperate with others and contribute to an environment of cooperation, the more likely they are and all involved are to have a positive experience and outcome. Even further, consultants are often looked upon to bring a spirit of cooperation to a situation where none previously existed. The best way to do that is always through example.

In many situations a consultant is expected to perform with a team. A cooperative spirit is especially important when working under these conditions. Helping other team members be successful and even taking a back seat to another team member in order for them to have an opportunity to shine can have a long-term positive result on the team, the outcome, and the reputation of a consultant. A consultant is most effective and successful when they are not trying to be a superstar but instead are working to make superstars of those around them. A key people skill for a consultant is creating a win-win environment and situation for all parties involved.

Observation

Consultants are required to figure out the lay-of-the-land very quickly. They need the ability to quickly and efficiently evaluate the political, social, and organizational environment they are in. Good consultants hone their observation skills by watching and learning the interactions, politics, personalities, and competency levels of the people around them. The more effective a consultant's observation skills the quicker they can fit in to contribute and share their expertise with those around them.

Articulation

Articulation is the ability to speak and communicate clearly, distinctly, and effectively. Articulation is not about accent. We all have accents whether we think we do or not. Articulation is the ability to speak fluently using language that is easy to understand.

A consultant does not need a barrage of words, overly-sophisticated language, or jargon to convey their thoughts, ideas, or concepts. In fact, when too many words or abstract words are used to communicate it is referred to as "gobbledygook," and the thought, idea, or concept is completely lost in the language used to try to convey it. Using jargon or gobbledygook will often make the listener or audience suspect that the speaker needs to use it to hide the fact that they really do not know what they are talking about.

There are times when an audience or listener does not have a strong command of language either because the language being used is not their first language or because they simply do not excel in language skills. When a consultant is not articulate it can leave that audience or listener feeling unjustly inadequate or diminished because they did not understand. A good consultant will always use concise, clear, relatively simple language. The audience will appreciate it and the message will have a much better chance of being received, understood, and retained.

Communication

Good communication skills are essential in the consulting world. Consultants are frequently expected to work unsupervised and with that comes the responsibility of being able to communicate with others when the need arises.

Communicating issues, risks, or challenges that can affect the outcome of a task or overall project is very important for the consultant and the client and/or staffing company. When to communicate can be a fine line. While a consultant does not want to cry wolf, they do want to make others (especially management or direct supervisors) aware as early as possible so everyone has an opportunity to resolve the situation and minimize any risk. No one ever wants to be blindsided, especially not management who are ultimately responsible for a deliverable or project's outcome. An open dialog with supervision, management, and a consultant's team will help everyone be successful.

How a consultant communicates with others is equally as important as the act of communication itself. Client and/or staffing company guidelines and procedures can often dictate the method of communication, but which avenue to use can sometimes be a gray area. A general rule of thumb is to verbally share any concerns with an immediate supervisor or manager. If an issue or risk is serious, there are often procedures in place to deal with communicating it to others. Most often this will involve documenting the issue or risk in some way. That documentation can be as simple as an email describing the issue and/or risk, or a formal internal system for logging it where others can access it, follow up, and manage it.

Another form of communication that is often overlooked is providing positive feedback when things are going right or someone is doing a good job in helping make a task or project successful. Even if a consultant is not in a client's formal chain of command, a word to a manager or supervisor about another team member's positive contribution is a win-win situation. It can provide a third-party perspective for the manager or supervisor to consider. It can speak to the character and confidence of the consultant when they give others kudos and credit without expecting something in return. It also helps strengthen camaraderie and good will within a team environment. Just think about how good it feels when someone notices and appreciates it when you are doing a good job.

Reliability
Reliability is a fundamental soft skill for a consultant. Consultants are paid very good money and are expected to be where they say they will be when they say they will be there and do what they say they will do when they say they will do it. The reliability of a consultant is a key element of their integrity and a major factor in their reputation and ultimate success.

When a consultant is reliable everything goes more smoothly in the task or project they are involved with. Conversely, when a consultant is not reliable it can have a substantial effect on a task, a project, their success, and the success of any team they are working on or with. It also can have long-term consequences for the consultant. Whether a consultant is reliable or not it will follow them wherever they go.

There can be significant impacts and unintentional consequences when a consultant is unreliable. Imagine a consultant who has not done what they said they would do when they said they would do it. This can affect several down-stream tasks that are dependent on what the consultant said they would do. For example, if a software development consultant has not completed the development or coding, they committed to complete in a specific time frame, it can impact a team of testers waiting to receive the code for testing. This can impact when the final software is released which can impact end-user training and the end-users themselves who are waiting for the software to be up and running. In many cases, this can ultimately introduce new risks to a project, task, or deliverable and have a significant negative impact on overall timelines and budgets.

Another example of the impact of not being reliable is being late for a meeting or not showing up at all. While this may not seem like a big deal, it can be very costly to a client and/or company. Every person sitting waiting for the consultant is being paid a salary whether they are sitting there waiting or being productive and working on the goal of the meeting. The cost associated with the consultant not being on time or showing up is the prorated salary or hourly wage of each of the attendees, times the amount of wasted time spent waiting or having to reschedule another meeting to accomplish what was intended to be accomplished in the original meeting. When there are three, five, ten or more other attendees this figure can quickly become substantial. This does not take into account the time each attendee loses when they could be working on other tasks and the frustration it can produce. This is an intangible cost that will remain part of the impression a consultant makes on each of these individuals. In the case of causing a meeting to be rescheduled, the impact can also include the direct and indirect costs of reserving a conference room for a second meeting.

A good consultant always strives to be reliable.

Presentation Delivery
For those consultants in fields where presentations are used as a primary form of communication, in addition to the hard skill of being able to create a presentation slide deck a consultant must be able to deliver the presentation and speak to each slide in it. Slides are used as a visual queue for the narrative component of a presentation.

The style of delivery will be based on the unique delivery style of a consultant and the specific circumstance. The presenter might interactively solicit comments and questions during the presentation of each slide. Alternatively, the presenter might want to keep a certain pace and hold all comments and questions until the end of a presentation after the material has been presented.

Whatever the approach, a private script should be developed to articulate what will be said while narrating the presentation. The script sets the stage for the pace and tone of the presentation. It is used to fine-tune the narrative and as a tool to practice the presentation before it is formally delivered. It helps the presenter to become familiar with the tone and flow of the presentation and become comfortable with speaking about its content. Typically, a script is written around each slide in the deck.

The level of detail of a presentation script depends on the consultant. It can be a word-for-word script or a broad outline of speaking points for each slide. As part of the script or practicing the script the consultant should include pauses for the audience to absorb the information being presented. The consultant should also identify and anticipate any spots that may invoke questions, comments, or reactions. The presenter should always keep their audience in mind, not only as they create the presentation content, but as they script it or speak to it.

If a consultant does not possess the skills to both put together a set of slides and be able to speak to them, it is highly recommended that you take a class and learn these skills. Presenting can make or break a consultant. It is commonly the primary communication tool for articulating ideas to clients and management.

If a consultant does not possess the skills necessary to narrate a presentation with confidence, it is highly recommended they look into a class such as a public speaking class to learn these skills. How a slide deck is presented or narrated can sometimes make or break a consultant. It can leave an audience with a great sense of confidence or a great sense of confusion and doubt in a consultant's abilities. A consultant can be extremely knowledgeable in their area of expertise but if they cannot convey confidence in that knowledge to a client or audience it can leave the client or audience irreparably doubtful of a consultant's expertise.

Logistics
Logistics is the detailed planning, coordination, and implementation of things. Logistics constantly come into play for most consultants. Logistics frequently begin long before a consultant walks out the door to begin a new project, assignment, or client visit. Logistics can also last long after that project, assignment, or client visit ends.

When traveling, logistics can begin with finding and booking an economical flight and/or hotel and determining whether it is more economical to rent a car or use taxi or public transportation services. When traveling to multiple destinations in the course of a week, as some consultants often do, the logistics become exponentially more complicated. It can become very frustrating when one missed or delayed flight negates hours of logistical planning. Good logistics practices include looking at some what-if scenarios, just in case.

After working out airline, airport, and car rental logistics, the consultant must find the client site if not relying on a taxi or public transportation to get them there. In some cases, a taxi might be more economically feasible than renting a car. It can save the stress of driving in an unknown area to the client site but might greatly limit the consultant's mobility. This could affect and limit where the consultant finds lodging and what and where they eat.

Often a client site turns out to be an expansive campus and it can be a logistical nightmare for a consultant to find their way around. It can also be a logistical nightmare getting from Point A to Point B when going from one meeting to another on a large campus or shuttling between multiple sites.

Along with the logistics of getting from point A to point B, the logistics of luggage; a place and time to write and file required reports such as expense and time reports; and arranging times, places, and accommodations for meetings are other examples of this soft skill that is required of many consultants on an everyday basis.

When a consultant is responsible for larger scale, more complex arrangements, good logistical skills become even more important. Planning for such things as events, workshops, and training sessions involve many more details and planning. A good consultant can easily maneuver between the most simplistic logistics and the most complex.

Calendars and Scheduling

Another important soft skill in the world of consulting is the ability to effectively manage time. A calendar is a consultant's roadmap through the day, week, and month. If a consultant is working on more than one project at a time a calendar is exponentially more important and often the only way a consultant can navigate through a day, especially when meetings are added to their calendars by others. Even when working on one project at a time it is not unusual for a consultant to be double and even triple-booked on any given day. A calendar is often the only way a consultant knows where they are expected to be at any given time during a day.

Shared calendars are usually standard functionality for those companies and clients using enterprise mail applications such as MS Outlook. Shared calendars can help a client or team locate others. They also provide a means for others to add meetings or meeting invites to the consultant's calendar. Sometimes a consultant's calendar is the only way a client, supervisor, or manager knows where the consultant is or is expected to be throughout the day.

Calendars can be viewed by the year, month, week, and day. When a consultant is in the middle of a complex project, a daily view of their calendar is sometimes all they can deal with - although they also need to keep an eye on the bigger weekly and monthly picture views. When planning broader tasks such as travel, a weekly or monthly view can be more practical.

It is common sense that when working on a short-term task or project it is highly recommended that a consultant not plan on taking time off, unless necessary. On longer assignments of six months or more, a consultant sometimes has personal or other commitments they must schedule. When a consultant is going to require time off it is important to let their client, supervisor, manager, and/or team(s) know as far in advance as possible so that required tasks and activities can be planned around that time.

After notifying a supervisor, manager, client and/or team(s), the consultant should always block the time on any shared calendars so activities and meetings are not subsequently scheduled during this time off. If activities and meetings are already scheduled during a time-off block, it is the responsibility of the consultant to inform the activity/meeting scheduler that they will not be available. A consultant should always communicate and be considerate of others in any situation.

An automated "Out-of-Office," message is a standard feature with most calendar applications and should be set up and used when a consultant is not available. The message should include when the consultant is expected to return or once again be available. It should also include an alternate contact or delegate's email address and phone number so if a critical or time-sensitive situation arises there is someone who can be contacted to help in the consultant's absence.

It is often difficult to find free time on a calendar when clients are adding meetings to it. It can be equally as challenging to find a free block of time on a client's or team member's calendar to book an activity or meeting when they have a full calendar. Most shared calendars have the functionality to compare schedules and offer times when all invitees are available. However, there are times when it is impossible to find a common time when all attendees are free. In those cases, a discussion with the attendee(s) will usually result in them adjusting their calendars to accommodate important, time-sensitive activities and meetings.

Local versus Travel

Some consultants do not care for the travel aspects that are often associated with a career in consulting. This is often the case of senior consultants who are in demand and will only accept positions local to them after burning out on years of traveling. When a consultant decides to remain local there may be trade-offs involved. The consultant may have to be more flexible on how often positions become available, the level of a position, duration of a project, and the rate of pay they can expect.

While travel can be a major part of a consultant's life, many consultants either stay local or temporarily relocate. Some technologies lend themselves better to remote/telecommute work such as mobile development and working within a cloud environment. In many of those cases a consultant may only be required to travel to a client site for a project kickoff or major deliverable.

Transportation

A consultant must figure out the best way to get to and from their assignment or client site. Their geographic location, assignment, and client or company will factor into how best to do this. For many assignments the only practical method of transportation may be to fly due to distance. For assignments within a close metropolitan area public transportation may be an option. In some cases, the consultant may have the option of using their own transportation to get to and from an assignment or client facility.

Whether being reimbursed for travel expenses or not, original receipts are required for all expenses claimed. The exception to this rule is when a consultant uses their own transportation to go to an assignment or client location. In this case, original receipts are required for any tolls or parking claimed (based on company or client policy for reimbursable expenses), but mileage is calculated based on the total round-trip miles times the current IRS standard mileage rate. No receipt is required to claim the standard mileage rate, however, a log of actual miles driven is usually required and gas costs cannot be claimed when using this deduction or reimbursable expense. Conversely, when renting a vehicle, standard mileage rates cannot be claimed but actual gas purchased (along with original receipts) can be.

The Consultant at Home

Working from Home
One of the most elusive forms of employment is a work-at-home job. Often, consultants get to do just that when they are not on site with a client. While working from home can be an envious circumstance, it is not without its challenges. At times it can be very difficult to focus on work with the daily happenstance and distraction of home life swirling all around. A consultant cannot stop in the middle of an international teleconference because the baby is screaming, something is boiling over on the stove, or the dog just threw up on the living room carpet.

Whether at the office or at home, deadlines are deadlines and due dates are due dates. A company, and certainly a client, is not interested in the dog-ate-my-homework story, they are interested only in results. Is that a steadfast rule? Of course not, there will always be extenuating circumstances that merit flexibility, but it must be the rare exception and not the rule. Working from home can become very comfortable but it is always a privilege and never something that should be taken for granted.

Environment
A professional consultant must create a home work

environment that is conducive to work productivity.   The level of a consultant's focus will determine the degree of boundary needed to be productive. Some consultants work and focus best when there is absolute quiet and no distractions swirling around them. Others can have complete chaos all around them and be able to detach fully and concentrate.

Like an office that is visited every day at a staffing company office or client site, the home work area must have at least a minimum set of tools necessary for the consultant to do their job. This will vary greatly based on the type of consulting being done and specific tasks. It can range from a telephone and a flat surface to a full-blown, fully-equipped dedicated office space.

Whatever the environment, the consultant must be able to work efficiently and professionally within it. They must be able to work on their tasks and when they interact with others, it should be transparent to others where the consultant is working from.

Balancing Work and Life
Balancing work and life, and effective time management is always an important part of a consultant's existence and lifestyle. When working from home time management can often become an issue. While it can be a luxury to walk into your own kitchen and grab a glass of water or cup of coffee, it can quickly take a consultant out of what they are working on. Dishes in the sink, meal planning, making a grocery list or a myriad of other distractions, if not managed, can completely derail a day's productivity. During work hours, a consultant must always remember that their work tasks are their priority.

When working on projects from home it is sometimes easier to put off working on individual tasks until the minute before they are due. Along with providing unnecessary stress, this practice devalues what the consultant could have contributed had they given the task the attention that it deserved and the time that was allocated for it.

On the other side of the work-at-home time management challenge consultants often find it difficult to manage their non-business time when working from home. It can sometimes become a challenge to walk away from work at the end of a day when work is just steps away. This can be especially true when there are pressing tasks or deadlines looming. It can sometimes be very difficult to stop working simply because it is 5:00 pm, or after a consultant has worked for eight hours. Many consultants are workaholics driven to working very long hours. A good consultant learns to balance their time for their health, well-being, and the well-being of those around them.

Phone calls and emails that need attention at odd hours or during meals are routine prices to pay for working from home. In some cases, business interruptions are a necessary evil, especially when engaged with international teams in different time zones. However, a good consultant learns to differentiate and prioritize between what needs immediate attention and what can wait for them to give their full attention to during regular business hours.

Cooperation
Cooperation is a must-have for anyone not living alone who is thinking of working from home. This is true whether a consultant has a family or roommates that they share their home with. Even when a consultant has a separate home office, working from home requires cooperation within the rest of the household. When a consultant is working the rest of the household typically finds themselves constantly needing to make adjustments,

some big, some small. Simple adjustments such as quiet time during work hours can be easier said than done. Larger adjustments such as routine meal preparation or children's playtime can be challenges that need to be worked out to everyone's satisfaction. When a roommate is involved these adjustments can include when a roommate enjoys relaxation time with their friends.

The door of cooperation swings both ways. When a consultant is working, they need the household's cooperation, but the household also needs cooperation and compromise. A consultant cannot expect all household activities to stop simply because they are working. Working through these challenges, communicating with each other, compromising when necessary, and considering others are keys to creating a cooperative home work environment that everyone can live with.

The Home Office
Some consultants can sit on their sofa or at their kitchen table with a television on, family activities going on around them, and still be able to completely focus on the tasks they are working on. However, this is not an easy thing to do. More typically it is necessary to create a separate work area within the home that is a dedicated work environment. It can be that sofa, kitchen or dining room table, or other area, but during work hours it needs to be the consultant's domain. A dedicated work area provides an invisible or visible boundary between home activities and work activities.

There are several advantages to creating a home office dedicated to business activities. It is usually a spare room or an area partitioned off for business only. This helps provide a dedicated space where the consultant can focus exclusively on work, and it helps create a healthy work routine for "going" to the office each day. A dedicated space provides a visible boundary to leave work at the end of the day and be able to walk away from it.

There are financial benefits to a dedicated work area or home office. When a consultant has a home-based office the cost of the office translates to an annual tax deduction when filing income taxes. Generally, the deduction is based on a couple of factors. One factor is the percentage of time the consultant uses the office space versus total time worked. For example, if a consultant works from home 100-percent of the time, the total cost of the area and all related expenses are deductible. If the consultant works 50-percent from home and 50-percent in a client's office, only half of the cost of the area and expenses associated with it are deductible.

The other factor used to calculate a home office tax deduction is the amount of space used versus the total square footage of the home. For example, if a consultant works 100-percent of the time from a home office, the office is 250 square-feet in size, and the total size of the home is 1000 square-feet, 25-percent of the the mortgage payment or rent and 25-percent of associated utilities are deductible.

Items such as a dedicated phone line that is only used for business purposes and office supplies are also deductible.

The equipment needed for a work-at-home consultant will vary greatly depending on the specific area of consulting the consultant is involved in. For example, a software developer might need a powerful enough computer to be able to write, compile, run, and test code. A marketing consultant might need high bandwidth for uploading and managing marketing material. A writing consultant might only need a laptop to create content. However, at a minimum, a consultant typically needs a phone (land-line and/or cell), a laptop computer, desktop or tablet computer, and a reliable high-speed Internet connection.

At Home Between Trips

Organization

Consultants who routinely travel, especially those who travel every week, need to be organized. When juggling a consulting career, a home life, and traveling regularly, organization helps reduce overall stress and provides much needed extra time at home. The less time used during time home cleaning up from the last week and preparing for the next week, the happier and more relaxed the consultant and those around them are going to be.

When a consultant arrives home, they usually have a week's worth of paperwork and laundry to catch up on. The sooner these tasks are out of the way, the sooner the consultant can relax, enjoy their time at home, and enjoy their family and loved ones. Paperwork can include weekly reporting of status, expense, and time. When these tasks can be accomplished at the hotel, during lunch, or while waiting at an airport it gives the consultant more time at home. When laundry is tackled right away it not only removes that task from the weekend to-do list, it can also expedite the task of packing for the next trip by repacking work clothes when the laundry is done.

Routines like packing help make travel a lot easier. Having a set pattern of what and when to pack makes life that much easier. In some cases, having extra items that are dedicated just for travel such as extra deodorant, shampoo, shavers, and hair brushes make it unnecessary to unpack and repack everything every time the consultant arrives home.

Identifying and organizing what and when weekly tasks are done and creating routines around them can make the life of a consultant run a lot more smoothly.

Departing and Arriving

If someone had to break down what the pain points of a traveling consultant are, two major ones are departing and arriving. They both have their challenges and recognizing these challenges can help overcome them.

Departing on Sunday night, Monday morning, or whenever departure falls can be extremely difficult. When traveling three to five or six days a week, a day or two leaves little time to stop and smell the coffee, nurture relationships, or resolve issues that arise. For consultants with partners, often the consultant is grabbing their bags and running out the door before their partner has had a chance to discuss an issue let alone have time to work as a team toward resolution. The realization of separation can be paralyzing for everyone. There are, however, the consultants whose relationships are based on separation and who would likely separate or divorce if they were in the same house for any length of time. When a consultant walks out the door an almost invisible transformation takes place from being at home in the nucleus of a home or family dynamic to being alone and in unfamiliar surroundings.

Arriving home after traveling and being on the road is another pain point. With a partner and/or family there is little time to decompress from a week filled with assignments, tasks, issues, and meetings. Walking through the door after a trip can often mean stepping into the middle of a drama or mood that the consultant is ill-prepared for. It can mean stepping into the middle of a situation without knowing the rules or into an expectation that the consultant did not get the memo on.

A consultant can become frustrated when they arrive home seeing that the family has become used to them not being there. It can leave a consultant feeling like they are under foot and making the home feel a lot smaller. As wonderful as arriving home can be after a trip it can also mean a major adjustment on everyone's part. Home and the road operate at different speeds with different rhythms and it can take major adjustments and compromises to arrive at a speed and rhythm that works for everyone.

On the Road

Most companies have established corporate policies and guidelines for travel. Travel policies and guidelines often include airline, ground transportation, rental car, and hotel preferences. They may also state maximum allowable reimbursements. Some companies have internal travel groups or external travel agents they require consultants to work with. These groups or agents may book some or all aspects of a business trip. Costs for a consultant's travel may be billed directly to the company or reimbursed after travel is complete.

Consultants who are left to make their own travel arrangements should always ask for corporate rates when booking car rentals and hotels. Often car rental agencies and hotels have corporate rates in place for business travelers, or they sometimes have discount agreements with larger companies where employees or consultants travel often.

A consultant must always observe and comply with any established policies and guidelines when making their travel arrangements or when a travel group or agent does so on their behalf.

Life Without a Consultant

For those who are single the life of a consultant can be a great fit, but even single consultants can be affected when they travel frequently. For the consultant with a partner and/or family, it takes major adjustments on everyone's part to accommodate a consultant's lifestyle. Life without a consultant is just that – it can be a single existence 85 to 90 percent of the time. For those couples with a family that means single-parenting most of the time.

Unattached Consultants

A single person may look like a perfect fit for consulting. Except for immediate family ties they do not have the obligations of intimate relationships to balance or reconcile their absences with. However, even an unattached, single person may feel the strains of consulting on their lives. It can be difficult to maintain social contacts at home when a consultant finds themselves away so much of the time. A consultant can find themselves an occasional visitor to their own circle of friends due to frequent and prolonged absences while they travel.

Spouses and Partners

With a consultant in the household spouses and partners live as unconventional a lifestyle as the consultant. All tactical household decisions are left to the consultant's spouse or partner. When the toilet backs up, the roof leaks, the car needs repairs, or the kids need a ride, the consultant can be hundreds or thousands of miles away. A spouse or partner cannot usually ask a traveling consultant to pick up a loaf of bread on the way home from the office. Even special occasions can often be celebrated alone because the consultant is traveling. Life with a consultant can be a very lonely existence.

Life is not easy for the spouse or partner that is left behind when a consultant travels frequently. The normal rhythm of a family and household is foreign to a consultant by the time they come through the door after being away for a few days, a week, a month, or sometimes longer. It can sometimes be very difficult going from a fast-paced, highly charged energetic environment during the day to a solitary, lonely existence at night in a hotel room. Juggling this on/off wave of energy can easily lead to insomnia and can make it very difficult to assimilate back into another rhythm when the consultant is back at home.

For the spouse or partner the assimilation is equally as challenging. The consultant isn't going to routinely come through the door Friday night and be the spouse, partner, parent, lover, or roommate everyone is expecting. The home environment naturally evolves from the last time the consultant was home. All the phone calls, emails, and text messages in the world cannot prepare a consultant for the reality of walking back into their home environment which has now evolved days, weeks, or even months without them. It is the point at which relationships are cemented or torn apart.

It is easy for a spouse or partner to resent living with a consultant. They are left to maintain the household and raise the children alone the majority of the time. When the consultant comes home it would be nice if they took over for awhile and gave their spouse or partner a break. Some do. Many do not, or, should we say, cannot. The demands on a consultant's time are weighty and exhausting. It is not a nine-to-five job. Many consultants work more than eight hour a day followed by hours spent in airports and on flights to and from home. Many work on international projects involving Europe in the early morning hours and the Pacific Rim in the late evening hours along with US hours during the day. It can be so all-consuming at times that rest, completing and filing reports, and laundry are all the consultant can muster up in a day or two before getting on a plane and doing it again. That's if they are lucky.

Consultants are typically thrown into high-pressure environments where expectations are high, budgets are low, and timelines are unrealistic. Stress is a way of life. That energy will likely bleed over into the consultant's home life to some degree. When it meets the stress of a spouse or partner who has had a difficult week at home, it can be volatile.

As difficult as a consultant's lifestyle can be there can be times when the very fact that the consultant and their spouse or partner have been apart will make for a very exciting time together, proving the old adage, "Absence makes the heart grow fonder." These times can be wonderful for a relationship and give the couple the feeling they got during the honeymoon period of their relationship.

There are many consultants who have very strong relationships with a spouse or partner that are based on being apart from one another. When a consultant in this type of relationship hasn't traveled for a period of time it can cause great friction. Each participant in the relationship maintains their own habits, routines, and identities separate from the other, and it can be difficult adjusting and sharing responsibilities and challenges that they would typically approach and deal with on their own.

Consulting is often the "other person" in a relationship. However, it can easily be far more demanding than another person. This is not by choice. The consultant doesn't have to answer that call, doesn't have to attend that meeting, doesn't have to make that flight, but there are people on the other end of that call, that meeting, and that flight who are depending on the consultant and paying premium rates for their services. When a client has an issue, a consultant is expected to perform miracles in record time. When the email comes in, the pager buzzes, the meeting request arrives, or the phone vibrates, a consultant is expected to respond. A romantic anniversary dinner will often take a back seat to the latest client emergency.

There are times when a consultant will be distant and impossible to approach. The more flexible and understanding a spouse or partner can be the easier it will be for the consultant to work through it and find their way back. Consultants are usually highly-educated and highly-motivated individuals, and generally over-achievers. These are not always the easiest individuals to live with.

For a spouse or partner who is the parent at home they must become both mother and father to their children only to be replaced by the other parent when they return. One set of rules prevails when the consultant is away, another kicks in when the consultant arrives home. The parent at home gets the full-on brunt of a child's day, good or bad. They get the days where one look or action by their child makes life worth living. Then there are the days when they want to leave the children in their spouse or partner's care and put some distance between them and their children but find themselves without that support system in place.

Children
When children are involved, things can be (and usually are) exponentially more difficult. A consultant can miss a baby's first step, a birthday, a school play, parent-teacher meeting, and countless other milestones in their child's life. They may not be there to share in their child's successes or to deal with their child's misbehavior and consequences. It is not uncommon for a consultant to walk through the door weighed down with guilt when children are involved.

Children of consultants have a different relationship with

both their parents. With the consultant, children learn to communicate via technology at an early age. A consultant does many things other parents do with their children daily; only the consultant often does it alone, remotely. The consultant often speaks with their children in the mornings before work and school via phone or other technology, encouraging them in their day. In the evening, the consultant hears about their children's day and maybe even reads them a bedtime story from afar. They tell them they love them as often as they can but there is no substitute for a parent's hug and presence.

Much like children of divorced parents, children of consultants will often try to play one parent against another. Rules that are followed when the consultant is away may be challenged by a child when the consultant is home, playing on their guilt. Consultants often unknowingly adopt the role of a grandparent; someone who is fun to be around but not there to discipline them. It is difficult to balance the true role of a parent when a consultant is absent a great deal of the time. It takes a strong, cooperative team effort for a consultant and their spouse or partner to avoid these types of child-rearing pitfalls. A consultant maintaining the role of a parent is a skill that should not be underestimated.

The children of consultants live very special lives and have very different life experiences from other children. Because of their parent's occupation they hear first-hand experiences of people and places they would not normally be exposed to. They often get to travel more than other children and typically have exposure to the latest technologies. The downside to this is an absentee parent. A gift from Japan or vacation to Europe cannot make up for a child's parent missing from the audience for their first ballet recital or school play.

The Single Person Lifestyle
Consultants and their spouses or partners spend a great deal of time operating as single people. Unattached consultants spend much of their time away from their friends. Consultants spend many days and nights alone, often eating meals and enjoying other activities alone. This can take as much getting used to as the adjustments that are made when the consultant returns home.

Consultants can sometimes become isolated and depressed needing the support of those around them. This can be as innocent as needing a pat on the back by a team member or reminder that they are not alone. Attached consultants can sometimes be at a greater risk of infidelity. Being alone most of the time when not working can make a consultant vulnerable to seek out company or be open to another person who seeks their company. If there is friction at home, it can isolate and alienate a consultant further and sometimes lead them astray even quicker.

There are usually many opportunities to meet someone while living alone in a hotel and eating out alone or socializing alone with colleagues and clients. Many of the people a consultant meets and spends time with are doing the same things. They have a common ground between them and can be equally lonely so there is sometimes an opportunity to form a bond with others.

For the consultant's spouse or partner the same can be true. Meeting someone they can spend time with can become very attractive when they spend a great deal of time alone. When the consultant isn't present to help take care of things another person can sometimes take advantage of a spouse or partner's vulnerability, especially if there is already tension in a relationship. Sometimes someone comes along who can fill the weekly void left when the consultant heads out the door to the airport.

It takes respect, consideration, understanding, a strong bond, and hard work on both parts to make a relationship with a consultant work and be successful.

Lifelines Home
It is very lonely being away from home. The longer the absence, the harder it becomes. Lifelines home help a consultant get through the lonely periods. Of course, phone calls, texting, Skype, and emails help keep the lines of communication open but other lifelines can help as well. Bringing a favorite picture, finding a note from a loved one in a suitcase, or other home-based ties can sometimes mean all the difference for a consultant and can contribute greatly to a good trip. Sometimes making plans for activities to share when the consultant returns home can keep them grounded and help them feel just a little less lonely. Little things like this can go a long way when someone is so far from home.

Long-Term Travel

Some consultants work on long-term assignments that can last from 6 to 24 months or longer. When working on a long-term assignment that requires regular travel a consultant is typically traveling every week or at regular intervals during that time. They must figure out the best way to maintain and balance their at-home life during these extended time periods. They must also figure out the best, most cost-effective logistics of getting to and from these assignments, living away from home for long periods of time, and meal planning during those times, among other things.

Travel expenses are typically reimbursed by the consultant's staffing company or client whether they involve long-term or short-term travel. Reimbursable travel expenses can include transportation, lodging, and food expenses. Other travel expenses may be applicable and are usually governed by Internal Revenue Service (IRS) rules and guidelines. If travel expenses are not reimbursed, the consultant can claim travel-related expenses to and from an assignment or client site as a business expense deduction on their annual income tax return. In either case, any expenses claimed must be accompanied by original receipts. If the consultant is claiming the expenses as an income tax deduction they do not submit original receipts with their income tax return, but must keep them as part of their personal tax record in the event of an IRS audit.

Housing
Consultants who travel long-term must figure out, analyze, and arrange both the most cost-effective means of living away from home for a longer duration and the most comfortable. While cost is important for keeping down expenses, the comfort of a consultant is important to keeping them from crashing and burning after a month or two.

Corporate housing and short-term rentals can be options when traveling long-term, depending on geographic location. Corporate housing typically involves a corporate housing agent finding and securing an efficiency, studio, or one-bedroom apartment where they provide all the furnishings and regular housekeeping services.

Some hotels will make it easier for regular long-term guests by allowing them to store some items over weekends until they check in the following week.

Transportation
It is always a balance whether to use a personal vehicle, public transportation (when available), a rented vehicle, or hire a taxi when traveling to client sites. The more research done up front, the easier the choice becomes. It is never

recommended to wait until arrival at a destination to make arrangements. Depending on location, typically when public transportation is not available, a car rental usually works out best.

There are usually several options for getting to and from an airport when embarking on a trip and arriving back home. These options can include the consultant driving their personal car and using long-term parking; an airport shuttle service; taking a taxi; public transportation; or hiring a private car and driver. The option the consultant chooses will depend on cost and convenience. When looking at these options it might seem some would be more costly than others, but there are times and circumstances when a seemingly more costly mode can be less expensive than other alternatives.

Airports – Not for the Squeamish

If a hotel room is not a home-away-from home for a traveling consultant, airports often are. Consultants sometimes spend more time in an airport than they do on site at a client's facility. Even an hour-long round-trip commuter flight can result in three to four hours of airport time. A good consultant will make the most of their airport time, taking advantage of free Wi-Fi services and getting some work done. Some consultants who have conquered the art of focus routinely use airport time to catch up on their weekly reports, prep for upcoming meetings when they land, work on assigned tasks, or catch up on phone calls and correspondence.

Airports, however, are not for the squeamish. If someone is not comfortable in a crowded, loud, manic atmosphere, an airport is the last place they want to be. People are constantly rushing to catch flights, collect baggage, rent cars, and catch ground (or public) transportation. Layovers are frequently an hour or more and many times when taking connecting flights an arriving flight gate can be across an airport terminal or in another terminal building from the next departing flight.

Knowing and observing airport and airline rules will make the airport experience a much smoother one. For example, knowing and observing carry-on luggage rules and regulations will speed up going through security checks and flight boarding times. Little adjustments such as wearing slip-on shoes to the airport and not wearing accessories which contain metal can greatly reduce the time it takes to go through security checks.

Mondays and Fridays are especially challenging at most airports. Those are typically the days regular travelers or commuters travel. When those passengers are added to the normal flow of casual travelers it can make for a very crowded, chaotic experience. It is not unusual on a Monday and a Friday for the line of passengers waiting to go through the security check to extend the length of a terminal and beyond. Often the lines extend outside the terminal and sometimes all the way into an airport parking lot or garage.

Airports are also especially crowded during high-volume travel periods such as Summer months and holiday weekends and seasons when many families are traveling. Navigating through airports becomes especially challenging during these periods. A savvy consultant will avoid traveling on Mondays, Fridays, and during holidays and Summer months whenever possible. When frequent travelers such as consultants must travel during those periods, they know to arrive at the airport especially early to compensate for the extra crowds. They also know that they can expect delays, flight cancellations, and general mayhem.

Frequent travelers know that morning flights are typically more apt to be on time than afternoon or evening flights. Morning flights usually have planes already waiting at their gates for the first flights of the day. As the day goes on there are more opportunities for flights to experience delays. Often, one flight delayed on one side of the country can cause a daisy-chain effect on many other flights all the way to the opposite coast because of connecting flight; plane, gate and crew availability; flight path; and other inter-dependencies along the way.

Trying to get something to eat or drink in an airport can be expensive and challenging. Airport restaurants and shops are a monopoly with a captive audience of customers. Often crowded airport shop cash register lines are three and four people deep and restaurants have long lines waiting to be seated or served. Conversely, when taking red-eye (night) flights an airport can be a quiet, abandoned, lonely, deserted place with all the shops and eateries closed.

Airlines
There are usually several airline carriers to choose from when traveling to and from major destination points. A consultant should be familiar with airline terms like direct flight and non-stop. A direct flight is a flight that will go directly from Point A to Point B but may include one or more stop-overs along the way that make the total flight time longer. A non-stop flight is faster and goes from Point A to Point B without any stop-overs but is usually more costly than direct flights. An indirect flight usually offers the cheapest fare but requires transferring between airplanes and flights one or more times along the way to the destination.

Consultants should familiarize themselves with airline hubs for better pricing and more flight options. Hubs are airports used as transfer points by each major airline to get passengers to their destination. Each airline has their own designated hubs and larger airline carriers will have several hubs across the country based on geographic region. Hub airports offer more airline-specific choices in final destinations than non-hub airports.

Consultants often have a favorite airline they use, but their carrier choice should factor in a cost comparison to other carrier options. Other factors a consultant will consider when choosing an airline include departure and arrival times, layover times, the reputation of the airline based on passenger reviews, on-time percentage rates, and their own personal experience with an airline. Upgrade options can also factor into a consultant's choice of airline especially when they frequently travel long distances. Free or low-fee upgrades to Business or First-class seats can be attractive to frequent fliers when taking long flights. Loyalty or rewards program perks can also factor into a consultant's decision on airline carrier.

Baggage

Consultants should always check and comply with any client or staffing company travel policies and guidelines addressing reimbursement for checked baggage fees and maximum weights.

Unless a consultant is going to be traveling for more than a week, it is highly recommended they find a way to pack everything they need in a carry-on bag(s) whenever practical. This practice makes life a lot easier on both ends of the trip saving a great deal of time avoiding long checked baggage lines, baggage carousel wait-times, and the delays associated with them.

Packing carry-on bags can become an art form. When packing carry-on bags, always observe airline rules and regulations. The size and quantity of carry-on baggage allowed can vary based on the airline carrier. Items such as purses and computer bags are each considered single carry-on items and count toward maximum allowable bags. Airline websites provide specifics of their carry-on baggage policies. In addition, these websites also provide a list of items prohibited and limited from being contained in carry-on bags. A good consultant makes a point of being familiar with these restrictions and packs accordingly. Traveling tricks like packing clothing in a computer bag along with a computer or packing a purse in a piece of carry-on luggage can help comply with existing rules.

Checked baggage has its own set of restrictions and limitations. Certain items are prohibited and there are typically weight limits on checked bags. When checking bags, a consultant knows to never pack cash, valuables, or prescription drugs in checked bags because bags can get lost, delayed, or looted before reaching their destination. When checking bags, consultants who travel regularly know to always allow extra time for check-in lines and procedures when arriving at the airport, and extra time retrieving luggage when they arrive at their destination.

Security
Airport security forever changed after September 11, 2001. Before 2001, friends and family could accompany a passenger to the boarding gate and wait with them until they boarded their flight or wait at the gate for a passenger's flight to arrive. Today, airport security is high and anyone without a boarding pass is rarely allowed in an airport terminal. Good-byes must be said before passengers step into line to go through airport security checks.

Security checks are forever challenging and forever changing. At a minimum, a valid boarding pass and government-issued identification are required to advance through security. From there, passengers are required to pass through metal detectors, have their carry-on luggage passed through a scanner, and are subject to search along with having any laptop computers and equipment scrutinized. Although there is a basic national standard set of rules and regulations regarding security checks, local airport rules and regulations can vary and be even more stringent. Security equipment calibration thresholds can mean the difference between a smooth walk through an airport security check or being singled out and scrutinized further. The most innocent of items can set off some sensing devices.

Consultants are professional travelers who routinely pass through airports and airport security. They keep up with the latest rules, give themselves plenty of extra time, and do everything they can to make their trip through security checkpoints and the airport as smooth and easy as possible.

Professional travelers such as consultants are often offset by occasional, casual, or even worse – first-time travelers who have no idea how to navigate through an airport or its security checks. This has the greatest impact during high-volume travel periods. While this can become very frustrating very fast the best way a savvy traveling consultant can handle the situation and make the experience as smooth as possible for all concerned is to have patience and provide guidance whenever practical to help the inexperienced traveler maneuver their way through.

The Hotel

Consultants can sometimes spend more time in hotel rooms than they do at home. While it is a great idea to check out all available options, there is much to be said for using one hotel chain whenever possible.

Many clients and staffing companies have established

travel policies and guidelines that address lodging including preferred hotel chains. Some will cite acceptable extra expenses that qualify for travel reimbursement including Wi-Fi services.

Comfort and Functionality
Cost is always a major consideration when choosing a hotel to stay at during an assignment. However, it is not the only consideration for a consultant. Comfort and functionality can be equally important.

Frequent travel is very hard on most people both physically and mentally. Staying in an establishment that does not provide comfortable lodging can lead to short and long-term physical ailments. For a consultant to be their most effective, they need to maintain their physical health. A sore back, muscle spasms, or a pinched nerve due to inadequate accommodations can lead to a consultant losing time on an assignment, being less effective, or being in a negative state of mind due to the pain.

Functionality is also very important when choosing a hotel. Amenities such as Wi-Fi service, a comfortable desk to work at, and a common business center with a printer are minimum requirements for most consultant's needs. For some consultants, access to a fax machine is also very important.

Location
The location of the hotel can be very important to a consultant. A hotel with a few less amenities can sometimes be more workable than one with everything a consultant could need if the hotel is located very close to a client facility. Many times a consultant can find a hotel that meets all their needs and is close to where they need to go. However, depending on circumstances, there are times when even though a hotel is located near a facility, it is not available, and the consultant must look for

accommodations further away. Booking early whenever possible can help ensure securing accommodations in the right place, with the right amenities, for the right price.

Making the Most of Hotel Time
Making the most of hotel time is often a sign of a successful, driven consultant. Some consultants will finish their day and go back to their hotel rooms to enjoy happy hour at a hotel bar, surf the Internet, watch television, play video games, or sit pool side while enjoying several nice cold drinks. While this can be very relaxing these activities may not be the best way of making the most of their hotel time.

A good consultant usually uses their hotel time to prepare for the next day with their client, touch base with their home office, write reports, review material, and often prepare for upcoming status meetings or work on key presentations they cannot find time to work on during normal business hours. This does not mean a consultant doesn't take time to relax.

A good consultant learns to balance relaxation with ensuring they are doing their consulting homework and completing any next-day preparations necessary to keep up with a sometimes full and busy schedule. When a consultant is under strict time constraints, they may forego happy hour or have just one drink to relax, allocate a set amount of time to catch up on personal tasks and obligations, or take advantage of room service to save time going out to eat. They save the fun things they can do for after they have finished non-business hours work-related tasks.

Rewards Programs

Travel rewards or loyalty programs are one of the major perks of being a consultant who travels frequently. Airline carriers, major hotel chains, and some car rental companies offer their regular customers memberships in these programs. Many major airlines, hotel chains, and car rental companies have cooperative partner agreements in place that allow participants the option of having their points converted between participating programs. The basis for accumulating points varies greatly. Most consultants will sign up for all programs offered but lean toward using one or two airline, hotel chains, and car rental companies on a regular basis. This allows them to accumulate the most points in the shortest period of time and reap the maximum benefits of memberships.

Consultants who travel frequently quickly accumulate large amounts of loyalty or rewards points and enjoy the perks of these programs. Many accumulate and hold their point balances and use them for free or highly discounted non-business or family vacation airfares, hotel stays, and car rentals.

Airlines
Major airline carrier rewards programs allow participants to accumulate points based on number of flights, air miles traveled, or number of point-to-point legs flown. When a consultant is long-distance commuting by flying even twice a week, these rewards accumulate quickly. Depending on the program, the rewards points can be used for future flights, seat upgrades, merchandise, and/or conversion to other partner programs.

Hotel Rewards
Most major hotel chains offer loyalty programs for staying at their establishments. A program member accumulates points based on either the number of nights they stay in a participating hotel or by the dollar amount of their hotel room and sometimes other room charge amounts incurred during their stay. When staying in a hotel every week for

three to six months or more these points begin to accumulate quickly. Hotel points can typically be used for future upgrades, free stays, transfer to participating partner programs, and/or merchandise. Many major hotel chains also include tiered memberships based on a participant's frequency staying at their hotels. The higher the tier reached in these programs the better and more frequent the free perks.

Car Rental Rewards

Major car rental companies offer rewards program memberships for customers renting vehicles on a regular basis. Points are accumulated based on either number of rental days, number of rentals, or per rental dollar amounts depending on the program. Points can typically be redeemed for free upgrades, rental days, transfer to participating partner programs, and/or merchandise.

Credit Card Rewards

Many major credit cards also offer membership rewards programs. These work similarly to other types of programs. The more a participant uses their credit card to pay for goods and services, the more points they accumulate. Credit card points can also sometimes be converted to partner programs. Points can usually be redeemed for goods, services, and sometimes more favorable interest rates on the credit card. A consultant traveling frequently and using the same credit card for their expenses can quickly accumulate high account point balances.

Meals

Many clients address meal reimbursement in their corporate travel policies and guidelines. Meals are typically reimbursed based on actual receipts up to a maximum per meal (breakfast, lunch, and dinner), a daily total maximum, or a daily per diem meal rate. Per diem rates are fixed daily amounts a company will reimburse regardless of actual receipts. Alcoholic beverages are typically not included in reimbursable meal expenses although some company policies will allow one alcoholic beverage with a dinner meal.

Most major hotel chains offer an array of food service options ranging from free breakfast buffets or grab-and-go breakfasts to paid services such as full meal menu offerings, breakfast buffets, room service, or access to local restaurant delivery services. Many hotel locations have attached restaurants or are in close proximity to local restaurants. Some hotels have partnerships in place and offer discounts for their guests to attached or local restaurants. Front desk personnel will usually know if this is the case and have details on how to take advantage of these programs.

Eating every meal out may sound or seem glamorous at first but when it is the only option and a long-term practice it can be very unhealthy and become very repetitious and boring depending on options available and the geographic location a consultant finds they are in.

Some hotel chains offer studio rooms or suites with kitchenettes. These rooms provide the consultant an opportunity to prepare some of their own meals versus eating every meal out.

On the Bench

Staff consultants are those lucky enough to be full-time employees of a staffing company or agency. These consultants receive full benefits like any other employee whether they are assigned to a client or project or whether their time is billable or not. When their time is not billable to a client they are often referred to as being "on the bench." Staff consultants not working on a billable project are still expected to be productive while they are on the bench. Staff consultants on the bench are expected to be available for such tasks as supporting internal projects, proposal efforts, mentoring, and furthering their own skills development and those of others. They are also expected to be readily available for any billable tasks that may come up.

While it may seem attractive not to be under the pressure of working with deadlines, the first time and often every time a staff consultant finds themselves on the bench it can be very intimidating and somewhat frightening. In the world of consulting everything revolves around billable hours – it defines a consultant's worth. Long periods of being on a virtual bench can jeopardize a staff consultant's position due to the high cost of their salary and compensation package and lack of revenue the company is receiving because the staff consultant is not billable.

However, how a staff consultant focuses their efforts while on the bench is key to their overall worth and success as a staff consultant. This is especially true for those staff consultants who work remotely and may offer little management visibility into what the consultant is filling their time with while on the bench. The added value a staff consultant on the bench can contribute to the staffing company or agency can be paramount to their overall value.

While it can become easy to be lazy while on the bench, especially after rolling off of a long, difficult project, how a staff consultant conducts themselves on the bench reflects on them and affects them more than they might realize. It is during these non-billable times that management can sometimes be watching, observing and evaluating most carefully and closely.

Opportunities
Being on the bench can be an opportunity with the right approach. Bench time can be a time to catch up with

fellow consultants and conduct informal knowledge transfers of experiences they have had with various challenges and how they resolved them. It can provide time to work on exciting homegrown internal projects and it is an excellent opportunity to catch up on industry, field, and technological advances. The staff consultant probably does not have time for these activities while billable but while they are on the bench, they can add great value to their future ability to be billable and increase their billable rate.

The bench can provide a staff consultant with great opportunities not afforded a nine-to-five employee. The more a consultant makes of their time on the bench the more valuable a consultant they become to their staffing company or agency and future clients.

Catch Up
Bench time can give a staff consultant the opportunity to catch up on work placed on the back burner while billable. Lower priority tasks and projects are often put on a back burner while a consultant is billable. Bench time can offer an excellent opportunity to work on, catch up, and finish those tasks and projects.

Exploration and Research
Bench time can provide the opportunity to explore and research new developments and technologies. Internet surfing is often looked upon as a waste of time and resources. However, for a consultant the Internet is an important research tool that can be used during periods on the bench to read relevant publications, white papers, and brush up on and become familiarized with the latest industry developments, advancements, and technologies.

Staff consultants often author white papers within their areas of expertise. White papers are detailed reports or guides written by authorities with experience on a specific subject. Conducting thorough research to author and publish a white paper can be an excellent use of bench time. White papers are often used as marketing tools for sales teams and can sometimes be packaged and offered as a product to clients.

Training and Certification
Professional and technology staff consultants often have specific certification and training requirements and periodic recertification requirements they must meet. Being on the bench can allow a consultant time to catch up on keeping current with these requirements.

Bench time is also a great opportunity for senior staff consultants to mentor and train more junior consultants and share their experiences and expertise with them. This practice can add value to the overall team of consultants the staffing company or agency has to offer its clients.

Marketing and Sales Support
Staffing companies or agencies are constantly soliciting new clients and business partners. Due to their direct experience on assignments and projects with client staff, consultants on the bench can contribute their experience and expertise to marketing campaigns, sales proposals efforts, and the teams that conduct these activities. It is not unusual for a staff consultant to temporarily join a sales team as the Subject Matter Expert (SME) when the team writes a proposal or visits a potential new client to deliver a sales presentation. Their presence can sometimes tip the scales for the team, offering the potential client a glimpse of what level of consulting expertise the company or agency actually has.

In-House Project Contributions
Some staffing companies or agencies will utilize their

bench teams to collectively work on internal projects or products that, once completed, may be marketed to yield a company significant profit. Besides the obvious bragging rights afforded by a successful project or product launch, working on these projects can add invaluable experience to a consultant's tool bag while working in a less constrained environment than a billable project sometimes allows. It can also provide team members who normally work alone or with client teams an opportunity to build a sense of camaraderie alongside other consultants that they rarely see or work with otherwise.

Time Management
There are many factors that will make or break a consultant. Time management is one of those single point of potential failures. When a staff consultant is on the bench time management can be even more important then when they are working with a client. Effectively managing bench time will help make what might look like down time become productive quality time almost as valuable as billable time.

Often, a staff consultant's management will dictate how a consultant uses their bench time. But being proactive and putting a good plan in place for upcoming bench time can help management in planning the consultant's bench time and help the consultant make the most of the their time on the bench. Allocating and balancing bench time between tasks can maximize a consultant's effectiveness while keeping time spent from becoming monotonous and singularly focused. For example, a balanced plan of authoring and publishing a white paper, participating in training, and providing sales support can not only be value-added for a staffing company and increase the worth of the staff consultant but can also give the consultant a variety of productive tasks to focus on.

Good time management habits both on and off the bench will yield a less stressed consultant and contribute to their steady growth.

Making the Most of the Bench – The Extra Step
Bench time is routinely scrutinized very carefully by management. On a company balance sheet, a consultant on the bench does not have an entry in the asset column when they have no billable hours to report. Depending on the staffing company there may be a very prescribed schedule of how a consultant uses their bench time. Other staffing companies may leave it to the consultant to recognize how their bench time is best spent to better themselves and their consulting worth.

In either case going the extra step at all times, but particularly when on the bench, can mean the difference of a bonus, raise, a future promotion, or ultimately, a consultant's job.

What is the extra step? In the case of bench time, it is focusing on things that will best benefit the staffing company. For example, focusing on what skill sets a company's consulting pool might be light on and using bench time to master these skills will give added value not just to the consultant but to the organization as a whole. Volunteering for an internal project that is manned from the bench where a consultant can see their skills and expertise having a significant impact can help the project team reach their goals and the project reach fruition and success. Lending support to sales pipeline efforts can contribute to future projects, more revenue for the company, and ensure future billable hours not only for the consultant but for the teams that may also support winning proposals.
Developing a proposal for an internal project that results in a marketable end-product can provide focus, a goal, and a future marketable product for the consultant, the rest of the

bench team, and the company. For more senior consultants, bench time can be used to share expertise and experience with less experienced consultants, making it an ideal opportunity to mentor others on the bench. All of these suggestions can add value to the staffing company while not logging billable hours.

A successful consultant always takes the extra steps most consultants may not. They always looking for opportunities to create and add value, always looking for win/win situations for themselves and others.

The Company Office

If a staff consultant is local to a company branch office, the staffing company may require them to report for work each day to an office when they are not on a billable project. Consultants tend to lead a lonely, lone wolf professional existence. Normally staff consultants are on the road or at client sites. An organization's staff consultants do not typically cross paths unless they are working on the same project team. Often the only time a staff consultant may meet or see their colleagues in person is at an annual office party, if then.

When a staff consultant reports to the company office it can provide a rare glimpse into the rest of the world's normal nine-to-five work world. It may also require some adjustment for the consultant who is used to a more unconventional professional existence. Suddenly they are required to be at the same desk or cubicle for an undefined period of time. Often, they are required to share an office or space with one or more other benched staff consultants. They must contend with regular traffic commuting to and from the office, regular lunch periods, and see the same faces day-in and day-out. Management is suddenly in close-proximity when typically the closest they are is a phone call or email away. However, there are opportunities when reporting to a company office.

Opportunities
Time in a company office can provide staff consultants opportunities they do not often get. Spending time in a company office can give a staff consultant a sense of community and grounding that is sometimes otherwise illusive. It can be a rare opportunity to share experiences, knowledge, and camaraderie with other consultants. Sharing project challenges and solutions can help increase the staff consultant's knowledge base without direct experience. Sharing experiences can lead to an understanding of potential challenges, how others resolved them, and can often come back to help in future projects when a similar challenge arises. Having a solution in hand when a challenge arises greatly adds to a consultant's value even when the solution comes not through direct experience but through a knowledge transfer with another consultant.

Being in the office creates an opportunity to socialize with colleagues, often over lunch. Keep in mind when in the company office, lunch is on you, not a client. Many companies recognize the importance of consultants sharing experiences and ideas and will sponsor office luncheons when traveling consultants are on temporarily on the bench.

The Client Site

When a consultant is working at a client's facility there are written and unwritten rules of conduct a consultant is expected to adhere to. Although each client experience will be different, consultants are constantly under the watchful eye and scrutiny of the client.

The Client-Consultant Agreement
The agreement an independent consultant signs or a staffing company signs when placing a consultant with a client company outlines what a consultant is agreeing to do, what a client is agreeing to provide to support the consultant's efforts, and the time frame and form a product or service is to be delivered in. The agreement documents the expectations of both parties. This is the easy part of any assignment because expectations are written in black and white. Either party can refer to the agreement if there are any questions. If additional tasks or deliverables arise that are not mentioned in the agreement, the agreement can always be amended to include the extra requirements along with the time, cost, and specifics associated with it.

What may not be as straightforward are the unspoken agreements between parties that involve a consultant's performance, behavior, and interaction within the company's existing culture. These unspoken agreements are very important to be aware of and adhere to while at a client site. A good consultant understands these unspoken agreements without having them spelled our for them or having to have the client enforce them.

Mostly Second-Class Citizens
Consultants are almost always second-class citizens within the client company cultural and hierarchy structure. Even when a consultant is placed in a management position, the team they are managing may usurp their authority by

simple virtue of their being full time employees of the client company.

Consultants are typically relegated to the least desirable locations within a client facility floor plan. They are often required to share small spaces with other consultants, have the least desirable work space and equipment to work with, yet are expected to perform at a higher standard than that of full time employees.

In some client cultures consultants are literally thought of as second-class citizens and frequently suffer the disrespect and inconsideration of the full--time employees around them. There can be many reasons for this attitude when it arises that can range from preconceived ideas about consultants or a past bad experience with a consultant to feelings of job insecurity because of the presence of a consultant. Whatever the motivation, if this negative attitude arises it is up to the consultant to remain focused on performing their tasks to the best of their ability and not letting someone else's attitude affect them. Sometimes helping a full-time employee shine or be recognized for their contributions can completely change their attitude and create a win-win situation for all involved.

Meetings

Meetings are a way of life for a consultant. It is not unusual for a meeting to be held to decide whether to hold a meeting. A consultant should always be as prepared as possible for meetings they attend. They should be familiar with the meeting's agenda and the goals of the meeting so they can contribute to those goals. If a consultant has been tasked with providing input to a meeting, they should always have that input prepared and ready before the meeting starts.

Logistically meetings can be a real challenge for a consultant as they maneuver their way through the labyrinth of a client site to find meeting locations. The consultant must quickly learn client common knowledge such as the best way to get to the Sequoia conference room in building 726 on the 4th floor. Consultants are expected to quickly learn the idiosyncrasies of a client's culture like knowing that conference room names starting with the letter "F," such as Fiesta, Fission, and Freedom indicate the first floor of a given building while conference room names beginning with the letter "S" such as Sycamore, Sunset, and Spencer indicate they are located on the second floor. The quicker the consultant acclimates themselves to the logistics of a client site the quicker they blend into the client culture and become more productive and efficient. Meeting locations are often one of the first trial-by-fire challenges they encounter.

Showing up for meetings on time is important in building trust with the client and in building and maintaining a reputation of reliability. Getting lost on the way to a meeting is no excuse to the client even when the meeting location can be very confusing. If other attendees can find the location and show up for a meeting on time the consultant is expected to be able to as well.

Hygiene and Appearance

Hygiene, appearance, and wardrobe should not be a subject that needs addressing but it is astounding how many consultants require the discussion.

Personal Hygiene

It goes without saying that personal hygiene is very important. But it is also important in making a positive impression on colleagues and clients. A well-groomed consultant conveys that they care about themselves and others. A consultant with bad body odor, bad breath, or unbrushed hair is not only unflattering but can be offensive to those around them. A consultant who indulges in heavy use of perfume or cologne can be equally offensive and can cause a health concern for those who may be allergic to artificial scents or have chronic breathing health issues.

A good consultant practices good daily healthy hygiene. They are clean, neatly groomed, and have no overpowering natural or artificial odors.

Appearance and Dress Codes

Everyone enjoys making statements about their individuality based on their appearance. However, as a consultant there are certain unspoken rules and taboos when it comes to appearance and wardrobe. While there are exceptions, most consultants will adhere to these codes because while a consultant might want to make a statement with their appearance, it may inadvertently offend a client and leave them with a negative impression of the consultant regardless of their performance.

Successful consultants use makeup and jewelry to enhance their overall appearance but do not use them in excess. Makeup and jewelry used tastefully and sparingly can contribute to an overall professional appearance but are not necessarily required.

Tattoos are not always appreciated by others. If a consultant has tattoos it is usually best to wear clothing that conceals them whenever possible. Tattoos are an expression of a person's individuality and artistic preference. Consultants remembered more for their tattoos and less by the product or service they delivered are usually less likely to get the next project or assignment.

The same holds true of a consultant's choice in hair styles. While an unconventional hair style might be desirable in making an individual personal statement, it may not be the best way to make a positive impression on a client.

Dressing for success is more than a cliché for a consultant.

The clothing a consultant chooses to wear when interacting with clients and colleagues can leave a lasting impression. Dress codes have changed over time and suits are not required as often as they were in the past. Many company dress codes are now "business casual." Business casual for men means slacks, a buttoned shirt, and, depending on a client's preference, a sports jacket and/or tie. For women business casual means a dress; skirt and blouse; or slacks and blouse. Except on rare occasions business casual never means jeans, shorts, tee shirts, flip flops, or tennis shoes.

The goal of a consultant's appearance is to have the client remember a job well done and not their appearance. A non-conventional appearance can distract the client and can indirectly and inadvertently derail a consultant from reaching that goal.

Fitting In
Fitting in with an existing corporate culture can be a challenge but is very important. Part of fitting in is to observe and respect the client culture and dress accordingly. Asking questions before arriving at a client site can help make the transition easier. If a client states that the environment is business-formal, the consultant knows a suit or jacket and tie are required and will know how to dress. If the client cites a business casual environment the consultant may need to ask some more detailed questions to determine what the client's definition of business casual is.

Following a client's cultural practices is also important to fitting in. For instance, if employees observe "Casual Fridays," where employees are allowed to wear jeans on Fridays; or "Hawaiian Shirt Day," a consultant dressed in formal business attire might stick out and it could be seen as a sign of disrespect of their culture.

Fitting in by doing what the natives do will help a consultant be more readily accepted into the existing culture. However, a consultant must be able to distinguish when it is appropriate to follow the crowd and when it is appropriate to maintain a level of professionalism. Employees are going to remain at their jobs long after a consultant is gone. Once a consultant completes an assignment or project and leaves the only thing that remains are the products of their work and the impressions they left on the client and client team.

Professionalism

Consultants are professionals and are expected to act as professionals no matter what anyone around them might be doing. By definition, getting paid to be a consultant is what makes a consultant a professional. But what defines the professionalism of a consultant is how they conduct themselves in business and casual circumstances.

Consultants often work under little or no supervision. Whether someone is watching or monitoring them or not should have no bearing on how a consultant works, performs their tasks, or conducts themselves. A consultant who exhibits a high degree of professionalism always shows up where they need to be on time, is prepared for the tasks at hand, is prepared for the unexpected, completes tasks on time as promised, looks professional versus casual, is reliable, dependable, and always exhibits a positive, cooperative attitude.

Performance

How a consultant performs is a measure of the product, service, or completed tasks they deliver and whether deadlines and budgets were met. Other criteria and factors used to measure performance can include such things as how well challenges or difficult situations were handled, whether solutions were provided to mitigate those situations, and how effectively a consultant communicates with others.

Performance is like a line on a graph or chart. It transcends projects and assignments and is continuous over long periods of time and multiple product, service, or task deliveries. Overall performance is a contributing factor in a consultant's worth and what kind of hourly rate they can charge a client for their services.

Breaks and Lunch

Consultants do not punch a clock like many employees. Most of their time is spent on the honor system. If a consultant takes breaks during the day they should be limited to no more than two fifteen minute breaks during a normal eight-hour day. Taking excessive amounts of breaks or unusually long breaks will get the consultant noticed in a less than favorable light. A consultant's time comes at a premium price and they are expected to spend their time on assigned tasks, not on excessive breaks.

Lunchtimes can vary for a consultant depending on the circumstances, client, and assignment. There are times when a consultant will find themselves sharing lunchtime with others in a meeting, eating while they work. At other times a consultant may find themselves eating alone, either bringing a bag lunch, running out and getting a quick box lunch, or eating alone at a local restaurant or company-sponsored cafeteria.

In some instances when a consultant is part of a team the team may choose to spend their lunchtimes together, staying in as a group or going out together. In a team environment this can build camaraderie, a cooperative environment, a team spirit, and can provide a chance for team members to exchange assignment-related ideas and solutions.

A consultant should always observe a client's rules for lunchtimes. Sometimes a company will want a consultant to take their lunch break at a specific time each day. At other times a consultant may be left to take their lunch break at the most convenient time based on their schedule, so they may find lunchtimes earlier or later than a conventional period. A client will also indicate how long lunch periods are (usually a half hour, forty-five minutes, or an hour). Whatever the time period allocated the consultant should always be back from lunch at their desk or work station on time and ready to work.

Many larger companies offer their employees and consultants access to company cafeterias. Many company-sponsored cafeterias provide a variety of menu choices and healthy foods at discounted prices. When a cafeteria is present there are usually weekly or monthly menus posted on a company's Intranet site or available through a department's administrative assistant where a consultant can check what is being served along with any specials being offered. Some cafeterias are only open for lunch while others also offer breakfast items. In some rarer cases a company cafeteria may also offer full dinner menus. Company-sponsored cafeterias provide quick and easy access to meals for the convenience of their employees and consultants.

Company-sponsored cafeterias run the gamut of dining experience and food quality ranging from gourmet menus in dining room style settings to basement cinder block rooms with nothing more than vending machines. If there is a cafeteria present it is usually worth at least investigating. At a minimum they are usually a good place to pick up a quick cup of coffee, tea, or a cold drink.

Full-Time Employee Dramas

When a consultant finds themselves placed in a team environment consisting of regular full-time employee (FTE) members there are inevitably dramas and personality conflicts that come into play. Some environments are worse than others in this regard, but it is always important for a consultant to stay out of company employee dramas and not take sides. FTEs often try to share their perspective and want a consultant to lend a sympathetic ear or perspective. There are times when an FTE may have issues with a consultant for no other reason but that they are a consultant and view the consultant as infringing on their "territory." A good consultant will gracefully decline involvement and stay focused on the task at hand.

In-house company dramas are never in the best interests of the company and can greatly affect the success of the team and the consultant. If a situation arises that begins to interfere with a consultant's ability to do their job, it should be reported as soon as possible without emotional involvement to management for resolution.

Conduct Off-Site While on Travel Status
When a consultant is traveling for business whether they are at a client facility or having a drink at a bar after hours they should always consider how they conduct themselves and how their behavior appears to others. A consultant can never be sure when someone from the client company, someone they may not even be working with directly, could be at that same bar and unintentionally observing their behavior.

Client facilities are often located in localized areas where many company employees frequent local businesses or have relatives who own or frequent them. If a stranger patronizes the business and causes a scene, is loud, rude, or becomes intoxicated and obnoxious, someone is going to notice and it will reflect on the consultant, the staffing company they may represent, and the client they are working for. Therefore, consultants should always consider themselves "at work" to an extent, even during off business hours when they are on travel status and conduct themselves accordingly.

Socializing

Being a consultant is not always all work and there are times when a consultant will occasionally or regularly socialize with others, especially when a consultant finds themselves away from home. Socializing with others is a great way to relax and de-stress. It is also a great way to enjoy local offerings and see local sights while traveling.

A good professional consultant will always conduct themselves in a respectful, courteous manner when socializing with others. They should always remain friendly while enjoying themselves and the company of others, and never over-indulge.

Socializing with Colleagues and Other Consultants

Consultants who find themselves traveling to new places where their client's facilities are located are often not alone. Often, many consultants will converge from different areas of the country or world to join together as a team and find themselves in new surroundings together. Sometimes consultants will converge from different geographical locations, not to work together, but to all work on different projects for the same client. In either case this can be a great opportunity to get together when they are away from work. It can help all of them combat the feelings of loneliness and isolation they may feel being so far away from home.

Sometimes a group of consultants will meet up for lunch and take turns choosing a different new place to eat together. Along with companionship this can provide a means to critique local eateries together and enjoy finding consensus on their favorites.

When a group of consultants are away from home over weekends it can be an opportunity to explore and learn about local customs, enjoy seeing local sights together, and share in trying local cuisines that a consultant alone might otherwise feel awkward pursuing. It can also be a great way to have a shared experience with others. Often, a group of consultants will use public transportation or chip in to rent a car or taxi to visit local tourist attractions or other points of interest together.

Socializing with Clients

There are times when a client or members of a client team will seek out the company of a consultant. These can be great opportunities for the consultant to bond with client team members, experience local customs, and see local sights with residents as their guides. Whenever these opportunities arise the consultant should always remain casually professional while enjoying themselves. They should also always be gracious and remember to express their gratitude to a host for their time and efforts.

A Consultant's Office Can Be Anywhere

Airport Gates

Consultants do not have the constraints of a cubicle everyday, but they also do not always have a stable place to get their work done. Consultants sometimes need to make do with where they are to get their work done.

Often consultants get stuck in airports for hours at a time. When they have strict deadlines that they need to meet, airline gates sometimes become their temporary offices. Most airports offer free or low-cost Wi-Fi connections so a consultant can send and receive emails and upload and download material when needed. Many consultant tasks do not require an Internet connection and can be worked on at any airport gate using their laptop and installed software.

One consultant found themselves delayed at an airport on their way to a major Fortune 100 company client. There they were supposed to have most of the day to work on a very important presentation that was due to be given late in the afternoon. Instead of arriving more than a half day before their meeting with the client they found themselves scheduled to get to the meeting within fifteen minutes of the meeting start time.

The consultant spent the better part of the day at the airport creating the presentation, using the free Wi-Fi to share it with colleagues, and making notes for later in the afternoon. Once the presentation was complete the consultant was able to email it to a team member already at the client site who made copies for handouts to the participants. During the rest of the time at the airport the consultant practiced their talking points for the meeting.

When the consultant landed, they took a taxi from the airport to the client site, went to the conference room, and unpacked and plugged in their laptop as the client participants were beginning to gather. The meeting and presentation went off without any issues and the client never knew the circumstances the consultant had to work with to successfully participate in the meeting and deliver the presentation.

Hotel Lobbies
Often, when a team of consultants are working on the same project and staying at the same hotel, the hotel lobby can become an excellent pop-up office for them to meet and work together.

A group of consultants were collaborating on a technical design for a software system. The seating arrangements the client had arranged at the client site did not take into consideration that the team needed to be working together, so they were spread out in different locations. None of their hotel rooms would accommodate all six of the team members, but the hotel had several large comfortable sitting areas arranged in quite nooks around the hotel lobby. The team decided to assemble in the lobby at a pre-agreed time after dinner each evening with their laptops. There they were able to work together and discuss the design amongst themselves and divide up individual tasks they needed to complete to finish the design. During the day at the client site they could each be productive working on individual pieces of the task. The team successfully delivered a coherent design while the client never knew the circumstances of where or how they worked together to deliver it.

Cafeterias

Most larger clients have on-site cafeterias for their employees and temporary contract help. One busy consultant working as a project manager was constantly in demand due to the nature of the project. When the consultant wasn't triple-booked in meetings and could be at their desk there were constant interruptions from people dropping by, along with being barraged with project-related phone calls.

The consultant was responsible for reviewing very complex documents and conducting highly confidential meetings with little to no conference room availability. The consultant found that during cafeteria off-hours there were no meals being served. Traffic volume during the off-hours was very, very low as only a few people went through the cafeteria to stop and pick up snacks or drinks to return to their offices with. There were many private, quiet tables available where the consultant could take documentation to review or conduct confidential meetings with others in privacy, without interruption, over a cup of coffee.

Expectations

Consultants constantly live in the spotlight of expectation. Expectations can become a very burdensome load while trying to perform a task or deliver a product or service. It is very important to realistically set expectations whenever possible at the beginning of an engagement. It avoids misunderstandings later, undue pressure, and stress.

As a consultant there will inevitably be times when the expectations of others will far exceed the reality of a situation. Even worse, there are times when there are expectations placed on a consultant that the consultant has no idea exist. In either case, the best first and foremost rule of thumb to follow is for the consultant to always do their best in every situation.

Managing other people's expectations can sometimes be a full-time job in and of itself for a consultant. However, the better the consultant communicates and manages these situations the better the chances of a positive, successful outcome.

Your Expectations

A consultant's expectations should always be simple, straightforward, and as close to the reality of a situation as possible. Ultimately, the best a consultant can hope for is that by doing their best every moment they are working on a task, product, or service, the more likely they are to be successful. A successful consultant understands that their best will vary from day to day and sometimes from moment to moment. They also understand that no one is perfect and when they do not do as well as they would like to it is best to learn from those times, accept them, and move forward.

Their Expectations

While working to deliver a task, product, or service, a consultant will have different levels of expectation placed on them by various other people.

A consultant's management, if they work for a staffing company, will have a set of expectations based on the consultant's performance and outcome. A client will have a set of expectations based on the time, budget, quality, and outcome of a consultant's efforts. Team members will have yet another set of expectations based on the consultant's contributions to overall team efforts.

In all cases, a consultant must manage these multiple expectations and provide the best services and performance they can. When a consultant cannot meet the expectations of others, effective communication is important to mitigate and manage the gap between expectations and what it is possible for a consultant to do.

Ultimately, the goal of a consultant should always be to meet or exceed the expectations of those they have a commitment to whenever possible.

Someone Else's Expectations
There are sometimes expectations placed on a consultant by others regarding what the consultant is expected to do, how they do it, and within what time frame. Examples of someone else's expectations include a client's upper management expectation of a deliverable; an account's expectation of time or material-related costs; and an end-user expectation of what a delivered product will look like or how it will function.

A consultant must be able to quickly analyze and prioritize which expectations they need to meet to accurately measure their efforts for success. They must also be able to manage the expectations of everyone to the best of their ability with a professional, positive, and cooperative attitude.

The Rest of the World's Expectations
The rest of the world will sometimes place expectations on a consultant just because they are a consultant. A consultant is often expected to make a great deal of money even if they are starting out in a more junior position. They may be expected to be more worldly than others even when a consultant may not normally travel outside their local area. Consultants are expected to constantly be working on an engagement or project, even when there may be periods when the economy slows or other circumstances arise

where there are no new engagements or projects to work on.

Ultimately a consultant should focus on their own expectations and understand who else has expectations that are important to the success of what they do. It is unrealistic to think that a consultant can continuously manage the expectations of everyone else. When a consultant can meet or exceed the expectations of someone else, it is often a bonus and not a goal.

Consultant Reporting

Reporting requirements are a part of the every day routine for most consultants. Whether it is status reporting, time reporting, expense reporting or other reports, regular reports are sometime the only means of communication to let others know what has transpired or what a consultant has done. Accuracy is extremely important no matter what type of report is required. Inaccuracies can cause miscommunication, delays, ineffective management, risks, billing errors, and delays in payments.

Time Reports
Time reports are used to account for a consultant's time. They are used by independent consultants and staffing companies to bill clients for time worked, and they are used as proof of actual hours or blocks of time worked. Clients use Time Reports to verify billed consultant hours and to reconcile billing with how many hours or what block of time the consultant reported to have worked. The information in a Time Report will vary based on staffing company and/or client policies and procedures. Some may only require reporting hours or blocks of time worked, while others may require a brief description of the tasks performed along with the hours reported working on them. Others may require start and end times for each day or block of time reported. Some larger companies may have

accounting codes that need to be included in Time Reports, so clients or departments are billed correctly for the consultant's time.

In some instances, due to differing reporting systems, a consultant may be required to submit multiple Time Reports, one to their staffing company and one directly to their client. Companies try to consolidate these reporting requirements whenever possible but differing formats and systems can sometime override convenience.

Time Reports can be submitted in many ways and with differing frequencies, depending on staffing company and/or client policies and procedures. The most common reporting period for submitting billable time is on a weekly basis, sometimes with daily details included.

Time Reports are almost always required when a contract with a client is based on Time and Materials (T&M). T&M contracts are agreements where a client will pay for a consultant's time and any materials that may be needed to perform the agreed-to tasks.

In the event a contract is based on a deliverable versus a T&M contract, a client may still require regular Time Reports so they can gain a better understanding of actual costs for future planning. Deliverable contracts are based on the final end-product regardless of how much time or money it costs to produce it.

Based on a company's policies and procedures Time Reports may need to be approved by an immediate supervisor, manager, or team lead. Tracking down authorized approvers on a Friday or at the end of a work period can sometimes be challenging, so it is always best to keep Time Reports up-to-date and ready for approval when they are required to be submitted.

There can be different methods required to submit a Time

Report. Some companies have online reporting systems that the consultant is given limited access to so they can submit their Time Reports for approval. Some companies require Time Reports be emailed, some require faxing, and some require they be submitted directly to a manager, supervisor, lead, or designated person for processing. Whichever way a Time Report is submitted, a consultant should always keep a copy of their reports for their own records and reference. In the event of a lost or missing report, or a later dispute in hours reported, these records may come in handy. Hours reported in a Time Report should never be recorded before the actual hours have been worked.

Billable versus Non-Billable Hours

It can sometimes be confusing, especially for someone new to consulting, what billable time is defined as, and how it reported versus non-billable time. Is travel time to a client site billable? Is half of travel time billable? Are meetings with clients billable? Are breaks billable? If you attend a working lunch is the time billable?

Billable time is the time spent on a client task, project, product, or service. It is based on the mutual agreement (or contract) between a client and either the staffing company or independent consultant. Billable time can be based on actual hours worked during a day (either reported based on start and stop times or total hours worked per day) or on a daily rate.

Billable time based on daily rates when working for a staffing company is usually reported only to the staffing company for accounting purposes, if required. The staffing company in turn bills the client a set amount for each day the consultant works for the client. Independent consultants do not bill their clients for hours worked but bill them at the set daily rate for each day worked. Daily rates mean it does not matter whether a consultant works four, eight, or twelve hours a day, the client pays the same daily rate for each day worked.

Travel time is something defined in a client contract if it is billable. Travel time is sometimes paid for by larger-sized clients who cannot get the expertise they need locally. It can be considered billable time as the actual time traveled, a daily rate, or in some cases by mutual agreement as half of the total travel time a consultant requires to get to the client site. Consultants should always be aware of travel time agreements and policies before charging their travel time.

Client meetings are always billable unless the meetings are part of sales and marketing efforts. When an independent consultant works with a staffing company and participates in a sales or marketing meeting with a client, whether their time is billable or not is mutually agreed on by the staffing company and consultant.

Breaks are generally part of a regular work day and are a part of the billable hours reported unless they exceed fifteen minutes; are more frequent than one break for every four hours worked; or, are specifically addressed as non-billable in a client contract.

Lunch breaks are generally not considered billable time. The exception to this is if a consultant is working on tasks during their lunch break. When a consultant works during their lunch break it is important that the client agrees to this practice in advance and that the practice does not violate any client company policies. When a client orders lunch in or takes a consultant or team out to participate in a working lunch the consultant's time is typically billable because although they are having lunch their time while eating is being used to work on a billable task.

Status Reports
Status Reports are not always required, but when they are

their frequency, format, and level of detail can vary widely and will be governed by staffing company and/or client policies and procedures. Consultants are required to submit Status Reports due to the often independent, entrepreneurial nature of the way they work.

The most common frequency for submitting Status Reports is weekly. Depending on the level of detail required and the complexity of a consultant's tasks or deliverables it is a good habit to maintain an ongoing Status Report during the week, updating it once a day. This helps capture activities while they are still fresh and saves scrambling at the end of a reporting period to capture and recreate activities and work performed.

Using a previous period's Status Report as a template or boilerplate can save time and effort. This practice also helps provide continuity between reports. For example, if a task is reportedly in progress one week and not addressed the next, it leaves the reader or reviewer wondering if anything is happening on that task. Was the task completed, is it still in progress, are their issues, is it on hold? Does the reader or reviewer have to make assumptions, or go back to the author for clarification? Gaps in reporting can be confusing and can make updates or rewrites to the originally submitted Status Report necessary.

The format, content, and level of detail of a Status Report will vary based on many factors. A Status Report can take the form of an email, memo, form, or presentation. Following set policies and procedures will help the intended audience better process this type of documentation and helps demonstrate the level of professionalism a consultant maintains.

While Time Reports are sometimes the only visibility for management to see how much time a consultant works on a task or product, Status Reports are often the only communication device a consultant has to report their activities, achievements, challenges, and any potential risks that may arise as the results of their work. For example, a consultant may be challenged to complete a task because a prerequisite dependent task or item expected to be completed or in place is late or missing. This can pose a potential risk to budgets, deadlines, and/or deliveries. Communicating a situation as soon as possible is important; but documenting it so others are aware of it and can track and manage it is equally as important. At times a Status Report may be the only means available to a consultant for reporting such things.

It is very important when Status Reports are required that they be submitted on time. Those responsible for reviewing these reports usually have a predefined time that they set aside for review. If a Status Report is late it can mean a reviewer has to stop working on another activity to review a late report and manage any resulting issues it might have documented in it.

Expense Reports
Expense Reports are the way a consultant is reimbursed by a staffing company or client for business-related expenses they incur. Most expenses are usually travel-related, however, there are other types of expenses a consultant may be reimbursed for such as mobile phone bills, business-related office supplies, and postage. The types of allowable business expenses are determined by the Internal Revenue Service (IRS) and specific reimbursable expenses are governed by staffing company and/or client corporate policies and procedures. Expense Report submittal time frames and formats are also governed by these corporate policies and procedures.

Expense Reports are usually submitted on a weekly or sometimes monthly basis. There are often deadlines associated with Expense Reports that a consultant must observe if they want to be reimbursed. It is very important to submit Expense Reports as soon as possible. There is always a lag in the time a report is submitted and the time that a consultant receives payment. However, expense reports should never be submitted prior to when a reported expense is incurred.

Expense Reports often go through a review and approval cycle once they are submitted and depending on the process it can be lengthy. Lag times for receiving payment can range from a week to more typically a month or longer. This means that any payments made for reimbursable expenses, especially those made using a credit card, may have to be paid for and then carried by the consultant because of their credit card billing cycles.

How an Expense Report looks will be determined by the staffing company and/or client and the means by which the report is submitted. Some companies have electronic systems that a consultant has limited access to where they report their expenses. Some companies require a faxed report based on a standardized template, while other companies require an original hard copy of the report be submitted via mail or other courier. In all cases, original receipts must accompany the report or be sent to the company after the report is filed. It is always a good practice to keep copies of all Expense Reports and receipts submitted for the consultant's records, in the event they are lost during transit or processing.

While the information required in an Expense Report may vary, there is a core set of information that every report will contain: 1) The date the expense was incurred; 2) A description of the expense; 3) The amount of each expense to be reimbursed; 4) An accompanying receipt with this information; and 5) A total of all reported expenses. Additional information may be required such as attendees in the case of reimbursable meeting or meal expenses.

When submitting expenses to a staffing company, expenses are typically reported based on the client that will be billed for those expenses. If a consultant has reportable expenses for more than one client, they are usually required to submit separate reports for each one.

In some instances, a consultant may be required to submit more than one Expense Report for the same expenses. Although this is not common, when it is required an original Expense Report is submitted to the staffing company and a copy is submitted to the client. In these cases, it is usually standard practice to submit any original receipts to the staffing company, not the client, so they can be passed on when the client is actually billed. When multiple reports are required, it helps the client more quickly reconcile and pay for expenses when they receive the actual billing from the staffing company.

Payments for expenses are usually either included in regular pay checks or direct deposits. In the case of independent consultants, expenses are usually paid by check separately from billable time unless bills submitted to the client include both.

The most important aspects of expense reporting are to follow the rules put in place by the staffing company and/or client, submit reports in a timely manner, submit original receipts with the reports, and ensure all information submitted in Expense Reports is accurate. Inaccuracies can cause delays in receiving reimbursement payments.

Other Reports
Consultants may be required to submit other types of regular reports depending on the industry, staffing company, and/or client. Additional reports can include regular reports on patients, testing activities, bug or issue reports, inspections, survey, and management reports.

Keys to Success

The keys to a consultant's success rest in the consultant's skills, experience, education, attitude, flexibility, reputation, and behavior. The more a consultant is directly involved with successful outcomes, the more successful they will be. When the good reputation of a consultant precedes them, it is an excellent indicator that the consultant is doing the right things and word-of-mouth is helping to further their success.

Good Habits, Practices, and Skills
Learning, developing, and following good habits and practices early in a consultant's career is the path of least resistance to a successful career as a consultant. When a consultant has to relearn or redevelop their regular habits and practices after a negative situation or outcome, it is a far more difficult task and can result in having to live with the consequences for a long time to come.

Common sense is something that is not found in textbooks or taught in school, yet it is something very important to a consultant's success. The ability to quickly assess a situation, logically analyze it, formulate a rational approach, and develop realistic conclusions while considering intentional and unintentional impacts of a conclusion is one of a consultant's greatest keys to success. Common sense is a simplistic, uncomplicated methodology to this cognizant thought process.

There are inevitably going to be times when a consultant comes across a client, client employee, colleague, or other consultant that is impossible in their expectations, attitude, and/or behavior. When this happens, it is a test and challenge for the consultant in how they handle the situation. If there is abuse involved or the consultant feels threatened or cannot effectively deal with the situation it is time for them to get management involved. If a consultant is working directly for a client that means reporting the situation directly to client management. If a consultant is working for a staffing company, it means reporting the situation to their staffing company management. When a consultant works for a staffing company it is the staffing company management, not the consultant, who is responsible for discussing the issue with the client.

It is always better for a consultant to find an acceptable resolution, but ultimately management is responsible and trained to deal with conflicts. A good consultant will recognize when it is time to step back and let others deal with a situation instead of potentially exacerbating it.

Expertise

Expertise is another key to a consultant's career success. Expertise is based on a formula of experience and time. A consultant builds their expertise in a given area over the course of time and specific experiences they have. Expertise translates to being highly familiar with specific subject matter, having deep understanding of it, having extensive experience with it, and being able to share knowledge with others in the given area of expertise.

As a consultant builds their expertise over time and a wide breadth of experience, they ultimately become Subject Matter Experts (SMEs). SMEs are go-to individuals who have greater knowledge than most in a specific area. SMEs are almost always in great demand and can command salaries and hourly rates at the high-end of a salary tier.

Reputation

The reputation of a consultant is a major key to their success. As a consultant builds more experience in their given field, they are also simultaneously building a reputation. Reputation is not always something a consultant considers, but people involved with consultants talk to one another. Managers, supervisors, team members, administrative support people, colleagues, and other consultants contribute to forming and broadcasting a consultant's reputation. A successful consultant will have a sterling reputation that precedes them wherever they go.

When a consultant has a good reputation, they will often hear clients, new teams, colleagues, and consultants remark that they have heard of them. These individuals will be excited about working with and next to a consultant because of the good things they have heard about them. Conversely, a consultant with a poor reputation will be invited to work for clients and join new teams less frequently. Their poor reputation will precede them, and it will be an uphill challenge to overcome it whether it is warranted or not.

Location
We often hear the phrase: location, location, location. It is usually used in the context of real estate or geographic areas of greatest career opportunity. Location considerations can also have a major affect on the career of a consultant.

Being in an area that has the greatest consultant career opportunities is one consideration. The best locations for consultant career opportunities are usually larger, urban areas where many large to medium-sized companies are located. There are some career fields where small companies will provide the best opportunities for a consultant. However, the companies that will consistently sustain a consultant's career are usually found in medium to large-sized companies because they use consultants more frequently. Being in an area where many of these larger sized companies are located and concentrated can be a key to a consultants' success.

Locations where many high-tech companies are concentrated can be important to how successful a consultant is depending on their field or industry. For example, a medical research consultant will have a far greater number of opportunities in an area where many research centers, pharmaceutical companies, and biopharmaceutical companies are located than in a rural area. The same is true of a software consultant being located near a high concentration of high-tech software product or services companies.

Another factor in where a consultant is located is often their proximity to a major international airport. When a consultant is required to travel frequently it is important that they can get to an airport within a reasonably short amount of time. There are sometimes situations or emergencies that may arise when a consultant is called on to travel with little or no notice. If these situations arise, a consultant should be able to respond quickly.

Being located near an airport also saves a great deal of wear and tear on a consultant as they depart and arrive from their frequent trips. Many consultants travel on Mondays and Fridays, two of the busiest days for commuting. Traveling great distances and dealing with traffic delays on the way to an airport can cause missed flights, high stress, and elevated anxiety levels to for a consultant. After dealing with hours of airport lines, hustle, and bustle on the way home from a trip, dealing with traffic delays exiting an airport and long commutes home can be exhausting.

Make It Look Easy
A consultant always tries to make whatever they are doing look easy no matter how difficult a task, situation, or challenge may be. People are constantly looking to a consultant to solve problems for them, mitigate risks, and provide solutions quickly, reasonably, and economically. The easier a consultant makes what they are doing seem, the more confidence it instills in those around them. Making something look easy and not dwelling on the difficulties or challenges of a problem, risk, or given

situation can sometimes instill the confidence in a team that ultimately leads to success. That success might not otherwise be achieved when focus is directed at how hard or impossible something is.

Keys to Failure

Along with keys to success there are keys to failure that a consultant should always avoid. A very easy gauge for failure is for the consultant to put themselves in the staffing company, client, colleague, team member, or other consultant's shoes. Seeing attitudes, behaviors, habits, and words through other people's eyes is a sure way to see and understand what might be going, or has gone, wrong. Another good gauge for determining potential failure is if something does not feel right, it probably isn't.

Attitude
A negative attitude will be noticed and noted by colleagues very quickly. It will be discussed and noted whether anything is said to the consultant or not. Attitudes such as "you won't be able to do that," "this is doomed," "that team member is not contributing, is lazy, inept, or incompetent," "I can't work with that person," "I don't want to be here, I want to go home," "I have better things to do than this task," or "My way is best, I am the expert," will affect everyone around the consultant in a negative way. It can have a direct impact on the successful outcome of the task or project, and in most cases will not be tolerated for very long. A negative attitude, just like a positive one, will follow a consultant long after they leave a client, company, or project.

The customer is always right, even when they are wrong. For example, there may be times when a consultant, through direct knowledge or previous experience, might know that an intended approach is going to lead to a negative outcome. In those instances, the best the consultant can do is try to share their experience without emotion. However, if a client chooses to continue doing things the way they see fit, the best the consultant can do is respect the client's decision, try to make the best of the situation, and contribute in any way they can to change the inevitable outcome. This is achieved through a positive and cooperative attitude, not a bad one.

In Over Your Head

A consultant can sometimes find themselves "in over their heads," due to a staffing company over-selling the consultant, a circumstance where a stronger or different skill set is required, or situations far more complicated, complex, or dire than anyone may have anticipated. This is not just reserved for a new consultant starting their career, but it can also happen to a seasoned consultant. While a consultant should always have a can-do attitude, there may be times when attitude simply isn't enough for a successful outcome.

In these circumstances the worst thing a consultant can do is wing it, think they can overcome obstacles they may be ill-equipped to overcome, or not communicate to management the risks of a situation. In extreme situations, the best thing a consultant may do is request to be removed from a situation to avoid being the reason for a failed venture.

Motivation

Lack of motivation is another key to failure. Almost everyone has days when they just do not want to get out of bed, go to work, or work on a given task or project. When a consultant is not motivated and brings that lack of motivation to a client or team it makes it much more difficult on the consultant and all those around them to be successful. Consultants are typically looked upon to be the motivators on a team, even when they aren't feeling it. When a consultant lacks motivation, it can spread like wildfire. Others who look at the consultant may think, "If this highly paid consultant has no motivation or low motivation for completing a task or project, why should I be excited about it."

A good consultant will set the bar and example for others, even when they don't feel like it, to motivate themselves and others.

Ten Things Not to Do

The following ten items are some keys to failure that a consultant should never do. They are not presented in any prioritized order but are all important behaviors and things a good consultant will always avoid.

One – Disrespect and Inconsideration
Disrespect and/or inconsideration directed at anyone is something that should never be an issue. A good consultant will never disrespect others and will always consider others before speaking or acting, whether they are a client, management, a colleague, or another consultant.

Two – Superior Attitude
A good consultant will never think, speak, or act in a superior manner. The terms superior and inferior are not a part of their regular vocabulary or thought process. Consultants often have a unique opportunity to empower and help build the self-esteem of those around them. A consultant should never allow themselves to feel that others are a threat to them, so they need to be competitive or feel superior. Everyone deals with their own private struggles. Respecting and considering others can help make those struggles just a little easier for others.

Three – Lies and Misrepresentation
Consultants should never lie or misrepresent themselves or a situation. The truth always comes to light and when it does the damage to a consultant and/or situation can be

irreversible and have unintended long-term effects for a very long time to come. Lies and misrepresentation are always exponentially worse than any truth they are hiding.

Four – Conducting Personal Business
A consultant that conducts personal business during business hours, especially while at a client site, is not the sign of a professional consultant. It is the sign of someone with poor work ethics and someone who does not take their career very seriously. If a consultant does not take their career seriously, why should or would anyone else?

Five – Absenteeism and Lateness
Not showing up when or where expected is an absolute taboo in the consulting world. Consultants have a small window of opportunity to deliver their product or service. That small window includes the opportunity to make a positive impression on a client, but absenteeism and tardiness narrows that window. Absenteeism and tardiness are perceived as a sign of disrespect. They are also a indication that a consultant does not take their position or responsibilities seriously.

Six - Sharing Proprietary Information
Sharing or discussing staffing company or client proprietary information is unacceptable in any circumstance. Many companies require a consultant to sign a Non-Disclosure Agreement (NDA) before sharing proprietary information or details about themselves. Whether a consultant signs an NDA or not, it is never acceptable to discuss or share a client's information or situation with anyone other than those authorized, such as team members working on a product or service for the client.

Seven – Incomplete or Missing Tasks
Incomplete or missing tasks are not what a consultant is paid for and will not be tolerated by a client or staffing

company for very long. Consultants are expected to be professional and perform the work they are tasked with; within the time frame they are given. When this is not the case it can impact entire teams, product and project outcomes, and overall budgets and timelines. In highly complex technical environments where tasks are interdependent with each other, an incomplete or missing task can have a negative ripple affect on many other tasks in a work plan and many other people depending on the task being complete.

Eight – Unprofessional Appearance

The old saying, "Don't judge a book by its cover" may be very true when it comes to judging people, but the reality is that in the consulting world a consultant is often judged by their appearance and how they dress. While most companies and clients do not expect a consultant to be dressed in a three-piece suit (although some industries do have those expectations), they do expect a consultant to look professional. Not bathing, having unkempt hair, wearing tee-shirts, shorts, flip-flops, and in most cases, jeans, is typically not acceptable to staffing companies and clients. An unprofessional appearance can create an immediate negative impression and be perceived as a sign of low self-worth. An unprofessional appearance can greatly hinder securing a consulting position.

Nine – Arguing or Fighting

Arguing or fighting are never acceptable behavior in any situation. It is always a sign of poor self-control and, even in the case someone is right, is never tolerated or considered acceptable behavior. A consultant is expected to be diplomatic in all circumstances and to get along with others, even the most difficult and contrary of people or situations. If a situation is heated a consultant is expected to have the sense to distance themselves and gain a calmer, more productive perspective and to seek an amicable solution.

Physical altercations are absolutely taboo under any circumstances and never tolerated. It is extremely important that a consultant always maintain a professional attitude and never engage in a physical altercation with another person. If someone is aggressive or threatens physical abuse, a consultant should immediately report it to management for them to address and resolve.

Ten – Inebriation and Incapacitation
Being inebriated or incapacitated by alcohol or drug consumption is a sure way to be immediately removed from a client or staffing company. If an individual cannot manage their alcoholic intake or dependence on drugs, it is important that they seek professional help to overcome it. If they are a full-time employee of a staffing company, they almost always offer confidential programs to help in dealing with these issues. An individual with these types of issues will not last as a consultant for very long.

Diving In, Head-First

Still want to be a consultant? Now that we have shared the ins and outs, up and downs, and dos and don'ts of consulting it is time to dive in and join the thousands of consultants who enjoy rewarding, lucrative careers across the world and across many industries.

No one can have more confidence or belief in themselves or their abilities than you. Your confidence and belief in your abilities will give confidence to a potential staffing company and/or client to take a chance and give your capabilities and skills a try. You can do this! Remember, make it look easy. Believe you can meet the goals of a client and can find practical solutions to their challenges and they will too.

Do not become discouraged if you do not succeed at first

and someone else is chosen for a position. Use the experience as a lesson. Realistically look at how the other consultant was chosen instead of you. Do not make excuses or use the experience as a weapon against yourself but instead consider it a learning opportunity. Solicit any feedback an interviewer or potential client may be willing to offer and always be sure to thank them for taking the time to share their insights with you. Look at what you could have said or done differently (if anything) to make yourself a stronger candidate, and do not look back on the experience with negativity. If a position or situation is meant to be, it will be. No matter how perfect a situation might look, if it does not work out there is a reason it didn't. Another opportunity, usually a better one, will come your way that would not come to you if it had. It is important to stay positive and trust that the right situation will always present itself to you and work out.

Stories from the Consultant Trenches

So many consultants who heard of this book while it was being written and reviewed commented, "Boy, the stories I could tell!" The following sections are taken from actual consultant experiences and shared here.

The Scapegoat
Consultants sometimes become scapegoats for the actions and poor decisions of full-time employee (FTE) team members. The following story comes from a consultant assigned to a long-term International project. The project was a software implementation across International teams and involved a number of consultants, most software developers, and two Business Analysts (BAs).

The married client project manager (PM) was rumored to be having a relationship with the married lead business analyst. Then rumor had it that the relationship ended. Behind closed doors there were many hushed meetings involving each of them that ultimately resulted in the client PM suddenly no longer being involved with the project. The void that this left was interestingly filled by the client lead business analyst who moved to the PM position. The FTE was in over their head and did not have the experience to properly manage a complex project or have the personality to effectively work with diverse internal International teams.

As part of the team two consultants were hired as BAs and reported to the client lead BA FTE. Both came with extensive experience successfully delivering complex International software implementation projects. When the lead business analyst ignored the business needs of the International business team, it required significant functional and technical rework to get the project back on track. One of the consultant BAs became the scapegoat for the problem as the FTE refused to take responsibility for their decisions and direction. Along with the significant budget and schedule impacts, the consultant left the project out of frustration and the client lost an excellent, valuable, and experienced resource.

The FTE PM continued to make errors in judgment and not consider the International team repercussions of their decisions. When the International teams met separately and jointly approached management with their concerns and issues, the FTE PM tried to place the blame on the second BA consultant. The International team members came to the defense of the consultant who was exonerated. The FTE PM was replaced by an experienced internal PM but the significant negative impact to the project's budget, schedule, and momentum was almost unrecoverable.

Perception Is Nine Tenths of the Law
Perception can be the make or break of a successful consulting engagement. Often in the Information Technology (IT) field, implementing a technology solution

brings with it preconceived perceptions of the technology. One example was a technology project introducing new technology in a highly regulated manufacturing environment to electronically manage manufacturing records that were being created and managed manually.

The consultant on the project was told on their first day by client management that they had zero confidence in the proposed solution and did not believe that it would work or be of any benefit. The project sponsor shared this belief, having had a very unsuccessful experience trying to implement a similar technology a few years earlier. He also shared that the executive Vice President (VP) responsible for the project knew the project would fail but was forced to fund the project due to regulatory requirements.

In even the best of circumstances it usually takes a strong commitment by management to implement new technology. End-users are very often leery of change, suspicious of technology, and can feel threatened that the technology will replace their jobs. Strong executive and management commitment are often needed to help counter these concerns. When management is also leery of a solution or has no confidence in it, the solution has little hope of success.

This presented a great challenge to the consultant. The consultant considered the challenge and decided a combination of public relations and education were needed to put the project on the right track and obtain management and end-user buy-in. The consultant worked with the project team to develop an executive workshop and brought management and the project sponsor together in an effort to change preconceived perceptions. The consultant walked the group through the new technology and discussed the differences and advances in technology since the project sponsor's poor experience a few years earlier. Then the consultant walked the executives step-by-step through the proposed solution, how it would work, how it would be implemented, and how the consultant planned to gain end-user buy-in to the solution. Along the way the consultant continually pointed out the benefits the new solution would bring the organization and the return-on-investment (ROI) the executives could expect. The consultant also discussed and reinforced the importance of management's support in gaining end-user confidence.

The consultant completed the workshop with a demonstration the technical team created of the proposed solution. A small prototype of the solution was demonstrated where the executives could actually see their processes working within the new technology solution. At the end of the session the perception of management, including the project sponsor, went from completely and vocally against the project to, while still leery, somewhat optimistic and hopeful. The VP still considered the project to be a disaster waiting to happen but was impressed by what he saw. The main concern of the group went from the solution being able to work to being able to gain end-user acceptance of the solution.

Next the consultant set up an end-user workshop. They took the workshop presented to management, looked at what worked and what didn't, and created a similar approach for end-users. Before the workshop was given the consultant had meetings with the project sponsor and VP. In them the consultant conveyed the importance of their role in the project and invited them to speak at the beginning of the end-user workshop.

When the consultant gave the end-user workshop, the project sponsor and VP stepped in at the beginning of the session to say a few words of encouragement to the users. During the end-user workshop, the consultant reinforced how the solution would benefit the end-users personally.

They gave examples of the end-users learning new skill sets, and how much more streamlined, efficient, and less frustrating their jobs would be. The project sponsor was so impressed with the response of the users that he stayed for the entire session.

A few days after the end-user workshop, the consultant was summoned to the VP's office. The consultant was convinced the VP was going to withdraw funding and end the project before it began. Instead, the VP shared a conversation he and the project sponsor had after the sessions. The project sponsor was so impressed by what he had seen, his perception completely changed. He had met with the VP and was now so excited about sponsoring the project he asked the VP to make the implementation of the solution one of the goals his bonus would be based on. The VP also shared that end-users had stopped him in the hallways to tell him how excited they were about the new solution and couldn't wait for it to be built and implemented. They thanked him for funding the project and for making their jobs easier and more efficient. The VP began using the project as a talking point in meetings with other VPs and senior executives.

Management, the project sponsor, and the VP gave the project significant support during its implementation. End-users were so excited about the project they volunteered important information needed by the project team to best meet their needs, and gave their time to user test the solution once it was built.

The end result was an extremely successful project and a very happy client. By addressing everyone's perceptions and concerns the consultant turned a failing project around to a successful one. The consultant was so successful that the client hired them for several additional projects, recommended them for two other internal projects in other groups, and became an excellent reference for future positions.

An Expensive Degree Does Not a Good Consultant Make
So often staffing companies and clients are completely
dazzled by Ivy League degrees. Often, they look at the
person but only see the Ivy League degree they carry.
While a degree from a highly prestigious college is
impressive, it does not guarantee that person will make a
good consultant.

During a difficult phase of a technology implementation
project, an over-extended project team was tasked with
creating test scripts for thoroughly testing the software to
be implemented before bringing it online. The staffing
company that provided the consultants working on the
project was contacted for additional, short-term assistance
to write the test scripts based on client specifications and
direction.

Although the client was already highly impressed with the
consulting team in place, the staffing company wanted to
further impress the client in an effort to secure future
business. They chose an inexperienced junior consultant
with a Harvard degree to complete the task. After talking
up the Harvard degree, the staffing company flew the junior
consultant across the country at great expense to work for
three days on the test scripts.

The junior consultant arrived half a day late for the
assignment dressed in a tee-shirt and jeans. The main aisle
at the client's facility was lined with file cabinets
surrounded by client FTEs in their cubicles. As the
consultant project manager and project team lead walked
the junior consultant down the main aisle, the junior
consultant stopped midway down the aisle when he noticed
a newspaper on top of one of the file cabinets. He picked
up the newspaper and began reading it as he and the other
two consultants continued walking down the main aisle

toward his temporary cubicle.

Shortly thereafter the three met to discuss the junior consultant's task, what was required, the extremely short time frame given to accomplish the task in, and how the client wanted the task completed. The junior consultant immediately questioned the task, the time frame, and the way in which the task was to be completed. When it was explained that this was something set by the client and already agreed upon by the team to deliver, the junior consultant became challenging and indignant. They stated that they had a Harvard degree and that they had a better way of doing things although it was at the client's direction that the task be done in the manner it needed to be accomplished in the time frame given. The junior consultant even suggested talking to the client about it directly although there was a consultant project manager from their own staffing company team who had already gained work plan approval from the client.

After a day and a half, the junior consultant continued to challenge the consultant project manager and could produce no test scripts that they had completed after being given all of the documentation and instructions needed to do so. On the afternoon of the second day the project manager had a telephone conference with staffing company management and had the junior consultant immediately removed from the project. The consultant project manager and staffing company management were left to conduct damage control while the staffing company scrambled to replace the junior consultant with someone who could and would get the task done in even less time than the unrealistic three days they were originally given. Another consultant was brought on board, one with a less impressive degree, who was able to not only make up for the lost time the consultant with the Harvard degree wasted but put in extra time and effort to successfully complete and deliver the task within the original time frame.

While an expensive degree is very attractive to clients and staffing companies, it is the person behind the degree that ultimately makes a good consultant.

Caught in the Middle
There are times when a consultant finds themselves caught in the middle of disputes between clients and their vendors. Things can get exponentially complicated when a vendor is a partner of the consultant's staffing company.

A vendor sold a client a multimillion-dollar suite of software that needed to be implemented. The vendor was responsible for initially installing and implementing the core pieces of the software. After eighteen months and several million dollars the software had not been implemented. Out of extreme frustration the client released a Request for Proposal (RFP) to staffing companies for a Project Manager (PM) to assess the situation and make recommendations on whether to continue the project, how to proceed, or to shut the project down and sue the vendor for breach of contract.

One staffing company submitted a winning proposal and a staff consultant was chosen to join the project team and represent the client as a PM. The consultant PM was intimately familiar with the vendor's software because the staffing company was a partner with the vendor and did significant work for them implementing their software.

The consultant began the engagement by studying the project documentation including the original contract between the client and vendor, the statement of work the vendor had agreed to deliver, and the project team's documentation of what they had done to-date. Then the consultant observed the vendor's project team, what they had done, how they were doing it, and why they were doing it based on what they had promised to deliver.

Next the consultant met with the client and the client project team. The client shared their experiences over the previous eighteen months with the vendor and vendor project team and they voiced their concerns and frustrations.

The consultant took all of the information they had gathered and assessed it based on what both the client and vendor had agreed to in their contract, along with what the goals of the project were.

What the consultant discovered was that the vendor had sold the client several software components that were not relevant to their industry but were used in other industries. The vendor project team had no experience in the industry the client was in, and in some cases no experience with the software components they were trying to install and implement.

On the client side of the equation the consultant found that the client project team had no experience in the technology they were trying to implement and in some cases very little technical experience at all. The consultant also found that the end-users were very opposed to the software being implemented and very unhappy with the existing vendor project team for wasting so much of their time.

The consultant found themselves in the middle of a very serious multimillion-dollar dispute. The first thing the consultant had to establish was where their loyalty lay. In being hired by the client to represent them the consultant had to put the client's best interests above the vendor, above their staffing company, and above their own interests. At the same time, the most important thing for the consultant to accomplish was how to make a win-win situation out of the existing lose-lose one.

The consultant completed their assessment and put together a presentation of what was assessed and how. Instead of looking for blame, the consultant focused on how to save the project, make it work, and how to help the vendor reconcile their relationship with the client and avoid a nasty lawsuit. Next the consultant put together a list of recommendations on how the client, the vendor, and the project could move forward and be successful. The presentation the consultant created included the consultant's findings along with their recommendation of how to successfully move forward.

First the findings were shared with the client. The consultant recommended that the vendor project team be replaced by one that had the right experience for what the client needed to implement the software, at the vendor's expense. The consultant recommended the new project team perform a gap analysis – a formal look at where the project was and what was needed to get it back on track - so the new project team could familiarize themselves with what had been done, if any of it could be used to move forward, and what the next steps were to continue the project.

The consultant recommended that the client's technical team be scheduled for formal training in the software technology so they could become more familiar with the capabilities and constraints of the software. Recommendations for gaining end-user confidence and cooperation were also shared.

Next the consultant modified the presentation and shared it with the vendor. In it the consultant shared where the vendor stood with the client contractually. The consultant made recommendations to replace the existing project team and avoid a major lawsuit. They also recommended providing the client with some training credits to help educate the client's technical team and show a sign of good faith.

The consultant arranged for the management of the client

and vendor to meet and discuss the recommendations and how to work together to move the project forward.

Once both parties agreed to continue to work together the consultant invited end-users to a project update workshop. In it the consultant reviewed what had been done, what was going to be done to get the project on track, and how important the end-users were to the ultimate success of the project. The end-users were given the chance to voice their frustrations and concerns. Then they were given a chance to voluntarily participate in future workshops to provide input into decisions that would directly affect them and how the system would appear and work for them.

Finally, a schedule was put in place for the vendor to provide regular project updates to client management. This provided a means for the vendor to show progress and successes to the client and to help successfully rebuild their relationship.

The result was a new, productive working relationship between the client and vendor. The project was restarted, the software was successfully implemented, and a multimillion-dollar lawsuit was prevented. The consultant became a hero with the client, the vendor, and the partner staffing company that placed them. This project also resulted in both the client and the vendor recommending the consultant and their staffing company for several large, high-visibility, lucrative projects afterward.

Master-Slave Mentality
The ideal situation for a successful outcome when utilizing consultants is an atmosphere of cooperation and common goals. However, there are sometimes situations when FTEs feel a sense of superiority because they have what they think is a secure, long-term position with a company. They perceive consultants as transient, short-term resources hired to not only meet their needs, but also their whims. This

master-slave mentality can be extremely difficult for a consultant to deal with, and when taken to the extreme can lead to a great deal of wasted time and money for the client.

A consultant is usually hired, and their fee is based on, delivering a specific product or service or to perform agreed-to tasks for a client. The work that is to be performed is typically detailed in a Statement of Work (SOW) or work plan. The SOW and/or work plan is a part of the contractual agreement between the client and either the staffing company or independent consultant. When a master-slave situation rears its ugly head a consultant can get caught up in performing unrelated tasks that can result in not delivering what was contractually agreed to and even sometimes being blamed when expected goals are not met.

One independent consultant found themselves in a master-slave situation that quickly escalated to a difficult and almost impossible situation to deal with. A client FTE felt a consultant was their personal resource, there to perform whatever tasks the FTE wanted them to do. As a result, the consultant was frustrated, miserable, and had to constantly refer the FTE back to the SOW and what tasks had been agreed on. When significant additional tasks were assigned to the consultant the FTE became infuriated when the consultant referred to the SOW and recommended amending it to add the additional tasks and time it would take to complete them. When the first set of project milestones were not completed on time, the FTE blamed the consultant. The situation deteriorated to the point where the independent consultant abruptly withdrew from the project in an effort to save their sanity, keep from wasting any more of the client's budget on performing non-critical tasks, and remove themselves from a no-win situation. Subsequent consultants came and went with regular frequency costing the client significant losses in money and time until the FTE was ultimately replaced.

Budget Cuts and Redirection

Consulting can be a very unstable career path. Economic trends, a company's financial performance, and internal budgets often factors into whether a consultant has an ongoing position with a client or staffing company. All these factors are out of the control of the consultant. A consultant seldom has visibility or prior knowledge of important factors that can influence the fate of their continued employment.

There are times when a client or staffing company may revisit their overall or original business plan or roadmap. They may decide that they need or want to take a different approach or direction. They may redefine their business goals or how they plan to achieve them. There are times when a consultant will get caught in the middle of these changes and become their victim.

Budget cuts and redirection are not personal. When a consultant is directly affected by decisions based on these considerations, it is important they remember these types of decisions are in no way personal. When a consultant does not take these situations personally, they can often create a future win-win situation from what might seem like a losing one at the time.

A consultant that does not take these situations personally makes it easier for a client or staffing company to meet their business needs. Companies make these decisions based on need, not desire, and they are seldom easy decisions to make.

Consultants who are flexible, understanding, and realize it is no way a reflection of their performance leave the door open for future opportunities when a company's situation improves, or new consultant opportunities arise within the organization.

An example of this type of situation was a consultant

Project Manager (PM) who was managing an extensive, long-term system implementation and roll out for a client. Midway through the project the client decided to replace the consultant with a member of their internal project management team. It in no way reflected on the performance of the consultant PM but was a decision based on the client's redirection on how they utilized their internal PMs, along with sudden budgetary constraints. The consultant was told on a Friday afternoon that their services would no longer be needed on Monday morning.

By not taking the decision personally and understanding and exhibiting cooperation, the consultant took the remainder of the Friday afternoon to perform knowledge transfer with the incoming PM. Two years later when a new consulting opportunity arose with the client, the same consultant was chosen to fill the position because of the client's previous positive experience with them. In the meantime, the consultant went on to other projects, gaining invaluable experience that they could use on their new assignment.

Becoming a Subject Matter Expert
Consultants can often find themselves in situations where they have no expertise in a given area but are required to perform as if they have. Some staffing companies will market a consultant as having more skills or expertise than they actually have. There are also times when a consultant is up front with a client and admits to not having experience in a given area but the client (who always knows best) chooses to take a chance, anyway, usually based on past performance or reputation. A consultant has two choices when this happens: 1) Fail miserably while standing by their position of not having the experience or expertise required; or 2) Do everything within their power to learn what they need to learn to produce a successful outcome and become an expert on the subject. The second

145

choice, which is obviously more desirable for the consultant to deliver a successful product or service, will also open them up to future opportunities based on the knowledge, expertise, and experience they gain through these experiences.

One consultant was hired to help an organization roll out a new computer system to end-users. Their responsibility was to write end-user instructions for users to refer to when using the system, provide them with handy tips for the things users would be doing frequently, and support training efforts.

The client was implementing the system within a very short time frame. They needed users to be up and running on the system from the moment it went live. Due to technical constraints, the consultant did not have direct access to the system for the first three weeks of the engagement. However, by the end of the first week they had published their first tip sheet for users and had begun writing a user instruction manual for the system having never actually seen the system or used it.

How did they do it? They took the initiative to read up on the technology being used, how it worked, and asked for all the system documentation that had been produced by the technical team. The consultant talked with the technical resources who had built the system and to several end-users who would be using the system heavily (super users) to learn what they would be using it for. Then, based on the information from the vendor documentation, system documentation, and discussions, the consultant wrote the first tips for the system. The consultant had the development team review the tips to ensure they were accurate, and then had the super users review them to ensure that they made sense based on what they needed the system to do.

The result was a very successful engagement with the client that lead to the consultant becoming a subject matter expert in the technology and system being used. The consultant went on to deliver many additional successful projects using the technology and knowledge gained through that experience. The vendor recognized the consultant's intimate understanding of their software and also recommended them to several clients. The consultant became well known in the field as a subject matter expert in many aspects of the complex software and went on to write several industry white papers (informative industry reports) on the subject.

The Client Always Knows Best
We have all heard the old saying, "The customer knows best." When it comes to consultants and clients, the same is true – the client always knows best... even when they do not.

A consultant working on what might have seemed like a simple software upgrade soon discovered that the customer had written pages and pages of custom code that would be incompatible with the software once it was upgraded. The client wrote custom code every time an end-user wanted to process information in the system a different way. No one looked at a standardized method to process information or whether the end-user understood the system well enough to make custom requests and demands. The technical department simply received the request and wrote the code to accommodate the end-user.

When the consultant realized that so much custom code had been created, they analyzed the processes affected and recognized commonalities amongst the separate processes. The consultant recommended a standardized method for processing information within the system based on technical constraints within the software once it was upgraded and the business needs of the client. This would have saved significant amounts of time upgrading the software, maintaining it, and significant amounts of money by having one method for end-users to interact with the system. Going against logic the client decided they wanted the end-users to continue to have their custom methods for processing information in the system. The result was converting over 200 custom processes to work with the software upgrade and a custom program for end-users to use for entering data in the system. The cost of the custom solution was over twenty times more than a standardized solution would have been.

Although the consultant tried to offer a solution that followed best practices and was far more cost effective, the client always knows best what they are willing to do and pay for. While costly, the client was very happy with the end-result.

One Thing Leads to Another
Consultants sometimes find that their experiences with one client can often open many future doors for work with other clients. A consultant may gain related experience and knowledge as an additional bonus that translates to experience another client is looking for, even though the original work was focused elsewhere.

One consultant was hired to work on a large project in a federally regulated environment based on their experience with the technology being used. The project had many federal regulations governing what could and could not be done. The consultant had no experience with the regulations that governed the project but was expected to learn them and comply, so the consultant did just that – they did their homework, learned the regulations, and complied with them.

After the project was completed the consultant was hired by many other clients within the industry because of their familiarity with the regulations and compliance governing their actions. Through their experience with regulatory requirements and compliance in that one industry the consultant was able to apply their general knowledge to regulations and compliance in other industries and greatly broadened the types of clients interested in their expertise. At the same time, along with the experience and expertise they already had and were adding to, they also gained experience and expertise to become a subject matter expert in the areas of government regulations and compliance.

Acronyms

BA – Business Analyst

CV – Curriculum Vitae

ECM – Enterprise Content Management

EIN – Employee Identification Number

ERM – Enterprise Records Management

FTE – Full Time Employee

GMO – Genetically Modified Organism

GPS – Global Positioning System

IRS – Internal Revenue Service

IT – Information Technology

NDA – Non-Disclosure Agreement

PDF – Portable Document Files

PM – Project Manager

PMI – Project Management Institute

RFP – Request For Proposal

ROI – Return on Investment

SME – Subject Matter Expert

SOW – Statement of Work

SSN – Social Security Number

T&M – Time and Material

About the Author

Flo DiBona is a retired Principal Information Systems Consultant and subject matter expert in the functional architecture, design, project management, phasing, implementation and delivery of highly regulated global Enterprise Content Management (ECM), Enterprise Records Management (ERM), and advanced capture systems. Her wide range of expertise spans from the pharmaceutical, biopharmaceutical, and medical device sectors, to U.S. and Canadian state, province, county, and city government environments. She began her career providing proprietary technical editing and writing services, and material shelf life management to the aerospace industry.

Flo has written, edited, and published numerous proprietary technical guides, manuals, and white papers. She has also written articles for CNN iReports and blogs.

Along with writing, Flo is an award-winning photographer. She has over 40 years of experience in freelance photography.

Flo is a daytime soap opera activist helping to champion canceled daytime soap operas and the soap opera genre. She is also a supporter of the emerging independent web series genre.

Flo lectures, offers webinars, and conducts workshops on various subjects. "The Consultant's Handbook" is her first commercially published work. She currently lives in Northern California with her husband, daughter, and two rescue cats.

Flo DiBona Online

Facebook: https://www.facebook.com/FloDiBona/

Pixel: https://pixels.com/profiles/flo-dibona.html

Twitter: http://www.twitter.com/anobid

Smashwords:
http://www.smashwords.com/profile/view/FloDiBona

Blog:
https://www.blogger.com/profile/16883345527101121235

CNN iReports: http://ireport.cnn.com/people/anobid

eMail: Flo.DiBona@gmail.com

L'HUMANITÉ

face à la

TECHNOLOGIE

Homme / machine
le choc à venir

Gerd Leonhard

www.techvshuman.com

Je dédie ce livre à ma chère épouse, Angelica Feldmann, qui m'a tant appris sur l'humanité, a supporté mes absences avec tendresse durant son écriture, m'a offert ses commentaires bienvenus et n'a jamais cessé de m'encourager.
Sans toi, ce livre n'existerait pas.

TECHNOLOGY vs. HUMANITY
The coming clash between man and machine
Titre en Français :
L'Humanité face à la Technologie
Homme / machine: le choc à venir

Traduction Française (2018)
Nicolas Finet
Serge Uebersax
Révision finale : Nicolas Finet

Publié pour la première fois au Royaume-Uni
par les éditions Fast Future Publishing Ltd. 2016

Tous droits détenus par
The Futures Agency GMBH, Suisse

Pour tous contacts
books@thefuturesagency.com
www.techvshuman.com

ISBN 978-1721603091

Directeur artistique, lecteur : Jean-François Cardella
Mise en page : Gabriele Ruttloff-Bauer.
Secrétariat d'édition : N2agency.com

Couverture : www.angellondon.co.uk

Sommaire

Introduction

*Comment le souci de l'humanité peut-il prévaloir, confronté
à un changement technologique exponentiel
et toujours plus global ?*

Notre monde entre dans une période de profondes transformations, à une échelle et une vitesse de développement que la plupart d'entre nous n'avions tout simplement pas anticipées. Ces avancées technologiques exponentielles sont riches d'un potentiel considérable, mais ces opportunités ne vont pas sans responsabilités nouvelles, considérables elles aussi.

Le plus grand défi de l'humanité

Je crois que l'ampleur du changement causé par des événements récents et imprévus comme le Brexit (la décision du Royaume-Uni par référendum, en juin 2016, de quitter l'Union européenne) sera dérisoire comparé à l'impact d'une avalanche de changements technologiques qui pourrait remodeler non seulement l'essence même de l'humanité, mais aussi chaque aspect de la vie sur notre planète.

Par le passé, chacun des changements radicaux vécus par la communauté humaine a fondamentalement été engendré par l'émergence d'un unique facteur clé : d'abord le bois, la pierre, le bronze et l'acier, puis la vapeur, l'électricité, l'automatisation à l'échelle industrielle et enfin l'internet. Aujourd'hui en revanche, je vois un bouquet de sciences et de technologies convergentes donner naissance à des changements de paradigmes, qui vont redessiner non seulement le commerce, la culture et la société, mais aussi notre biologie et notre éthique.

Un manifeste pour contribuer à l'épanouissement humain

Qu'on me comprenne bien : *L'Humanité face à la technologie* n'est ni la célébration d'un révolution technologique galopante, ni une lamentation sur la chute de la civilisation. Si, comme moi, vous êtes accro au cinéma, vous en avez probablement déjà plus qu'assez des visions utopiques comme des cris d'alarme dystopiques d'Hollywood. On ne peut façonner le futur ni sur la base d'un optimisme aveugle ni en fonction d'une peur panique !

Mon but, avec ce livre, est d'amplifier et d'accélérer le débat sur la manière dont nous pourrons, à l'avenir, nous assurer de guider, encadrer et contrôler les développements scientifiques et technologiques afin qu'ils s'acquittent de leur objectif initial : servir l'humanité et contribuer à son épanouissement.

Mon ambition est de susciter la discussion au-delà des cercles de technologues exubérants, des tenants de l'académisme et des analystes en col blanc, et d'exprimer un ensemble de préoccupations sur lesquelles la population au sens large devrait être sinon alertée, du moins informée, ce qui est loin d'être le cas. En tant que prospectiviste – quoique je me sente de plus en plus un *présentiste* –, j'espère également aider concrètement au déchiffrement d'un futur qui semble échapper à l'entendement de beaucoup – quant il ne paraît pas tout simplement indigne de leur attention. J'ai conçu ce livre comme une plate-forme de discussion passionnée autour de ce que je considère être le sujet de débat le plus important de notre monde. J'estime que mon rôle est d'ouvrir et de catalyser ce débat. C'est pourquoi j'ai préféré donner à ce livre la forme d'un manifeste engagé plutôt que d'un guide. Afin de contribuer à stimuler et nourrir ce débat, j'approfondirai également les thèmes abordés dans le livre au cours de mes conférences, films et contributions en ligne à venir.

Ce n'est pas parce que nous pouvons que nous devrions

Il est temps, me semble-t-il, de nous extraire des débats d'experts sur ce qui est potentiellement possible et sur la manière de le concrétiser. En la matière, je pense que nous devons mettre en

chantier une réflexion plus fondamentale sur le rôle que nous entendons faire jouer à ces technologies transformatrices, afin qu'elles servent effectivement l'humanité ; *pouvoir* faire ne signifie pas forcément que nous *devrions* faire…

Pour guider cette réflexion, j'expose dans ce livre ce que je crois être les forces motrices du changement, ainsi que l'évaluation de leur impact et implications potentiels. Je mets en relief nombre de questions fondamentales soulevées par le rythme de développement accéléré – et bien souvent exponentiel – dans de multiples domaines de la science et de la technologie.

Je soutiens que nous devons placer la question du bonheur et du bien-être humains au cœur des processus de décision et de gouvernance, car ce sont eux qui vont déterminer les investissements futurs dans la recherche scientifique et technologique, puis leurs retombées commerciales. Et parce qu'en dernier ressort, ce qui définit la technologie n'est pas ce que nous cherchons, mais comment nous le cherchons.

Je poursuis en présentant toute une gamme de scénarios possibles sur la manière dont les choses pourraient tourner, selon les options de développement futur que nous aurons privilégiées. Et je conclus avec une palette d'idées d'inspiration humaniste, pour amorcer les débats sur le choix du meilleur chemin pour l'humanité et des meilleures décisions à prendre tout au long de ce cheminement.

Afin d'amorcer puis nourrir cette ambitieuse conversation collective, j'ai structuré ma réflexion en douze chapitres clés.

Chapitre 1 : Un prologue au futur
À mi-chemin de la deuxième décennie du siècle en cours, nous avons atteint un seuil critique dans l'évolution technologique, une période charnière au cours de laquelle le changement deviendra non seulement combinatoire et exponentiel, mais également inévitable et irréversible. Je soutiens que la période présente incarne notre dernière chance de nous interroger sur la nature de

ces défis à venir – de l'intelligence artificielle au séquençage du génome humain. Trouver le bon équilibre sera la clé.

Chapitre 2 : La technologie et nous

Dans ce chapitre, j'explique pourquoi la technologie peut simuler et remplacer, encore et toujours plus – mais qu'elle ne peut en aucun cas se substituer à nous. La technologie n'a aucune éthique et c'est précisément pourquoi son entrée imminente au cœur même de nos vies et de nos processus biologiques les plus intimes doit absolument faire l'objet d'un examen collectif et citoyen prioritaire. J'examine en particulier la nature de l'éthique en tant que marqueur et différenciateur humain essentiel, par-delà les différences de religions et de cultures.

Chapitre 3 : Les méga-changements

Dans les entreprises comme dans le secteur public, on nous a vendu la mutation numérique généralisée comme le changement de paradigme majeur – alors qu'il ne s'agit en fait que de l'un des dix bouleversements systémiques qui demain vont interagir avec la vie humaine, et l'altérer pour toujours. J'explore ces méga changements – de l'hyper mobilité numérique et l'automatisation jusqu'à la robotisation. Il n'y aura pas de processus évolutionnistes lents qui nous laisseront le temps de les intégrer et de nous y adapter. Bien au contraire, ces changements vont impulser un véritable tsunami disruptif, l'équivalent potentiel d'une extinction de masse pour la plupart des infrastructures commerciales globales existant à l'heure actuelle.

Chapitre 4 : Automatiser le monde

Ce chapitre remet en cause le mythe envahissant et vraiment trompeur selon lequel l'automatisation ne perturberait finalement que le « travail en col bleu » – ou même en col blanc. Mais la prochaine vague d'automatisation à venir déferlera bien au-delà de nos usines ou de nos infrastructures publiques, jusqu'au cœur de nos fonctions biologiques, comme le vieillissement ou

l'enfantement. Je pose la question de savoir si nous, en tant que communauté, sommes prêts à renoncer à notre souveraineté humaine face aux forces sans visage de la technologie, habitués que nous sommes à des transformations graduelles annoncées par les vagues de changement antérieures, et avec des temps de réponse et d'adaptation qui s'expriment souvent en décennies. Vous personnellement, vous sentez-vous préparé(e) à la plus grande perte de libre arbitre qu'on ait vue dans l'Histoire ?

Chapitre 5 : L'internet des objets inhumains
Ce chapitre explore les défis que pose l'internet des objets – autrement dit le discours dominant en vogue sur les transformations numériques, porté par des milliers de stratégies d'entreprise qui surfent sur la tendance. Avons-nous seulement pris le temps de nous interroger sur la différence entre les algorithmes et ce qui fait de nous des humains – et que j'appelle *androrithmes* ? L'internet des objets inhumains va-t-il nous conduire, d'abord progressivement puis abruptement, à renoncer à notre humanité en nous mécanisant toujours plus, simplement pour rester dans le coup ? Alors que l'informatique se fait mobile, puis portable et bientôt ingérable et implantable, allons-nous sacrifier à un succès numérique illusoire notre avantage planétaire spécifique en tant qu'espèce ?

Chapitre 6 : Magique, maniaque… toxique !
J'examine ici de quelle manière notre *love affair* avec la technologie suit souvent une progression prévisible qui, de la magie aux comportements maniaques, aboutit finalement à l'intoxication. En acceptant de faire de l'expérience de la vie une séquence de rencontres toujours plus médiatisée et informatisée, nous pensons y prendre plaisir. Mais en réalité, nous sommes simplement chauffés à blanc par nos hormones – lesquelles font de plus en plus figure de cibles pour les gentils fournisseurs de « pop tech ». Alors que nous nous abandonnons à la grande fiesta sans fin que nous offre le progrès technologique, il serait salutaire

de réfléchir à la gueule de bois qui guette – et au prix à payer le lendemain, et après.

Chapitre 7 : Nouvelle pandémie : l'obésité numérique

Ce chapitre s'interroge sur la manière dont l'obésité numérique, qui ne nous est peut-être pas aussi familière que son pendant physique, est en train de prendre les proportions d'une pandémie d'ampleur sans précédent. Vautrés en nous goinfrant d'actualités et d'infos saturées d'algorithmes et constamment mises à jour, nous nous distrayons au sein une bulle technologique bourgeonnante dont on peut pourtant douter des vertus divertissantes. Compte tenu de la déferlante annoncée de nouvelles technologies et de plates formes numériques en tout genre, il est plus que temps d'aborder nos nutriments numériques exactement de la manière dont nous le faisons déjà pour nos nutriments biologiques.

Chapitre 8 : Précaution contre proaction

Ce chapitre examine l'argument selon lequel le futur le plus sûr – et qui reste le plus prometteur – est celui où nous ne repoussons pas l'innovation, sans pour autant ignorer les risques exponentiels qu'elle implique désormais, et sans nous en débarrasser comme s'il s'agissait du problème de quelqu'un d'autre. La facture de nos paris technologiques d'aujourd'hui, telle que nous l'avons transmise aux générations futures, ne peut être reportée – sous peine d'un dérapage immédiat, d'une ampleur sans précédent.

Je soutiens que précaution et proaction, les deux principes les plus souvent déployés à ce jour, sont l'un comme l'autre totalement insuffisants pour affronter un scénario combinatoire et exponentiel où la prudence s'avère aussi dangereuse que la précipitation. Le transhumanisme – avec ses allures de course de lemmings aux frontières de l'inconnu – représente à mes yeux l'option la plus effrayante de toutes celles qui s'offrent à nous aujourd'hui.

Chapitre 9 : Le bonheur au risque du hasard

L'argent est roi, certes, et pourtant la poursuite du bonheur demeure la grande affaire. Le bonheur n'apparait pas seulement comme le but ultime de l'existence humaine tel que le proclament les philosophies et les cultures de part le monde, mais il reste également un facteur insaisissable, qui persiste à résister à toute quantification, à toute tentative de reproduction technique.

Alors que la technologie de pointe s'efforce de simuler de brefs moments de plaisir hédoniste, distributeur appliqué de dopamine, comment pouvons-nous protéger les formes plus profondes du bonheur impliquant empathie, compassion et conscience ? Le bonheur entretien également des correspondances avec la chance, le hasard ; alors, de quelle façon devrons-nous user de la technologie pour qu'elle limite les risques inhérents à la vie humaine tout en continuant à préserver son mystère et sa spontanéité ?

Chapitre 10 : Éthique numérique

Dans ce chapitre, je soutiens qu'à mesure que la technologie se répand dans toutes les dimensions de la vie et de l'activité humaine, l'éthique numérique va s'imposer comme un sujet brûlant et impossible à ignorer, tant pour les individus que pour les organisations politiques, économiques et culturelles. Pour l'heure, nous ne disposons même pas d'un langage commun pour en parler, si ce n'est d'un consensus sur des droits et responsabilités partagées.

La question du développement durable a souvent été écartée comme un enjeu tiers-mondiste par les économies développées, et toujours laissée de côté lors des périodes de récession économique. Par contraste, il est désormais certain que l'éthique numérique va acquérir un statut permanent et central dans l'arène économico-politique. Le temps est venu d'ouvrir le débat éthique sur les technologies numériques – une menace à l'encontre de l'épanouissement humain, potentiellement bien plus grande que la prolifération nucléaire.

Chapitre 11 : La Terre en 2030 : paradis ou enfer ?

En voyageant par l'imagination en direction d'un futur proche ou plus lointain, nous pouvons aisément nous représenter certains des gigantesques changements qui altèreront le travail et la vie dans des proportions insoupçonnées – c'est ce que je m'efforce d'explorer dans ce chapitre. Nombre de ces bouleversements doivent être, en eux-mêmes, accueillis avec bienveillance – par exemple la perspective de travailler par passion plutôt que par nécessité. Toutefois, la plupart des privilèges les plus élémentaires que nous avons un jour ou l'autre tenus pour acquis, comme le libre arbitre dans nos choix de consommation ou de style de vie, pourraient bien devenir de simples échos d'une époque enfuie, ou la prérogative exclusive d'une poignée d'ultra-nantis. Paradis ou enfer ? Faites votre choix – mais faites-le maintenant.

Chapitre 12 : Le temps de la décision

Dans ce chapitre de clôture, je soutiens que nous vivons un moment crucial au regard de l'adoption des technologies – pas tant pour ce qui tient à l'usage de la technologie elle-même, mais pour ce qui touche à l'intégration toujours plus profonde de la technologie dans la vie humaine. Bien des sujets éthiques, économiques, sociaux ou biologiques ne peuvent plus attendre le prochain forum ou la prochaine génération. Il est temps de réglementer l'application des technologies de masse, exactement comme nous le ferions de n'importe quelle autre force de transformation similaire, comme l'énergie nucléaire.

Ce n'est pas là la conclusion d'un dialogue abouti, mais plutôt le début d'une conversation somme toute urgente dont il faut qu'elle devienne centrale dans nos médias, nos écoles, nos gouvernements et, encore plus immédiatement, dans nos cercles de réflexion et de décision. Le temps où les technologues et les technocrates se contentaient de transmettre les questions éthiques en d'autres mains est révolu.

J'espère que ce livre vous encouragera à réfléchir en profondeur aux défis que nous affrontons et je vous invite à contribuer à cette conversation collective en devenant membre de la communauté techvshuman/TVH sur www.techvshuman.com

Gerd Leonhard
Zurich, Suisse,
Août 2016

Chapitre 1
Un prologue au futur

L'humanité va changer davantage dans des 20 prochaines années qu'au cours des 300 années précédentes.

Les êtres humains ont l'habitude d'extrapoler le futur à partir du présent, ou même du passé. L'hypothèse, c'est que ce qui a déjà bien fonctionné pour nous jusqu'à présent devrait, avec quelques légers aménagements dans la forme, nous être également profitable à l'avenir. La nouvelle réalité pourtant, c'est que, compte tenu de l'impact toujours croissant de changements technologiques exponentiels et combinatoires, il est très peu probable que le futur s'avère un prolongement du présent. On peut même, au contraire, s'attendre à ce qu'il soit entièrement différent – tout simplement parce que le cadre de référence de nos hypothèses ainsi que leur logique sous-jacente ont changé.

C'est pourquoi, dans mon travail de prospectiviste, je m'efforce d'imaginer de manière intuitive notre proche avenir (de cinq à huit ans) et de m'immerger dans ces projections, puis, partant de cette extrapolation, de revenir au présent.

À partir de ce type de rapport sur le futur proche, ce livre explore les défis qui nous attendent et esquisse un manifeste – un appel passionné à prendre le temps de la réflexion avant que nous ne soyons tous balayés dans le vortex magique de la technologie, et finalement conduit à devenir non pas des plus qu'humains, mais des moins qu'humains. C'est une bonne occasion de se souvenir que le futur n'est pas quelque chose qui advient – nous

le créons, chaque jour, et par conséquent nous devons être tenus pour responsables des décisions que, précisément, nous prenons ici et maintenant.

Un tournant historique

Mon sentiment est que nous sommes en train de vivre l'une des époques les plus exaltantes dans l'histoire du genre humain, et d'une façon générale je me sens très optimiste à propos de l'avenir. Néanmoins, il nous faut absolument définir et mettre en œuvre une approche plus holistique de la gouvernance technologique, afin de sécuriser ce qui constitue l'essence de l'humanité.

Nous nous trouvons au tournant d'une courbe exponentielle dans de nombreux domaines de la science et de la technologie (S&T), à un point où le doublement quantitatif de chaque période de mesure par rapport à la précédente devient extrêmement signifiant.

Au cœur de la théorie du changement exponentiel, on trouve la loi de Moore – un concept apparu dans les années 70 selon lequel, pour le dire simplement, la vitesse de traitement informatique (autrement dit la capacité de puissance disponible dans une seule puce) accessible pour 1.000 dollars américains double tous les 18 à 24 mois. [1]

Ce rythme de développement exponentiel est manifeste dans des domaines aussi divers que l'apprentissage profond, la génétique, la science des matériaux et la production industrielle. De même, le temps nécessaire pour atteindre le prochain niveau de performance exponentielle ne cesse de décroître dans de nombreux domaines, ce qui ne fait qu'alimenter le potentiel de mutation majeure de chaque activité sur notre planète. En termes concrets, nous sommes maintenant en train de dépasser ce point de la courbe où il était difficile de percevoir que des changements étaient en cours : l'époque où nous ne progressions qu'à petits pas, de 0.01 à 0.02 ou de 0.04 à 0.08, est derrière nous.

Dans le même temps, nous n'avons heureusement pas encore atteint le point où ces doublements quantitatifs seraient devenus si considérables que leurs résultats submergeraient nos facultés de compréhension, inhibant nos capacités à agir. Pour mettre les choses en perspective, nous en sommes selon moi, dans la plupart des domaines, à un niveau de performance de quatre, et le prochain saut exponentiel, plutôt qu'une progression linéaire vers cinq, nous emmènera à huit ! C'est précisément à ce moment que les progrès exponentiels commencent à peser vraiment, étant entendu que la technologie suscite des changements de cette nature dans chacun des secteurs de nos sociétés, de l'énergie aux transports et à la communication en passant par les médias, la santé ou l'alimentation.

En témoignent, par exemple, les récents changements dans l'industrie automobile : au cours des sept dernières années, nous sommes passés de véhicules électriques offrant une autonomie de moins de 50 miles (80 km) à la dernière génération des Tesla et des BMWi8, qui affichent une autonomie de plus de 300 miles (500 km) à partir d'une seule mise en charge. [2] [3] Nous sommes également passés d'une poignée de stations de recharge au constat, stupéfiant, que l'agglomération de New York compte désormais davantage de stations de recharge électrique que de stations service essence. [4] Nous vivons dorénavant presque chaque mois une nouvelle percée dans les performances des batteries – dont les limitations ont constitué, pendant des décennies, l'un des principaux obstacles à l'adoption de masse des véhicules électriques (VE). Bientôt, nous ne rechargerons nos voitures électriques qu'une fois par semaine, puis une fois par mois et finalement peut-être seulement une fois par an – et alors sans doute ne subsistera-t-il qu'une toute petite population pour s'intéresser encore à de grosses voitures de luxe équipées de bons vieux moteurs à essence !

En témoigne, aussi, la baisse des coûts encore plus spectaculaire du séquençage du génome humain, avec un prix dégringolant d'environ 10 millions de dollars US en 2008 à

approximativement 800 dollars aujourd'hui. [5] Imaginez ce qui pourrait advenir quand de super-ordinateurs à la puissance exponentiellement décuplée, présents dans le *cloud*, deviendront accessibles à chaque unité médicale, chaque laboratoire ; alors, le coût du séquençage du génome d'un individu pourrait rapidement chuter en deçà de 50 dollars US. [6]

Maintenant, imaginez que les profils ADN de quelque deux milliards de personnes soient téléchargés dans un *cloud* sécurisé (et de manière anonyme, espérons-le) à des fins de recherche, développement et analyses – la plupart de ces tâches étant assurées par des intelligences artificielles (IA) tournant sur ces mêmes super-ordinateurs. Les possibilités scientifiques qui en découleront dépasseront de loin tout ce dont nous aurons pu rêver, mais impliqueront simultanément des défis éthiques gigantesques : accroissement spectaculaire de la longévité pour ceux qui en auront les moyens financiers, possibilité de reprogrammer le génome humain et, potentiellement, fin du vieillissement, peut-être même fin de la mort. Est-ce à dire que les nantis deviendront éternels tandis que les pauvres n'auront toujours pas les moyens de s'offrir des pilules anti-malaria ?

De tels développements potentiels suggèrent que persister à se représenter notre avenir de manière linéaire nous conduirait probablement à des hypothèses catastrophiques, erronées quant à l'échelle, la vitesse et l'ampleur des impacts du changement. C'est peut-être aussi la raison pour laquelle tant de gens paraissent si peu en mesure de se confronter aux inquiétudes nées de la surenchère de la technologie sur l'humain – après tout, cela semble si loin et, au moins pour l'instant, relativement inoffensif puisque nous n'en sommes qu'à quatre sur la courbe des changements. Des sujets comme l'accroissement de la perte d'intimité, la mise au chômage pour cause technologique ou la déqualification humaine ne nous paraissent pas encore suffisamment incarnés – et pourtant tout cela est sur le point de changer très vite.

Il est également important de réaliser que les plus grandes mutations surviendront sous l'effet d'innovations combinatoires, c'est-à-dire par la mise en œuvre simultanée de plusieurs méga-changements et éléments disruptifs. Par exemple, au chapitre 3 de ce livre, nous discuterons de l'emploi combiné et de plus en plus fréquent, par les entreprises, des méga-données, de l'internet des objets, de l'intelligence artificielle, du *cloud* et de la mobilité pour créer de nouvelles offres extrêmement disruptives.

Rien ni personne en tout cas ne sera épargné par les changements d'ores et déjà en cours, qu'ils soient pleins de bonnes intentions, issus de la négligence ou de l'ignorance de possibles conséquences involontaires, ou même inspirés par l'intention de nuire. D'un côté, des percées technologiques inimaginables pourraient spectaculairement améliorer nos vies et stimuler un épanouissement humain de très vaste ampleur (cf chapitre 9) ; de l'autre, certains de ces changements technologiques exponentiels sont en situation de menacer le tissu de nos sociétés, et finalement de remettre en question ce qui fait notre humanité.

En 1993, l'informaticien et célèbre auteur de science-fiction Vernor Vinge écrivait : « D'ici à 30 ans, nous aurons les moyens technologiques de créer une intelligence supra-humaine. Et peu de temps après, l'ère humaine aura pris fin. Est-on en mesure d'éviter un tel progrès ? Et, à défaut, sommes-nous en mesure d'influer sur les événements de manière à pouvoir survivre ? » [7]

Bienvenue en Enf...aradis !

Il devient de plus en plus clair que l'avenir des relations homme / machine dépendra en très grande partie du système économique qui les crée. Nous faisons face à ce que j'appelle un défi *infernalisiaque* – un mélange d'enfer et de paradis. Nous nous déplaçons à vitesse accélérée en direction d'un monde qui ressemble au Nirvana, où nous pourrions ne plus avoir à travailler pour subsister, où la plupart des problèmes seraient résolus par la technologie et où nous profiterions d'une sorte d'abondance universelle – ce que d'aucun appellent l'économie *Star Trek*. [8]

Toutefois, l'avenir pourrait aussi annoncer une société dystopique orchestrée et supervisée par des super-ordinateurs, des outils interconnectés et des interfaces informatiques super-intelligentes – machines et algorithmes, cyborgs et robots – ou par ceux qui en seraient propriétaires. Un monde où les humains non-augmentés ne seraient plus tolérés que comme des animaux domestiques, au mieux une nuisance nécessaire, au pire esclaves d'une cabale de dieux cybernétiques. Une funeste société devenue sans talents, insensibilisée, désincarnée et au bout du compte déshumanisée.

> *« Vous pourriez, de votre vivant, voir des horreurs façonnées par l'homme dont vous n'avez même pas idée. »*
> – Nikola Tesla [9]

Une vision paranoïaque ?

Examinons ce dont certains d'entre nous sont d'ores et déjà témoins dans notre vie quotidienne : des technologies numériques peu chères et omniprésentes nous ont donné la possibilité d'externaliser nos pensées, nos décisions et nos souvenirs, à l'aide d'appareils toujours moins onéreux et des *clouds* intelligents auxquels ils sont adossés. Ces « cerveaux externes » sont experts en profilage express, de « je te connais » à « je te représente » à « je suis toi ». En fait, ils ont déjà commencé à devenir un double numérique de nous-mêmes – et si ce constat n'a pas encore réussi à vous inquiéter, dites-vous que la puissance de ce cerveau externe sera multipliée par cent dans les cinq prochaines années.

Circuler dans une ville étrangère ? Impossible sans Google Maps. Du mal à choisir où dîner ce soir ? TripAdvisor va me conseiller. Pas le temps de répondre à mes e-mails ? Le nouvel assistant intelligent de Gmail le fera pour moi. [10]

Bien sûr, nous n'en sommes pas encore à ce niveau de convergence homme / machine où nous pourrions rester à la maison pendant que nos doubles cybernétiques vivraient nos vies à notre place, comme dans le film de Bruce Willis *Surrogates*. [11]

Pas plus que nous ne sommes déjà capables d'acquérir des créatures de synthèse à apparence humaine qui pourraient prendre en charge un large éventail de nos tâches et nous procurer de la compagnie, comme dans la série télé d'AMC *Humans* [12] – mais nous ne sommes plus très loin ni de l'un ni de l'autre.

Dans ce livre, j'expliquerai pourquoi je ne pense pas que le scénario dystopique puisse se produire. Mais dans le même temps, je soutiendrai que nous faisons désormais face à des choix fondamentaux, dès lors qu'il s'agit de décider et de planifier jusqu'où nous laisserons les technologies influencer et façonner nos vies, celles de nos proches et celles des générations futures. Certains experts prétendent que nous sommes déjà au-delà du point où nous aurions pu prévenir de tels changements, et qu'il s'agit simplement de la nouvelle étape de notre évolution « naturelle ». Je suis en profond désaccord avec cette opinion et j'expliquerai comment les humains peuvent sortir vainqueurs de ce choc annoncé entre l'homme et la machine.

Quand la convergence de l'humanité et de la technologie atteint son point de bascule...

Alors que je commençais à écrire ce livre et à diffuser ses thèmes dans mes conférences, trois mots importants se sont imposés avec force : exponentiel, combinatoire et récursif.

1. **Exponentiel.** La technologie progresse de façon exponentielle. Même si les lois fondamentales de la physique s'opposent à ce que les puces électroniques deviennent significativement plus petites que ce qu'elles sont déjà aujourd'hui, le progrès technique en général continue d'être soumis à la loi de Moore. [13] La courbe des performances poursuit son ascension exponentielle, plutôt que de suivre l'évolution graduelle et linéaire que les humains préféreraient comprendre et attendre. C'est pour nous un sérieux défi cognitif : la technologie progresse de

façon exponentielle, tandis que les humains – avec un peu de chance, ajouterais-je – demeurent linéaires.

2. **Combinatoire.** Les avancées technologiques sont combinées et intégrées. Certaines avancées à impact systémique comme l'intelligence artificielle, l'apprentissage profond, l'internet des objets et l'édition du génome humain ont commencé à interagir, s'amplifiant les unes les autres. Elles ont cessé de ne s'appliquer qu'à un seul domaine spécifique – et au contraire se répercutent maintenant dans une multitude de secteurs. Par exemple, certaines technologies avancées de séquençage du génome humain comme CRISPR-Cas9 pourraient finalement nous permettre de vaincre le cancer et d'allonger spectaculairement notre longévité. [14] Ces développements pourraient bouleverser toute la logique de nos systèmes de santé, la sécurité sociale, le monde du travail et jusqu'au capitalisme lui-même.

3. **Récursif.** Des technologies comme l'intelligence artificielle, l'informatique cognitive et l'apprentissage profond peuvent finalement conduire à des progrès récursifs (c'est-à-dire auto-féconds). Nous sommes par exemple en présence des premiers spécimens de robots capables de se reprogrammer eux-mêmes ou de s'auto-monter en gamme, ou encore de prendre le contrôle du réseau électrique qui les maintient en fonction – ce qui mène potentiellement à ce qu'on appelle une explosion d'intelligence. Certains, comme l'universitaire Nick Bostrom d'Oxford, pensent que cela pourrait conduire à l'émergence d'une super-intelligence – autrement dit un système d'intelligence artificielle qui pourrait un jour apprendre plus vite et surpasser les humains sur à peu près n'importe quel terrain. [15] Si nous sommes capables de concevoir des IA avec un QI de 500, qu'est-ce qui nous empêcherait d'en fabriquer d'autres avec un QI de 50.000 – et que se passerait-il si nous le faisions ?

La super-intelligence récursive, heureusement, ne fait pas encore partie de notre horizon immédiat. Cependant, même sans avoir à affronter des défis d'une telle envergure, nous nous débattons déjà avec des sujets en voie d'expansion rapide comme le traçage permanent de nos vies numériques, la surveillance passive, la restriction de notre sphère privée, la perte d'anonymat, l'usurpation d'identité numérique, la sécurisation de nos données personnelles, et bien d'autres encore. C'est bien pourquoi je suis convaincu que les fondements du futur de l'humanité – qu'il soit positif ou dystopique – sont sous nos yeux, ici et maintenant.

Nous sommes parvenus à un carrefour crucial et nous devons agir avec d'autant plus de clairvoyance, de vision globale et holistique délibérée et de maîtrise affirmée de nos ressources que nous sommes confrontés à des technologies qui finalement pourraient bien acquérir une emprise sur nous infiniment supérieure à ce que nous aurions jamais imaginé.

Si nous voulons conserver le contrôle de notre destinée et des développements qui pourraient contribuer à la façonner, il n'est plus temps d'attendre passivement de voir ce qui pourrait advenir. Bien au contraire, nous devons porter autant d'attention à ce que signifiera le fait d'être et de demeurer humains (autrement dit, ce qui nous définit en tant qu'êtres humains) qu'au développement de technologies toujours plus puissantes, qui transformeront l'humanité pour toujours.

Nous devrions également prendre grand soin de ne pas laisser ces décisions dans les seules mains du « marché », du capital-risque, des grands acteurs de la « Big Tech » ou des plus puissantes organisations militaires de la planète. L'avenir de l'humanité ne devrait pas être dépendant d'un paradigme industriel standardisé reposant sur la croissance et le profit à tout prix, ou de tel ou tel impératif technologique qui nous a peut-être bien servi dans les années 80, mais qui est aujourd'hui dépassé. Ni la Silicon Valley ni les nations technologiquement les plus en pointe ne devraient se voir investies de la « mission de gestion de

l'humanité » au prétexte que les technologies qui s'y développent génèrent des profits colossaux.

Heureusement, je crois que nous en sommes encore aujourd'hui à un rapport de 90/10 : 90% des étonnantes possibilités induites par la technologie pourraient jouer un rôle positif pour l'humanité, tandis que 10% pourraient d'ores et déjà être perturbatrices ou négatives. Si nous pouvons maintenir ce rapport, ou même l'emmener à 98/2, alors nous n'aurons pas fait d'efforts en vain. Mais en même temps, ces inquiétants 10% (quoiqu'aujourd'hui largement involontaires) pourraient rapidement gonfler jusqu'à 50% ou davantage si nous ne nous mettons pas d'accord sur la manière exacte dont nous souhaitons que ces technologies servent l'humanité. Bref, ce n'est clairement pas le moment de se contenter d'« aller de l'avant et voir ce qui se passera ».

Intelligence artificielle et séquençage du génome humain : les deux technologies qui changent la donne

En matière de technologies exponentielles, la toute première force est l'intelligence artificielle, que l'on peut simplement définir comme la conception de machines (logiciels ou robots) qui sont intelligentes et capables d'auto-apprentissage – autrement dit des machines pensantes à l'image de l'homme. On estime en général que les capacités de l'IA peuvent croître deux fois plus vite que les autres technologies, dépassant ainsi la loi de Moore et la croissance globale de la puissance informatique. [16]

> *« Le plus grand danger de l'intelligence artificielle, et de loin, c'est que les gens concluent prématurément qu'ils la comprennent. »* Eliezer Yudkowsky [17]

L'autre facteur de changement majeur est l'ingénierie du génome humain : altérer l'ADN humain pour mettre un point final à toutes les maladies, reprogrammer nos corps et peut-être même vaincre

la mort. Dans un tel contexte de reprogrammation, l'IA pourra jouer, de façon décisive, un rôle facilitateur.

Le couplage de ces deux technologies et des sciences connexes va avoir, en moins de vingt ans, un impact énorme sur ce que sont et pourraient devenir les humains. Dans ce livre, je me concentrerai en particulier, dans un souci de concision, sur l'IA et l'apprentissage profond, du fait de leur pertinence immédiate pour notre avenir et de leur effet accélérateur sur d'autres disciplines à fort potentiel de changement, comme le séquençage du génome humain, les nanotechnologies et la science des matériaux.

Devenir Dieu ?

Le Dr. Ray Kurzweil, actuel patron de la recherche chez Google, exerce une grande influence sur la pensée prospectiviste en général ainsi que sur mon propre travail, néanmoins je me verrai souvent conduit, dans ce livre, à remettre en cause certaines de ses opinions. Kurzweil prédit que les ordinateurs vont surpasser la puissance de traitement d'un seul cerveau humain vers 2025 et que vers 2050, [18] un seul ordinateur pourra surpasser la puissance de tous les cerveaux humains combinés.

Kurzweil suggère que ces développements annonceront l'avènement de ce qu'il appelle la Singularité, c'est-à-dire le moment de bascule où les ordinateurs auront définitivement surpassé les esprits humains en termes de puissance de traitement. À compter de ce moment, l'intelligence humaine pourrait progressivement devenir non-biologique, tandis qu'il deviendrait possible pour les machines de dépasser d'elles-mêmes et de manière récursive leur programmation originelle – un moment décisif dans l'histoire humaine.

Fin 2015, voici ce qu'a déclaré Ray Kurzweil à son auditoire de l'Université de la Singularité :

« *À mesure que nous évoluons, nous nous rapprochons de Dieu. L'évolution est un processus spirituel. Il y a de la beauté et de*

*l'amour et de la créativité et de l'intelligence dans le monde –
tout cela provient du néocortex. C'est pourquoi nous allons
travailler à étendre le néocortex cervical et devenir plus proches
du divin.* » [19]

Je pense moi aussi que le point où les ordinateurs pourront égaler
les capacités du cerveau humain n'est plus très éloigné, mais,
avec ou sans Dieu, et contrairement au Dr Kurzweil, je ne pense
pas que nous devrions renoncer volontairement à notre humanité
en contrepartie de la possibilité d'accéder à une intelligence non-
biologique illimitée. Cela m'apparaît comme un très mauvais
marché, un déclassement plutôt qu'une amélioration ; et c'est
pourquoi j'expliquerai dans ce livre pourquoi je crois
passionnément que nous devrions éviter à tout prix d'emprunter
ce chemin.

Pour l'heure, en 2016 (*époque à laquelle a été achevée la
rédaction de ce livre, ndlr*), les ordinateurs ne disposent tout
simplement pas de la puissance nécessaire pour concrétiser la
vision de Kurzweil. À mon sens, les puces électroniques sont
encore trop volumineuses, les réseaux pas assez rapides, et les
réseaux électriques n'ont tout simplement pas la puissance
suffisante pour alimenter de telles machines. Mais de toute
évidence, ces obstacles ne sont que temporaires : on entend
chaque jour des annonces de percées scientifiques majeures, sans
parler des nombreuses avancées qui restent dans l'obscurité, mais
dont on peut être sûr qu'elles surviennent secrètement dans des
labos du monde entier.

Il faut se préparer à la Singularité : soyons ouverts mais
critiques, scientifiques mais humanistes, aventureux et curieux
mais précautionneux, inspirés par l'esprit d'entreprise mais
soucieux de l'esprit public.

La science-fiction devient réalité scientifique

Très bientôt, les machines seront en mesure d'accomplir des
tâches qu'auparavant nous aurions pensé être l'apanage des seuls

travailleurs humains – qu'il s'agisse de cols bleus ou de cols blancs –, comme comprendre le langage, reconnaître des images complexes, ou se servir de nos corps de façon flexible et adaptative. À ce stade, nous serons à n'en pas douter devenus entièrement dépendants des machines, dans tous les aspects de nos vies. Nous assisterons également à une rapide fusion de l'homme et de la machine via de nouveaux types d'interfaces comme la réalité augmentée (RA), la réalité virtuelle (RV), les hologrammes, les implants, les interfaces cerveau-ordinateur (ICO), sans oublier l'ingénierie corporelle, avec les nanotechnologies et la biologie de synthèse.

Si des perspectives comme des nanorobots dans notre flux sanguin ou des implants communicants deviennent un jour possibles, qui décidera de ce qui est humain et de ce qui ne l'est plus ? Si (comme je l'affirme souvent) la technologie n'a pas (et ne devrait probablement pas avoir) d'éthique, que deviendront nos normes, notre contrat social, nos valeurs, notre morale, quand des machines s'occuperont de tout pour nous ?

À l'échelle d'un futur perceptible, et quoi qu'en disent les évangélistes de l'IA, je pense que l'intelligence des machines ne se préoccupera pas d'émotions ou d'éthique, tout simplement parce que les machines ne sont pas des êtres – ce ne sont que des duplicateurs ou des simulateurs. Et si finalement les machines deviennent capables de lire, d'analyser ou même de comprendre nos systèmes de valeurs, nos contrats sociaux, notre éthique et notre foi, elles ne sont en revanche jamais capables d'existence ou d'appartenance au monde comme nous le faisons nous humains – ce que les philosophes allemands aiment qualifier de *dasein*, littéralement « être là », « être présent ».

Mais tout de même, allons-nous vivre dans un monde où les données et les algorithmes triompheront de ce que j'appelle les *androrithmes*, c'est-à-dire tout ce qui fait de nous des humains ? Plus loin dans ce livre, je définirai exactement ce que j'entends par *androrithmes*.

Une fois encore, des doublements successifs de 4 à 8 puis de 16 à 32 sont totalement différents, en termes d'impact, que des doublements de 0.1 à 0.8. Et c'est bien l'un de nos défis les plus difficiles aujourd'hui : nous devons faire en sorte d'imaginer un avenir exponentiellement différent, et nous devons devenir les régisseurs d'un futur dont la complexité dépasse peut-être de loin l'entendement humain actuel. D'une certaine manière, nous devons devenir exponentiellement imaginatifs.

Graduellement, puis soudainement

Cet extrait d'Ernest Hemingway dans *le Soleil se lève aussi* décrit parfaitement la nature du changement exponentiel : [20]

« Comment as-tu fait faillite ? »
« En deux temps. D'abord graduellement, puis soudainement. »

Quand on réfléchit à la manière de façonner notre avenir, il est essentiel de comprendre ces deux mêmes jumeaux de l'exponentialité, graduellement puis soudainement – l'un et l'autre sont au nombre des messages clés de ce livre. De plus en plus, nous allons être mis en présence d'amorces modestes à des phénomènes de très grande ampleur – qu'il s'agisse de menaces ou d'opportunités : soudain, abruptement, elles peuvent disparaître et tomber dans l'oubli, ou au contraire s'imposer dès à présent, et dans des proportions bien plus grandes qu'on ne l'aurait imaginé. Pensez à l'énergie solaire, aux véhicules autonomes, aux monnaies numériques ou aux *blockchains* : toutes ont eu besoin de temps pour émerger, mais soudain elles sont là, et avec fracas. L'histoire nous enseigne que ceux qui s'adaptent trop lentement ou échouent à anticiper les points de rupture devront en subir les conséquences.

L'attentisme n'est souvent qu'une autre manière de dire « hors de propos » ou, encore plus simplement, « à oublier », obsolète, disparu. Par conséquent, nous avons besoin d'une autre stratégie

pour définir et préserver ce qui fait de nous des humains dans un monde qui se numérise à tout-va.

J'ai tendance à penser que les marchés ne vont pas s'auto-réguler et qu'ils seront tentés, pour traiter de ces sujets, de faire appel à la « main invisible ». Les marchés ouverts traditionnellement basés sur le profit et la croissance se contenteront de surenchérir sur les défis que suscite la confrontation de la technologie et de l'humanité, tout simplement parce qu'il est probable que les technologies génèreront des opportunités de profit de l'ordre de plusieurs trillions de dollars par an. On ne remet pas en question de telles opportunités d'affaires au nom des idiosyncrasies, interactions et qualités humaines. Ainsi Peter Diamandis, membre du conseil d'administration d'une société de Californie judicieusement baptisée Human Longegity Inc., proclame-t-il souvent que l'allongement de la longévité humaine génèrera un marché global de 3,5 trillions de dollars. [21] On peut comprendre que ces nouvelles frontières tellement irrésistibles tendent à prendre le pas sur des considérations aussi mineures que le futur de l'humanité…

Au-delà de la mission de contrôle

En dernier ressort, c'est bien de la survie et de l'épanouissement de l'espèce humaine dont nous parlons, et je crois que nous ne nous en sortirons pas si nous laissons les capital-risqueurs, les marchés financiers et les militaires mener le bal comme ils l'entendent.

Dans un futur proche, nous sommes certains de voir émerger des conflits très durs entre d'une part les tenants d'une vision paradigmatique et mondialisée, et d'autre part de gigantesques intérêts économiques, face à face – quelque chose comme une épreuve de force entre humanistes et transhumanistes. Maintenant que le pétrole et les autres énergies fossiles ont décliné au point de ne plus être les forces motrices des préoccupations politiques

et militaires, les Etats-Unis et la Chine ont déjà pris position à l'avant-garde d'une course accélérée à l'armement technologique.

Les prochaines guerres seront numériques et l'affrontement se joue déjà sur la maitrise du leadership en matière d'avancées systémiques exponentielles comme l'IA, les transformations du génome humain, l'internet des objets, la cybersécurité et l'informatique militaire. L'Europe (y compris et tout particulièrement la Suisse, où je vis) est en quelque sorte coincée quelque part au milieu, davantage tournée vers ce que bon nombre d'entre nous tiennent pour de nobles enjeux comme les droits de l'homme, le bonheur, l'équilibre, l'éthique, le bien-être collectif et durable. Comme je l'expliquerai plus loin, je crois que mettre l'accent sur de tels enjeux constitue en effet l'une de nos grandes opportunités ici en Europe.

Il existe d'ores et déjà, à l'échelle globale, des tribus de leaders d'opinion, entrepreneurs en série, scientifiques, capital-risqueurs et techno-gourous divers (ainsi que certains prospectivistes, mais oui !) engagés tous ensemble dans la promotion active d'un abandon de l'humanité. Ces techno-progressistes nous pressent de « transcender l'humanité » pour embrasser la prochaine étape de notre évolution, qu'ils présentent, bien entendu, comme une fusion du biologique et du technologique, l'altération et l'augmentation de nos esprits comme de nos corps aboutissant, de ce fait, à une superhumanité ayant vaincu la maladie et même la mort. Une quête aussi singulière qu'attrayante.

Il y a assurément un intérêt croissant autour de cette notion de transhumanisme, et cela constitue à mes yeux l'un des développements les plus troublants observés en quinze ans de pratique de la prospective. Mais franchement, tenter d'atteindre le bonheur humain en cherchant à transcender l'humanité par des moyens technologiques me semble plutôt illusoire.

Afin de vous donner une idée du contexte, je vous propose d'examiner deux points de vue contrastés à ce sujet, tels qu'exposés d'un côté par l'avocat du transhumanisme et ancien

candidat à la présidence des Etats-Unis en 2016, Zoltan Istvan, et de l'autre par le philosophe Jesse I. Bailey :

Le militant. Istvan écrit dans son roman de 2013 *The Transhumanist Wager* (*inédit en français, ndlr*) :

« Le code audacieux du transhumaniste va s'imposer. C'est un fait indéniable, inévitable. C'est inscrit au cœur de la nature non-démocratique de la technologie et de notre propre avancement évolutionniste téléologique. C'est l'avenir. Et nous sommes l'avenir, que ça vous plaise ou non. Ce qui nécessite d'être façonnés, guidés, pris en main correctement par la force et la sagesse de nos savants transhumanistes, accompagnés et encouragés par leurs nations et leurs ressources. Nous avons besoin d'être soutenus, de manière à assurer une transition réussie vers cet objectif, sans avoir à nous y sacrifier nous-mêmes – et sans craindre cette puissance démesurée, ni redouter de l'exploiter.

Vous devez mettre vos ressources au service de la technologie. Du système éducatif. De nos universités, de nos industries, de nos idées. Mais aussi du plus fort, du plus brillant, du meilleur de nos sociétés. Ainsi pourrons-nous réaliser l'avenir. » [22]

L'humaniste. Contestant cette position, Bailey écrit dans *The Journal of Evolution and Technology* :

« Je soutiens qu'en menaçant de mort les fondements possibles du dasein (l'existence humaine), le transhumanisme nous expose au danger d'occulter le besoin de développer une relation libre et authentique à la technologie, à la vérité, et en dernier ressort au dasein lui-même.

Les transhumanistes rassemblent souvent deux revendications en une seule : soit le corps que nous habitons sera en mesure de vivre des centaines d'années, soit notre conscience pourra être téléchargée sur de multiples supports biologiques. Chacune de ces deux hypothèses (selon des modalités subtilement différentes,

mais néanmoins importantes) est une aliénation de l'expérience humaine, dans l'intégrité de sa finitude incarnée.

Heidegger situe l'être vers la mort comme un élément central de l'appel à l'authenticité, loin de sa propre perte (et dont l'enjeu technologique tient lieu). En menaçant la conscience de notre propre mortalité, le transhumanisme menace du même coup d'occultation l'appel à l'authenticité, tout comme il en occulte la nécessité. » [23]

Il est clair que le déterminisme technologique n'est pas la solution, et que l'idéologie dominante de la Silicon Valley – « Pourquoi n'inventerions-nous pas la meilleure façon de tirer notre épingle du jeu, en nous amusant follement et en amassant des tonnes d'argent, tout en améliorant les vies de milliards de personnes grâce à ces incroyables technologies ? » – est, en germe, aussi improductive et dangereuse que le Luddisme.

Par respectueux contraste avec les vues plutôt cartésiennes ou réductionnistes de certains transhumanistes à propos de l'avenir de l'humanité (c'est-à-dire très simplificatrices et aboutissant à considérer le monde, et les gens, comme une sorte de machine géante), ce livre s'efforcera de dessiner les contours d'une philosophie de l'âge numérique que j'appelle parfois l'humanisme exponentiel. À travers cette approche philosophique, je crois que nous pouvons faire émerger un chemin équilibré qui nous permettra de *profiter* de la technologie sans *devenir* la technologie, de l'utiliser non pas comme un projet, mais comme un outil.

Pour sauvegarder le futur de l'humanité, il nous faut mobiliser autant d'énergie pour rester humains que nous en avons investi dans le développement des technologies. Je suis persuadé que si nous voulons un monde qui demeure plaisant pour les humains, avec toutes nos imperfections et nos insuffisances, nous devons mobiliser des ressources significatives (monétaires et autres) dans la définition de ce qu'un nouveau type d'humanisme exponentiel pourrait entrainer. Il ne suffira pas de se contenter d'investir dans

les technologies qui nous promettent de faire de nous des surhommes – dans la mesure où nous chevaucherons bientôt des machines auxquelles nous ne comprendrons plus rien.

Si nous ne faisons pas preuve de plus d'implication dans de tels sujets, je redoute qu'une explosion d'intelligence exponentielle, sans entrave et sans contrôle dans les domaines de la robotique, de l'IA, de la bio-ingénierie et de la génétique ne finisse par nous conduire à une négation pure et simple des principes fondamentaux de l'existence humaine, tout simplement parce que la technologie est dépourvue d'éthique. Or une société sans éthique court à sa perte.

Cette dichotomie se fait jour partout : pratiquement tout ce qui peut être numérisé, automatisé, virtualisé et robotisé le sera vraisemblablement, bien qu'il existe des choses que nous ne devrions pas laisser numériser ou automatiser, précisément parce qu'elles nous définissent en tant qu'humains.

Ce livre explore les directions où devraient nous mener les technologies exponentielles et convergentes dans les dix prochaines années, met l'accent sur les enjeux et indique ce qu'en la matière nous pouvons faire aujourd'hui. Quelles que soient vos convictions philosophiques ou religieuses, vous conviendrez probablement que la technologie a d'ores et déjà pénétré au cœur de nos vies quotidiennes, à un degré tel que tout progrès exponentiel ultérieur exigera assurément que nous débattions de leurs fondements et de leurs orientations. Alors que la technologie s'apprête, littéralement, à pénétrer l'intimité de nos corps et de notre biologie, il est temps de lancer une sorte de grand pow-wow tribal – peut-être bien la conversation collective la plus importante que l'humanité ait jamais eu à organiser.

Chapitre 2
La technologie et nous

Arrêtons-nous un instant pour considérer notre humanité

La capacité cognitive d'un être humain est déterminée, parmi beaucoup d'autres choses, par ses dispositions génétiques ainsi que par les 100 milliards de neurones de son cerveau.

Si tous ces neurones se trouvaient simultanément améliorés par la technologie, simplement en termes de performances ou de connectivité, il deviendrait rapidement possible d'atteindre, pour résumer à grands traits, un écart-type supérieur à 100. Ce qui conférerait à l'humain moyen un Q.I. de plus de 1.000, à comparer au niveau actuel de 70 à 130 qui concerne globalement 95% de la population. [24]

Il est difficile d'appréhender le niveau d'aptitudes que représenterait un tel niveau d'intelligence, mais on peut être certain que cela serait très supérieur à tout ce dont nous avons pu être témoins, ou même simplement imaginer. L'ingénierie cognitive, par l'entremise de modifications directes apportées à l'ADN humain embryonnaire, pourrait aboutir à produire des individus dont les capacités cognitives dépasseraient celles des plus remarquables intellects humains de l'Histoire. D'ici 2050, ce processus aura certainement débuté. Reconfigurer le système d'exploitation d'une machine est une chose, mais qu'en sera-t-il de la reprogrammation d'un être sensible, avec ses souvenirs et sa capacité au libre arbitre (à supposer que cela importe encore dans trente ans) ?

Commençons par regarder ce qui définit un être humain. D'innombrables philosophes se sont confrontés à cette question ; mais maintenant que nous sommes en train d'atteindre le point où la technologie nous offrira la possibilité d'augmenter, d'altérer, de reprogrammer ou même de modifier la façon dont les humains sont conçus, le sujet est devenu brûlant. De nombreuses voix, au sein de la communauté du transhumanisme et de la Singularité, estiment que nous sommes en route vers la fusion de l'homme et de la machine, de la technologie et de la biologie. Si en effet il s'avère que c'est bien le cas – et que cela soit ou non une perspective excitante –, alors définir les fondements de l'humanité à l'ère numérique n'en sera que plus essentiel.

Éthique et valeurs : l'essence de l'humain

Nous en arrivons aujourd'hui à ce défi fondamental : la technologie ne connaît ni éthique, ni normes, ni croyances, alors que le fonctionnement effectif de chaque humain et de chaque société repose entièrement sur ces valeurs. Il est possible que les machines finissent par apprendre à déchiffrer ou appréhender nos considérations morales et sociétales, ainsi que nos dilemmes éthiques, mais parviendront-elles pour autant à mettre en œuvre compassion et empathie dans une perspective holistique, ainsi que nous le faisons ? Nous cheminons dans nos vies en fonction de nos valeurs, de nos croyances et de nos mentalités, pas selon des données et des algorithmes. Même si les machines parviennent finalement à analyser ou même simuler la manière dont nous nous y prenons, il s'en faudra de beaucoup qu'elles mettent en œuvre leur existence ainsi que nous le faisons.

Nous parvenons aujourd'hui au point de bascule d'une courbe exponentielle, avec pour prochaine perspective un très grand saut de quatre à huit, puis à seize. D'où il ressort que nous faisons face à un énorme écart entre ce que la technologie peut effectivement faire (et il semble que la réponse soit : à peu près tout ce que nous voulons) et ce dont elle *devrait* être capable pour atteindre au bonheur humain global. Qui plus est, au-delà des causes les plus

évidentes de non-bonheur que sont les inégalités, l'absence de liberté, la pauvreté et les maladies, la réponse à la question de savoir ce qui définit le bonheur n'est jamais ni certaine ni universellement admise (voir chapitre 9).

Ce qui apparaît clairement, c'est qu'exceptée la capacité à simuler les interactions humaines de mieux en mieux, la technologie ne se préoccupe ni de bonheur ni de réalisation de soi, d'accomplissement, d'émotion, de valeurs ou de croyances. Elle ne connaît que la logique, l'action rationnelle, l'exécution des tâches, l'efficacité et les réponses de type oui/non ; parce que pour « connaître le bonheur », il faudrait en dernier ressort *être* heureux, ce qui selon moi exige d'être incarné.

La technologie est totalement nihiliste pour ce qui touche aux notions qui nous importent à nous autres humains. Je crois qu'on ne peut pas et qu'on ne devrait pas s'affranchir de la pyramide de la hiérarchie des besoins de Maslow, si ce n'est pour passer du stade des besoins élémentaires à celui de l'amour, de l'estime et de la réalisation de soi. [25] Oui, bien sûr, les réseaux neuronaux et l'apprentissage profond ont récemment permis aux ordinateurs d'apprendre eux-mêmes à exécuter des tâches complexes telles que jouer au go, [26] et j'imagine qu'il devrait, en théorie, être possible aux machines d'auto-apprendre comment agir en humains. Moyennant quoi la simulation n'est pas comparable à la duplication ; et médiatiser la réalité n'est pas la même chose que la réalité elle-même.

La technologie n'a pas d'éthique – il n'est d'ailleurs pas souhaitable qu'elle en soit dotée ! Et parallèlement, dans l'ère exponentielle qui est la nôtre, les cerveaux et les corps humains sont de plus en plus traités comme des objets machiniques, des défis en forme de *charniels* (l'équivalent incarné d'un logiciel) amusants. Et nous ne pouvons que frémir en imaginant ce qui se passerait si les ordinateurs étaient programmés pour copier ou même développer leurs propres valeurs et croyances artificielles. À mon sens, nous ne devrions vraiment pas emprunter ce chemin. L'idée même d'offrir aux machines la possibilité « d'être »

pourrait bien devenir, en dernier ressort, une incrimination de crime contre l'humanité.

Né(e) et élevé(e) à l'intérieur d'une machine ?

À titre d'exemple plutôt discordant, considérons le concept de plus en plus débattu et controversé d'ectogénèse – autrement dit l'idée de faire grandir un bébé à l'extérieur d'un corps féminin, dans un utérus artificiel. [27] Cette perspective, envisageable d'ici à 15 – 20 ans, offre le parfait exemple de ce en quoi une attitude technologique de type « faisons-le, puisqu'on peut le faire » outrepasse les considérations humaines les plus élémentaires. Bien que l'accession de la reproduction humaine à ce genre de technique futuriste soit probablement moins pénalisant pour les femmes, plus efficace et en dernier ressort plus économique qu'une grossesse naturelle, je considère aussi qu'il serait tout à fait déshumanisant et préjudiciable pour un bébé de naître de cette manière. Je ne sais pas ce que vous en pensez, mais pour ma part je peine à comprendre quelle serait la prétendue rationalité de ceux qui développent et promeuvent de tels concepts.

Est-ce bon pour l'humanité ? Un test de base

Face aux changements exponentiels, et de ce fait toujours plus lourds d'enjeux, qui se présentent à l'humanité, je propose de concevoir une batterie de questions grâce auxquelles nous pourrions évaluer les nouvelles percées scientifiques et technologiques, par exemple :

- Celle idée viole-t-elle les droits humains de quiconque y est impliqué ?
- Cette idée tend-elle à remplacer les relations humaines par des relations artificielles, ou à promouvoir ce concept ?
- Cette idée cherche-t-elle à faire porter l'efficacité sur ce qui est humain, ou bien cherche-t-elle à automatiser ce qui ne devrait pas l'être, comme les interactions humaines fondamentales ?

- Cette idée place-t-elle la pensée productiviste (croissance et profits) au-dessus des références éthiques élémentaires ?
- Cette idée tend-elle à substituer de simples biens de consommation à la recherche humaine du bonheur ?
- Cette idée tend-elle à automatiser des activités humaines essentielles qui ne devraient pas l'être – par exemple un ecclésiastique automatique ou un thérapeute issu de l'intelligence artificielle (IA) ?

L'un de mes auteurs de science-fiction favoris, William Gibson, a un jour noté que « les technologies sont moralement neutres, jusqu'à ce que nous nous en servions ». [28] Et en effet, sa remarque inspirée et souvent citée s'avère particulièrement pertinente face à ce qui se profile précisément aujourd'hui, alors que la définition même de l'humanité est de plus en plus affectée par des avancées technologiques exponentielles.

Le défi 90 / 10 : le point de bascule
Parce que nous atteignons aujourd'hui le moment charnière d'une courbe exponentielle, nous bénéficions de ce fait d'une chance unique d'agir sur notre avenir. Saurons-nous positivement tirer parti de ces progrès technologiques, à 90%, les 10% restants représentant des risques et défis gérables ? Ou tout cela échappera-t-il à notre contrôle, pour éclater inexorablement en un monde dystopique 10 / 90 ?

Beaucoup de développements technologiques actuels demeurent essentiellement positifs. Les améliorations constantes des technologies des piles et du solaire représentent un progrès considérable dans le mouvement global vers une énergie renouvelable et plus durable, tandis que les plus récentes applications de l'Internet des objets ouvrent la voie d'un véritable mouvement de fond dans des domaines comme les ports et villes connectées ou l'agriculture intelligente.

Aujourd'hui, alors que nous enregistrons un solde technologique à 90% positif, les conséquences négatives, encore

relativement mineures, commencent à essaimer rapidement, tout simplement parce qu'il n'y a pas assez d'inventeurs, de scientifiques, d'entrepreneurs et d'acteurs des marchés pour songer à s'en soucier. Dans le cas d'un Internet des objets développé sans précaution, cela pourrait aboutir au plus grand réseau de surveillance globale jamais mis en œuvre. [29] Nous pourrions ainsi en arriver à être observés, surveillés et localisés sous tous les angles, partout et tout le temps et, par défaut, sans aucun contrôle ni recours.

Les technologies à dynamique exponentielle possèdent réellement un potentiel incroyable pour l'humanité, mais nous courons le risque de les dilapider si nous ne faisons pas l'effort de penser de manière globale, ou si nous perdons de vue que le propos de toute technologie ou de tout business en général devrait être l'épanouissement humain.

Technologie, pouvoir et responsabilité

Le pouvoir implique des devoirs – et pourtant, quoique nous jouissions aujourd'hui de la puissance démesurée des technologies, nous échouons souvent à agir de manière responsable lorsqu'il en résulte des conséquences inattendues et des changements fondamentaux pour la trame de nos sociétés.

Nous adorons nous connecter les uns aux autres ou nous mettre en avant sur Facebook, et beaucoup d'entre nous se délectent du frisson né de chaque *like*. Jusqu'à présent pourtant, ce pacte faustien spécifique né des réseaux sociaux, où nous échangeons nos données personnelles contre le libre usage d'une plate-forme excitante de partage global, n'a pas placé les grandes entreprises de la Tech comme Facebook en situation de responsabilité réelle pour leur usage de nos données numériques. Et bien sûr, Facebook est passé maître dans l'art d'éluder ce sujet, car nous concéder davantage de contrôle sur nos propres données aboutirait à contrecarrer leurs efforts de monétisation, étant entendu que leur *business model* sous-jacent est de nous vendre au plus offrant.

Facebook voudrait que nous nous sentions responsables de ce qui se passe lorsque nous nous délectons de son puissant piège addictif et, exactement comme la National Rifle Association (NRA), s'entête à soutenir que ce sont les utilisateurs qui génèrent de mauvais usages de la technologie, pendant que les entreprises technologiques elles-mêmes n'auraient rien à se reprocher. De même que pour le slogan de la NRA, « Les armes ne tuent personne, ce sont les gens qui tuent d'autres gens », j'estime que c'est une manière vraiment bas de gamme de se défausser de ses responsabilités.

De la même manière, nous adorons utiliser Google Maps, Google Now et sans doute même Google Home (un équipement domotique auquel il est désormais possible de parler, exactement comme à un serviteur robotisé), pour anticiper les fluctuations de la circulation automobile ou mettre à jour notre agenda. Toutefois, nous ne paraissons pas en mesure de trouver comment incriminer les gens de Google pour la façon dont ils extraient puis vendent nos méta-données (en général grossièrement anonymisées) à des sociétés de marketing, ou les cèdent à n'importe quelle agence gouvernementale arborant le sceau de la FISA (Foreign Intelligence Surveillance Act). Très bientôt, nombre d'entre nous utiliserons à coup sûr des assistants numériques à commande vocale depuis nos terminaux mobiles, sans que quiconque soit tenu pour responsable de ce qu'ils seront capables de faire en coulisses. Ces équipements nous écouteront en permanence, mais nous n'aurons aucun contrôle sur eux. Autrement dit, nous sommes en train de créer des machines pensantes sans aucun gage de responsabilité, sans surveillance ni recours.

Nous entrons dans un monde où des automates logiciels robotisés intelligents issus du *cloud* (les *bots*) peuvent prendre en charge toutes sortes de tâches pour le compte de leurs utilisateurs, du type organisation de réunions ou réservations au restaurant. Nous ne serons même plus capables de saisir de quelle manière nos *bots* auront échafaudé leurs prises de décisions – et pourtant ils géreront de plus en plus nos vies.

Nous sommes témoins d'un manque généralisé d'anticipation et de précaution quant à l'utilisation et à l'impact de la technologie. Principalement parce que le sentiment de responsabilité à l'égard de ce que rend possible la technologie est très largement considéré comme un facteur externe par ceux qui la créent et la vendent – ce qui est une attitude totalement intenable vis-à-vis de notre avenir. Cela me rappelle la manière dont les compagnies pétrolières se sont très longtemps exonérées de tout sentiment de responsabilité vis-à-vis des questions de pollution et de réchauffement climatique, comme si celles-ci étaient totalement extérieures à leur business. Il va sans dire que ce genre d'approche de notre avenir est néfaste, et certainement ruineuse.

Je suis convaincu qu'il nous faut d'urgence dépasser les notions de profit et de croissance lorsque sont en jeu des technologies qui peuvent spectaculairement altérer l'existence humaine. Cet impératif moral surpasse même celui de l'âge nucléaire. Comme le disait J. Robert Oppenheimer, l'un des co-inventeurs de la bombe nucléaire, après les bombardements d'Hiroshima et Nagasaki : « Maintenant, je suis devenu la Mort, le destructeur de mondes. » [30] En citant ainsi les écrits sacrés hindous de la Bhagavad-Gita, Oppenheimer proclamait notre entrée dans une nouvelle phase de l'évolution humaine. Or aujourd'hui, nous faisons inconsciemment l'expérience de quelque chose d'encore plus vaste.

« Je prétends que l'intelligence artificielle, comme la fission nucléaire, est une technologie à usage dual. Nous savons la fission nucléaire capable d'illuminer des villes entières, tout comme les réduire en cendres. Sa puissance terrifiante était inimaginable pour la plupart des gens avant 1945. Avec l'intelligence artificielle avancée, nous en sommes aujourd'hui aux années 30. Il est peu probable que nous puissions survivre à une mise en œuvre aussi abrupte que ne le fût naguère la fission nucléaire. » James Barrat : Notre ultime invention : l'intelligence artificielle et la fin de l'ère humaine. [31]

La technologie, ce n'est pas ce que l'on cherche, mais *comment* on le cherche

La technologie, aussi magique nous apparaisse-t-elle, est un simple outil dont nous nous servons pour atteindre un but : elle ne se réduit pas à ce que nous cherchons, mais se réfère à la manière dont nous cherchons ! Le mot technologie lui-même trouve son origine dans le grec *techne*, soit « l'introduction du vrai dans le beau », autrement dit l'amélioration des compétences des artisans et des artistes par le maniement de tels outils. [32] Les philosophes grecs voyaient également la technologie comme quelque chose d'essentiellement inhérent aux activités humaines : nous inventons des outils et nous les perfectionnons sans cesse, tout simplement parce que c'est dans notre nature.

Aujourd'hui pourtant, nous mettons le cap sur un avenir promis à un formidable renversement de cette quête d'outils. Le philosophe et intellectuel Herbert Marshall McLuhan a un jour suggéré que les outils que nous fabriquons ont commencé à nous transformer nous-mêmes, et peut-être même à nous inventer. [33] Si l'on poussait le raisonnement de manière exponentielle jusqu'à ses extrêmes, on aboutirait à une perversion de l'intention originelle de la *techne* – et alors il ne nous resterait que bien peu de temps pour jouer à Dieu !

Bien sûr, vous pourriez me rétorquer qu'après tout, la technologie a toujours affecté et transformé l'humanité, alors qu'y a-t-il de nouveau, pourquoi s'en faire ? N'est-ce pas tout simplement une nouvelle incarnation du même flux de *techne* ?

Considérons que la technologie, dans son sens originel de *techne*, était avant tout un outil pour améliorer nos capacités, nos performances, notre productivité, nos ambitions et nos possibilités. Nous pouvons en trouver trace dans des inventions comme la machine à vapeur, le téléphone, l'automobile et l'Internet. La technologie, en l'espèce, ne nous a pas améliorés dans notre globalité, mais seulement dans nos actions et dans notre élan vers de nouvelles possibilités. Aucune de ces avancées technologiques ne nous a véritablement transformés,

matériellement, de manière profonde et irréversible, que ce soit en termes neurologiques, biologiques ou même psychologiques ou spirituels. L'utilisation de ces technologies ne nous a pas rendus exponentiellement plus puissants – en tout cas pas au point d'atteindre le moment de bascule sur la courbe.

L'invention de la machine à vapeur a certes créé une forte rupture lors de la révolution industrielle, mais nous en étions encore aux prémisses de cette courbe exponentielle. Par contraste, l'irruption de la robotique avancée et de ses effets démultipliés sur l'automatisation du travail survient à un moment clé de cette courbe (le stade 4, qui lui-même précède le stade 8) – là réside toute la différence. Et c'est une différence de magnitude, pas seulement de style ou de forme.

Algorithmes contre Androrithmes

Le fait d'être humain a beaucoup à voir avec tout ce que nous ne savons pas calculer, mesurer, définir algorithmiquement, simuler ou comprendre dans sa globalité – en tout cas pas dans un avenir prévisible. Ce qui fait de nous des humains n'est ni mathématique ni même simplement chimique ou biologique. Cela implique toutes ces choses qui pour une large part restent fugaces, non-dites, subconscientes, éphémères, subjectives. Ce sont ces caractéristiques essentiellement humaines que j'aime qualifier d'androrithmes, et que nous devons absolument préserver même si elles nous semblent maladroites, compliquées, lentes, risquées ou inefficaces comparées aux systèmes non-biologiques, aux ordinateurs et aux robots.

Nous ne devrions pas tenter de corriger, réparer, améliorer ou même éradiquer ce qui fait de nous des humains ; bien au contraire, nous devrions configurer la technologie pour qu'elle sache reconnaître, respecter et protéger ces différences. Hélas, la lente diminution – voire la pure et simple mise à l'écart – du champ des androrithmes, ces traits insaisissables qui fondent notre humanité, a déjà débuté, tout autour de nous. Ainsi, les réseaux sociaux nous permettent de créer nos profils au gré de nos

envies, et de nous délecter de ces identités fabriquées, plutôt que d'affronter le réel avec celle dont nous sommes dépositaires dans notre vraie vie incarnée.

Cela peut paraître un bien, mais pourrait pourtant devenir très négatif si cela allait trop loin. Car tandis que se multiplient les chevauchements entre nos identités réelles et en ligne, le face-à-face social et incarné des androrithmes tend de plus en plus à être remplacé par des écrans séduisants et des algorithmes fûtés, qui prennent en charge mise en relation et échanges de contenus. Parvenus à ce point, il nous est aisé de nous reconfigurer à notre guise grâce à des technologies puissantes et pour la plupart gratuites, pour bientôt nous percevoir nous-mêmes, ainsi que le décrit le philosophe Dr. Jesse Bailey, comme « les produits technologiques de notre propre contrôle numérique rationnel ». [34] Évidemment, sans surprise, de plus en plus de gens se sentent seuls, et même déprimés, sur les réseaux sociaux. [35]

Le philosophe allemand Martin Heidegger, souvent brillant quoique politiquement quelque peu fourvoyé, a noté dans son ouvrage *Être et temps* (*Sein und Zeit*) que « l'être humain est la seule entité qui se soucie de la question existentielle de l'Être ». [36] Le terme allemand *dasein* (« être là ») permet de mieux cerner cette idée.

Dasein en effet, expression de la différence fondamentale entre l'humain et la machine, est un motif important qui court tout au long de ce livre : c'est l'être sensible qui est au cœur de nos désirs humains – l'intellect, l'esprit, l'âme, cette part insaisissable de nous-mêmes que nous ne sommes pas en mesure de définir précisément ni même de localiser, mais qui en dernier ressort guide nos vies.

STIM ? CORE !

L'idée maitresse, c'est que la magnitude des mystères humains – autrement dit les interactions entre corps et esprit, entre biologie et spiritualité, celles qui ne sont ni rationnelles, ni calculables, ni duplicables, ni quantifiables – persiste à rester hors de portée, et

de très loin, de la science, de la technologie, de l'ingénierie et des mathématiques (STIM). Nous devrions donc, par conséquent, ne pas trop anthropomorphiser nos technologies, et ne pas trop mélanger nos priorités lorsqu'il est question d'opérer des choix et décisions sociétales importants ; bref, ne pas oublier nos responsabilités lorsque nous nous risquons à créer des technologies qui à terme pourraient nous dominer.

J'ai beau être captivé par les percées des STIM, je n'en crois pas moins qu'il nous faut d'urgence créer un contrepoids qui soit à même d'amplifier l'importance des facteurs véritablement humains. Par contraste avec l'acronyme STIM, j'ai donc récemment commencé à les qualifier de CORE : Créativité / compassion, Originalité, Réciprocité / responsabilité et Empathie.

La préoccupation immédiate, ce n'est pas tellement l'annihilation potentielle de l'humanité par les machines, mais plutôt le risque d'être captés par un vortex de technologies, de mondes virtuels et de simulations si fascinants que cela affaiblisse puis finalement détruise tout ce qui justement fait de nous des humains.

Serait-il possible que nous en venions à privilégier la technologie aux dépens de l'humanité ?

À l'échelle de notre présent et d'un futur prévisible, même les plus admirables de nos technologies seront uniquement capables de simuler d'une manière ou d'une autre le fait d'être humain (*dasein*), plutôt que de réellement devenir humaines. Néanmoins, avec le temps, le défi majeur ne tiendra pas tant à l'aptitude de la technologie à remplacer ou même annihiler l'humanité, qu'à notre propre désir de préférer les simulations performantes – fournies avec talent et à peu de frais par les machines – à notre « vraie » réalité incarnée. Pour le dire autrement, préférerons-nous finalement entretenir des relations avec des machines plutôt qu'avec des gens ? [37]

Trouverons-nous bientôt l'épanouissement dans nos conversations avec nos assistants numériques, nos repas imprimés en 3D, nos voyages instantanés dans des mondes virtuels et nos

commandes personnalisées à la demande livrées dans nos maisons intelligentes par drones ou via le *cloud*, jouissant d'être littéralement servis par nos robots ? [38]

Commodité accrue, très bas prix et facilité d'usage généralisés (on n'en est plus très loin, n'en doutons pas), combinés à une tendance humaine assez marquée à la paresse, finiront-ils par triompher de notre besoin d'interactions et d'expériences incarnées ? Difficile à imaginer aujourd'hui, peut-être, et pourtant cela pourrait devenir extrêmement probable dans moins de dix ans. Peut-être bien que « et si ? » est déjà devenu « et maintenant ? ».

Nous voyons déjà certaines technologies comme la réalité augmentée (RA), la réalité virtuelle (RV), les hologrammes et les interfaces cerveau-ordinateur (ICO) faciliter considérablement des extensions ou des simulations de réalité qui jusqu'alors restaient du seul apanage des sens humains. Graduellement puis soudainement s'accroit la probabilité que les unes et les autres commencent à se confondre.

Interfaces et éthique

Je prédis que dans quelques années seulement, se servir de la réalité augmentée (RA) et de la réalité virtuelle (RV) sera devenu aussi banal que de s'envoyer des messages ou de communiquer avec les apps d'aujourd'hui. Imaginez simplement de quelle manière nous percevrons le monde si des centaines de millions de gens commencent à utiliser ces équipements. Sera-t-il encore humain de vivre ainsi en état d'augmentation perpétuelle ? Qui aura la charge de définir les règles d'augmentation des sens humains ? Sera-t-il par exemple légal (ou éthique, en l'occurrence), durant une conversation, de superposer au corps visible d'un(e) interlocuteur/trice une image sexuelle simulée artificiellement ? D'être viré(e) pour avoir refusé de travailler dans une réalité simulée ? Ou, encore pire, serez-vous prêt(e) à retourner dans un monde dépourvu de toute RA / RV une fois que

ces outils immersifs et omniprésents seront partout devenus disponibles ?

Enfin et surtout, qui seront nos administrateurs dans cette ère annoncée d'augmentation des sens tous azimuts ? Les technologies existantes de voyage virtuel comme Oculus Rift de Facebook, VR de Samsung et HoloLens de Microsoft commencent tout juste à nous offrir un aperçu de ce que peut être la sensation de descendre l'Amazone ou escalader le Mont Fuji. Ce sont des expériences très intéressantes, qui vont à coup sûr affecter notre manière d'appréhender la réalité, la communication, le travail ou l'apprentissage. Mais pouvons-nous, ou devrions-nous, empêcher les fournisseurs de ces expériences à venir de ne nous présenter que des versions « expurgées » de la réalité – par exemple, nettoyer les bidonvilles de Mumbai à chaque fois que nous les traversons en taxi ?

Serons-nous encore humains si nous commençons à systématiquement préférer de telles mises en scène du monde ? Y a-t-il quelque chose que nous puissions faire pour empêcher la VA / VR de devenir un outil standard de notre société, comme le sont déjà nos mobiles et nos réseaux sociaux ? Pouvons-nous proposer d'en modérer l'usage, comme on le ferait d'un bouquet de programmes télé, ou bien serons-nous enclins à considérer comme ennuyeux le monde normal non-augmenté ? Songez simplement au nombre d'ados d'aujourd'hui qui vivraient comme une corvée le fait d'aller à la plage sans wi-fi. Ce sont des dilemmes, en effet, et on ne les résoudra pas par des réponses de type oui ou non. Il nous faudra mettre en œuvre des approches équilibrées, contextualisées et ethnocentrées.

Pour l'heure, considérons qu'il subsiste encore une grande différence entre ces nouvelles manières d'expérimenter les réalités alternatives et la vraie vie. Imaginez-vous, un court instant, debout en plein milieu d'un marché bondé à Mumbai, en Inde. Puis comparez les souvenirs que vous auriez ainsi accumulés lors de ce très bref épisode avec ceux qui seraient issus d'une expérience beaucoup plus longue, mais simulée à l'aide des

outils les plus avancés d'aujourd'hui ou de notre proche avenir. Les odeurs, les sons, les images, les réactions de votre corps, la saturation générale de vos sens... autant d'éléments mille fois plus intenses que ce que pourraient espérer simuler même les gadgets les plus avancés, issus de progrès technologiques exponentiels.

Voilà exactement ce qu'est la différence entre une expérience humaine holistique, incarnée, contextuelle et intégrale, et une simulation générée artificiellement. Bien sûr, une simulation réussie n'est pas mauvaise en soi – aussi longtemps que nous avons conscience de ce qu'elle est. Dès lors qu'elle ne cherche pas à nous donner envie de la préférer à nous, sans doute pouvons-nous l'utiliser à des fins satisfaisantes.

Les technologies visuelles sont appelées à devenir infiniment plus performantes dans un très proche avenir, rendant de plus en plus floues, au fil du temps, les frontières entre l'homme et la machine. Une fois que nous pourrons littéralement sauter à l'intérieur d'une scène de film grâce à la réalité virtuelle, nos capacités mentales et notre imagination seront définitivement surpassées. [39] Et c'est exactement ce qui m'excite et m'inquiète profondément à la fois. Sommes-nous voués à accomplir cela ? Sommes-nous câblés pour ce genre de virtualité ? Nos réseaux mentaux devront-ils se transformer en conséquence, et comment faut-il nous y prendre pour y parvenir ? Faudra-t-il, pour cela, faire appel à de nouveaux circuits non-biologiques ?

Peu importe la manière de répondre à ces questions : s'il advient que le progrès technologique exponentiel conduise nos corps à ne plus être le référent central de notre identité, alors nous aurons franchi le seuil nous amenant à devenir nous-mêmes des machines. Notre humanité s'en trouvera-t-elle amoindrie, si nos capacités biologico-informatiques réclament de constantes remises à jour pour demeurer utiles ? Il se pourrait bien qu'alors, nous ayons renoncé à 95% de notre potentiel pour « devenir semblables aux outils que nous aurons créés. » [40]

L'intelligence artificielle et l'effacement des frontières humaines

Compte tenu de l'envergure de son impact potentiel, nous devrions vraiment prendre en compte le rôle de l'intelligence artificielle dans l'effacement progressif de la distinction homme / machine. Prenons l'exemple de DeepMind, une entreprise londonienne leader du secteur IA, dont Google a fait l'acquisition en 2015. Dans une interview au *Guardian* de février 2016, Demis Assabis, PDG de DeepMind, mettait ainsi en lumière le potentiel de l'intelligence artificielle :

« *La surcharge d'information est telle que sa maîtrise devient difficile même pour les humains les plus intelligents, tout au long de leur vie. Comment passer au crible ce déluge de données pour en extraire les idées pertinentes ? L'une des manières d'envisager l'intelligence artificielle en général, c'est de l'envisager comme un processus permettant de convertir automatiquement l'information non structurée en connaissance exploitable. Ce sur quoi nous sommes en train de travailler, c'est potentiellement une méta-solution à n'importe quel problème.* » [41]

Que signifie en pratique cette ambitieuse déclaration ? Imaginez une société où la technologie – et singulièrement l'intelligence artificielle – fournirait des méta-solutions à tous les grands défis sociétaux, les maladies, le vieillissement, la mort, le changement climatique, le réchauffement global, la production d'énergie, la nourriture et même le terrorisme. Imaginez l'intelligence d'une machine qui pourrait aisément calculer plus d'informations que nous ne pourrions jamais espérer en comprendre, une machine qui pourrait littéralement lire toutes les données du monde en temps réel, partout et tout le temps. Cette machine (et conséquemment ceux qui en seraient les propriétaires ou les opérateurs) deviendrait ainsi une sorte de cerveau global, incroyablement puissant et bien au-delà de l'entendement humain. Est-ce bien dans cette direction que des entreprises comme DeepMind et

Google voudraient nous emmener et si oui, quelles seraient nos possibilités de conserver nos qualités humaines dans un tel scénario ?

> *« Le fait d'attribuer de l'intelligence à des machines,*
> *unitaires ou en réseau, ou à d'autres déités allumées du*
> *même type, crée davantage d'obscurité que de lumière.*
> *Quand on dit aux gens qu'un ordinateur est intelligent, ils*
> *tendent à modifier leur propre comportement pour que*
> *l'ordinateur paraisse mieux travailler, plutôt que d'exiger*
> *que l'ordinateur soit modifié pour devenir plus utile. »*
> Jaron Lanier, You Are Not A Gadget. [42]

La technologie peut-elle s'emparer de ce qui compte vraiment ?
Imaginons qu'une telle machine, une « intelligence artificielle dans le *cloud* », accède à l'existence (et en réalité nous n'en sommes plus très loin). Serait-elle vraiment capable de déchiffrer, comprendre et apprécier les interactions entre humains qui ne seraient pas exprimées sous forme de données ? Pourrait-elle appréhender *dasein*, l'être ?

En dépit des avantages technologiques exponentiels dont on peut être assuré qu'ils adviennent, la façon dont les humains font l'expérience de l'être et de leur environnement diffère spectaculairement de la manière dont les technologies captent ces moments qui nous importent. Même les meilleures photographies, vidéos ou données ne sont que de simples approximations de ce à quoi a pu ressembler le fait d'être vraiment là – car ce sont le contexte, l'incarnation et la profondeur qui, d'une manière ou d'une autre, nous rendent un moment unique.

Certains philosophes ont avancé qu'il n'est jamais réellement possible de saisir, retenir ou reproduire ce qui compte vraiment. Si cela est exact, alors comment pourrions-nous seulement espérer capturer ne serait-ce qu'un fragment d'humanité simulée à l'intérieur d'une machine ? Ne nous exposerions-nous pas au

risque, très élevé, de perdre 95% de ce qui nous rend humains en « dépassant les limitations de la biologie », ainsi que le suggère le transhumanisme ?

Voici la définition que donne Wikipédia du transhumanisme :

«...Mouvement international et intellectuel prônant la transformation de la condition humaine par la création et le développement de technologies sophistiquées et largement diffusées, dans le but d'accroître significativement les aptitudes humaines intellectuelles, physiques et psychologiques. » [43]

Cette sinistre promesse de « grand accroissement » est exactement ce qui me soucie le plus à propos du transhumanisme. Aussi séduisante que soit la perspective d'accroître mes capacités, il me semble que les fournisseurs de ces améliorations, entreprises, plates-formes et technologies, seront précisément les premiers bénéficiaires de ce concept. Ils verront fortement s'accroître leur puissance, leurs profits et leur valeur marchande, tandis que les humains ordinaires devront encore et toujours continuer à lutter pour se maintenir au niveau de leurs semblables augmentés. Les perspectives économiques du remplacement de l'expérience intrinsèquement humaine par des algorithmes, des logiciels et un niveau d'intelligence artificielle nous promettant une puissance quasi-divine sont évidemment immenses – mais constituent-elles en elles-mêmes un plus ? Faut-il que nous laissions les clés de notre avenir à ceux qui veulent en faire un gigantesque système d'exploitation dans le *cloud* sous prétexte que cela va générer des montagnes d'argent ?

« Ce que je dis, c'est que nous sommes désormais comme des dieux, et que nous avons intérêt à être bons dans ce boulot. » Stewart Brand [44]

En la matière, de nombreux évangélistes transhumanistes sont prompts à souligner que les humains ne seraient au fond que de simples entités incarnées nécessitant d'importantes réparations et une sérieuse remise à niveau. Pour eux, nous ne sommes pas assez intelligents, pas assez rapides, pas assez grands, pas assez agiles. Ils prétendent que ce dont ont besoin les humains, c'est d'une mise à jour logicielle et matérielle, qui leur permettra dès lors de mettre fin au vieillissement, et peut-être même de vaincre la mort. Le fait de se transformer tout ou partie en machines représente-t-il la prochaine étape logique de notre évolution ? L'abandon de nos limitations biologiques et l'augmentation de nos capacités grâce à la technologie sont-elles inscrites dans notre destinée ?

L'idée de comparer les êtres vivants et les machines n'est pas nouvelle. Le grand philosophe rationaliste René Descartes, au XVIe siècle, a comparé les animaux à des automates très complexes. [45] Aujourd'hui, nombre de technologues rafraichissent ce concept, que j'aime qualifier de pensée-machine, en avançant que tout ce qui nous entoure – y compris ce qui est *en nous* – peut être appréhendé comme un appareillage susceptible d'altération, de réparation et de duplication. Pour eux, l'existence humaine ne serait finalement rien d'autre qu'une expérience scientifique amusante.

Prendre par exemple des médicaments pour abaisser notre niveau de cholestérol ou notre pression artérielle, ou pour éviter une grossesse, représente pourtant déjà une intrusion significative, quoique largement acceptée, dans les mécanismes naturels de notre corps. Et désormais, les prochaines étapes dans l'innovation médicale pourraient en accroître les proportions beaucoup plus fortement. Témoins par exemple l'implantation de composants non-biologiques à l'intérieur du corps humain (notamment des nano-robots dans notre flux sanguin pour traiter nos problèmes de cholestérol), l'altération de nos gènes eux-mêmes pour nous prémunir des maladies (ou pour programmer la naissance de nos

bébés), ou encore l'implantation de dispositifs de stimulation cognitive dans nos cerveaux pour en accroître les performances.

S'agit-il simplement de notre évolution inéluctable, ou bien est-ce une quête bizarre de super-pouvoirs qui met au défi l'essence même de notre nature, de nos conceptions et de nos desseins ? L'humanité est-elle vraiment destinée à se recréer et reprogrammer elle-même, et ainsi à se doter d'options sans limites – être ce que nous voulons, ne jamais mourir et... devenir divins ? Même si vous n'êtes pas croyant (et, à titre de clarification, assurément je ne le suis pas), cette question est au cœur de notre sujet.

L'accroissement du bonheur humain et l'épanouissement collectif ne résulteront pas d'un renforcement de notre artificialité, même si cela peut effectivement nous procurer une sorte de super-pouvoir (ce qui ne sera de toute façon pas envisageable à court terme). Je soutiens au contraire que nous devrions remettre en question les hypothèses fondamentales du transhumanisme (comme l'idée de dépasser nos limitations biologiques), plutôt que de les accepter comme inévitables.

Et il est tout aussi important de réaliser et d'accepter que notre humanité est en fait quelque chose avec lequel il nous faudra composer ; quelque chose qu'il nous faut protéger, et travailler dur pour préserver. Les relations humaines les plus intenses sont souvent le produit de luttes et de conflits, et l'amour ne se nourrit pas de passivité. Le fait d'être humain n'est pas quelque chose que nous pouvons – ou devrions – simplement nous contenter de consommer par l'entremise de technologies séduisantes. Il n'existe pas d'app pour cela.

À quoi pourrait ressembler notre futur, à la croisée des attentes des transhumanistes et de celles des humanistes exponentiels tels que moi ? Existe-t-il une voie médiane entre la technologie et l'humanité, et à quoi pourrait-elle bien ressembler ?

Je crois qu'il en existe une en effet, et je suis en mission pour la définir.

Chapitre 3
Les méga-changements

Les bouleversements systémiques méga-changements
technologiques reconfigurent le paysage social

Je crois que le clash à venir entre l'homme et la machine va s'intensifier de manière exponentielle par l'effet combiné de dix grands changements – des méga-changements. À savoir :

1. Numérisation
2. Mobilité numérique exponentielle
3. Monitorisation
4. Désintermédiation
5. Transmutation
6. Intelligisation
7. Automatisation
8. Virtualisation
9. Anticipation
10. Robotisation

À l'image des changements de paradigme dans le monde de la pensée et de la philosophie, un méga-changement, ou bouleversement systémique, représente un saut évolutionniste majeur pour la société, qui à première vue peut sembler graduel... avant de déployer ses effets de manière très soudaine. J'explore ci-après la nature de ces bouleversements systémiques avant de décrire chacun d'eux, dans toutes ses implications potentielles.

Exponentiel et simultané

Nombre des innovations majeures de notre monde ont vu le jour il y a des décennies, parfois des siècles, avant de finalement déferler sur les sociétés humaines. Elles ont souvent été élaborées de manière relativement séquentielle, chacune d'elles adossée à celles qui l'avaient précédée. Par contraste, il est fréquent que les bouleversements systémiques naissent au même moment, même s'ils se sont d'abord déployés lentement. Ils sont aujourd'hui au seuil de leur expansion, et vont déferler de plus en plus vite sur nos sociétés.

Les défis qu'ils représentent sont pressants et complexes ; ils diffèrent par leur nature des forces qui par le passé ont impacté sociétés et activités économiques. L'une des différences clé, en l'occurrence, c'est que parmi les organisations ou individus capables d'anticiper, d'exploiter ou de traiter les méga-changements, peu sont en mesure d'y déceler des opportunités et d'en tirer des bénéfices substantiels. Vous êtes peut-être déjà familiers de ces termes, mais essayez de vous représenter de quelle manière ces différentes forces technologiques peuvent se combiner pour générer une véritable tempête. Technostress ? Les défis que nous avons eu à affronter jusqu'à présent n'ont aucune espèce de commune mesure avec ce qui s'annonce…

Méga-changement 1 : la numérisation

Tout ce qui peut être numérisé le sera. La première vague a inclus la musique, puis les films et la télé, puis les livres et les journaux. Désormais, la numérisation touche l'argent, les banques, les sociétés d'assurance, la santé, les produits pharmaceutiques, les transports, les voitures et les villes. Bientôt, ces changements se feront sentir dans la logistique, le transport maritime, l'industrie, l'alimentation, l'énergie. Notons, c'est important, que lorsque quelque chose est numérisé dans le *cloud*, ce quelque chose tend à devenir gratuit, ou en tout cas bien meilleur marché. Observez ce qui s'est passé avec Spotify : en Europe, un CD d'une douzaine de titres s'achetait autour de 20€ (environ 22 US$) – alors que

maintenant, vous pouvez avoir accès à 16 millions de titres pour 8€ par mois (environ 9 US$), ou les écouter gratuitement sur YouTube.

Je suis certes un abonné satisfait et fidèle de Spotify, et heureux d'y avoir recours, mais il faut bien reconnaître que ce type de darwinisme numérique destructeur de marges bénéficiaires introduit une énorme rupture dans les modèles commerciaux, et contraint la plupart des opérateurs en place à s'adapter ou périr. Dans mon livre de 2005 *L'Avenir de la musique* (*The Future of Music*, Berklee Press), j'ai longuement débattu de ce qui me semblait alors une certitude – à savoir que les grands labels qui avaient contrôlé l'industrie de la musique durant des décennies allaient cesser d'exister tout simplement parce que la distribution de la musique n'était plus une activité viable. [46]

De son côté, dans une réflexion restée fameuse, Sir Paul McCartney a comparé les labels musicaux installés à des dinosaures se demandant ce qui allait bien pouvoir se passer après la chute de l'astéroïde. [47] Une image en effet exacte du trauma psychique vécu par les institutions établies de ce royaume naguère prospère, mais qui ne donne pas d'indication sur la vitesse de l'extinction. Après tout, les crocodiles ont survécu et certains dinosaures se sont métamorphosés en poulets – mais les bouleversements systémiques ne se préoccupent guère de l'Histoire, et ne font pas de prisonniers.

En 2010, j'ai forgé l'expression « ceux qu'on appelait hier les consommateurs » ; pour eux, la numérisation est souvent synonyme de produits meilleur marché, dont la disponibilité s'est améliorée. [48] C'est généralement considéré comme un point positif, mais, une fois de plus, n'oublions pas que des produits meilleur marché peuvent aussi signifier raréfaction de l'emploi et baisse des salaires. Témoin par exemple la numérisation de la mobilité avec Uber et ses concurrents de par le monde, comme Lyft, Gett ou Ola Cabs en Inde. Il nous est désormais possible de commander une course en taxi via une application sur notre

smartphone, et souvent ce sera moins cher que via des opérateurs traditionnels. Mais cette nouvelle économie sera-t-elle viable à long terme pour les chauffeurs de taxis, ou bien nous dirigeons-nous vers une économie darwinienne de type loi de la jungle, où nous devrons tous nous résoudre à une multitude de petites missions mal payées en *freelance* plutôt que d'avoir des emplois stables ? [49]

Quelle que soit l'ampleur des défis sociétaux qu'elles impliquent, la numérisation, l'automatisation et la virtualisation rapides de notre monde sont probablement inévitables. En pratique, la cadence pourra parfois en être freinée par les lois fondamentales de la physique, à ce jour encore non-dépassées, comme par exemple les besoins en énergie des supercalculateurs ou la plus petite taille minimale possible d'une puce informatique – souvent cités parmi les raisons pour lesquelles la loi de Moore ne prévaudra pas éternellement.

Quoi qu'il en soit, l'hypothèse d'une pénétration continue et envahissante de la technologie nous laisse entrevoir un futur où ce qui ne pourra pas être numérisé et/ou automatisé (voir « Société automatisée », chapitre 4) pourrait devenir extrêmement précieux. Comme je l'ai évoqué au chapitre 2, ces androrithmes sont l'expression de qualités humaines essentielles telles que les émotions, la compassion, l'éthique, le bonheur et la créativité.

Tandis que les algorithmes, les logiciels et l'intelligence artificielle (IA) « dévoreront le monde » encore et toujours plus (ainsi qu'aime à le rappeler le capital-risqueur Marc Andreessen) [50], il nous faudra protéger la valeur des androrithmes – ces choses impalpables qui, de manière unique, nous rendent humains.

À mesure que des produits et services auparavant coûteux deviendront bon marché et abondants, les androrithmes devront être valorisés au même titre que la technologie – pour autant que nous voulions perpétuer une société prônant l'épanouissement humain. Car nous ne voudrons certainement pas passer d'un monde où les logiciels nous dopent à un monde où ils nous dupent !

Je prévois par exemple que dans un proche avenir, nous serons témoins d'un changement dans la manière dont les organisations perçoivent les outils de mesure tels que les « Indicateurs clés de performances » (en français ICP, d'après l'anglais Key Performance Indicators, KPI) – une référence largement utilisée pour l'établissement des objectifs commerciaux ainsi que dans les ressources humaines. Il se pourrait tout simplement que les ICP du futur ne soient plus basés du tout sur la quantification et la qualification de nos réalisations professionnelles en fonction de faits et de données tels que les unités vendues, les contacts clientèle, les indices de satisfaction ou les taux de conversion réussie ; mais qu'à la place, on voie monter en puissance ce que j'appelle les Indicateurs clés humains (ICH), qui reflèteront une approche beaucoup plus holistique et écosystémique de l'évaluation des contributions individuelles. En d'autres termes, on ne devrait plus privilégier l'employé quantifié, mais l'employé humainement qualifié !

Comme tous les bouleversements systémiques, la numérisation est autant un bienfait qu'une malédiction, mais quoi qu'il en soit, il ne s'agit pas d'un phénomène dont nous pourrions simplement décréter l'arrêt, ou programmer le report. Par conséquent, il est impératif de nous y préparer.

Méga-changement 2 : mobilité numérique et médiatisation

L'informatique n'est plus un univers que nous côtoyons uniquement sur nos ordinateurs et d'ici 2020, cette idée même nous semblera fossile. L'informatique est devenue invisible et encodée dans nos vies, greffée sur ce que nous appelions encore, il y a peu, nos téléphones mobiles. La connectivité est notre nouvel oxygène, tandis que l'informatique est notre nouvel élément liquide. Connectivité et capacités de calcul, les unes et les autres pratiquement sans limites, vont devenir la nouvelle norme.

La musique est mobile, les films sont mobiles, les livres sont mobiles, la banque est mobile, les cartes sont mobiles... et la liste continue de s'allonger. La mobilité exponentielle signifie

également que la technologie se déplace encore plus près de (et bientôt à l'intérieur de) nous : ordinateur mobile dans ma main, puis autour de mon poignet via des équipements connectés comme des montres, puis sur mon visage grâce à des lunettes ou des lentilles de contact de réalité augmentée (RA) ou de réalité virtuelle (RV), et bientôt directement dans mon cerveau grâce à des interfaces cerveau-ordinateur (ICO) ou à des implants.

Comme le suggère Gartner, synchronise-moi, connais-moi, suis-moi, regarde-moi, écoute-moi, comprend-moi... sois moi – voilà où nous emmène la mobilité exponentielle. [51]

> « *Un jour viendra où ce ne sera plus* « *Ils m'espionnent à travers mon téléphone. Ce sera devenu : Mon téléphone m'espionne.* » – Philip K. Dick [52]

La société Cisco Systems prédit qu'en 2020, pratiquement 80% du trafic internet mondial passera par l'entremise d'équipements mobiles, qui seront capables de prendre en charge quasiment tout ce que nous avions pris l'habitude de n'accomplir qu'avec nos ordinateurs. [53] C'est déjà le cas pour des métiers aussi divers que designer graphique, ingénieur télécom, gestionnaire en planification ou logisticien. Et la plupart de ces tâches s'accompliront par commande vocale, tactile, gestuelle ou intelligence artificielle – finis les claviers !

L'essor rapide de la numérisation et de la mobilité a entraîné la médiatisation et l'enregistrement, sous forme de données, de toutes sortes d'informations qui auparavant existaient en version analogique – par exemple les informations médicales personnelles partagées avec mon médecin – et désormais ont migré dans le *cloud* sous forme de fichiers électroniques. La majeure partie de ce qui jusqu'alors était partagé ou vécu sans beaucoup d'apport technologique, sous forme d'interactions entre individus, est désormais saisi, filtré ou transmis sur des équipements intelligents dotés de puissants écrans.

Les images et les souvenirs qu'historiquement nous avions pris l'habitude de ranger exclusivement dans notre hippocampe biologique sont dorénavant aspirés par nos équipements mobiles et partagés en ligne de matière routinière, à la cadence de plus de deux milliards d'images par jour. [54] La société Deloitte Global estimait qu'en 2016, la communauté humaine aurait partagé en ligne plus d'un trillion (mille milliards) d'images. [55]

Les infos qui auparavant étaient imprimées sont maintenant diffusées en flux par applications interposées, devenant ainsi liquides et malléables. Les rencontres sociales qu'auparavant nous amorcions dans des cafés et des bars sont aujourd'hui facilitées en quelques glissements sur une app. Les restaurants qu'on découvrait naguère sur les recommandations éclairées de bons amis sont dorénavant identifiés et notés sur des moteurs de recherche et des sites internet en ligne proposant à leurs utilisateurs commentaires et visites des cuisines à 360° – sans oublier la nourriture !

Les conseils médicaux reposaient autrefois sur médecins de famille et infirmières de quartier ; aujourd'hui, ils sont dispensés par des équipements qui vous promettent, pour une fraction du prix, un meilleur diagnostic délivré directement chez vous. Ainsi Scanadu, un outil de diagnostic à distance qui mesure vos flux vitaux – y compris votre pression sanguine – et se connecte au *cloud* pour une analyse instantanée. [56] Bien des expériences qui ne survenaient que par l'entremise d'une communication d'individu à individu passent désormais par un média.

On peut considérer, bien sûr, que tout ce qui pourra être mobilisé en votre faveur le sera probablement, mais est-ce à dire pour autant que toute expérience ainsi mobilisée devrait en conséquence être médiatisée ?

Il nous faut prendre en compte la possibilité que l'impératif technologique « on doit le faire parce qu'on peut le faire », qui continue à prévaloir aujourd'hui, n'est peut-être plus une preuve d'intelligence. Les avancées technologiques exponentielles vont

nous donner la possibilité d'accomplir des tâches plus lourdes et plus complexes, incluant des activités qui auront un impact matériel sur nos comportements et nos expériences d'humains – et pas toujours de façon positive.

Considérons la possibilité, auparavant irréaliste, de tracer via ses gadgets mobiles chaque utilisateur / utilisatrice d'Internet. Certes, nos appareils perpétuellement branchés présentent l'avantage d'une connectivité totale et d'un suivi constant de notre état de santé, via nos applications dédiées et nos compteurs de pas. Mais de ce fait, nous allons aussi devenir extrêmement traçables, mis à nu, prévisibles, manipulés et, en dernier ressort... programmables.

Voici quelques questions critiques que nous devrions prendre l'habitude de nous poser lorsqu'il s'agit de déterminer jusqu'à quel point nous voulons laisser la technologie intervenir dans notre vécu d'humains :

- Avons-nous vraiment besoin de photographier ou d'enregistrer tout ce qui nous entoure afin de créer une mémoire intégrale de nos vies dans le *cloud* ?
- Avons-nous vraiment besoin de partager le moindre aspect de nos vies sur les plates-formes numériques et les réseaux sociaux ? Cela nous conduit-il à ressembler (et à ressentir) davantage à des machines, ou davantage à des humains ?
- Doit-on vraiment se fier à des applications de traduction en temps réel telles que SayHi ou Microsoft Translate pour dialoguer avec quelqu'un dans une autre langue ? Bien que cela puisse s'avérer utile en cas de manque de temps, cela aboutit finalement à intercaler un média entre nous et les autres, et cela médiatise un processus qui devrait pourtant rester le propre des humains. Encore une fois, ce qui est en question est la recherche d'un nouvel équilibre, et pas seulement une réponse de type oui / non.

Méga-changement 3 : (R)Évolutions dans la monitorisation et les interfaces

De la frappe au « *touch and talk* », pratiquement tout ce qui était traditionnellement consommé sous forme de papier imprimé est aujourd'hui en train de migrer vers les écrans. Cette (r)évolution des interfaces signifie que les journaux auront très probablement cessé d'être lus sur support papier d'ici seulement dix ans. Et le même sort attend sans aucun doute les magazines, mais peut-être un peu plus lentement dans la mesure ou odeur et sensations tactiles font encore partie, dans leur dimension charnelle, de l'expérience de lecture de nombreux magazines.

Les cartes et plans papier sont déjà en train d'intégrer nos outils mobiles et vont sans doute presque totalement disparaître d'ici quelques petites années. Les opérations bancaires, jusqu'alors accomplies au guichet ou sur des automates spécialisés, sont en train d'être dématérialisées dans le *cloud* à une cadence effrénée. Quant aux appels téléphoniques, naguère effectués sur des téléphones, ils se transforment aujourd'hui en appels vidéo sur écrans, via des services comme Skype, Google Hangouts et FaceTime.

Les premiers robots utilisaient comme interfaces boutons-poussoirs ou télécommandes ; aujourd'hui, c'est le règne des écrans auxquels on a donné figure humaine – et il nous suffit de leur parler. De même, il y avait sur les voitures des interrupteurs, des boutons, des cadrans et des tableaux de bord personnalisés ; désormais, le contrôle des véhicules s'effectue entièrement par l'entremise d'écrans tactiles. Et la liste ne va pas se contenter de s'allonger : elle est sur le point d'exploser !

Alors que des instruments d'augmentation visuelle toujours plus puissants inondent le marché, nos yeux aussi sont en passe de se « *screenifier* ». Mais quoiqu'il y ait des gens pour suggérer d'en améliorer les performances grâce à la technologie, je pense que dans un proche avenir, nous continuerons à voir avec nos bons vieux yeux humains 1.0. Il est néanmoins possible, dans le même temps, que beaucoup d'entre nous aient recours à des

lunettes augmentées, à des lentilles de contact connectées à Internet, ou encore à des visières améliorant spectaculairement ce que nous sommes capables de voir, ainsi que la manière d'y réagir. Bref, notre manière de regarder le monde est en passe de changer pour toujours – une situation typiquement *infernalisiaque*.

La monitorisation est une tendance clé de la convergence homme / machine, ainsi que du débat de plus en plus intense sur ses limites : jusqu'où nous faut-il aller en la matière ? Bien entendu, tout cela préfigure aussi l'essor de la RA / RV et des hologrammes.

Nous aurons des écrans pour tout, partout, et il est possible que ces écrans, alimentés par énergie solaire ou par piles longue durée à faible coût, deviennent bientôt moins chers que du papier peint fantaisie. De ce fait, il deviendra très simple de franchir l'étape suivante et d'utiliser ces écrans comme surface additionnelle à la « réalité véritable » – autrement dit pour superposer des infos ou n'importe quelle image contextuelle à la réalité de ce que nous verrons autour de nous. Je suis prêt à parier que d'ici dix ans, avoir recours à la RA et à la RV sera devenu aussi normal que d'utiliser WhatsApp aujourd'hui. Ce qui est une pensée à la fois grisante et effrayante : car parvenu à ce point, qui pourra dire ce qui est réel et ce qui ne l'est pas ?

Considérons ce en quoi nos perceptions, en tant qu'êtres humains, en seront affectées. Imaginez-vous atteindre à une telle « super-vision » et à l'omnipotence visuelle simplement en coiffant la visière HoloLens de Microsoft, pour seulement US$ 250. Imaginez votre chirurgien équipé d'un casque VR Samsung lors de sa prochaine intervention chirurgicale, limitant les risques de poursuites judiciaires pour erreur médicale simplement parce qu'il aura eu un accès renforcé à vos données.

Le monde que nous voyons ainsi se dessiner peut paraître infiniment plus riche, plus rapide et plus interconnecté – mais alors, ne pourrait-il pas aussi devenir plus confus, plus addictif ? Et pourquoi n'aurait-on pas envie de voir ce qui nous entoure sans

tous ces super-dispositifs d'amélioration ? Il est plus que probable que ces questions deviennent centrales, lorsque les fournisseurs de ces produits déploieront à l'avenir des armées de neuroscientifiques et d'experts comportementaux pour nous rendre ces écrans encore plus accrocheurs et plus pratiques. Si l'on se souvient qu'un *like* sur Facebook fait grimper votre taux de dopamine, alors quels seront les effets, considérablement plus puissants, que suscitera une vision haute définition ?

> *« Ici toutefois, il n'y a pas d'oppresseurs. Personne pour vous forcer à faire ça. Vous vous enchaînez de plein gré vous-même. Et vous devenez de plein gré socialement autiste. Vous ne recherchez plus les signes de la communication humaine de base. Vous êtes attablé en compagnie de trois humains, dont chacun vous regarde et s'efforce de vous parler, et vous, vous restez les yeux rivés à un écran ! À la recherche d'inconnus... à Dubaï ! »* –
> Dave Eggers, The Circle. [57]

Méga-changement 4 : Désintermédiation

L'une des tendances clés du commerce en ligne, des médias et de la communication est de supprimer les intermédiaires humains : introduire la disruption par l'échange direct. On a déjà vu le phénomène se produire dans le monde de la musique numérique, où de nouvelles plates-formes comme Apple, Spotify, Tencent, Baidu et YouTube perturbent puis délogent les cartels du disque qui jusqu'alors avaient l'habitude de capter 90% des revenus des artistes.

C'est également en train de se produire dans l'univers du tourisme et des hôtels : Airbnb nous donne la possibilité de séjourner dans des résidences privées et de réserver directement auprès des propriétaires, sans avoir besoin de recourir à un hôtel classique.

C'est aussi le cas de l'édition, puisque les auteurs peuvent désormais utiliser directement Amazon Kindle Publishing, et ainsi

récupérer 70% des revenus d'un e-book plutôt que les 10% d'un éditeur traditionnel. A-t-on idée de ce qu'aurait été l'impact, la popularité et les gains de Tolstoï s'il avait pu bénéficier de ce genre d'accès direct ?

Idem encore dans le monde des transactions bancaires, où les clients peuvent désormais utiliser des outils comme PayPal, M-Pesa en Afrique, Facebook Money ou TransferWise pour faire des virements dans le monde entier. Fréquemment, ces services contournent les banques ainsi que les dispositifs traditionnels de transferts financiers et les commissions scandaleuses qu'ils osent prélever. Ajoutez à cette équation la distribution, le secteur des assurances et bientôt l'énergie, et vous pouvez voir où cela nous mène : à chaque fois qu'une relation directe sans intermédiaire ou d'individu à individu sera possible, cela se fera. La technologie en sera le garant.

Mais le défi majeur est aussi celui-ci : oui, la disruption est motivante, excitante et potentiellement génératrice de grands profits – ainsi qu'en témoignent les parcours très médiatisés de start-ups réussissant des valorisations de milliards de dollars en seulement quelques années –, mais au bout du compte nous aurons aussi besoin de structuration. [58] En apparence, il peut sembler valorisant de rejoindre les rangs des entreprises valorisées de un (les « licornes ») à dix (les « decacorns ») milliards de dollars. Néanmoins, il nous faudra creuser davantage et nous assurer de bâtir des infrastructures sociétales différentes et de meilleure qualité, plutôt qu'une capitalisation boursière de haut vol, qui ne crée rien et se contente d'écarter ce qui existait auparavant.

Uber a ainsi « désintermédiatisé » le marché des taxis et des limousines, ce qui a représenté un bénéfice majeur à la fois pour les clients et pour les chauffeurs et autres travailleurs d'Uber. Toutefois, en se transformant ainsi peu à peu en acteur important et puissant de ce secteur, Uber est lui-même devenu un intermédiaire d'un genre nouveau. Certains experts n'hésitent pas à parler de « capitalisme de plate-forme » et de « féodalisme

numérique », à cause de la manière dont Uber traite ses chauffeurs, comme des matériaux hautement malléables – sans conteste un inconvénient de l'économie de la précarité. [59]

L'exemple d'Uber montre bien qu'il ne suffira pas de simplement remiser de ce qui ne marche plus très bien, comme l'industrie des taxis, ou de réinitialiser les activités dont les titulaires actuels ne sont plus suffisamment motivés. Il sera tout aussi nécessaire de recomposer un nouvel écosystème complet, d'essence numérique, qui sera en mesure de prendre en compte toutes les pièces du puzzle, et pas seulement certaines d'entre elles. Se contenter d'écrémer ce qui subsistera du chambardement des modèles économiques devenus obsolètes ne serait pas tenable. Ce qui est en jeu n'est pas uniquement la disruption, mais aussi la construction.

De ce point de vue, la désintermédiation est clairement la résultante des technologies exponentielles, et nous en verrons à coup sûr bien d'autres effets. Les plus gros tsunamis se produiront dans les secteurs de la santé et de l'énergie. Et il sera alors essentiel de se souvenir que la disruption seule ne suffira pas et ne durera pas. Il nous faudra aussi élaborer de véritables valeurs humaines, ainsi qu'un écosystème holistique générant de la valeur à long terme pour chacun(e) d'entre nous. Autrement dit, pas seulement davantage d'algorithmes, mais aussi des androrithmes revivifiés. Seule une vision holistique fera la différence.

« Avant de devenir envoûtés par ces magnifiques gadgets offrant des contenus fascinants sur écrans HD, permettez-moi de vous rappeler que l'information n'est pas le savoir, que le savoir n'est pas la sagesse et que la sagesse n'est pas la clairvoyance. Chacun de ces phénomènes procède des autres, et nous avons besoin d'eux ensemble. » –
Arthur C. Clarke [60]

Méga-changement 5 : Transmutation

Au-delà du simple changement, le plus grand meme de 2015 a été la notion de « transformation numérique », une formulation qui nous apparaît déjà vaguement défraichie, avec son parfum de *social media*. Cependant, le terme présente cet avantage de dépasser de loin la simple notion de changement ou d'innovation. Il suppose, littéralement, une mutation, comme de se transformer de chenille en papillon, ou de voiture-jouet en voiture-robot, ou encore de constructeur automobile en fournisseur de mobilité. Pour la plupart des entreprises et des organisations, à mesure que les conséquences du changement technologique exponentiel se feront sentir, la transformation va devenir la priorité numéro un. Se transformer en quelque chose qui sera fonctionnel d'ici cinq ans réclame à la fois du courage et beaucoup de clairvoyance, sans oublier bien sûr le soutien de tous les actionnaires et des marchés financiers.

Mais n'en oublions pas pour autant que la matrice de toutes les transformations sera notre propre méga-changement : passer d'un régime de séparation physique à celui d'une connexion directe avec nos ordinateurs et nos machines.

Méga-changement 6 : Intelligisation

Voilà l'une des raisons majeures pour lesquelles l'humanité est aujourd'hui aussi profondément mise au défi : les objets sont en train de devenir intelligents.

Chaque objet autour de nous, qui auparavant était déconnecté et dépourvu de contexte dynamique, est désormais connecté à Internet via des réseaux de capteurs et continuellement mis à jour et interrogé par un réseau global de périphériques interconnectés. Dorénavant, tout ce qui pourra être rendu intelligent le sera, tout simplement parce que maintenant, nous en avons les moyens.

L'apprentissage profond, à cet égard, est un facteur clé d'intelligisation, et un puissant générateur de changements. Plutôt que de se reposer sur l'approche traditionnelle de la programmation, qui conduit les machines à exécuter des

instructions pour réaliser une tâche, le nouveau paradigme émergent consiste à mettre à leur disposition rien moins qu'une gigantesque puissance de calcul, un accès à une énorme quantité d'historiques et de données en temps réel, un éventail de base de règles d'apprentissage et une simple commande de type « découvrez comment gagner à tous les coups au jeu de go, aux échecs ou au backgammon ». La machine en vient ensuite à poser des règles et des stratégies que nous autres humains ne pourrions probablement jamais découvrir par nous-mêmes.

Les laboratoires DeepMind AI de Google ont fait en 2015 la démonstration de la puissance de l'apprentissage profond en montrant comment un ordinateur pouvait vraiment apprendre entièrement par lui-même comment jouer et gagner aux jeux de casse-briques d'Atari, et ensuite évoluer vers une totale maîtrise de ces jeux en un très court laps de temps. [61]

Peu après cette démonstration Atari, DeepMind a développé AlphaGo – un ordinateur auto-apprenant qui a acquis la maîtrise du jeu de go traditionnel chinois, [62] infiniment plus complexe. Voilà bien le Graal de l'intelligence informatique : non pas la perfection mathématique manifestée par Deep Blue lorsqu'il a battu Gary Kasparov aux échecs, [63] mais la capacité pour la machine de comprendre son environnement et de concevoir elle-même la meilleure action à appliquer – y compris de façon récursive. En mettant en œuvre de façon répétée le même processus, ces IAs pourraient exponentiellement devenir bien meilleures, et très rapidement.

Méga-changement 7 : Automatisation
La grande promesse de bien des technologies exponentielles est que nous pourrons numériser n'importe quoi, le rendre intelligent et ensuite l'automatiser et le virtualiser. L'automatisation est l'un des ressorts de l'idée d'hyper-efficience, car elle rend possible de substituer des machines à des humains. J'explorerai ce méga-changement dans mon chapitre 4 sur l'automatisation de la société.

Méga-changement 8 : Virtualisation

La virtualisation, pour le dire simplement, est l'idée de créer une version numérique non-physique de quelque chose, plutôt que d'en avoir une copie tangible sur site. Parmi les services virtuels les plus communément utilisés, il y a par exemple la virtualisation sur serveurs des fonctions de bureau, qui implante mon poste de travail dans le *cloud* et auquel il n'est possible d'avoir accès que via un terminal sur mon bureau ou une application sur mon *smartphone*. Autre exemple, les communications en réseau : plutôt que d'utiliser du matériel de mise en réseau tel que routeurs et commutateurs, les échanges vocaux ou de données s'effectuent de plus en plus par l'entremise du *cloud*, via des réseaux à définition logicielle (« software-defined networking » ou SDN). Outre les bénéfices qui en découlent, notamment d'importantes réductions des coûts et une vitesse de service accrue, cela introduit une disruption dans les *business models* d'acteurs globaux importants comme Cisco.

D'après certaines estimations, la virtualisation via le *cloud computing* pourrait permettre d'économiser jusqu'à 90% des coûts. [64] Plutôt que de livrer par bateau des livres imprimés tout autour du globe, Amazon a fait le choix de virtualiser la librairie, et d'envoyer à ses lecteurs des fichiers numériques sur leur liseuse Kindle. Les transports de marchandises sont également sur le point de se virtualiser. Imaginez les économies que vous pourriez réaliser grâce à une imprimante 3D capable de fabriquer l'étui de votre iPhone directement dans votre salon ; il vous suffirait simplement d'en télécharger le design. Imaginez une future imprimante 3D capable de fabriquer directement dans votre centre commercial préféré même les produits les plus avancés grâce à des centaines de matériaux composites ; tout ce que vous pourrez désirer depuis votre paire de tennis jusqu'aux derniers modèles de poupée Barbie, en passant par des myriades de produits.

La décentralisation est souvent une composante majeure de la virtualisation, car nous n'avons pas besoin de point de distribution central dès lors qu'un produit peut être fourni dans le

cloud. Les systèmes SDN se dispensent de tout le câblage conduisant à tel ou tel interrupteur ou modem ; toutes les commandes peuvent être actionnées à distance, débouchant sur des économies substantielles. Naturellement, les questions de sécurité deviennent lourdes d'enjeux lorsqu'on entreprend de virtualiser ou de décentraliser des actifs financiers, car les point de contrôle physique sont moins nombreux. [65] Cela représente de belles opportunités d'affaires pour les entreprises innovantes, mais également un sérieux défi pour les gouvernements et le personnel politique. Comment en effet nous mettrons-nous d'accord sur les règles et les impératifs éthiques à adopter dans la mise en œuvre des solutions à ces défis techniques ?

Dans un proche avenir, la virtualisation va se répandre dans tous les secteurs d'activité, banque, services financiers, santé, industrie pharmaceutique – et tout particulièrement dans la mise au point de nouveaux médicaments. La thérapeutique numérique visera à compléter ou même remplacer les médications traditionnelles, en suggérant des modifications comportementales pour réduire ou même vaincre une pathologie donnée. Autre instance en phase de montée en puissance, la biologie du *cloud*, où des logiciels intègrent les résultats des laboratoires et les fusionnent avec d'autres données pour accélérer la découverte de nouveaux médicaments.

Maintenant, imaginez les effets exponentiels et combinés de la virtualisation et des autres méga-changements. Des robots virtuels installés dans le *cloud* pourraient tout simplement rendre n'importe quel processus considérablement plus rapide et plus fiable, et de ce fait aboutir à ce que la numérisation des changements comportementaux devienne une alternative aux médicaments. [66]

Il va aussi sans dire que la virtualisation sera l'une des principales forces motrices du conflit entre la technologie et l'humanité, en provoquant des pertes d'emplois et en accroissant la probabilité d'une emprise prochaine des logiciels sur la biologie, ainsi que la tentation croissante de virtualiser les

humains par le téléchargement de leur cerveau ou leur « cyborgisation » – le rêve de bien des transhumanistes. [67]

Méga-changement 9 : Anticipation

Les ordinateurs sont également devenus très bons pour anticiper nos besoins avant même que nous n'ayons réalisé nous-mêmes ce qu'ils pourraient bien être. Google Now et Google Home sont les assistants numériques intelligents (ANI) de la société Google, et constituent une part non négligeable de son pari sur l'intelligence artificielle. Ils seront chargés d'anticiper les moindres changements dans vos agendas quotidiens – qu'il s'agisse d'un vol retardé, de difficultés de circulation ou de réunions qui s'éternisent – et pourront utiliser l'information dont ils disposent pour prévenir vos prochains rendez-vous de votre retard ou même réserver un autre vol. [68]

La prévention du crime fondée sur les algorithmes devient également un thème à la popularité croissante auprès des responsables des forces de l'ordre. Ces programmes exploitent principalement des mégadonnées telles que statistiques de crimes, médias sociaux ou informations de géolocalisation, ainsi que les données de trafic routier, pour prévoir où des crimes pourraient survenir, afin que les patrouilles de police potentiellement concernées puissent être mobilisées. Dans certains cas, qui étrangement ne sont pas sans nous rappeler les « précogs » de *Minority Report*, [69] des individus ciblés reçoivent même la visite d'un travailleur social ou d'un officier de police, parce que le système a fait savoir qu'ils étaient très probablement sur le point de commettre un crime.

Imaginez où cela pourrait nous mener lorsque l'Internet des objets sera globalement opérationnel, avec des réseaux de capteurs interconnectant des centaines de milliards d'objets tels que feux de signalisation, voitures et caméras de surveillance. Imaginez ce que sera le potentiel d'anticipation prédictive lorsque nous disposerons d'outils d'intelligence artificielle capable de donner sens à toutes ces données. En matière de découverte de

médicaments, un logiciel d'IA tournant sur un ordinateur quantique pourrait dresser la carte de trillions de combinaisons moléculaires et ainsi identifier celles qui pourraient être opérationnelles pour un traitement donné, ou même aider à prévenir le déclenchement de maladies.

Imaginez ce qui pourrait advenir une fois que les billets et les pièces de monnaie seront devenus numériques, et lorsque le moindre achat pourra être tracé instantanément – beaucoup plus efficace, mais aussi beaucoup plus invasif. Doit-on parler de transformations numériques lucratives ou bien du *Meilleur des mondes* ?

En dépit des promesses terriblement attrayantes que les technologies anticipatrices semblent nous offrir, je vois très rapidement émerger un certain nombre de questions éthiques inquiétantes – dont voici les plus critiques :

• **Dépendance** – Abandonner notre pensée aux logiciels et aux algorithmes, tout simplement parce que c'est beaucoup plus pratique et rapide.

• **Confusion** – Ne plus savoir si la réponse reçue à mes e-mails émanait de leur destinataire humain, ou de son assistant numérique intelligent (ANI). Ou même ne plus savoir si j'ai pris seul(e) telle ou telle décision, ou si j'étais manipulé(e) par mon ANI.

• **Perte de contrôle** – Ne plus être en mesure de savoir si l'anticipation de mon IA était correcte ou pas, étant donné qu'il nous serait devenu impossible de tracer la logique du système, ou même de comprendre les principes de fonctionnement d'un ordinateur quantique auto-apprenant. En d'autres termes, nous serions dès lors placés devant une alternative de type 100% confiance / aucune confiance, tout à fait comparable au dilemme auquel doivent déjà faire face certains pilotes d'avions confrontés à leurs systèmes de pilotage automatique.

• **Abdication** – Être tentés de déléguer à nos systèmes davantage de tâches que nécessaire, qu'il s'agisse d'organisation d'agenda,

de prises de rendez-vous ou de réponses à des e-mails. Alors, bien sûr, en cas de survenue d'une erreur, il serait très probable que nous nous contentions d'en rejeter la faute sur notre *cloud* / notre *bot* / notre IA.

Méga-changement 10 : Robotisation

Les robots sont l'incarnation même de tous ces méga-changements, le point de convergence où toutes ces mutations donnent lieu à de nouvelles créations spectaculaires – et elles surgiront absolument partout, que cela vous plaise ou non. Alors que la science réalise de grands progrès dans la compréhension du langage naturel, la reconnaissance d'image, la puissance des batteries et les nouveaux matériaux permettant l'accomplissement de mouvements plus fluides, nous pouvons nous attendre à ce que le prix des robots diminue spectaculairement, tandis que leur utilité – ainsi que leur convivialité – monteront en flèche. Il est même possible que certains robots puissent être imprimés en 3D, exactement comme le sont aujourd'hui les premiers modèles de voitures presque entièrement fabriqués de cette façon. [70]

Le point clé de tout cela, c'est que, tandis que nous sommes engagés dans le changement exponentiel, il nous faut impérativement coopérer autour des questions d'éthique, de culture et de valeurs. À défaut, il est certain que la technologie, d'abord graduellement puis soudainement, deviendra le centre même de nos vies, plutôt qu'un simple outil pour en découvrir le sens.

Chapitre 4
Automatiser le monde

Une productivité accrue, de meilleures marges mais moins d'emplois, davantage de techno-milliardaires et une *middle class* en déclin ?

De tous les méga-changements décrits dans le précédent chapitre, l'automatisation mérite une attention particulière. Elle a été un puissant facteur de changement tout au long de l'Histoire, par exemple lorsque les métiers à tisser manuels ont cédé la place à de nouveaux métiers mécaniques, provoquant en retour en Grande-Bretagne, entre 1811 et 1816, les insurrections de ceux qu'on a appelés les Luddites, qui craignaient que la technologie ne menace leur survie même. [71]

Historiquement, les bénéfices de l'automatisation se sont souvent traduits en nouvelles opportunités pour ceux qu'elle perturbait ou remplaçait. Les marchés sont devenus plus profitables, les coûts ont chuté, l'industrie et l'économie en ont tiré parti, de nouveaux secteurs d'activité ont fait leur apparition ; au fil du temps, la société industrielle n'a pas réellement subi de sous-emploi persistant du fait des nouvelles technologies ou de l'automatisation. [72] À chacune des vagues successives d'industrialisation, les technologies nouvelles ont donné naissance à de nouveaux secteurs d'activité, et finalement créé suffisamment d'emplois nouveaux pour remplacer les emplois périmés qu'elles avaient rendu redondants. Les salaires ont également crû à mesure que la productivité progressait – jusqu'à ce qu'Internet débarque !

Maintenant, progressons jusqu'à l'époque dite de l'économie de l'information – aujourd'hui un terme vraiment désuet qui servait à désigner la première vague de l'Internet – et examinons comment s'y sont articulés progrès technologique et création d'emplois. Les inégalités se sont accrues au sein des économies dominantes – Etats-Unis en tête –, ceux qui détenaient les leviers et les outils de la numérisation se trouvant en situation de réduire considérablement leurs ressources humaines, dans une proportion jamais vue auparavant. [73] [74]

Par la suite, le passage de l'économie de l'information à l'économie de la connaissance s'est avéré beaucoup plus court, et potentiellement plus disruptif. Aujourd'hui que nous abordons l'étape suivante, et que nous nous précipitons tête baissée dans l'économie de l'intelligence des machines, on s'attend à ce que l'emploi décline, avec une disparité probablement croissante entre productivité et niveaux de salaire. En exploitant les méga-changements, les entreprises sont en mesure de réaliser de meilleurs produits, bien plus vite et à moindre coût. Je m'attends à ce que l'accroissement disruptif des plans sociaux et du chômage devienne la norme plutôt que l'exception.

Certaines des tendances préoccupantes du monde du travail ont été relevées dès le début des années 80, lorsque se sont manifestés les premiers effets de l'automatisation, avec des machines capables d'accomplir notre travail à notre place, des équipements agricoles aux centres d'appels automatiques en passant par les robots soudeurs. Mais l'échelle de ce défi nous apparaît mieux désormais. Aux Etats-Unis, selon le Bureau des statistiques du travail, la productivité américaine d'ensemble a, depuis 2011, progressé dans des proportions significatives, mais pas l'emploi ni les salaires. [75] Conséquence, ce sont les profits des entreprises qui se sont accrus depuis 2000. [76]

Dans le même temps, les inégalités ont partout explosé : d'après le site d'information *The Huffington Post*, les 62 personnes les plus riches de la planète ont amassé plus de richesse que la moitié de toute la population mondiale. [77]

La question clé est de savoir si le progrès technologique exponentiel continu va exacerber cette tendance préoccupante ou bien si, d'une manière ou d'une autre, il va s'y confronter.

Je crois pour ma part que les statistiques américaines sont peut-être révélatrices d'une tendance plus marquée, appelée à s'amplifier spectaculairement sous l'effet des méga-changements : le progrès technologique n'est plus le catalyseur de revenus et d'emplois qu'il était durant l'ère industrielle, ni même dans les premiers temps de l'âge de l'information et de l'Internet. Oui, certes, les marges et les profits d'ensemble s'accroissent pour la plupart des entreprises à mesure que les machines se substituent de plus en plus aux hommes. Mais pour autant, ces millions de travailleurs licenciés n'en verront sans doute pas mieux les bénéfices de l'automatisation ; il ne sera pas si simple de transformer des chauffeurs routiers en concepteurs d'interfaces mobiles !

Maintenant, essayez de vous représenter où cela va nous emmener, sur la base d'un progrès technologique exponentiel. Une étude de 2013 de l'Oxford Martin School suggère que quelque 50% des emplois pourraient être automatisés au cours des deux prochaines décennies. [78] Du coup, les grandes firmes se trouvant en situation de pouvoir faire décroître le nombre de gens qu'elles emploient à l'échelle globale, les profits des entreprises pourraient monter en flèche, et cela dans tous les secteurs de l'industrie. En d'autres termes, en s'appuyant prioritairement sur l'automatisation et les neuf autres méga-changements, les grands acteurs économiques seraient potentiellement en mesure de faire beaucoup plus d'argent avec beaucoup moins de main-d'œuvre. Bien sûr, nous verrons aussi se créer de nouveaux métiers qui n'existaient pas auparavant, comme les concepteurs d'interfaces homme-machine, les biologistes du *cloud*, les superviseurs d'intelligence artificielle (IA), les analystes du génome humain ou les gestionnaires de la sphère privée. Néanmoins, des centaines de millions de tâches abrutissantes et d'emplois routiniers auront disparu à jamais – en particulier ceux qui sont les plus répétitifs et

qui ne requièrent pas beaucoup de compétences typiquement humaines telles que la négociation, la créativité ou l'empathie. La question n'est pas de savoir si cela va advenir, mais quand.

Voilà ce que sera la substance même du défi technologie contre humanité : il nous faut absolument prendre conscience de la vitesse croissante à laquelle ce changement va probablement se produire, et ce qu'il pourrait signifier en termes d'éducation, d'apprentissage, d'enseignement, de stratégies gouvernementales, de systèmes de prestations sociales et de politiques publiques, partout sur la planète.

Tandis que les intelligences artificielles, d'abord graduellement puis brusquement, se substitueront aux scientifiques, aux programmeurs, aux médecins, aux journalistes, les perspectives d'emploi intéressantes pourraient devenir si rares que très peu d'entre nous seront en mesure de décrocher un job – en tout cas tels que nous les connaissons aujourd'hui. Dans le même temps, la plupart des fournitures les plus élémentaires de la hiérarchie des besoins de Maslow – nourriture, eau, abri – seront progressivement devenus bien meilleur marché. Les machines accompliront la majeure partie des travaux difficiles, rendant du même coup beaucoup moins chers les services tels que les transports, la banque, l'alimentation et les médias. Il est tout à fait possible que nous nous dirigions d'un côté vers un territoire d'abondance économique, inconnu jusqu'alors, et de l'autre vers la fin des emplois « gagne-pain ». À terme, il n'est pas exclu que nous en venions à devoir dissocier argent et travail ; un tel basculement remettrait alors en question nos hypothèses fondamentales sur la nature de nos valeurs et de nos identités. S'agira-t-il d'une bonne ou d'une mauvaise chose ? Comment les gens privés d'emploi s'y prendront-ils pour payer les biens et services produits par les machines, même si c'est à bien moindre coût qu'aujourd'hui ? Est-ce la fin de la consommation en tant que logique centrale du capitalisme ? Sommes-nous témoins du début de la fin du travail rémunéré tel que nous l'avons connu ?

Les hommes politiques, les responsables publics et les gouvernements en général doivent être beaucoup plus au fait du défi de l'automatisation, et devenir de bien meilleurs organisateurs alors que les échéances se rapprochent à toute allure. Être dépositaire d'un *leadership* éclairé deviendra une exigence cruciale, et tout responsable public qui ne comprendra pas la nécessité de devenir un « régisseur du futur » aura d'emblée perdu la partie.

Dans un très proche avenir, la raison majeure pour laquelle nous voterons pour tel(le) ou tel(le) candidat(e) tiendra à son aptitude à gérer le présent, le réel, tout en sachant nous montrer qu'il (ou elle) a une compréhension profonde des potentialités du futur.

Automatisation[2] – Les cinq A
J'ai pour habitude d'évoquer l'automatisation sous la forme des cinq étapes suivantes, qui s'aggravent progressivement :

1. Automatisation
2. Assentiment
3. Abdication
4. Aggravation
5. Abomination

L'automatisation, une destination inéluctable
J'estime que l'automatisation exponentielle est une certitude, tout simplement parce qu'elle devient réalisable et qu'elle réduit spectaculairement les coûts – un objectif primaire dans presque toutes les entreprises et organisations. D'ici les cinq à dix prochaines années, nous allons voir apparaître dans la plupart des industries de nouvelles formes de *low cost* et d'hyper-efficacité – mais songez à ce qu'en seront les conséquences pour l'emploi. L'efficience devrait-elle vraiment prévaloir sur l'humanité ? Devons-nous réellement automatiser les choses simplement parce que c'est possible ? Les entreprises qui investissent de façon

agressive dans le remplacement des hommes par des machines ne devraient-elles pas être astreintes à payer une sorte de taxe sur l'automatisation, dont le bénéfice irait à ceux qui n'ont plus d'emploi ? Telles sont les questions auxquelles il nous faudra répondre très bientôt.

Considérons simplement le fait que les forces combinées des méga-changements – tout particulièrement la numérisation, la virtualisation, l'intelligisation (apprentissage profond et intelligence artificielle) et la mobilité numérique – créent de nouvelles possibilités pour l'automatisation chaque jour qui passe. Au début de 2016, lorsque le système GoAlpha de Google a percé le code du jeu de go, il n'était pas programmé pour jouer au go, mais davantage pour apprendre le jeu en partant de rien, par lui-même. [79]

Il ne s'agit pas d'une IA limitée ni d'un ordinateur pré-programmé capable de surpasser les humains dans des domaines plus ou moins mathématiques ou logiques comme les échecs. Il s'agit ici d'une IA capable d'imiter le mode de fonctionnement du cerveau en se servant de réseaux neuronaux proches de l'humain, et capable aussi de s'adapter et se programmer elle-même. Imaginez ce genre d'IA s'attaquant à des défis et tâches humaines très complexes à grande échelle, capable de concevoir la manière de les résoudre et de les automatiser pour notre compte – et au bout du compte de manière infiniment plus performante que nous ne l'aurions jamais été face à des tâches mettant en jeu la connaissance.

Dans son livre *Smarter Than Us: The Rise of Machine Intelligence*, Stuart Armstrong écrit :

« Si une IA possédait l'une quelconque de ces compétences – aptitudes sociales, développement technologique, potentiel économique – à un niveau surhumain, il est très probable qu'elle en viendrait rapidement à dominer notre monde d'une manière ou d'une autre. Et, ainsi que nous l'avons vu, si elle avait été en

mesure de développer ces aptitudes à un niveau humain, alors elle les développerait probablement bientôt à un niveau surhumain. Par conséquent, nous pouvons supposer que la programmation d'une seule de ces compétences dans un ordinateur nous conduirait dans un monde dominé par des IA ou des humains augmentés par IA. » [80]

Prenons comme exemples la sécurité sociale, le rembour-sement des frais médicaux, les retraites et les prestations de chômage pour, potentiellement, des centaines de millions de personnes. En déployant l'intelligence artificielle, il pourrait bientôt devenir possible de disposer d'un superordinateur intelligent définissant ce que devraient être les règles de la sécurité sociale et de quelle manière elles pourraient être mises en œuvre, débouchant ainsi sur des économies substantielles pour les gouvernements, fût-ce au prix d'une possible déshumanisation citoyenne.

Aux Etats-Unis, une IA avancée pourrait fonder ces règles sur l'exploitation de toutes les données d'assurance sociale des quelque 80 années écoulées depuis la fondation du système de sécurité sociale, en 1935. [81] Elle pourrait par ailleurs tirer parti de toutes les autres informations connexes disponibles, telles que dossiers médicaux, profils sur les réseaux sociaux, antécédents juridiques et bases de données gouvernementales ou locales. Il pourrait ainsi en résulter une IA de sécurité sociale en constante évolution (appelons-la SécuBot), capable de prendre en charge ces très complexes transactions avec seulement 10% à 20% du personnel actuel. Mais dites adieu à l'empathie humaine et à la compassion : les machines seules détermineraient les prestations auxquelles vous pourriez prétendre, et il n'y aurait plus guère la possibilité de les discuter.

Je me demande souvent ce qu'il adviendra lorsque ces concepts seront devenus réalité, graduellement puis soudainement. Voici une chaine probable d'événements qui joue déjà un rôle dans les situations de surcharge des réseaux sociaux : confrontés à l'automatisation tous azimuts, nous commençons par

consentir, c'est-à-dire par accepter la supériorité des décisions du système décisionnel – à contrecœur, mais avec le sourire. Ça ne nous plaît pas réellement, mais nous n'allons pas non plus en faire toute une histoire.

Et puis, par la suite, il se peut que nous commencions à abdiquer – autrement dit nous « renonçons au trône » et abandonnons le pouvoir au système. Dès lors, très bientôt, nous cessons d'être l'entité la plus importante au sein de ce système : c'est la machine elle-même qui en est devenue le nouveau centre de gravité – nous sommes devenus un contenu plutôt qu'une raison d'être. L'outil est devenu le but ; quant à nous, nos actions commencent à être motivées par la satisfaction du système. Lequel « système » consistera principalement en autres nœuds raccordés au réseau, autrement dit les humains également interconnectés au même écosystème électronique global.

Facebook incarne aujourd'hui le meilleur exemple de ce principe d'abdication : plutôt que d'entreprendre de vraies actions au sens politique, qui pourraient probablement devenir embarrassantes et souvent inopportunes, nous nous contentons de « liker » ce qui passe à notre portée sur Facebook, de partager une vidéo avec nos amis, de signer une pétition ou, au mieux, de faire don de quelques dollars (ou euros) à une campagne de Kickstarter ou sur Causes.com…

Assentiment

Nous sommes d'ores et déjà les témoins de multiples phénomènes d'automatisation de choses qui ne devraient pas l'être – par exemple user de logiciels « améliorant » la qualité de nos messages, c'est-à-dire capables de collecter pour nous davantage de « likes » sur les réseaux sociaux. Nous donnons fréquemment notre assentiment *a posteriori*, après avoir consenti sans trop y réfléchir à continuer à surfer, par procuration, parce que c'est simple et pratique. Ça fait le boulot. Autre exemple, ajouter un nouvel ami Facebook à votre liste, simplement parce qu'il est un ami d'ami d'un autre ami qui a récemment « liké » l'un de vos

posts. Pourquoi pas, après tout, aucun mal à ça ? Oui, il serait difficile en effet de prétendre que cela peut vraiment nuire.

Abdication

Mais ensuite, il se pourrait que nous nous trouvions, la plupart du temps par inadvertance, en situation d'abdiquer les responsabilités qui étaient les nôtres, en nous en déchargeant sur la technologie. Plutôt que de régulièrement vous déplacer chez votre grand-mère, peut-être pourriez-vous lui installer Skype et ainsi lui rendre visite plus souvent, par écran interposé ? Bon ou mauvais résultat ?

Ou bien, dans un très proche avenir, plutôt que de vous assurer qu'elle consulte régulièrement son médecin, peut-être lui enverrez-vous un appareil de diagnostic à distance capable de mesurer son état de santé toujours et partout, ce qui vous évitera de l'y emmener vous-même à chaque fois ?

L'abdication (soit, littéralement, « renoncer au trône ») de notre propre pouvoir de contrôle au profit de la technologie est devenue un motif récurrent partout autour de nous. Je me sers souvent de TripAdvisor, qui m'indique d'autorité que tel restaurant est le meilleur, et bien que nous ayons le nez sur 25 autres options alléchantes, nous nous contentons d'aller là où la machine nous le dit.

D'une certaine manière, nous transférons notre autorité et notre capacité de jugement à un algorithme. Là encore, lorsqu'il ne s'agit que de TripAdvisor, rien de bien grave ; mais imaginez donc que cette tendance se développe de manière exponentielle ! Alors nous pourrions vraiment en arriver à ne plus rien décider ni même faire de notre propre chef : les choses nous arriveraient, et voilà tout. Ça nous rendrait la vie tellement plus simple, n'est-ce pas ? Se laisser aller demande beaucoup moins d'efforts que se prendre en main.

J'ai eu ce débat spécifique sur TripAdvisor avec de nombreux amis et auditoires ces dernières années, et j'en suis arrivé à la conclusion que si je l'utilise comme source d'information parmi beaucoup d'autres, tout en étant averti de l'attrait trompeur de

l'assentiment et de l'abdication, alors TripAdvisor peut s'avérer assez utile. Une fois encore, tout est question de mesure. Mais que pourrai-je faire si TripAdvisor devient une IA, un robot-futé-dans-l'espace dont il me sera impossible d'évaluer effectivement et facilement les performances et l'impartialité ? Qu'en sera-t-il si cette IA est devenue si intelligente que je n'aurai d'autre choix que de la croire sans réserve – ou pas du tout ?

Google Maps est un autre exemple de la facilité avec laquelle nous autres humains pouvons abdiquer notre trône. Combien de fois vous est-il arrivé, en utilisant Google Maps, de vous tenir perplexe à une intersection dans une ville étrange, en train de chercher sur l'écran une chose qui était littéralement sous vos yeux ? Hélas, nous ne faisons plus confiance au témoignage de nos sens – et pas davantage aux passants qui pourraient nous aider. Nous ne croyons plus qu'à ce que nous dit le cerveau dans le ciel. Va-t-il pleuvoir, faut-il que je prenne un parapluie ? Google OS va me le dire, plutôt que ma propre intuition météo, ou un coup d'œil rapide par la fenêtre.

C'est en l'occurrence un exemple banal, mais examinez les effets d'amplification à venir, issus des technologies exponentielles.

Existera-t-il un jour un cerveau médecin global susceptible de décider si nous devrions ou pas avoir des enfants, en fonction de notre ADN et de milliards d'autres facteurs ? Les sociétés d'assurance se refuseront-elles à nous couvrir si nous nous obstinions à n'en faire qu'à notre guise ? Conserverons-nous la liberté de prendre des décisions qui ne soient inspirées ni par la logique ni par les algorithmes ? Pourrons-nous encore faire des choses stupides comme conduire trop vite, forcer sur la boisson ou mal nous nourrir ? Le libre arbitre est-il sur le point de disparaître ?

Maintenant imaginez Abdication[2] : l'oubli exponentiel de nous-mêmes

Qu'arriverait-il si la technologie continuait à nous encourager à renoncer encore plus au contrôle de nos existences, simplement parce que c'est pratique, parce que c'est efficace, parce que c'est magique (et je ne parle même pas du gain de temps : 95% plus vite !) ? Et si nous n'avions encore entrevu que le sommet de l'iceberg de l'abdication ? Et si nous n'en étions qu'au niveau cinq sur une échelle graduée de zéro à cent ? En arriverions-nous à terme, ainsi que l'auteur Stephen Talbott le suggère dans *The New Atlantis*, à « abdiquer notre conscience » même, en permettant aux machines d'agir en arbitres ultimes de nos valeurs et de notre morale ? [82] Si, comme Talbott l'argumente, « les technologies nous invitent puissamment à nous oublier nous-mêmes », que se passera-t-il quand nous mettrons en œuvre des technologies exponentiellement toujours plus puissantes ?

Cette attraction vers « l'oubli de nous-mêmes » nous poussera-t-elle à progresser comme des somnambules à travers la vie numérique, ouvrant ainsi la porte à une sorte de féodalisme numérique global, où les seigneurs de la technologie nous gouverneront d'une manière dont nous n'avons même pas idée ?

Une chose est certaine : la technologie et la plupart de ses plus grands fournisseurs déploient tous leurs efforts pour nous faire aimer les chemins de l'assentiment et de l'abdication, que ce soit intentionnellement ou par inadvertance. Nous n'essayons même pas de manger différemment ; à la place, nous prenons des médicaments contre l'hypertension. Nous ne cherchons pas à tirer profit de l'ennui pour nous abandonner à la contemplation ; à la place, nous remplissons le vide avec nos tablettes chatoyantes, en nous aventurant dans le vortex numérique. Nous ne cherchons pas à ce que nos enfants se fassent de nouveaux amis ; à la place, nous les laissons jouer avec des amis virtuels en forme de robots animaux ou d'Hello Barbie – la première poupée capable de se connecter au *cloud* pour parler aux enfants comme une vraie personne. [83] C'est tellement plus facile !

Dans un tel contexte, des assistants numériques intelligents (ANI) comme Amazon Echo ou Google Home pourraient-ils bientôt se comporter en moteurs d'abdication ?

Dans le cas de la sécurité sociale évoquée plus haut, cette « compulsion abdicationniste » pourrait bien conduire les pouvoirs publics à abandonner leurs responsabilités au système décisionnel. Supposons par exemple que ce « SécuBot » imaginaire prenne graduellement en charge les tâches humaines, tout simplement parce que ce serait 90% moins cher et 1000% plus rapide : quand bien même cette hypothèse ne serait vérifiée qu'à 90%, il y aurait alors toutes les chances pour que les gouvernements considèrent que c'est tellement mieux ainsi...

Aggravation

L'étape suivante de cette spirale descendante pourrait bien être l'aggravation, tant pour les quelques agents humains restants que pour les utilisateurs du système, les usagers et les clients. Il est certain que la frustration ferait rage, mais on n'y pourrait probablement pas grand-chose, puisque le système serait toujours plus rapide, plus efficace, plus modulable. Il serait bien sûr possible de traiter les frustrations, mais compte tenu de la présence écrasante du système dans chacun des compartiments de nos vies, il n'y a presque aucune chance que nous puissions effectivement cesser de l'utiliser. À nouveau, Facebook nous en offre le meilleur exemple actuel : nous ne cessons de recevoir un flot toujours plus abondant de notifications et mises à jour de statuts émanant de personnes dont nous avons peine à nous souvenir, simplement par peur de perdre le contact avec ceux qui nous importent. Et là encore, l'extrême plasticité comme la puissance sans pareille de cette plate-forme nous rendent impossible d'intervenir au sujet de ce qui ne nous convient plus.

Abomination

Finalement, dans un environnement censé être dédié à la sécurité sociale, on peut être sûr que traiter les gens comme de simples

numéros, ou comme des données désincarnées, nous conduira finalement à une abomination, une perversion de l'intention d'origine du système, qui est de procurer des services sociaux aux citoyens humains. Voilà le stade final, quoique quelque peu déprimant, vers lequel tend le processus des cinq A, si nous n'en traitons pas correctement les deux premières étapes (assentiment et abdication) dans notre marche vers l'automatisation.

Espérons simplement qu'il résultera un moindre assentiment et de moins nombreuses abdications d'une automatisation technologiquement bien pensée et bien mise en œuvre, avec des dérives limitées. Car c'est bien ce qui inquiète dans l'automatisation exponentielle : nous ne nous rendrons même pas compte de la perte de notre pouvoir et de notre contrôle avant d'avoir atteint le point de bascule, et alors il se pourrait bien que nous ayons aussi perdu toute possibilité d'y réagir.

Un équilibre à trouver

Encore une fois, la question est de trouver le bon équilibre : que pouvons-nous automatiser qui ne remplacera pas les indispensables processus et échanges verbaux intrinsèquement humains, ou encore les flux que nous ne voudrions pas abdiquer ? Quand vous contactez un centre pour modifier votre réservation aérienne, avez-vous besoin, pour ce service, d'un agent humain pour vous prodiguer compréhension et empathie ? La plupart du temps, ce n'est pas le cas, mais dans certaines circonstances ça l'est – par exemple dans l'hypothèse où surgiraient des enjeux de politesse. Par conséquent, il se peut tout à fait que 90% des centres d'appels finissent par être automatisés dans les prochaines années, mais que dans certains cas spécifiques nous ayons encore besoin d'interactions humaines. Dans ce domaine en particulier, une automatisation bien pensée et sous supervision humaine constitue donc probablement une évolution positive, mais il n'en reste pas moins, quel que soit l'angle sous lequel on aborde le sujet, que des millions d'emplois seront perdus.

Maintenant portons le même débat sur un terrain connexe et dans un proche avenir : lors d'un vol en avion, vous sentiriez-vous en confiance avec un cockpit sans pilote et entièrement automatisé ? Seriez-vous rassuré(e) de savoir qu'un pilote humain est bien aux commandes ? Lorsque vous êtes soumis à un examen médical, avez-vous besoin qu'on vous témoigne compassion et humanité, ou bien vous contenteriez-vous d'une machine vous informant simplement des faits ? Lorsqu'il est question de grippe ou de maux d'estomac, il semblerait que les diagnostics à distance permis par l'automatisation soient utiles et socialement acceptables. Toutefois, lorsqu'il s'agit de diagnostiquer des affections complexes comme des symptômes de stress, de l'asthme ou du diabète, l'automatisation tendrait certainement à déshumaniser la prise en charge médicale.

Au fond, il ne s'agira pas de simplement dire oui ou non à l'automatisation ; il sera question de réponses graduelles et d'approche globale préventive, capables de maintenir un équilibre et de continuer à placer les préoccupations humaines au centre, toujours. La question clé n'est pas de savoir si et comment la technologie peut mettre en œuvre l'automatisation, mais de savoir comment nous en ressentirons le résultat nous autres humains, de savoir si l'automatisation sera en mesure d'encourager ou pas l'épanouissement humain. Et, au fond, de savoir si nous nous sentirons davantage en affinité avec le camp des humanistes ou avec celui des technologues.

Une invitation à l'automatisation intérieure ?

Parallèlement à toutes les choses qui s'automatisent tout autour de nous, il y en a aussi une bonne quantité qui sont probablement en cours d'automatisation à l'intérieur de nous-mêmes, affectant nos façons de penser et de ressentir. Considérez par exemple la manière dont les algorithmes, les logiciels, les assistants numériques personnels, les services du *cloud* ou encore les robots prennent de plus en plus en main nos affaires courantes, et comment certains d'entre nous ont d'ores et déjà automatisé

l'amitié, par l'entremise de réseaux sociaux ou d'applications de messagerie.

Que va-t-il par exemple rester de notre intelligence collective – autrement dit les dialogues par lesquels nous continuons à transmettre, débattre, discuter, décider et concevoir nos sociétés et nos démocraties ? Dans quelle mesure nos choix seront-ils façonnés si ce que nous voyons et entendons les uns des autres est exclusivement déterminé par des algorithmes dont la raison d'être est de vous faire ingurgiter autant de pubs que possible – et non par des hommes ? Et qu'en sera-t-il si ces outils ne sont pas supervisés, régulés ou placés sous contrôle public ?

Serons-nous à l'avenir sous l'influence de machines et d'algorithmes détenus par une poignée d'entreprises technologiques et de plates-formes géantes de l'Internet global ? Vont-elles devenir des « systèmes dispensateurs de dopamine virtuelle » programmés pour l'affirmation positive et envahissante, et conçus pour extraire le maximum de résultats au profit de leurs propriétaires, publicitaires et collecteurs de données, pressés d'analyser et d'exploiter vos données personnelles ?

Témoin Google News, [84] qui n'est pas directement géré par des personnes, pas plus d'ailleurs que ne le sont les applications « d'information » [85] de Facebook ou Baidu. [86] Dans presque tous les cas, il y a certes une dose de supervision humaine, mais ce sont des algorithmes qui font l'essentiel du vrai travail. Dans ces entreprises, très peu de gens sont effectivement confrontés à des contenus au sens journalistique du terme – ils se concentrent plutôt sur la conception d'algorithmes et de logiciels toujours plus intelligents, capables de répondre à chaque nouvelle attente. Rien d'un hasard si la formule de Marc Andreessen, « les logiciels bouffent le monde » a déjà muté en « Facebook bouffe le Net ». [87] Et Facebook n'a aucunement l'intention de partager le festin avec le peuple ! Exception faite des programmeurs, ingénieurs et chercheurs en intelligence artificielle, la compagnie entend

n'embaucher que le minimum possible d'employés, pour se concentrer sur *les clients* humains.

Peut-être même que bientôt, les logiciels ne se contenteront plus de « bouffer le monde », pour de plus en plus « berner le monde ». Je me sens moi-même un peu berné, ou disons manipulé, lorsque je suis mon fil d'info Facebook, parce qu'il m'est impossible de lui accorder la confiance que j'accorderais au *New York Times*, à *The Economist*, à *Der Spiegel* ou au *Guardian* – son unique projet étant de générer du profit pour lui-même. Non pas un média mais une tromperie – et quelque conscience que nous en ayons, cela ne nous empêche manifestement pas d'être fascinés.

Il est vrai que cela n'est pas entièrement à sens unique : le site d'actualité *Mashable* rapporte qu'Apple fait des efforts considérables pour associer des modérateurs humains à son application d'infos, à ses recommandations musicales et à son service de playlist – mais il s'agit certainement d'une exception, pas de la règle. [88]

L'automatisation explose car il est désormais clair que les humains sont chers, lents et souvent inefficaces, là où les machines sont économiques, rapides et ultra-efficaces – et qu'elles tendent à l'être encore plus. Il est difficile d'imaginer où tout cela va nous emmener dans les dix prochaines années. Mais avec l'explosion de la productivité, il semble inévitable que l'emploi humain tel que nous le connaissons décline spectaculairement. Nous pouvons être sûr d'avoir des professions à l'avenir, mais il est probable qu'elles soient déconnectées de l'idée de gagne-pain.

Il devient également très vraisemblable qu'avec des plates-formes médiatiques aussi largement automatisées, nous nous trouvions détournés d'informations autrement plus pertinentes. Les contenus seront plutôt sélectionnés par un robot et une IA évaluera ce que nous devrions regarder ou lire, sur la base de centaines de millions de faits et fragments de données analysés en temps réel. Le risque manifeste qui en découle, c'est que des

services de ce type soient de plus en plus dépourvus de l'éthique, des valeurs, des émotions et des références morales et artistiques qui, même éphémères, sont peu ou prou la base même du *storytelling* humain. Bien sûr, les robots et les IA seront également capables de comprendre nos émotions et nos sentiments dans un proche avenir, et il se peut même qu'ils puissent également simuler nos émotions et nos capacités au *storytelling* – mais ce n'est pas pour autant, me semble-t-il, qu'ils seront en mesure d'atteindre à un véritable *être* humain.

Je ne ressasse pas la gloire passée des journaux imprimés – ils étaient et sont encore peu pratiques, souvent monopolistiques, corrompus et mensongers. Pourtant, dans bien des cas, les journalistes étaient des gens dont le métier consistait à être mieux informés que nous, à percevoir les contextes et à déterminer leur pertinence. Leur mission, aussi subjectifs qu'ils l'aient parfois été, était de se concentrer sur ce que le public devait discerner.

Le fiasco retentissant des armes irakiennes de destruction massive – monté en épingle par *Fox News* et tant de ses semblables – a clairement démontré que les chaines et leurs correspondants humains pouvaient aussi se fourvoyer, sans clairvoyance aucune. Mais au moins, nous avons eu la possibilité de comprendre qui tirait les ficelles de cette histoire – ainsi que la possibilité de les interroger. Je pense que nous n'aurions pas la même latitude avec les IA et leurs *newsbots*. Et je suis certain de ceci : nous n'aurions pas le moindre indice sur la manière de les interroger.

Autre conséquence des fils d'info automatisés : nous ne pourrons plus voir, ou entendre, les contenus que ceux qui nous entourent – nos familles, nos conjoints, nos amis et collègues – voient ou entendent. Leurs sources seront 100% customisées, voire totalement différentes des nôtres. Car nous ne sommes finalement plus très loin du point où nous disposerons de suffisamment de puissance de calcul pour customiser chaque fil individuel selon des données entièrement personnalisées.

Sommes-nous aujourd'hui en train d'alimenter le problème de la « bulle filtrante d'Internet » si souvent décriée, créant ainsi par algorithmes interposés un phénomène de chambres d'écho, d'un individu à chacun de ses pairs, pour nous rendre cette expérience la plus plaisante possible ? Quels effets cela aura-t-il sur nos préjugés ? Les fournisseurs d'algorithmes aux si gigantesques implications, comme Google et Facebook, évaluent-il ces questions ? Ou bien les inquiétudes humaines sur le filtrage, la manipulation et les préjugés ne figurent-ils que tout à la fin de leurs listes de priorités ?

« Vous savez... c'est bien, d'avoir une éthique ; mais nous n'avons ni le temps ni les ressources pour nous en occuper maintenant » : voilà ce que j'entends dans les entreprises lorsque nous abordons le sujet. Je pense que c'est une grave erreur, car je crains qu'une société dotée d'un pouvoir technologique infini, mais dépourvue d'éthique, courre à sa perte.

Tâchons de nous représenter ce genre de NewsBot ou de MedIA migrant de nos ordinateurs à la télévision, ce qui arrivera à coup sûr. Et examinons le scénario possible : des programmes d'infos individuellement customisés pour chacun d'entre nous via une transmission *over-the-top* (OTT) adossée à l'Internet plutôt qu'à la télédiffusion terrestre ou par câble ; CNN ou la télé publique en Europe remplaçant votre flux vidéo Twitter ou votre fil d'actu Facebook ; et les apps, robots et autres assistants numériques personnels mettant fin au règne du câble et de la télédiffusion tels que nous les connaissions. En moins de dix ans, la télé et l'Internet auront complètement convergé, rendant possible un complet renversement de notre manière de consommer les médias. Et, oui, il y a bien de nombreux avantages aussi à l'adoption globale de l'OTT, alors ne jetons pas le bébé avec l'eau du bain !

Si, comme le directeur exécutif et fondateur franc-tireur de *Wired* Kevin Kelly l'a dit un jour, « les machines c'est pour les réponses et les humains c'est pour les questions », [89] alors où donc les machines nous emmèneront-elles pour ce qui est des

médias, des contenus et de l'information ? Vont-elles simplement construire un paysage de réponses magnifiquement fausses ou simulées, évacuant toutes les questions que nous aurions pu ou dû poser si seulement nous avions disposé d'un peu de marge de manœuvre ou d'espace vital pour la contemplation ?

> *« Les ordinateurs sont inutiles. Ils ne peuvent vous donner que des réponses. »* Pablo Picasso [90]

De mon point de vue, nous nous distinguons par des traits humains singuliers tels que l'aptitude à poser des questions, à imaginer des situations innovantes, à remettre en question l'ordre établi, à observer sous différents angles, à lire entre les lignes et à discerner ce qui n'est pas encore survenu. Et n'est-ce pas tout cela que ces médias et ces fournisseurs de contenus, ainsi que ceux qui les organisent, devraient avoir à cœur de faire ?

Je redoute sincèrement le moment où tous ces traits humains pourraient être écartés, tout simplement parce que chaque plate-forme ne programme jamais que ce qui nous concerne individuellement. Nous pourrions bien alors nous engager sur le chemin qui mène à l'abdication complète de notre conscience, et à la sous-traitance de notre humanité. Peut-être en viendrons nous à vivre dans une sorte de réalité programmée avant même de nous en être rendu compte – et sous la coupe de ceux qui possèdent ces programmes et ces serveurs.

> *« Les humains sont les organes reproducteurs de la technologie. »* Kevin Kelly, What Technology Wants [91]

Si les *bots* et les IA pensent et agissent de plus en plus en notre nom, qu'arrivera-t-il au processus même de nos prises de décision ? Si bon nombre de nos décisions apparemment banales, comme le choix du film que je vais regarder ce soir ou la nourriture que je vais acheter, peuvent en effet être prises en charge par des logiciels et des agents intelligents, qu'en sera-t-il

de l'effet de surprise, du mystère, des erreurs humaines et des heureux hasards de nos vies ? Ces ANIs pourront-ils être programmés pour agir en humains avec ce que cela suppose d'aléas, d'individualité, d'imperfections, de penchants particuliers – et néanmoins obtenir des résultats convaincants ? Et cela serait-il même souhaitable ?

Les *bots* finiront-ils par voter en notre nom, par nous représenter dans d'éminentes instances démocratiques comme les référendums ou même les parlements ? Nos ANIs se serviront-ils de nos historiques d'opinions, de comportements et de choix pour nous conseiller et nous convaincre sur la manière dont nous devrions voter ? Et si tout et n'importe quoi devient prévisible, alors le libre arbitre sera-t-il voué à devenir une relique du passé ?

> « *Réalisez-vous qu'il n'y a aucune marge pour le libre arbitre dans ce que nous créons avec l'intelligence artificielle...* » Clyde DeSouza [92]

Vortex informatiques maîtres du monde ?

Alors que la technologie nous offre la possibilité de nous plonger toujours plus profondément au cœur de son propre vortex, je discerne un danger significatif dans ce que l'automatisation exponentielle pourrait nous enseigner : il nous est en effet devenu possible de prendre des raccourcis pour à peu près n'importe quoi, dès lors que nous y affectons les ressources des combinaisons de données, de l'intelligence artificielle et de la robotique. Plus besoin de main d'œuvre laborieuse, lente et fastidieuse.

La technologie est passée de mes mains à mon visage, puis sur mes oreilles et finalement à l'intérieur même de boîte crânienne. Plus besoin pour les enfants d'apprendre à écrire, puisque les ordinateurs se chargeront d'écouter, enregistrer et transcrire tout ce que nous leur dirons. Plus besoin de composer avec les complexités des relations humaines dans la « vraie vie », dès lors que j'aurai le loisir d'entretenir des relations interpersonnelles et

même sexuelles avec leurs équivalents numériques, via robots et réalité augmentée ou virtuelle. Nul besoin d'apprendre à jouer d'un instrument de musique puisque mon interface cerveau-ordinateur (ICO) me permettra de faire de la musique simplement en y pensant. Plus besoin d'apprendre des langues étrangères, puisque mon traducteur automatique sera toujours là pour m'aider. Inutile de parler aux autres si je peux accéder librement à leurs dépôts de données. Et plus besoin de s'encombrer de nos émotions chaotiques et simiesques, si peu conformes au bel ordonnancement des IAs.

L'automatisation nous permet de considérablement réduire toutes les tâches nécessaires à la réalisation de la plupart des routines humaines, et d'obtenir le même résultat instantanément ou presque – en tout cas c'est l'idée. Sur n'importe quel sujet, il est désormais possible de scanner des milliers de commentaires Twitter et de regarder les meilleurs extraits de centaines de vidéos YouTube, et ainsi de se donner l'air d'un expert en un rien de temps. Nous pouvons apprendre tout sur tout « juste à temps » plutôt qu'« au cas où » - il suffit de disposer du bon mot-clé et du bon programme.

Du coup, nous sommes emportés par un flot continu de données plutôt que de télécharger et mémoriser de la connaissance. En un sens, nous avons l'opportunité de devenir surhumains. Mais est-ce si sûr ?

Pour qualifier tous ces concepts, j'utilise l'expression « trou de ver » parce que, comme les trous de ver cosmiques – un raccourci imaginaire à travers l'espace et le temps initié par le vaisseau *warp drive*, ainsi que le savent tous les fans de *Star Trek* –, il permet de contourner tous ces fastidieux facteurs humains et, par technologie interposée, d'atteindre ses objectifs beaucoup plus rapidement.

Mais n'oublions pas qu'abuser de ces vortex (trous de vers) nous éloignera de l'humain, en nous conduisant à devenir nous-mêmes des machines, au moins partiellement. Le psychologue lauréat du Prix Nobel Daniel Kahneman a souligné à plusieurs

reprises que « la cognition est incarnée : nous pensons avec le corps, pas avec le cerveau ». [93] Il nous faut réaliser et accepter que le fait d'être humain est une expérience globale ; que l'apprentissage dépend d'interactions entre de multiples facteurs, et pas seulement de l'acquisition de données ; que les réalisations réellement puissantes émergent de conversations humaines et non de flux de clics de souris, même si ceux-ci peuvent bien sûr s'avérer utiles aussi. En d'autres termes, si nous éliminons les processus des résultats, alors nous n'obtiendrons pas les mêmes résultats : nous aurons été abusés par le logiciel.

> « *Les relations humaines sont riches, désordonnées et*
> *exigeantes. Et nous les aseptisons à coup de technologie.*
> *Textos, courriels, publications, toutes ces choses nous*
> *permettent de nous présenter comme bon nous semble.*
> *Éditer à notre guise implique que nous pouvons aussi*
> *effacer, retoucher notre visage, notre voix, notre chair, notre*
> *corps – ni trop ni trop peu, juste ce qu'il faut.* »
> Sherry Turkle [94]

Si nous supprimions toutes ces tâches et comportements humains ennuyeux que sont la discussion, la réflexion et les émotions, quels en seraient les effets sur notre humanité collective ? Deviendrions-nous complètement dépendants de ces trous de vers et *warp drives*, sans nous arrêter au fait que tout ce qu'ils savent accomplir n'est que simulation de l'expérience humaine ?

Un immense défi nous attend, dans la mesure où les méga-changements (voir mon chapitre 3) s'articulent les uns aux autres de manière combinatoire : numérisation, automatisation et virtualisation croissantes entraineront sans doute encore plus d'automatisation. Chaque étape dans l'automatisation d'un processus contraint toutes les autres pièces à faire de même : l'automatisation d'une tâche actionne la suivante, l'automatisation de l'ensemble du processus déclenchant une réaction en chaine chez tous ceux auxquels il est lui-même relié.

Une logique qui ne peut être rompue, parce que l'entièreté du système est conçue à cette fin.

Résultat final : à force d'automatiser les nouvelles et l'information, à force d'automatiser les achats et le commerce, à force d'automatiser décisions financières et soins médicaux, nous pourrions bien en venir à terme à nous automatiser nous-mêmes, ne serait-ce que pour ne pas trop perturber le système...

Qu'il s'agisse de notre ordinateur, de notre smartphone, de notre ANI ou de notre IA, si nous permettons à nos outils de devenir notre raison d'être, en abdiquant et en leur déléguant toute notre autorité, alors nous pourrions bien prendre le risque de devenir dispensables puisque nous, humains, ne sommes au fond que des machines assez minables.

> « *L'argument majeur pour comprendre pourquoi une IA avancée a besoin d'un corps pourrait surgir de sa phase d'apprentissage et de développement – car les scientifiques, alors, pourraient bien découvrir qu'il n'est pas possible de faire croître une AGI* (pour « artificial growing intelligence, soit « intelligence artificielle organique », *ndt*) *sans le support d'un corps, quelle qu'en soit la forme.* »
> James Barrat, Our Final Invention : Artificial Intelligence and the End of Human Era. [95]

Comment définir, du coup, les limites acceptables de l'automatisation ? À partir de quel stade pourrait-on considérer avoir été trop loin à l'intérieur du vortex ? Afin de nourrir le débat, voici ce que je considère comme quelques exemples d'automatisation justifiée :

- comptabilité, archivage, administration financière
- sécurité aéroportuaire
- gestion d'agenda, planification de rendez-vous et réunions
- tâches routinières n'impliquant pas de prises de décision humaine

Et voici en revanche quelques-unes des tâches qu'à mon sens il ne faudrait pas automatiser (à supposer que l'on sache le faire) :

- nouvelles et médias publics
- messages à ses connexions personnelles
- *likes* et affirmations sur les réseaux sociaux
- amitié (par exemple l'auto-suivi de Twitter)
- embauche ou licenciement de personnel
- sélection de partenaires et établissement de relations interpersonnelles
- activités démocratiques (par exemple signature de pétitions en ligne en lieu et place d'activités politiques réelles)
- altération du génome humain
- naissance

Pour rappel, la définition traditionnelle de « automatiser » est, littéralement : « acte d'autoréalisation, agir sans concours extérieur ». [96] Il est clair qu'il existe nombre de tâches, actions et activités dont l'automatisation apporte valeur et bénéfice à tous. Il y a ensuite celles dont l'automatisation apporte des avantages à une majorité, celles dont ne tirent parti qu'une petite minorité et enfin celles qui, à long terme, disqualifient pratiquement tout le monde. Dans *La Machine à remonter le temps*, H.G. Wells a imaginé un futur nettement divisé entre les sauvages Morlocks et l'élite oisive des Eloi. [97] Même si nous parvenons à échapper au destin des Morlocks, nous sentirons-nous souverains et héroïques dans la peau des Eloi – machines incarnées mais passives, figées dans leur magistère ?

Chapitre 5
L'Internet des objets inhumains

L'Internet des objets inhumains nous conduira-t-il,
graduellement puis soudainement, à renoncer à notre humanité
et à devenir toujours plus mécanistes, simplement pour rester
dans la course ?

Ainsi que nous l'avons exposé auparavant, une conjugaison de développements technologiques divers nourrit l'émergence de l'Internet des objets (IdO, *Internet of Things* – IoT en anglais) – également appelé par l'entreprise Cisco Systems l'Internet de tout et par quelques autres comme General Electric l'Internet industriel.

La promesse est simple : lorsque tout sera connecté et les données collectées toujours et partout, alors nous serons en situation de découvrir de nouvelles vérités et même de prédire et d'anticiper la survenue d'événements. L'expert en sécurité et vie privée Bruce Schneier qualifie ce réseau-dans-le-ciel artificiel d'objets, senseurs, matériels et processus interconnectés de « Toile globale » (en anglais « World Sized Web »). [98] Et en effet, il est bien possible que cela aboutisse à une nouvelle ère d'optimisation et d'hyper efficacité – mais qu'arrivera-t-il aux interactions humaines ?

L'IdO nous promet d'énormes économies d'échelle via un futur d'une plus grande durabilité, au sein d'une économie circulaire où toute les ressources sont réutilisées, réparées ou recyclées après leur consommation initiale, et où les déchets sont effectivement éliminés. [99] L'IdO est rendu possible par

l'intégration de capteurs au sein de chaque objet, permettant ainsi de virtuellement connecter tout à tous. L'idée est ensuite, en déployant l'intelligence artificielle (IA) et l'analyse prédictive, de parvenir à une méta-intelligence par la capacité exponentielle à mieux lire, mieux comprendre et mieux exploiter les données.

Mes nombreuses conversations avec les partisans de l'IdO à travers le monde suggèrent que si celui-ci tient ses promesses, alors nous pourrions réaliser des économies allant de 30 à 50% sur les coûts de la logistique globale et du transport maritime, de 30 à 70% sur les coûts des transports et de la mobilité personnelle, de 40 à 50% sur les dépenses d'énergie, de chauffage et de climatisation – et ce n'est qu'un début.

Les avantages économiques potentiels de cette connectivité généralisée sont fascinants : l'IdC est véritablement une entreprise gigantesque et va certainement ridiculiser ce qu'on appelait jusqu'à présent « l'Internet des humains et des ordinateurs ».

> « *Rien de vaste n'entre dans la vie des mortels sans malédiction.* » - Sophocle [100]

L'IdO est voué à devenir incomparablement plus puissant que l'Internet humain d'aujourd'hui et, par conséquent, sans doute infiniment plus enclin à susciter des conséquences inattendues. L'impact du déploiement global de l'IdO pourrait signifier aussi bien le paradis que l'enfer, mais en tout état de cause la boussole pour ce voyage-là s'étalonne aujourd'hui même.

L'IdO pourrait-il nous transformer nous-mêmes en objets ?

D'ores et déjà, il nous faut aujourd'hui composer avec nombre d'effets négatifs d'Internet. Admettons que les conséquences imprévues de la surveillance des données, de la perte d'intimité et de « l'obésité numérique » ne soient pas intentionnelles. Mais face à l'essor mondial de l'IdO, on doit assurément commencer à s'interroger sur le pouvoir que nous sommes prêts à concéder (par exemple le degré de liberté d'accès à nos données et aux IA

chargées de les traiter) aux fournisseurs de ces solutions, outils, moteurs de recherche et plates-formes. Il nous faut également nous demander dans quelle mesure nous devrions, pour nous en prémunir, mettre en œuvre accords globaux, sanctions effectives, auto-régulation et supervision indépendante.

Aujourd'hui, les principales plates-formes, fournisseurs de service *cloud* et autres entreprises technologiques, pour l'essentiel basés aux Etats-Unis, semblent incapable d'empêcher la NSA, le FBI et autres instances officielles d'aller fouiller dans nos appareils et nos données. Alors qu'en sera-t-il d'ici cinq à sept ans, lorsque nous disposerons de plus de 200 milliards d'objets connectés ? Dans son anticipation la plus sombre, l'IdO pourrait représenter l'apogée de la pensée machinique – la plus parfaite des opérations d'espionnage numérique jamais conçue, le plus grand réseau de surveillance en temps réel jamais inventé, imposant une totale soumission humaine et éradiquant toute velléité d'anonymat qui pourrait encore subsister. [101]

Imaginez-vous un monde, pas si lointain, où :

- Votre voiture connectée transmet toutes ses données en temps réel, y compris son emplacement et tous les mouvements en cours dans son habitacle.
- Tous vos paiements s'effectuent par l'entremise de vos appareils intelligents, transformant ainsi argent liquide, portefeuilles et cartes de crédit en objets du passé.
- votre médecin peut aisément savoir à quel point vous avez peu quitté votre chaise et marché cette semaine, ou ce qu'était votre rythme cardiaque pendant que vous dormiez dans l'avion.
- Votre cerveau externe – autrement dit vos outils mobiles – est directement connecté à votre cerveau organique par l'entremise d'objets portables, interfaces cerveau-ordinateur et implants.

- Tout le monde et toute chose devient une balise de données générant chaque jour des milliers de gigabits, collectés, filtrés et analysés dans le *cloud* par des armées d'experts de chez IBM et de DeepMinds de chez Google, pressés de mobiliser les cerveaux affamés et auto-apprenants de leurs IA globales.

Dans un tel contexte, il est probable que l'efficacité technologique prendrait le pas sur l'humanité à la moindre occasion, et que nous finirions par être gouvernés par un système d'exploitation géant capable d'auto-apprendre et d'alimenter notre production, jusqu'à ce que notre propre contribution soit elle-même devenue superflue. Alors, arrivés à ce point, notre valeur serait devenue bien moindre que celle de la technologie que nous avons nous-mêmes créée et nourrie.

La souveraineté inhérente au genre humain, qui nous a définis depuis au moins plusieurs dizaines de milliers d'années, sera alors finalement compromise – et pas tant par des extra-terrestres ou d'autres créatures concurrentes que par des protagonistes technologiques et leur agenda hyper-mécanisé.

Si nous, aujourd'hui, ne sommes même pas capables de nous entendre sur les règles et l'éthique qu'il serait nécessaire d'appliquer à un Internet des gens et à ses instruments, comment pourrions-nous nous mettre d'accord sur quelque chose de potentiellement mille fois plus vaste ? Ne devrions-nous pas nous en inquiéter davantage, pendant qu'il en est encore temps ?

Qui est aux commandes ?

À l'heure actuelle, nous avons dans les domaines de la biotechnologie et de la bio ingénierie des standards, des méthodes, des accords et des traités sur ce qui est autorisé – lire les directives Asilomar de 1975 sur l'ADN recombinant. [102] Nous avons également des traités de non-prolifération nucléaire. Mais en revanche nous n'avons encore rien de cet ordre pour les données et l'intelligence – qui constituent le pétrole de l'Âge

numérique. En dépit du fait que les données sont en train de devenir le plus puissant des leviers économiques, et peut-être même le seul, nous ne disposons encore d'aucun traité global définissant les limites du traitement des données des 3,4 milliards d'utilisateurs d'Internet, [103] ou encore d'un traité sur l'informatique cognitive et l'intelligence artificielle en général. Exception faite des armes nucléaires, il est rarement arrivé dans le cours de l'histoire humaine qu'une aventure technologique ait été aussi rapidement entreprise avec aussi peu de recul. Car de fait, l'utilisation exponentielle des données, et désormais de l'IA, concurrencera bientôt les armes nucléaires en termes d'impact potentiel, alors que l'intelligence artificielle demeure pourtant un espace largement non-régulé.

Qui s'assurera que les sociétés leaders des données et de l'IA agiront correctement ? Qui s'assurera que les entités dépositaires du nouvel et si chatoyant IdO agiront correctement ? Et d'ailleurs que signifie agir correctement, qui le définira ? Serons-nous même encore capables de discerner le bien du mal ?

Les androrithmes et le principe de précaution

Qu'est-ce qui empêchera les nouveaux maîtres de l'univers non seulement de transformer les processus et les matériels en données, mais également de transformer les humains en objets, que ce soit par inadvertance ou à dessein ? Nonobstant le plaisir que les industries technologiques expriment vis-à-vis de l'IdO, pour ne rien dire de ses bénéfices manifestes, voilà un risque que nous ne devrions pas prendre sans exercer une prudence extrême.

À chaque étape d'une progression exponentielle de la technologie, il nous faut tempérer ses effets par le questionnement humain, en nous assurant de la mise en œuvre d'un développement qui interpose réellement une part d'aléas humains entre les « 0 » et les « 1 » qui commencent à dominer nos vies.

Je suggère humblement que nous opposions une version mise à jour du principe de précaution (voir mon chapitre 8) à tous ceux

qui ont pour projet de consacrer l'IdO en nous inondant de ses bienfaits. La charge de prouver et garantir que l'IdO ne nuira pas à ceux qui y seront assujettis devrait incomber à ceux qui en auront le contrôle – étant entendu que nous n'irons de l'avant qu'une fois que cette responsabilité sera clairement établie. Il nous faudra adopter des approches proactives et simultanément ne pas étouffer l'innovation.

Il n'est plus question d'affronter ces enjeux par des ou bien / ou bien – et pas davantage de se contenter de combiner les stratégies. Soixante-dix ans après avoir déchainé la puissance nucléaire sur la Terre, dans un contexte d'expérimentation militaire et de décision politique qui demeure sujet à controverse, *Homo Sapiens* pénètre sur un territoire entièrement nouveau. Sans nouvelle guerre mondiale pour justifier ou excuser notre progression tête baissée au « pays des données », nous nous comportons comme si toutes les options nous restaient ouvertes. Pourtant, l'Internet des objets inhumains pourrait bien encercler notre humanité et altérer son essence vitale – et de même insuffler un sentiment d'omnipotence divine à ses propriétaires. Nous devons être précautionneux *et* nous devons rester proactifs – mais nous ne pouvons plus faire comme si l'un et l'autre dépendaient de deux agendas séparés, conduits par deux tribus distinctes.

Chapitre 6
Magique, maniaque…toxique !

Alors que nous nous grisons de cette grande fête sans fin qu'est la technologie, il est salutaire de réfléchir au prix qu'il nous faudra payer demain, et après.

L'un des pères de la prospective, qui a eu une influence décisive sur mon propre travail, Arthur C. Clarke, est resté célèbre pour avoir dit en 1961 : « Toute technologie avancée est impossible à discerner de la magie ». [104] Aujourd'hui, ainsi que je l'ai souligné dans les chapitres précédents, nous commençons à percevoir ce que Clarke entrevoyait dans sa déclaration prémonitoire : nous sommes au cœur d'une véritable explosion de magie scientifique et technologique, dont les avancées dépassent nos rêves les plus fous.

Les effets magiques de la technologie sont devenus démesurés tant sur le plan commercial qu'économique ou social, propulsant à des niveaux météoriques les succès boursiers d'entreprises comme Google, Apple, Facebook, Amazon, Baidu, Tencent et Alibaba. La magie technologique est également le moteur et l'accélérateur de licornes et de decacornes majoritairement américains et chinois – des sociétés disruptives telles que Baidu, Dropbox, Uber ou Airbnb, arrivées relativement récemment sur la scène.

Lors des débuts de Google en 1998, trouver le résultat parfait à une requête Internet aussi douteuse que « vols à bas prix pour Londres » relevait pratiquement du tour de magie. Et il en était de même pour ce qui était de commander un livre n'importe où dans

le monde et de le voir livré sur votre pas de porte en seulement quelques jours. La vague suivante d'innovation a vu l'émergence, tout aussi magique et pourtant légale et très bon marché, de plates-formes de loisirs telles que Netflix, Hulu, ViaPlay, Spotify et YouTube, bouleversant à jamais notre manière de consommer – et payer, pour autant que nous l'ayons quelquefois fait – les médias.

De tels moments de magie sont partout désormais. Activez par exemple l'application Shazam et pointez votre smartphone vers n'importe quelle source de musique. Shazam va identifier le titre diffusé, puis vous connecter à votre plate-forme musicale préférée afin de stocker ce titre pour une diffusion ou un partage ultérieur. Auparavant, le simple défi consistant à identifier ou découvrir de la musique nouvelle était infiniment plus compliqué ; aujourd'hui, c'est encore plus facile que de passer un coup de fil.

Pour beaucoup d'entre nous, les outils et applications mobiles constituent bien sûr la manifestation numéro un de la magie technologique : le fait qu'il existe (ou qu'il doive exister) une application pour ceci ou cela est devenu une sorte de réponse par défaut à la quasi-totalité des petits enjeux de notre vie quotidienne – pour autant que nous soyons connectés à une source Internet mobile et que nous disposions d'un mobile performant (ce qui est presque toujours le cas).

Rien que sur l'Apple store, vous trouverez des milliers d'apps pour publier vos images et des centaines d'autres uniquement pour faire des rencontres. Il existe des apps sans nombre pour organiser votre agenda et prendre des rendez-vous, des apps qui vous aident à divorcer, plusieurs services très utiles qui vous alertent quand les couches de bébé sont mouillées (comme Tweetpee), de nombreuses applications vous permettant de pratiquer à distance le vaudou numérique et – très important – toutes sortes de simulateurs de pets.

Tout autour du globe, c'est la magie qui fait tourner la technologie et le business des outils mobiles, et c'est la raison pour laquelle un smartphone est aujourd'hui plus important qu'un

ordinateur. La hiérarchie des besoins de la pyramide de Maslow s'est modifiée en conséquence : aux besoins élémentaires que sont la nourriture, l'eau, les vêtements et un abri, il nous faut désormais ajouter les outils mobiles, les smartphones et la connectivité wi-fi – souvent classés au-dessus du sexe, de l'amitié et du prestige ! Dans un futur plus si lointain, il semble en outre inévitable que nous ajoutions aussi les assistants numériques intelligents (ANI) à cette hiérarchie.

Avec l'avènement de l'Internet des objets (IdO), des véhicules autonomes (voitures sans pilote), de l'intelligence artificielle (IA) et des assistants intelligents, même les choses et les activités de la vie de tous les jours prendront une dimension magique. Ainsi Libelium, l'un des fournisseurs « magiques » les plus en vue du B2B (*business to business*) a-t-il entrepris de réveiller le monde en développant fermes intelligentes, villes intelligentes et énergie intelligente. [105] Pour ce faire, l'entreprise a installé de vastes réseaux de capteurs capable de rendre intelligents pratiquement n'importe quelle machine ou équipement anciens, qu'il s'agisse d'un tracteur dans un champ ou d'un arbre dans un parc.

Grâce aux solutions intelligentes, n'importe quel pipeline connaît la température de ses tuyaux, la quantité de gaz ou de pétrole qui y circule, le niveau de bruit extérieur, etc. Chaque lampadaire urbain sait combien de véhicules et de personnes il voit passer, ce que montrent les adresses MAC (*media access control*) Bluetooth et quel est le niveau de pollution : vous lui donnez un nom, vous l'équipez, et l'environnement intelligent est en mesure d'identifier et de mesurer ce que vous lui avez demandé. Compte tenu des gains potentiels, il n'est vraiment pas surprenant que chaque entreprise technologique ait investi en masse dans l'IdO.

Une telle magie est sur le point d'engendrer une acceptation technologique dont l'échelle et la vitesse dépassent même nos attentes les plus extrêmes. L'iPhone est (a été ?) magique – pour une bonne part des gens en tout cas, il se rapprochait de la définition de ce qui est magique. De même, l'iPad est magique, la

réalité augmentée (RA) et la réalité virtuelle sont magiques (2016 aura marqué, à cet égard, l'essor graduel puis soudain de l'une comme de l'autre), les voitures Tesla sont magiques, les Hololens de Microsoft sont magiques… partout, à chaque minute qui passe, émergent de nouvelles incarnations de la magie.

C'est d'autant plus crucial que les coûts de toute cette magie sont en train de chuter : un mouvement décisif car, un peu à l'image des drogues illégales, les prix et la disponibilité d'une offre magique ont un effet matériel direct sur la vitesse et la profondeur de sa propagation. Dans cinq ans, des produits et services magiques auparavant très chers, comme l'analyse du génome humain ou même certaines variétés de superordinateurs, seront devenus ridiculement bon marché. Essayez simplement de vous imaginer de quelle manière cela affectera nos modes de vie : un royaume enchanté personnel accessible à chacun de nous. Chaque problème surmonté par la technologie. Le chemin de la divinité.

Des humains magiques – avec de l'intelligence à l'intérieur

La magie technologique a commencé à transcender le royaume des équipements et des objets. Il ne s'agit plus seulement d'outils, de gadgets, de services ou même de connectivité ; ce dont il est de plus en plus question, c'est de nous, de nos corps, de nos esprits, de notre humanité.

Un grand nombre de chercheurs ont mis en évidence de quelle manière l'Internet, en particulier pour ce qui touche aux réseaux sociaux, nous conduit en fait à développer des réactions très physiques. [106] Ils ont ainsi découvert que des poussées d'endorphines et de dopamine survenaient dans nos corps lorsqu'un(e) inconnu(e), parfois distant(e) de milliers de kilomètres, avait « liké » l'un de nos *posts* ou posté un commentaire qui nous donnait la sensation d'être valable et apprécié(e). Il s'agit apparemment d'une réaction biologique prédéterminée, qui survient sans effort et ne fait peut-être même pas l'objet d'un contrôle conscient – et qui pourrait être l'une des

raisons pour lesquelles de nombreux réseaux sociaux sont en train de devenir encore plus recherchés que bien des boutiques et des sites de e-commerce.

Faciliter l'activation de ce genre de piège à plaisir constitue l'un des ingrédients clés de la recette secrète des réseaux sociaux dominants. [107] Et c'est l'une des raisons majeures pour lesquelles, en janvier 2016, j'ai moi-même sérieusement entrepris de reconsidérer ma relation à Facebook : me sentir émotionnellement et intellectuellement manipulé par leurs algorithmes m'est alors apparu comme un chemin très confortable vers une forme bizarre d'inhumanité. Bien qu'après six semaines, j'aie réalisé que je ne pouvais pas me permettre d'ignorer le fait que Facebook draine 60% de la fréquentation de mes sites internet – un dilemme qui, manifestement, requiert d'être examiné plus avant. Pour l'heure, je continue à poster divers éléments, mais j'ai pratiquement cessé d'utiliser Facebook comme source d'infos et comme média.

Outre le rôle évident exercé par la magie technologique dans les réseaux sociaux, elle encourage de plus en plus à son adoption rapide, partout, en stimulant nos fluides et nos sens. En visionnant les vidéos que nos caméras GoPro ont tournées lors de notre grande virée nature en *mountain bike* dans l'Arizona, nous pouvons littéralement sentir la magie vibrer. Et c'est encore la magie de WhatsApp qui nous permet de nous connecter instantanément et gratuitement à ceux que nous aimons, partout sur la planète, et de partager avec eux ces moments magiques.

Alors, quel est le problème ?

Il est certain que nombre de ces technologies sont généralement les bienvenues, et bien sûr j'en profite assez souvent moi-même. L'addiction technologique, les abus et l'embarras social qui en résultent ont certes pu représenter un souci au cours des dernières années, mais la plupart du temps sur un mode bénin, attribué à diverses variétés de néo-Luddites ou aux tenants de la détox numérique. On me demande souvent quel est le problème, et en

quoi l'afflux de magie technologique serait un motif d'inquiétude – alors permettez-moi de partager avec vous quelques réflexions.

La technologie exponentielle est sur le point de déclencher une réaction en chaine de type bombe A

Je crois qu'aujourd'hui, nous sommes positionnés exactement au point de bascule de la courbe exponentielle du développement technologique, et que cela représente un moment-pivot dans l'histoire. D'un certain point de vue, nos scientifiques et technologues sont dans une situation similaire à ce qu'a du affronter Albert Einstein. Bien qu'il se considérât lui-même comme un pacifiste, en 1939 – 1940 il pressa le Président Roosevelt d'accélérer la construction que la bombe nucléaire, avant que les Allemands n'y parviennent. Et en 1941, Einstein contribua par inadvertance au développement de la bombe nucléaire en aidant Vannevar Bush à résoudre certains des problèmes mathématiques complexes qui ralentissaient le programme atomique américain. [108]

L'historien Doug Long relève :

« Le biographe d'Einstein Ronald Clark a remarqué que la bombe atomique aurait été inventée sans les lettres d'Einstein, mais également que sans les premiers travaux américains résultant de ces mêmes lettres, les bombes A n'auraient peut-être pas été prêtes à temps pour être utilisées lors de la guerre contre le Japon. » [109] En novembre 1945, cinq mois avant sa mort, Einstein a résumé ses sentiments à propos de son rôle dans la création de la bombe atomique :

« *J'ai fait une grande erreur dans ma vie… lorsque j'ai signé la lettre au Président Roosevelt recommandant que les bombes atomiques soient produites. Mais il y avait alors une justification : le danger que les Allemands ne les fabriquent.* » [110]

« L'esprit humain doit prévaloir sur la technologie. »
Albert Einstein [111]

Des arguments analogues à « Einstein 1939 » sont aujourd'hui avancés pour justifier le développement accéléré de technologies exponentielles extrêmement lourdes d'enjeux, telles que l'intelligence artificielle en général, la géo-ingénierie (c'est-à-dire le contrôle du climat par des moyens technologiques), le déploiement de systèmes d'armes autonomes et la modification du génome humain. D'après ce que j'entends, les arguments les plus couramment répandus seraient que « si nous ne faisons pas cela, quelqu'un d'autre (et probablement quelqu'un de mal intentionné) le fera sûrement à notre place, en nous laissant à la traine », ou bien « exception faite de tous ces dangers, ces technologies vont déboucher sur un monde meilleur, il serait stupide de ne pas s'y atteler », ou encore « il n'est pas possible de désinventer quelque chose, ou simplement de cesser d'inventer. Essayer de les créer va de soi, si tant est qu'elles puissent être inventées : c'est tout simplement dans la nature humaine ». Ma réponse est toujours la même : la technologie n'est ni bonne ni mauvaise – elle *est*, tout simplement. Et c'est à nous – ici et maintenant – de décider ensemble des usages de la technologie à proscrire ou pas.

Alors que vous lisez ces lignes, des technologies encore plus puissantes que l'énergie nucléaire ou les armes atomiques sont en train d'être inventées et testées dans de multiples domaines. En la matière, des progrès rapides semblent inévitables ; on ne les stoppera pas en se contentant simplement de souligner la nécessité d'appliquer le principe de précaution, ou de tenir ceux qui sont en train d'inventer une nouvelle technologie pour responsables de la preuve préalable de son innocuité (voir chapitre 8).

Je pense que le défi clé réside en ceci : comment faire en sorte que ces accomplissements technologiques inévitables demeurent à 98% magiques – autrement dit qu'ils puissent être utilisés pour le

bénéfice de l'épanouissement humain collectif plutôt que de sombrer soudainement du côté obscur ? Prenez par exemple des percées du type édition du génome, qui pourraient prévenir le développement des cancers. Et maintenant imaginez les usages potentiels d'avancées exactement semblables pour créer des chimères homme-animal, ou conduisant à l'essor spectaculaire des cyborgs (des créatures homme-machine), ou encore nous permettant d'auto-déterminer notre code génétique.

Ces tentatives pourraient s'avérer très comparables au recours à la puissance nucléaire pour fabriquer des bombes atomiques – l'éventualité de voir se multiplier des « Hiroshima numériques » devenant une possibilité bien réelle.

Quelles seront, dès lors, nos lignes directrices éthiques ? Sommes-nous seulement d'accord sur une sorte de fondation éthique globale ? Et comment amener toutes les nations à s'entendre sur la manière de définir ou de contenir les côtés sombres du développement technologique ? Qui sera en charge de la surveillance des violations et, plus généralement, comment conjurer la spirale fatale vers ce que l'auteur James Barrat appelle « nos ultimes inventions » ? [112] Telles sont les raisons pour lesquelles le débat sur l'éthique numérique est essentiel (voir chapitre 10).

La croissance exponentielle des données, de l'information, de la connectivité et de l'intelligence constitue le nouveau pétrole du monde numérique, alimentant des changements spectaculaires dans chacun des aspects de notre monde. En l'état, nous sommes en train de franchir le seuil allant de simples calculs mathématiques ou de codes informatiques à une puissance équivalente à une frappe nucléaire.

« Seize centimètres cube de circuit de nanotube, une fois complètement développés, seraient plus de cent millions de fois plus puissants que ne l'est le cerveau humain ».
Ray Kurzweil, La Singularité est proche : quand les humains transcendent la biologie [113]

La science et la technologie nous ont déjà dotés d'une puissance immense. Au cours des 20 – 30 prochaines années, nous allons être témoins d'une série de points de bascule sur la courbe exponentielle des technologies, tels que l'informatique quantique omniprésente et la survenue de la soi-disant Singularité. Tandis que nous progresserons sur la courbe à une allure de plus en plus grande, nous deviendrons infiniment plus puissants, acquérant des capacités dépassant nos rêves les plus fous. Pour paraphraser les propos que l'on prête à bien des acteurs de l'Histoire, de Voltaire au père de Superman : « Avec de grands pouvoirs viennent de grandes responsabilités. » [114]

D'abord et avant tout, comment s'y prendre pour que la puissance démesurée des technologies exponentielles reste subordonnée aux progrès du bonheur humain ? Comment peut-on s'assurer que les efforts nécessaires seront consentis pour nous éclairer puis bâtir les accords et les lois qui nous protègeront des dérapages maniaques ou toxiques ? Et comment devrions-nous définir là où s'arrête la magie ?

Bienvenue dans l'explosion magique

Une fois que ce que j'aime appeler le quotient magique sera déployé de manière exponentielle, les problèmes jusqu'alors latents liés à l'abus ou au dévoiement de telle ou telle technologie donnée ne feront que croître – peut-être de manière exponentielle aussi, en tout cas graduellement puis soudainement, une fois encore.

Je conserve un fond d'optimisme quant à nos capacités collectives à encadrer la puissance des technologies exponentielles, mais néanmoins je m'inquiète également à l'idée que dans presque chaque situation de changement exponentiel et combinatoire, il existe un vrai risque de basculement du magique au maniaque puis au toxique, en un très court laps de temps.

D'où il ressort que nous ne pouvons pas nous permettre une mauvaise gouvernance lors de périodes de ce genre. Le défi posé à notre humanité se précise un peu plus chaque jour, le quotient

magique explose et les dérapages potentiels ne sont jamais très loin.

La question clé n'est plus « si » ou « comment », mais « pourquoi ? »

Ainsi que nous en avons débattu, nous sommes désormais parvenus à un point de bascule du progrès exponentiel et combinatoire où la totalité du bien-être humain pourrait être aussi bien magnifié que grandement diminué par la technologie. Bientôt, la question ne sera plus de savoir si ou comment telle ou telle magie technologique pourrait effectivement se concrétiser – car la réponse sera toujours oui. Les questions clés, désormais, seront de savoir pourquoi elle doit s'accomplir, qui en sera responsable et en aura le contrôle, et ce que cela pourra bien vouloir dire pour le futur de l'humanité.

Pour maintenir un environnement vraiment favorable à l'épanouissement humain, il nous faut accorder une profonde attention aux conséquences inattendues des technologies, en y incluant les effets collatéraux envisageables. Ces effets collatéraux, tels que les incidences du réchauffement climatique en tant que conséquence de notre dépendance aux énergies fossiles, ne sont en général pas intégrés en tant que tels, on peut le comprendre, aux *business models* initiaux des entreprises. Il n'empêche que nous devons accélérer l'intégration de ces sujets cruciaux au sommet de l'agenda des entreprises, et mettre en œuvre la pensée holistique comme approche par défaut.

Une explosion de pure magie est sur le point de se produire, à mesure que la technologie gagne en super-puissance et en super-vitesse, bien au-delà de tout ce qu'on pouvait imaginer, faisant de nous des divinités. Nos assistants numériques intelligents deviendront bientôt super-intelligents, omniprésents, ridiculement bon marché, invisibles et embarqués dans absolument tous les supports – y compris à l'intérieur de nous-mêmes.

Le point où nous en sommes arrivés diffère fondamentalement des autres périodes historiques favorables à la magie

technologique. C'est particulièrement vrai des développements exponentiels et combinatoires en cours, dont le déferlement magique va dépasser en taille, en échelle et en nature tout ce dont nous avons été témoins jusqu'à présent, ou même tout ce que nous aurions pu concevoir. Se servir d'un moteur de recherche pour dégotter un bon plan pour une chambre d'hôtel est une chose, mais c'en sera une autre de voir l'ensemble des réservations d'un voyage complet pris en charge pour votre compte par les successeurs intelligents des outils que nous utilisons aujourd'hui, tels que Siri d'Apple, Cortana de Microsoft, M de Facebook ou Amelia de IPSoft. La génération des ANI actuellement en service ressemblera bientôt aux premières Ford Model T lorsqu'on les compare à nos Ferrari et Tesla d'aujourd'hui. Vous n'avez encore rien vu !

La technologie pénètre nos organismes, nous séparant du monde et accroissant notre déconnexion des expériences humaines

L'usage traditionnel d'un moteur de recherche consiste à se servir d'un outil externe, comme on pourrait le faire d'un marteau pour construire une maison, tandis que l'approche d'un ANI repose plutôt sur l'idée de laisser le marteau concevoir lui-même la maison. La technologie devient apparentée à notre cerveau, en se déplaçant à l'intérieur de nous. Et du même coup effaçant progressivement la distinction entre l'outil et nous.

Vous avez probablement déjà observé notre tendance à laisser nos ANI faire le travail à notre place. Siri est capable de répondre à nos questions et de nous diriger instantanément vers les ressources pertinentes, Alexa peut commander des livres pour nous puis nous les lire à haute voix, Amelia peut faire des réservations de voyage pour notre compte. Les assistants numériques intelligents incarnent la nouvelle vague des apps et deviendront omniprésents dans les prochaines années.

Maintenant, essayez simplement de vous représenter le degré de séparation, de disconnexion personnelle, de désengagement

créatif et d'abdication générale qu'il nous faudrait affronter face à nos assistants hyper-intelligents, omniprésents et gratuits :

- Ils sauront qui nous sommes – et je veux dire par là qu'ils connaîtront intimement chaque donnée, chaque communication, chaque mouvement, chaque fragment numérique de nous-mêmes.
- Ils connaîtront littéralement tout de nos centres d'intérêt, intentions et désirs à chaque instant, qu'il soit question d'une simple transaction, d'un rendez-vous ou de n'importe quoi d'autre.
- ils seront capables de communiquer avec des millions d'autres assistants similaires, et de créer ainsi un effet de réseau extrêmement puissant – un cerveau-global-dans-le-*cloud.*
- ils seront capables de communiquer de notre part dans cinquante langues et plus – et ça, ce n'est que le début.

« La numériphrénie – autrement dit la façon dont nos médias et nos technologies nous encouragent à être dans plus d'un endroit à la fois. » – Douglas Rushkoff, Present Shock : When Everything Happens Now [115]

Il ne fait aucun doute que la vitesse, la puissance, la séduction et la praticité absolues de ces ANI s'avèreront totalement irrésistibles – et je m'attends à ce que cela conduise presque certainement à un désengagement créatif et émotionnel d'une ampleur gigantesque. Les ANI entreront en scène là où s'arrêtent aujourd'hui les smartphones, introduisant les interfaces informatiques dans le royaume privé de nos pensées, de nos attentes et de nos comportements intimes. Dès lors, il ne restera plus qu'un petit saut à accomplir pour parvenir à des interfaces directement reliées au cerveau et à l'humanité hybride.

Regardez par exemple l'impression en 3D : s'il était possible d'imprimer un fantastique repas instantanément, continuerions-

nous à cuisiner ? Si nous pouvions compter sur un outil de traduction instantanée, continuerions-nous à apprendre des langues étrangères ? Si nous pouvions diriger le travail d'un ordinateur grâce à nos ondes cérébrales, continuerions-nous à taper sur un clavier ? Et si la nécessité est la mère de l'invention, le choix est-il alors le père de l'abdication ?

Détenir la puissance informatique d'un supercalculateur des années 70 de la taille d'un salon dans la seule paume de votre main, comme c'est le cas des iPhones et outils Android aujourd'hui, est déjà ahurissant. Alors imaginez la puissance quantique d'un million d'outils similaires disponibles dans le *cloud*, et auxquels il serait spontanément possible d'avoir accès par la voix, le geste ou même par l'esprit, via une interface cerveau-ordinateur (ICO).

Voici de quoi cette explosion de magie s'accompagnera :

- Pratiquement tout sera perçu ou défini comme un service, puisque tout sera numérisé, automatisé et intelligisé. Les conséquences économiques en seront immenses, puisque cela créera progressivement l'abondance dans presque tous les secteurs de la société – d'abord la musique, les films, les livres, suivis par les transports, l'argent et les services financiers et finalement par les traitements médicaux, la nourriture et l'énergie. Je crois que cette abondance finira par provoquer l'effondrement du capitalisme tel que nous le connaissons, ouvrant la voie à une ère de post-capitalisme restant à définir.
- Nous serons constamment soumis à la tentation de réduire voire d'abolir l'idiosyncrasie humaine, telle qu'elle s'exprime par exemple dans la contemplation ou l'imagination, parce que nous aurons l'impression qu'elle nous ralentit (ainsi que tous les autres).

- Nous serons bientôt en voie de devenir nous-mêmes des machines, ne serait-ce que pour fonctionner à l'unisson d'un monde mécanisé.
- Estaríamos a merced de la manipulación y de la influencia desproporcionada de cualquiera que supiera cómo utilizar el sistema.
- Nous serons bientôt en voie de devenir nous-mêmes des machines, ne serait-ce que pour fonctionner à l'unisson d'un monde mécanisé.
- À mesure que la biologie cèdera le pas à la technologie, nos systèmes biologiques deviendront de plus en plus optionnels, remplaçables et finalement vestigiels.
- La technologie devenant la plate-forme dominante du monde – distribuant aisément et à chacun(e) une « vérité technologique révélée » –, nos propres cultures, symboles, comportements et rituels pourraient, faute de continuer à être utilisés, tomber définitivement en désuétude.

Clairement, la question est de savoir si de telles technologies exponentielles resteront effectivement de simples outils. J'estime que non. Prenons l'exemple d'un marteau, ou encore celui de l'électricité ou d'Internet lui-même : être privés de tels outils serait effectivement un inconvénient – mais cela ne nous rendrait pas pour autant incapables de vivre. L'électricité ou l'Internet n'ont tout simplement pas la même importance que l'oxygène ou l'eau ; ils contribuent à améliorer grandement nos vies.

Mais en revanche, à l'instar de l'oxygène, nombre de technologies exponentielles ne seront bientôt plus considérées comme de simples outils ; au contraire, elles pourraient bientôt être perçues comme des nécessités vitales, au point de nous amener à ne plus être naturellement ou entièrement humains. Et c'est là, à mon sens, qu'il nous faut tracer la ligne rouge.

Car le chemin que nous sommes en train de prendre, c'est de devenir nous-mêmes la technologie, parce que celle-ci nous sera devenue aussi indispensable que le fait de respirer. Je pense que

c'est un seuil que nous ne devons pas franchir – en tout cas pas de manière délibérée. Et même s'il peut sembler raisonnable pour une victime d'accident ou de maladie de devenir partiellement une machine, par choix – mais dans une telle hypothèse, c'est tout à fait différent.

Imaginez à quoi ressemblerait la vie après une telle explosion de magie technologique – de nouveaux outils un million de fois plus puissants que ceux d'aujourd'hui, disponibles toujours et partout, pratiquement pour rien. Insondable. Irrésistible. Addictif. Devrions-nous, ainsi que de nombreux technologues le suggèrent, céder à un tel développement et nous abandonner à l'inévitable et totale convergence de l'homme et de la machine ? Ou bien privilégier un rôle davantage proactif, et donner effectivement corps à ce que nous créons – ou pas ?

Sommes-nous vraiment destinés à devenir nous-mêmes une technologie, du fait de l'entrée de la magie dans nos corps ? Posons-nous quelques questions simples : qui voudrait se priver d'une telle magie, pour toujours ? Nous sentirions-nous handicapés ou inférieurs si nos technologies magiques étaient absentes ou indisponibles ? Est-ce qu'alors nous nous sentirions aussi limités que si nous avions soudain perdu l'ouïe ou la vue ? Accepterions-nous naturellement ces technologies comme des extensions de nous-mêmes, tout comme nous l'avons déjà fait avec nos appareils mobiles intelligents ? Notre compréhension de ce qui est nous et ne l'est pas (autrement dit « eux » ou « ça ») aurait-elle complètement disparu ? Et quel impact aurait cette médiatisation totale sur notre expérience du monde environnant ? Sur nos prises de décision ? Sur notre état émotionnel ?

Comment allons-nous réagir à tout ça ?

Je m'inquiète à l'idée que nous ne commencions à confondre la magie de ces outils avec l'addiction qu'entraînent la connectivité constante, la médiatisation, la monitorisation, la simulation et la virtualisation. Cette magie a déjà commencé à se transformer en dépendance – addictive, tentatrice, envoûtante, exigeante –, alors que se passera-t-il lorsque le quotient magique

atteindra 1000, lorsque la technologie sera devenue encore plus puissante, meilleur marché et inséparable de nos vies ?

« D'abord nous construisons les outils, et puis ce sont les outils qui nous construisent. » Marshall McLuhan [116]

Je redoute que nous ne soyons en train d'entrer dans une période de développement potentiel qui, si on ne le restreint pas, pourrait ne pas se conclure par le bonheur humain tel qu'Aristote l'a défini, en évoquant le sens profond des relations et des contributions humaines : l'épanouissement (voir chapitre 9). Je crains qu'il ne s'agisse d'une régression de ce que nous sommes, et non d'une expansion ; non plus une responsabilisation, mais un asservissement déguisé en cadeau. Un cheval de Troie de proportions réellement jamais vues.

Magique, maniaque, toxique

Il semble désormais clair que la transition de la magie à la perversion puis à l'intoxication peut s'avérer assez rapide, avec des conséquences à la fois spectaculaires, nuisibles et involontaires. Considérez un instant le plaisir et la dimension magique de pouvoir facilement partager des photos de vacances en famille via Flickr – une évidence pour des centaines de millions de personnes. Un service qui de fait était déjà disponible bien avant iCloud, Dropbox ou Facebook (la plate-forme la plus maniaque à laquelle je sois capable de penser), et qui aujourd'hui permet le partage de mes contenus encore plus aisément.

Mais Flickr peut rapidement devenir super-flippant si un tiers se met à se servir de ce que j'ai béatement partagé avec mes amis et ma famille, sortant entièrement mes contenus de leur contexte et en totale contradiction avec leur propos initial.

Par exemple, quand en 2015 les dirigeants de la compagnie néerlandaise Koppie-Koppie ont voulu vendre des mugs décorés de mignonnes photos de bébés, ils se sont tournés vers Flickr pour pouvoir utiliser gratuitement des photos de familles librement

disponibles sous licence « Creative Commons » (CC). [117] Or Flickr considère que c'est un usage correct dès lors que vous avez téléchargé vos images sous licence CC. Surprise, surprise : nombre des propriétaires de ces images et leurs parents n'étaient pas d'accord. Aucun doute, voilà clairement une utilisation de la technologie en contradiction flagrante avec ses intentions de départ. Certaines conséquences involontaires peuvent prendre très vite de vastes proportions lorsqu'elles sont amplifiées par des technologies en réseau.

Pour certains utilisateurs en tout cas, la magie du partage sur Flickr s'est soudain fracassée sous l'effet d'une interprétation abusive des droits de diffusion et d'une exploitation néfaste d'un contexte inattendu – peut-être pas un acte illégal en soi, mais assurément assez élevé sur l'échelle du glauque. Koppie-Koppie est un « bel » exemple de la manière dont la magie peut rapidement se pervertir.

Les conséquences involontaires vont se multiplier en proportions égales des technologies qui les génèrent

Le cas Koppie-Koppie restera probablement un incident mineur n'ayant provoqué qu'assez peu de dommages (enfin, sauf si ce sont des images de vos propres enfants qui ont ainsi été diffusées). Cependant, cela soulève des questions : qu'en est-il si votre participation active à quelque chose qui semble inoffensif, pratique et utile à tous permet à ce quelque chose de devenir si puissant qu'il en vient à développer ses propres projets, ses propres raisons d'être, sa propre existence autonome ? Facebook en est le meilleur exemple – et c'est d'ailleurs pourquoi j'ai largement pris mes distances avec l'usage que j'en faisais.

Que se passerait-il si une entité toujours plus puissante commençait à empiéter sur nos désirs privés, tacites ou implicites, une entité si profondément installée au cœur de nos vies que nous n'y pourrions plus grand-chose ? Qu'en serait-il si, immergés dans ce nouveau média, nous commencions à perdre de vue où il commence et où il prend fin ?

Que se passerait-il si les capacités de technologie et d'intelligence d'une organisation devenaient mille fois, cent mille fois ou un million de fois plus puissantes que ce que nous en connaissons aujourd'hui – de même que les promesses de l'informatique quantique et cognitive, un million de fois plus rapide que n'importe quel boitier de connexion aujourd'hui, et tournant sur des logiciels qui ne seraient plus programmés, mais apprendraient d'eux-mêmes en fonctions de l'évolution de leurs besoins ?

Quelles seraient les conséquences involontaires de tels développements ? Ces nouveaux intermédiaires et nouvelles plates-formes seraient-ils finalement conduits à se montrer plus pressants dans leur quête discutable de profit à partir de l'exploitation de nos données, et avec notre participation, afin d'assouvir les attentes financières de leurs propriétaires ou des marchés ? Etant donné l'absence presque complète de législation sérieuse en matière de plates-formes numériques, de telles organisations, aussi puissantes, seraient-elles capables de résister à la tentation de franchir la ligne rouge qui sépare l'erreur involontaire du dévoiement intentionnel ?

Qu'est-ce qui nous permet, finalement, de penser que cela n'arrivera pas ? Nous ferions mieux de prendre en considération ces hypothèses déplaisantes, tout simplement parce que c'est sur ce chemin-là que nous sommes engagés – avec les technologies exponentielles pour carburant. La puissance des réseaux sociaux de l'ère du Web 2.0 ressemblera à des jouets d'enfants le jour où nous serons capables de connecter tout et tout le monde à un IdO dans le *cloud* immensément puissant, nourri de systèmes IA en état d'expansion et d'apprentissage permanent, comme Watson d'IBM ou DeepMind de Google. Littéralement toutes nos données, y compris nos informations médicales et biologiques les plus personnelles, deviendront ainsi disponibles, et nous ne pourrons plus cligner de l'œil sans que quelqu'un soit en mesure de le tracer, à la fois dans la vie réelle et au royaume du numérique.

Je pense sincèrement que la technologie et ceux qui en sont les pourvoyeurs, de manière exponentielle, vont devenir de plus en plus habiles à savoir exactement qui nous sommes, ce que nous pensons et comment se jouer de nous – et sans doute même à moindre coût. D'où la nécessité d'accorder un surcroît d'attention aux points de départ et d'arrivée – je veux dire par-là au point d'intersection entre mon humanité et leur technologie, et à la façon dont l'une et l'autre s'enchevêtrent.

Dans un tel monde, certains de ces sujets vont sans doute s'avérer menaçants. Par exemple, dans quelle mesure nos perceptions vont-elles être façonnées par l'effet de filtre consécutif au fait de ne voir ou de ne lire que des choses qui auront été tamisées et orchestrées pour nous par des algorithmes ? Comment pourrons-nous évaluer le risque de parti-pris et de manipulation, quand nous ne discernerons même pas la logique à l'œuvre derrière le fait de voir ou ne pas voir ?

Nous devrions saisir cette opportunité pour commencer à affiner nos talents pour observer et relever les défis, afin qu'une gouvernance humaine plus holistique puisse émerger. Un défi, aussi, pour les attentes que nous plaçons entre les mains des politiques et des responsables gouvernementaux.

Les assistants numériques intelligents et le *cloud* en tant qu'extensions de nous-mêmes

Aujourd'hui, nous utilisons déjà des machines intelligentes assez simples dans de nombreuses circonstances, par exemple des cartes routières connectées, des logiciels de messagerie ou des applications de rencontres. Néanmoins, si des applications comme TripAdvisor sont bien en mesure de nous dire ce que d'autres personnes ont pensé d'un restaurant qui nous intéresse, elles n'en connaissent pas pour autant nos historiques culinaires des vingt dernières années. Elles ne regardent pas à l'intérieur de notre frigo ou ne contrôlent pas nos toilettes ainsi que l'a récemment proposé un nouveau service au Japon, [118] et elles ne collectent pas toutes ces informations pour les comparer avec les 500 millions

d'autres bases de données d'utilisateurs qui sont aujourd'hui disponibles. Ce qui n'empêche d'ailleurs pas TripAdvisor d'être d'ores et déjà bien pratique, et un *must* pour pratiquement chaque hôtel et restaurant. Quoique son niveau d'intelligence soit modeste, c'est un outil utile pour autant que l'on ignore le contexte de son système de notations et de recommandations.

Ce type d'assistance élémentaire, simple et utile mais relativement mécanique, est sur le point d'être évincé par les progrès rapides du développement des ANIs. La nouvelle génération d'assistants sera principalement installée dans le *cloud* plutôt que sur nos appareils, et pourra superviser tout ce que nous faisons avec nos gadgets mobiles, nos systèmes domotiques, nos capteurs et nos ordinateurs. Imaginez la puissance quantique de Watson d'IBM accessible via vos appareils mobiles – et tout ce que vous aurez à faire, c'est de parler, sans même toucher le moindre clavier. Et maintenant, imaginez que tout ce que vous ayez à faire, c'est simplement de *penser*, en émettant des directives via votre interface cerveau-ordinateur (ICO). La super-humanité est à notre portée…

En 2016, Siri, Google Now et Cortana étaient déjà capables de répondre à des questions simples sur la météo ou sur la disponibilité d'un produit, et l'IA de gmail de répondre à notre place à certains de nos courriels. Bientôt, vos ANIs seront capables d'organiser la plupart de vos rendez-vous et de faire vos réservations aériennes, sans avoir besoin d'aucune supervision. Après-demain, ils deviendront vos fidèles-amis-dans-le-ciel. Et après cela, ils pourraient bien être devenus aussi importants que vos yeux et vos oreilles. Et ensuite ? Eh bien, vos intuitions valent sans doute largement les miennes, mais la question clé n'en reste pas moins : nous rendrons-ils heureux ? Et qu'est-ce que le bonheur, au fond (voir chapitre 9) ?

Dans son article de 2015 « Cortana incarne-t-il un pas dangereux vers l'intelligence artificielle ? », l'écrivain Brad Jones explique :

« *Les IAs développent leurs propres personnalités et deviennent plus intelligentes en collectant données et informations dans le monde qui les entoure. Toutefois, cette connaissance tend progressivement à mobiliser l'intégralité des ressources de calcul disponibles, au point qu'avec le temps, l'IA deviendra proliférante. Et une IA en état de prolifération considère les humains comme ses inférieurs, développant du même coup une perception délirante de sa propre puissance intellectuelle.* » [119]

La question clé sera de savoir si ces ANIs seront capables d'accomplir des tâches pour lesquelles ils n'auront pas été spécifiquement programmés – or nous avons vu que c'est exactement ce qu'est la promesse de l'apprentissage profond : une machine effectivement capable de s'auto-instruire, une machine pensante qui apprend plutôt que de suivre sa programmation.

Ces extensions de nous-mêmes exploiteront les pouvoirs exponentiels des réseaux neuronaux, de l'apprentissage profond et de l'informatique cognitive pour nous fournir des services extrêmement puissants, extrêmement personnalisés et à forte capacité d'anticipation. Il est presque certain qu'au cours de ce processus, elles soient également capables de développer des facultés pré-cognitives. Ajoutez la RA / RV et les ICOs à ce cocktail, et il n'y aura plus que le ciel pour horizon à ce que les futures générations d'ANIs pourraient être capables d'accomplir.

Car une fois que mon ANI ou mon « bot » connaîtra toute mon histoire, qu'il aura accès à toutes mes données en temps réel et qu'il pourra les comparer aux données de centaines de millions d'autres ANIs organisés en réseau, il lui sera alors tout à fait possible de prévoir mes actions et mes réponses. Bienvenue dans le crime putatif, avec cette idée de pouvoir prévenir la délinquance grâce aux capacités d'anticipation de nos robots, qui seraient capables de déceler une intention criminelle émergente, même à l'insu de la personne concernée. La société britannique Precobs développe d'ailleurs déjà un logiciel de cette nature, mis

à contribution dans le cadre des actions des forces de police locales. [120]

Bienvenue aussi dans un environnement numérique et médiatique propice à toutes les manipulations politiques, et où mon ANI serait chargé de toutes les représentations routinières de moi-même ; voire me remplacerait, au point de devenir moi-même. Mon ANI, dans un tel contexte, pourrait-il être victime de manipulation, ou bien délibérément être de mèche pour influencer mes décisions ?

Ainsi que la société d'étude Gartner l'a mis en évidence en 2013 : les appareils mobiles me synchronisent, me voient, me connaissent... et bientôt, ils seront moi. [121] D'où mes interrogations : tout ceci nous conduit-il à un épanouissement de l'humanité ? J'en doute sérieusement.

Il est possible qu'un jour pas si lointain, nous voyions notre ANI batailler ou négocier avec l'ANI du système de réservation aérienne afin d'obtenir dans les six prochaines minutes le meilleur prix possible pour notre vol à Hawaii. Et, bien sûr, la majeure partie de nos courses ne seront plus effectuées par nous personnellement – notre ANI étant devenu bien plus rapide et plus efficace, constamment à l'affut des bons de réductions et des annonces de soldes, et en mesure de prendre les bonnes décisions à la vitesse de la lumière. Tout ce que j'aurai à faire sera de penser à un achat... et mon assistant sera déjà en train de le commander en ligne. Satisfaction instantanée dans un monde d'abondance totale. Si nous sommes ainsi assurés de bénéficier d'une abondance extérieure totale, nous serons tout aussi assurés de vivre une pénurie intérieure croissante en termes de relations humaines, de communauté, de valeurs, de spiritualité et de croyances.

Croyez-le ou non, mais pour de nombreux experts et techno-déterministes de la Silicon Valley, la puissance des ANIs dans notre proche avenir sonne comme une perspective inoffensive : pas de quoi s'inquiéter de l'usage d'un ANI à peine plus évolué que mes apps d'aujourd'hui, n'est-ce pas ? Mais maintenant,

envisageons certains scénarios sous un angle un peu plus inquiétant, et qui incarnent d'ores et déjà un avenir possible à moyen terme.

Tout d'abord, considérons que pour être génial, rapide, prévoyant et intuitif, mon ANI – cette brillante entité, cette extension de moi-même, mon robot-personnel-dans-le-*cloud* – devra posséder une immense quantité d'informations à mon sujet. Je dirais même qu'il vaudrait mieux qu'il sache absolument tout de moi, extrayant des informations en temps réel à chaque source possible, en les remettant à jour en permanence. Beaucoup d'entre nous auraient probablement l'impression qu'un tel système, nourri de tous ces détails à notre sujet, serait souhaitable, parce qu'il améliorerait constamment la qualité de service dont nous bénéficions, rendant ainsi nos vies plus faciles – un prix apparemment mineur à payer, en effet, pour un tel niveau de confort et un pouvoir personnel à ce point décuplé.

Opter d'être constamment tracé, surveillé et poussé du coude – voilà où tout commence : des fonctionnalités populaires aussi couramment utilisées que « partager » ou « sauvegarder » montrent bien à quel point nous sommes piégés par ces plates-formes pour demeurer constamment connectés. Google est devenu un maître absolu en la matière, en nous maintenant à chaque instant à l'intérieur de son univers en expansion constante – et Google n'est qu'un exemple parmi d'autres de ces plates-formes globales visant à devenir une sorte de cerveau géant capable de dupliquer chacun des innombrables utilisateurs du *cloud*. Nous suivre ainsi à la trace est une façon de capitaliser, dans ces entreprises pour qui les données sont le nouveau pétrole, en particulier les plates-formes globales comme Google, Baidu, Alibaba et Facebook, qui ne commercialisent en fait aucun bien physique, mais agissent en extracteurs de données, en moteurs publicitaires et en super-nids d'informations. Représentez-vous ce concept amplifié des milliers de fois par l'IdO et les IAs, et vous entendrez avec quelle allégresse tintent leurs tiroirs caisses.

Tous sous surveillance totale ?

Alors, qu'est-ce qui pourrait mal tourner, avec les ANIs ? Voici quelques exemples de la manière dont ils pourraient nous planter.

- **Risques significativement accrus pour votre sécurité et votre vie privée** : votre ANI peut être piraté, abusé, mis sous pression ou corrompu en divulguant tout ou partie de vos informations personnelles à d'autres IAs actives en ligne. Il pourrait par exemple être conduit à divulguer les mots de passe permettant d'envoyer des e-mails, de faire des achats ou d'accéder en votre nom à certains médias et réseaux sociaux. L'étendue cumulée de telles fuites d'information pourrait être telle qu'elle vous causerait des dommages irréparables – et vous pourriez ne même pas vous être rendu compte que votre ANI a été corrompu !

- **Surveillance exponentielle** : votre ANI pourrait se comporter 24 heures sur 24 et 365 jours par an comme un enregistreur perpétuel de votre vie, numérique comme incarnée, sans plus de distinction. Quiconque muni des bonnes références, ou d'un niveau d'autorité suffisante, vraie ou fausse, pourrait ainsi accéder à vos données. Cela pourrait permettre à n'importe qui disposant des compétences robotiques requises de vous profiler, ou de vous signaler comme suspect(e), dissident(e) ou individu dangereux. De telles personnes pourraient également exploiter des fragments d'information hors-ligne ou décontextualisés pour vous cibler ou vous manipuler. Imaginez ce qui se passerait si la quantité de données à laquelle pourrait accéder votre *bot* s'avérait un millier de fois plus approfondie et pertinente, simplement parce qu'il serait en mesure de les corréler avec des millions d'autres flux de données, issues par exemple de réseaux sociaux. Les résultats pourraient rendre ridicules même les projections les plus dystopiques de George Orwell.

C'est la raison pour laquelle un scénario *cloud/bots*/ANI sans garde-fou me choque, car il m'apparaît comme une incitation ouverte aux abus et aux persécutions, qu'on le veuille ou non, surtout dans ces pays où la vie privée ne bénéficie déjà plus d'une véritable protection, ou qui ont déjà fait la preuve de leur mépris à l'égard des droits élémentaires à l'intimité de leurs citoyens. L'autre point à prendre en compte, c'est que nos gouvernements pourraient à l'avenir être de plus en plus en mesure d'accéder à nos ANIs et à nos identités numériques – soit légalement, de manière ouverte, ou plus insidieusement, via une lucarne à code d'accès ouvert. De ce fait, il me paraît raisonnable de supposer que toute entreprise de piratage sérieuse serait en mesure de faire de même. Je frémis à l'idée de ce qui pourrait survenir si nous nous retrouvions tous ainsi numériquement nus...

- **Déqualification humaine croissante** : Imaginez que je me sois tellement reposé sur mon ANI que j'aie commencé à oublier ou à désapprendre comment faire les choses par moi-même, par exemple trouver mon chemin dans une ville étrangère, comment trouver des informations fiables en ligne, comment effectuer une réservation aérienne, comment gérer une feuille de calcul ou même comment écrire manuellement – une éventualité tout à fait crédible. Il semble en effet parfaitement envisageable que nous perdions certains des talents autrefois inhérents au fait d'être humain, tels que communiquer sans intermédiaire, et sans nous soucier de la lenteur et des erreurs potentielles qui pourraient en résulter. Sommes-nous en train de rendre les humains de plus en plus remplaçables ? Faut-il tout automatiser sous prétexte que c'est faisable ?

- **Numériphrénie** (un néologisme de premier ordre forgé par Douglas Rushkoff, dont je vous recommande vivement les

ouvrages) [122] : l'un des principaux facteurs à l'origine de la déqualification humaine sous l'influence de la technologie est notre tendance croissante à l'ubiquité. Des technologies telles que la téléprésence, les systèmes de messagerie et les réseaux sociaux semblent amplifier ce phénomène de simulation, aboutissant à encourager certains d'entre nous à renoncer aux expériences authentiquement vécues.

Pour citer Douglas :

« La numériphrénie est l'expérience qui consiste à tenter d'exister simultanément en plusieurs versions de vous-même. Il y a votre profil Twitter, il y a votre profil Facebook, il y a votre boîte mail. Toutes ces multiples représentations de vous-même opèrent simultanément et en parallèle. Et ce n'est vraiment pas une situation confortable pour la plupart des êtres humains. » [123]

• **Etablir des relations avec des écrans et des machines plutôt qu'avec des personnes** : nombre de tâches et processus entrepris par les humains aboutissent fréquemment, même si ce n'est pas l'intention première, à établir des relations avec les autres – par exemple faire ses courses ou préparer un événement avec des collègues. Il est clair que certaines de ces interactions ne sont ni essentielles ni précieuses, comme de parler avec un agent de voyage pour réserver un vol ou dialoguer avec votre banquier à propos d'un investissement potentiel – deux choses que d'ailleurs je ne fais jamais personnellement.

Alors, oui, certaines de ces tâches mineures pourraient en effet être accomplies par des machines sans que les relations humaines en soient affectées – après tout je n'ai nul besoin de copiner avec mon banquier pour décider où je dois investir 5.000€. Mais en revanche, je pense qu'il nous faut remettre en question l'automatisation de certaines d'entre

elles, plus humainement impliquées, comme de rendre visite à son médecin – même si c'est seulement pour se convaincre que ce dont nous souffrons n'est qu'un simple coup de froid, et pas un emphysème pulmonaire. Dans certains cas en effet, d'accord pour laisser une machine gérer à distance votre diagnostic, sans quitter le confort de votre maison ; mais dans certains autres, cela pourrait en revanche déshumaniser la relation médecin-patient, parce que les actions qui ne devraient pas être automatisées ou prises en charge par des machines sont justement celles qui créent vraiment des relations importantes.

Imaginez par exemple que l'automatisation devienne une part substantielle de vos interactions professionnelles avec votre équipe ou vos collègues, ainsi que l'ont proposé des start-ups comme x.ai, avec ses apps d'assistants automatisés. [124] Il n'y aurait bien sûr aucun inconvénient à ce qu'un e-mail génère automatiquement un agenda partagé, mais imaginez que vous receviez une réponse d'un collègue à cet e-mail sans être en mesure de savoir si c'est lui ou son ANI qui l'aurait rédigé. Ou bien, en poussant la même logique un peu plus loin, que ressentiriez-vous si votre père ou votre mère passait par son ANI pour entrer en contact personnel avec vous ?

Et où tout cela finira-t-il ? Jusqu'où pousserons-nous les choses ? Qui décidera où s'arrête l'IA et où commence l'humain ? Mon ANI finira-t-il par choisir les invités de ma prochaine fête d'anniversaire, par commander à manger, choisir la musique, compiler un bon diaporama et peut-être même programmer un site web *ad hoc* pour l'occasion ? Va-t-il en venir à me dire comment être le plus heureux possible lors de cette fête ? Cela m'incitera-t-il à construire de meilleures relations avec les autres humains, ou me laisserai-je aller à déléguer ce travail, même au prix d'une perte de sens ? Est-ce qu'au fond nous n'irions pas jusqu'à

développer davantage de relations avec nos machines tout simplement parce que c'est pratique ?

• **La manipulation à une échelle inimaginable est réalisable et toujours plus probable** : si nous en venions à déléguer nos décisions à des ANIs toujours plus puissants, cela commencerait probablement par les questions de médias et de contenus – ne serait-ce que parce que les fonctionnalités de base en sont d'ores et déjà en place au sein de la plupart des réseaux sociaux. Nos ANIs pourraient aisément trouver et filtrer l'actualité et les films qui nous intéressent, et plus généralement mettre de l'ordre dans nos médias sociaux. Pour une large part, la technologie influence déjà, ou même décide, ce qu'il est bon que nous voyions, lisions ou écoutions. Mais une intelligence issue du *cloud* et impulsée par des technologies exponentielles rendrait basiques, par comparaison, les choix actuels.

Imaginez les possibilités ne serait-ce que d'une poignée de robots ou de plates-formes d'ANIs, contrôlant ce que regardent ou ce à quoi s'intéressent des milliards de gens. Imaginez ce que les marques et les annonceurs seraient prêts à payer pour être vus par les bonnes cibles, au bon endroit et au bon moment...

À mes yeux, l'essor des ANIs pose des questions fondamentales :

• Qu'en serait-t-il si une copie numérique de moi-même divulguait des informations à de mauvais interlocuteurs – par exemple ma compagnie d'assurances ou mon centre de sécurité sociale, l'une comme l'autre en mesure d'approuver ou refuser une prestation ?
• Qu'adviendrait-il si mon ANI devenait si performant dans la prise de décisions à ma place que j'en viendrais à suivre ses recommandations lors de choix de vie majeurs tels que mariage, déménagement, parentalité ou éducation ?

- Que se passerait-il si mon ANI filtrait toutes les nouvelles et informations de telle manière que je ne sois plus jamais amené à exprimer une opinion divergente, et qu'en serait-il si sa logique pouvait être manipulée ou achetée par une campagne visant à m'influencer ?

« *Gartner prévoit que d'ici fin 2016, des décisions d'achat plus complexes que celles portant sur les équipements de rentrée des classes, réalisées de façon autonome par des assistants numériques, atteindront annuellement 2 milliards de dollars. Soit approximativement 2,5% des utilisateurs d'appareils mobiles, qui délèguent à leurs assistants numériques des achats à hauteur de 50 dollars par an.* »
« Le monde des assistants numériques –Pourquoi les applications d'IA quotidiennes vont façonner l'IdO » [125]

L'essor météorique des ANIs va probablement me contraindre à remettre à jour l'une de mes plaisanteries de conférence favorites : « Google en sait davantage sur nous que notre mari ou notre épouse. » Qu'un ANI comme Google Now collecte des millions points de données me concernant – tels que mes déplacements, mes historiques de connexion, mes achats, mes « like », mes courriels, mes cartes, mes vidéos visionnées sur YouTube – va certainement considérablement faire monter les enchères. Comme j'aime à le rappeler, sur une échelle de 100 de ce qui pourrait être numérisé, nous n'en sommes guère qu'à cinq... et déjà à deux doigts de perdre tout contrôle.

De quoi revenir à une autre notion clé : « Nous n'avons encore rien vu ». L'essor fulgurant de l'IdO va impulser un élan supplémentaire aux plates-formes d'ANI – générant à leur tour encore plus de données à fournir au cerveau global auquel s'abreuvent tous ces systèmes. Progressivement, des pièces de matériels auparavant muettes telles que trépans, machines agricoles, pipelines, interrupteurs et connecteurs vont être équipées de capteurs et de réseaux de connexions sans fil. Et

bientôt, il deviendra possible d'obtenir directement des données de tout ce qui nous entoure, littéralement.

« D'après une étude récente, les réseaux sociaux – les vrais, ceux qui rassemblent des personnes physiques que vous connaissez et pouvez voir, pas comme sur Facebook et Twitter – sont aussi importants pour votre santé que de faire de l'exercice ou surveiller votre alimentation. Et, mieux encore, la quantité de liens sociaux que vous entretenez directement a un effet direct sur votre santé. » Charlie Sorrel – « Cessez d'être un solitaire, car cela vous tuera. » [126]

Alors, pourquoi si peu de gens se soucient-ils de tout cela aujourd'hui ?
Il y a de nombreuses raisons pour lesquelles si peu de gens se manifestent pour exprimer des commentaires critiques sur ce glissement du magique au toxique. En voici trois.

1. **Des profits considérables.** Connecter les gens les uns avec les autres et tirer parti du progrès technologique exponentiel en fournissant des appareils mobiles peu chers mais très addictifs constitue probablement l'une des plus grosses opportunités d'affaires qu'on ait jamais vues. Approvisionner les gens en magie numérique – autrement dit l'économie des données –, rend presque ridicules les secteurs de l'énergie et des transports – et personne ne veut manquer la fête. [127] Dans une société ou les valeurs de profit et de croissance occupent encore les toutes premières places, les effets pervers, et même les résultats toxiques, sont trop souvent considérés comme des facteurs externes : pas notre problème.

2. **Manque de règles contraignantes et ignorance politique.** À la différence de l'exploitation et de la fourniture de ressources naturelles telles que le pétrole, le gaz ou l'eau, il

existe très peu de réglementations globales qui s'appliquent à la mise en œuvre de l'intelligence artificielle, aux effets addictifs de la technologie ou à l'exploitation du *big data*, c'est-à-dire la commercialisation de nos données personnelles par les réseaux numériques. Il y a là un grand vide qu'il faut absolument traiter.

3. **La dépendance à la technologie (« Les appareils mobiles, ou la nouvelle cigarette »).** Les technologies exponentielles, qui semblent rendre nos vies plus faciles, jouent de notre paresse naturelle et de notre besoin de nous faire aimer, sont hautement addictives et ont souvent le même effet qu'une drogue. En la matière, les mauvaises habitudes se prennent très vite – jetez-vous un œil une dernière fois à vos courriels, vous aussi, avant de vous coucher ? Vous sentez-vous délaissé(e) lorsque vous n'êtes plus connecté(e) à votre réseau social favori, ou sans défense lorsque vous ne pouvez plus compter sur Google Maps ou sur vos applications de messagerie ?

Le fondement de tout cela, c'est que vendre de la magie numérique, puis passer au pervers ou au toxique est probablement la plus grosse opportunité d'affaires de l'Age Numérique, et que dans sa forme la pire, c'est exactement la même chose que d'ajouter des substances addictives à de la malbouffe ou à du tabac.

À mesure que nous progressons de manière exponentielle, sans doute faudra-t-il réexaminer et revoir à la baisse cette stratégie, si nous voulons effectivement voir advenir une société qui place la poursuite du bonheur humain au-dessus de tout le reste.

Ce que vise la technologie : transformer l'artificiel en naturel
Il nous arrive parfois d'utiliser la phrase « ceci est devenu pour moi comme une seconde nature » pour décrire l'usage d'outils ou de technologies qui donnent l'impression d'être naturels. Les gens

disent par exemple « Avoir toujours mon téléphone mobile avec moi est devenu une seconde nature » ou « Me connecter avec mes amis sur Facebook est devenu une seconde nature ». Cette phrase décrit quelque chose qui est devenu une habitude, quelque chose que nous faisons parce qu'elle nous paraît naturelle, nous n'y pensons même plus.

« Liker » des publications sur Facebook, partager des images et des vidéos sur WhatsApp ou des applications de messagerie similaires, être constamment joignable sur des appareils mobiles, est ainsi devenu une seconde nature. Google Maps est, de la même façon, devenu une seconde nature, et pour un nombre croissant d'utilisateurs de l'iPhone d'Apple, Siri est en train de devenir une seconde nature. L'expression « seconde nature » se rapporte au fait de faire quelque chose sans beaucoup y penser, une habitude enracinée (presque comparable à des actions « naturelles » comme le fait de respirer) sur laquelle nous ne nous interrogeons plus, quelque chose que nous réalisons de manière automatique. Dans une bonne partie des cas, on peut estimer qu'il s'agit déjà d'une manie un peu *borderline* – combien de fois avez-vous expérimenté le syndrome de la vibration fantôme en percevant une sensation vibratoire dans votre poche alors même que vous avez laissé votre appareil mobile à la maison ?

Mais maintenant que nous pénétrons avec empressement dans le vortex du changement technologique exponentiel, nous pouvons constater qu'un nombre croissant de technologies (ou de ceux qui les vendent) rivalisent pour s'imposer non pas comme une seconde, mais comme une première nature – autrement dit « la » nature, point. De toute évidence une opportunité d'affaires gigantesque. Si être « simplement humain » n'est plus satisfaisant, ou si être humain est simplement devenu trop lourdingue, pourquoi ne pas recourir à la technologie pour vous améliorer ou vous augmenter vous-même ? Pourquoi ne pas faire de la technologie une « première nature » et jouer sur le même terrain de jeu, nous et les machines ?

L'idée de parvenir à une augmentation de l'être humain par des moyens technologiques bascule souvent tout droit vers le monde des entreprises, qui veulent monétiser notre désir de devenir plus puissants, tout en nous rendant la vie plus facile. Pour une bonne part des gens, s'équiper de Fitbits et autres applications, accessoires, vêtements connectés et capteurs embarqués dans nos vestes et chemises participe déjà de cet élan vers la « première nature » (« Bien sûr que je trace mes paramètres vitaux et que je surveille mon corps de cette manière – c'est une chose tellement naturelle »). Ce qu'on appelle le *soi quantifié* est en pleine expansion, partout, et des pans entiers d'activités nouvelles se créent autour de ce concept. Néanmoins, je m'inquiète souvent à l'idée que ces offres ne nous transforment tôt ou tard en esclaves quantifiés ou, encore pire, en *soi stupéfiés*, en nous donnant effectivement la possibilité de nous déqualifier via la prise en charge de nos pensées (et de nos sentiments) par des technologies externalisées.

Imaginez simplement quelles autres augmentations humaines pourraient ainsi être aisément atteintes, passant de désirables à « seconde nature » puis nature – simplement parce qu'il serait devenu tellement bon de ne pas s'en passer, et parce qu'elles seraient devenues abondantes et presque gratuites. La liste de ces possibilités technologiques inclut la RA, la RV et les hologrammes, qui me permettront de me projeter dans un espace virtuel où il me sera possible d'interagir avec autrui comme si je m'y trouvais vraiment, comme avec Hololens de Microsoft. [128] De tels outils pourraient s'avérer très utiles lors de visites de musées, ou pour des chirurgiens en opération, ou pour des pompiers pénétrant dans un bâtiment inconnu. Mais je pense que nous devrions résister à la tentation d'en faire une « seconde nature » (et qu'on ne me parle plus de « première nature »).

Qu'on ne s'y trompe pas : la plupart de ces appareils, services et plates-formes – qu'ils l'aient fait ouvertement et intentionnellement ou par opportunisme – s'efforcent de restreindre ou même d'éradiquer complètement la différence

existant entre nous (la nature humaine) et eux (la « seconde nature »), tout simplement parce que s'ils parvenaient à leurs fins, cela les rendrait totalement indispensables et donc hautement profitables en termes commerciaux.

Dans un tel contexte, il ne me serait même plus possible de demeurer un être humain en bonne santé sans avoir recours à toute cette batterie d'appareils et d'apps – au point de me demander comment j'avais donc bien pu m'y prendre pour seulement exister jusque là ! Mission accomplie...

Pour ma part, je maintiens que nous ne devrions pas laisser la technologie dépasser ce stade de la « seconde nature » – quoique tout cela soit d'ores et déjà engagé dans une bien mauvaise passe. Une technologie qui aurait su se transformer en nature (c'est-à-dire nous) voudrait dire au fond que la nature humaine serait interchangeable avec la technologie – ce qui n'est pas un bon chemin pour atteindre au bonheur humain, ainsi que j'essaie de le montrer tout au long de ce livre.

Cet extrait d'une interview de 2016 dans *Nature Institute* avec l'auteur Stephen Talbott décrit très bien le défi à relever :

« *Ce n'est qu'en appréhendant ces technologies avec la plus grande attention possible portée au spécifique, au qualitatif, au local, à l'ici et maintenant, que nous serons en mesure de préserver les équilibres. C'est une règle générale qui, à ma connaissance, a été exprimée pour la première fois par Rudolf Steiner : plus nous nous engagerons de notre plein gré dans une existence mécanisée et plus il nous faudra avec détermination avancer vers les régions les plus élevées de nous-mêmes ; faute de quoi nous perdrons progressivement notre humanité.* » [129]

Il est de plus en plus probable que notre usage de la technologie nous fasse passer de magique à pervers à toxique, à mesure que des gains exponentiels sont atteints tout autour de nous. Combien de fois nous arrive-t-il de traîner plus d'une heure sur Internet ou

de nous égarer dans une nouvelle application futile, sans même nous rappeler ce qu'à l'origine nous étions venus y chercher ? S'aventurer individuellement en terre inconnue est une chose, mais qu'en sera-t-il si c'est la société dans son entier qui s'y laisse dériver ? Et quelles expériences exclusivement humaines sommes-nous déjà en train d'abandonner jour après jour à Internet, au téléphone mobile, au *cloud* et à nos robots et assistants intelligents ?

Comment pouvons-nous identifier à quels moments sont franchies les frontières entre magie et perversion ? Quand la perversion devient-elle toxique ? Et qu'en sera-t-il de cette toxicité lorsqu'il ne sera plus question de désintoxiquer seulement un individu, mais toute une culture ? Alors que la *techne* devient le *qui* autant que le *comment*, serons-nous seulement assez forts et suffisamment lucides sur nous-mêmes pour enfin nous réveiller ?

Chapitre 7
Nouvelle pandémie : l'obésité numérique

Vautrés dans une débauche d'actualités, de mises à jour et d'informations générées par algorithmes dont nous nous bâfrons, nous nous distrayons dans une bulle technologique en plein essor. Des distractions pour le moins douteuses.

L'obésité physique est un problème global qui, selon le cabinet d'audit McKinsey, se chiffre actuellement à 450 milliards de dollars par an uniquement aux Etats-Unis, à la fois en termes de coûts de santé et de perte de productivité. [130] Les Centres pour la prévention et le contrôle des épidémies ont établi en 2015 que plus des deux tiers des Américains sont en surpoids, et que 35,7% d'entre eux sont obèses. [131]

Je pense que nous allons faire face à un défi similaire, voire plus grand encore, à mesure que nous nous gavons de technologie, cause d'obésité numérique.

Je définis l'obésité numérique comme un ensemble de conditions mentales et technologiques par lesquelles les données, l'information, les médias et la connectivité numérique généralisée s'accumulent à un point tel qu'ils finissent par avoir un effet négatif sur la santé, le bien-être, le bonheur et la vie en général.

Comme on pouvait peut-être s'y attendre, et en dépit de ce constat sanitaire choquant, l'idée selon laquelle on pourrait appliquer des règles plus strictes à l'encontre de l'industrie agro-alimentaire pour qu'elle restreigne l'utilisation d'additifs chimiques facteurs d'accoutumance, ou qu'elle mette un terme à

ses campagnes marketing incitant à la surconsommation, ne rencontre encore qu'un soutien global assez restreint. Dans une Amérique qui s'entête dans sa guerre sans fin contre la drogue, il est surprenant qu'on fasse si peu allusion aux sucres et aux composants alimentaires nocifs. De la même manière que les produits bios semblent être aujourd'hui l'apanage des riches et des bien-portants, nous pouvons nous attendre à ce que l'anonymat et l'intimité deviennent des produits de luxe hors de prix – c'est-à-dire hors de portée de la plupart des citoyens.

Les consommateurs achètent désormais des gadgets et des applications censés les aider à réduire leur consommation alimentaire et à améliorer leur état de forme, comme FitBit, Jawbone, Loseit et maintenant Hapifork – qui vous alerte en vibrant lorsque vous mangez trop vite –, très utile, en effet. [132] Idée sous-jacente : acheter (ou télécharger) et consommer un produit ou un service supplémentaire qui va miraculeusement, et sans grand effort, faire disparaître le problème antérieur de surconsommation.

Générer le besoin : le chemin de la prospérité

Le principe de base, évident, est que plus les gens mangent et meilleur c'est pour tous ceux qui produisent et vendent notre nourriture – par exemple les maraîchers, les éleveurs les épiceries, les supermarchés, les fast foods, les restaurants, les bars et les hôtels. On peut trouver choquant d'apprendre que chaque année, chaque consommateur dans les pays développés ingère involontairement environ 70 kilos d'additifs divers – pour l'essentiel du sucre, des levures et des antioxydants, y compris des produits réellement dangereux comme le glutamate de sodium (MSG). [133] Ces substances constituent le lubrifiant de la surconsommation. Non seulement elles rendent la nourriture plus attractive et plus durable, mais elles en améliorent également le goût – aussi contestable que cela puisse être. Les consommateurs sont ainsi ingénieusement incités à suivre le mouvement par l'ingénierie du « j'en reprendrais-bien-encore-un-peu », de sorte

qu'il devienne très difficile de s'extraire de ce royaume de consommation heureuse et sans fin.

Et si vous trouvez que tout ceci sonne façon Facebook ou vous évoque votre *smartphone*, alors vous avez compris où je veux en venir. En fait, l'industrie de l'alimentation appelle ceci « la création de besoins ». [134] Dans le monde de la technologie, les *marketers* parlent de magie, de besoin d'adhésion, d'indispensabilité ou, de façon moins brutale, « d'engagement utilisateur ».

Engagement et addiction : le *business model* de la technologie
Le fait de générer ainsi ce genre de besoins, et de nourrir nos addictions numériques de manière apparemment inoffensive, constitue clairement un *business model* puissant. [135] On peut aisément appliquer le concept de la création de besoins aux entités dominantes du secteur *SoLoMo* (social-local-mobile) comme Google et Facebook, ou aux plates-formes comme WhatsApp. Nombre d'entre nous sommes littéralement accros à la connectivité dans la conduite de nos vies quotidiennes, et lorsque nous nous déconnectons, nous nous sentons incomplets.

Toutefois, je m'interroge : est-il vraiment de l'intérêt des grandes firmes de l'Internet qu'une importante proportion de leurs utilisateurs deviennent des obèses numériques ? Est-ce vraiment là l'intérêt bien compris de la technologie, essentiellement d'origine américaine, et des géants du Net ? [136] Simultanément, il ne faudrait pas non plus sous-estimer la forte tentation de rendre les consommateurs dépendant de ces merveilleuses nourritures numériques – de nous rendre accros à ce tsunami de *likes*, de commentaires et de remises à jour de nos listes d'amis, générateur de sérotonine.

Pensez à 2020 et représentez-vous des milliards de consommateurs hyperconnectés en train de devenir numériquement obèses, suspendus à une perfusion constante d'informations, de médias et de données – y compris le retour en boucle de leurs propres réactions. C'est une opportunité d'affaires gigantesque et

terriblement attrayante, qui surpassera de loin le marché global des additifs alimentaires – et qui devrait valoir quelque chose comme 28,2 milliards de dollars d'ici 2018, d'après les projections de Transparency Market Research. [137]

Pour une rapide comparaison d'échelle, le Forum économique mondial estime que la valeur cumulée de la numérisation pourrait atteindre 100 trilliards de dollars dans les dix prochaines années. Ces économistes soulignent que cela nous ouvrira la possibilité de « créer une future force de travail où les humains et les machines intelligentes travailleront de concert pour améliorer la manière dont le monde fonctionne et vit. » [138] Je dois admettre que je trouve l'idée séduisante, mais en revanche je vois mal comment nous pourrions encore préserver notre humanité au sein d'une société aussi techno-centrée.

Qui est responsable de l'obésité numérique ?

En revenant à la question alimentaire, vous pourriez demander : mais si l'industrie agroalimentaire fait tant d'argent avec une approche aussi discrètement (ou même clandestinement) perverse de l'addiction et de la création de besoins, pourquoi se soucier de ces quelques consommateurs qui semblent incapables de résister par eux-mêmes à la tentation ? La faute ne leur en incombe-t-elle pas, n'est-ce pas tout simplement de leur propre responsabilité ? Qui prétendrait que qui que ce soit d'autre que l'individu puisse être tenu pour responsable de sa propre consommation alimentaire ? Après tout, nous vivons dans un monde libre et à chacun son propre libre arbitre, non ?

Le problème, c'est que dans l'ère annoncée de l'information en croissance exponentielle et de la connectivité abondante, cette stratégie du laissez-faire est intenable, précisément parce que nous n'en sommes qu'au point de bascule de la courbe exponentielle – et que les plus grands chocs restent à venir.

Deux défis clés nous attendent : premièrement, la « nourriture numérique » est la plupart du temps gratuite ou très bon marché, et encore plus universellement disponible que la nourriture

« physique » – elle est distribuée et immédiatement accessible pratiquement à coût zéro. Deuxièmement, elle ne présente que très peu d'effets secondaires avérés ou de signaux d'alerte physiques. La plupart des consommateurs ne comprendront leur consommation numérique et leur sur-connectivité ou ne commenceront à s'en inquiéter que lorsqu'elles seront d'évidence devenues un problème sérieux, comme l'addiction au jeu des adolescents en Corée. [139] Une fois que vous êtes obèse, il est très difficile de redémarrer votre vie sur un autre paradigme.

Je crois qu'il nous faut d'urgence définir des politiques publiques fluides ; de nouveaux contrats sociaux ; des normes globales de santé numérique ; des cadres légaux modulables et localisés ; et un sens plus affirmé de la responsabilité et de l'engagement de la part des professionnels du marketing et de la publicité.

Les fournisseurs de technologie doivent (et je crois d'ailleurs que, d'ores et déjà, beaucoup le souhaitent) encourager l'émergence d'un manifeste global équilibré des droits et de la santé numériques, en s'engageant d'eux-mêmes à la retenue, et basculer vers un *business model* plus holistique, qui mette réellement les humains au premier plan. L'hyperconnectivité avant tout ne doit certainement pas devenir notre ultime objectif, pas plus que l'hyper-efficience ne doit être le seul objet des entreprises. Placer l'humain au premier plan signifie placer *le bonheur* au premier plan, et j'ajouterais que c'est la seule façon de créer des bénéfices durables, qu'il s'agisse du monde des affaires ou de la société en général.

> « *La différence entre la technologie et l'esclavage, c'est que les esclaves sont tout à fait conscients de n'être pas libres.* »
> Nassim Nicholas Taleb [140]

Un tsunami de données s'annonce

Tandis que la quantité de données, d'information et de médias disponibles croît de façon exponentielle, un immense défi lié à l'obésité numérique se dessine de plus en plus. Il nous faut le prendre au sérieux et nous en saisir à bras le corps, parce que la pression numérique s'annonce encore plus écrasante que l'obésité physique. Il y a aujourd'hui beaucoup trop de communication et d'information dans nos vies (il y en a en fait une quantité infinie, bien sûr) et le paradoxe du surchoix déferle partout autour de nous. [141]

Nous sommes confrontés à une déferlante de possibilités, toujours et partout, et elles sont toutes trop savoureuses, trop bon marché, trop riches. Il ne se passe pas un seul jour sans qu'on nous propose un nouveau service de mise à jour de nos listes d'amis – également croissantes ; sans qu'il ne nous soit offert davantage de façons d'être interrompus par les notifications incessantes de pratiquement n'importe quelle plate-forme – témoin par exemple la popularité grandissante des montres connectées, qui se vendent désormais en plus grand nombre que les montres suisses. [142] Nous faisons face à une croissance exponentielle des options de consommation – davantage d'actualités ; davantage de musique ; davantage de films ; davantage d'appareils mobiles, plus performants et moins chers ; et, en apparence, une connectivité sociale totale.

Nous sommes en train de nous noyer dans un océan d'applications – des applications pour se rencontrer, pour divorcer, pour signaler les nids-de-poule ou même (comme nous l'avons vu précédemment) pour surveiller les couches de bébé. [143] Nous subissons 24 heures sur 24 et 7 jours sur 7 l'assaut d'alertes de géolocalisation et de communications comme celles d'iBeacons, de coupons numériques, de nouvelles manières d'envoyer et de recevoir des messages à coût zéro, 500 millions de tweets quotidiens, [144] 400 heures de vidéo téléchargées chaque minute sur YouTube, [145] et la liste s'allonge, et s'allonge... C'est un véritable tsunami de données, qui déverse son abondance sur

le monde extérieur, mais qui crée aussi pénurie et absence de sens à l'intérieur de nous-mêmes. En d'autres termes, nous disposons de toujours plus d'options pour toujours moins cher, mais dans le même temps nous nous inquiétons sans cesse à l'idée d'être passés à côté de quelque chose que nous aurions pu vivre ou faire. Où tout cela nous mène-t-il ?

Abondance extérieure, pénurie intérieure – des vélos pour l'esprit ou des balles pour l'âme ?

Nous sommes soumis à un bombardement d'informations, et à bien des égards nous nous y vautrons de la même manière que nous l'aurions fait naguère dans les buffets *all you can eat* à 9,99$ de Las Vegas. Les seigneurs de l'alimentation numérique sont bien sûr les Google et autres équivalents chinois comme Baidu et Alibaba. Le génie de Google, c'est d'avoir su créer en douceur un paradis (ou à tout le moins un royaume) de consommation tous azimuts à partir d'une infinité de plates-formes très virales et très invasives telles que Gmail, Google Maps, Google +, Google Now, YouTube, Android et Google Search.

L'univers de Google est tellement hyper-efficace, tellement pratique et tellement addictif qu'il menace de gaver totalement non seulement nos cerveaux, nos yeux et nos oreilles, mais également nos cœurs et nos âmes. J'aime m'y référer en parlant de l'alternative abondance extérieure / pénurie intérieure, ou en évoquant le dilemme vélos pour l'esprit ou balles pour l'âme : tandis que nos esprits s'aiguisent grâce à Google et consorts, nos artères s'engorgent de toutes les scories issues de nos fêtes numériques sans fin, nos cœurs s'alourdissent de trop de relations sans issue et de connexions à distance qui n'existent finalement que sur écrans.

Si vraiment « Google me connaît mieux que mon épouse », alors sans doute faut-il commencer à se demander qui est au service de qui. [146] L'obésité numérique est-elle au fond partie prenante du système, a-t-elle un agenda caché ? Ou bien n'est-elle

rien de plus qu'une conséquence involontaire de l'activité de cette poignée d'entités qui régentent désormais nos vies numériques ?

« *Neurologiquement parlant, nous devenons ce que nous pensons.* » Nicholas Carr [147]

« Plus un patient se concentre sur ses symptômes et plus ces symptômes se gravent dans ses circuits neuronaux », écrit Nicholas Carr dans *Ce que l'Internet fait à nos esprits*.

Dans les cas les plus graves, le cerveau s'entraîne fondamentalement à tomber malade. De même, de nombreuses addictions se trouvent renforcées par la modification de la structure et de l'organisation des chaînes neuroniques dans le cerveau. Même de très faibles doses de drogues addictives peuvent spectaculairement altérer le flux des neurotransmetteurs dans les synapses d'une personne donnée, produisant des dommages durables dans les circuits et fonctions du cerveau. Il semble même que l'accumulation de certains types de neurotransmetteurs tels que la dopamine, une cousine de l'adrénaline source de plaisir, puisse parfois être en mesure de provoquer l'activation ou l'extinction de gènes spécifiques, qui à leur tour alimentent une appétence encore plus grande pour la drogue. La voie vitale devient fatale. [148]

Les nouvelles interfaces comme la réalité augmentée ou virtuelle intensifient le défi

Parvenir à établir un régime numérique équilibré deviendra encore plus difficile à mesure que la connectivité, les appareils et les applications seront exponentiellement moins chers et plus rapides, tandis que les interfaces informationnelles seront réinventées. Nous passerons de l'étape de la lecture et de la visualisation d'écrans à celle du dialogue avec des machines, puis tout simplement au fait de les diriger en pensée. Jusqu'à finalement en venir, dans un avenir plus si lointain, à considérer la

question ultime : est-ce nous qui vivons dans la machine, ou bien la machine qui vit en nous ?

Le « nouveau pétrole » des données : payez, ou alors devenez vous-même un contenu

J'en ai déjà parlé à de nombreuses reprises, mais cela vaut la peine de le répéter : les données sont réellement en train de se substituer au pétrole. Les grandes entreprises qui se nourrissent de *big data* et la soi-disant société connectée se transforment rapidement en nouveaux Exxon-Mobil, procurant avec empressement aux masses leur nouvel opium : nourriture numérique, connectivité totale, apparcils mobiles puissants, contenus gratuits, agrégats sociaux-locaux-mobiles (SoLoMo) en provenance du *cloud* par robots interposés et assistants numériques intelligents (ANI). Ils nous procurent le nutriment que nous autres internautes– ceux qu'on appelait naguère des consommateurs – contribuons en fait nous-mêmes à créer et partager par notre simple présence et participation. [149]

Certes, nombre d'entre nous se sentent au fond très à l'aise dans l'enceinte de ces jardins issus de Google, Facebook, Weibo, LinkedIn et tant d'autres. Nous consommons autant que nous le pouvons tout en acceptant volontiers d'être de la nourriture pour d'autres. Ainsi que l'auteur Scott Gibson l'a récemment déclaré au blog du magazine *Forbes*, « Si vous ne payez pas, alors c'est vous-même qui devenez le contenu ». [150] Nous nous nourrissons les uns des autres comme jamais auparavant et la majeure partie de cette activité est incroyablement enrichissante, satisfaisante et addictive. Mais s'agit-il d'un Nirvana, d'un pacte faustien futé, ou d'une recette désastreuse ? Ou alors cela dépend-il de qui pose la question ?

L'obésité numérique à l'horizon 2020

La société Cisco prévoit qu'aux alentours de 2020, 52% de la population globale seront connectés à l'Internet – soit environ 4 milliards d'utilisateurs humains. [151] À ce moment, chaque

fragment d'information, chaque image, chaque vidéo, chaque grain de donnée, chaque lieu et chaque parole prononcée par chaque humain connecté sera probablement surveillé, collecté, connecté et traité sous forme de médias, de *big data* ou d'intelligence commerciale. Des intelligences artificielles (IA) alimentées par des ordinateurs cognitifs quantiques génèreront des analyses de données en temps réel en zettabits (un sextillion (10^{21}) / 2^{70} de bits), aux perspectives renversantes. Plus rien, alors, ne restera très longtemps sans être observé.

Cela pourrait clairement être un paradis si vous êtes un(e) professionnel(le) du marketing, un fournisseur d'outils prenant ces tâches en charge, une agence gouvernementale impatiente ou tout simplement un super-*geek*. Mais cela pourrait aussi être un enfer, compte tenu de la possibilité manifeste que cette même information à haute densité puisse faire l'objet d'une surveillance perpétuelle globale, ainsi que les révélations de Snowden l'ont rendu douloureusement évident depuis 2013. [152]

Non seulement nous pourrions devenir obèses d'information, mais en plus nous serions tout nus – charmante perspective !

La question n'est plus « si nous pouvions », mais « si nous devions »

Je prédis que la question de savoir si la technologie peut ou pas résoudre un problème donné sera bientôt remplacée par la question, plus pertinente, de savoir si nous devrions faire ce que la technologie nous permet de réaliser, et pourquoi. C'est d'ores et déjà vrai pour nombre d'innovations et tendances récentes telles que les médias sociaux, l'auto-quantification, les Google Glass, l'impression 3D ou la Singularité, supposée imminente (voir chapitre 1).

Dans le contexte de l'obésité numérique, la question fondamentale est celle-ci : devons-nous absorber constamment tous ces médias, toutes ces données, toutes ces connaissances et même toute cette sagesse sous prétexte qu'elles sont devenues disponibles instantanément et gratuitement ? Avons-nous

vraiment besoin d'une app pour nous dire où se trouve la section musique ? Nous faut-il réellement comparer nos génomes avant de nous rendre à un rendez-vous galant ? Et avons-nous vraiment besoin de compter nos pas de telle manière que notre statut de forme grimpe d'un cran sur un réseau social ?

De « plus, c'est mieux » à « moins, c'est le mieux »

Finalement, on en arrive à ça : de la même manière qu'avec la nourriture, où la question de l'obésité apparaît plus évidente, il nous faut d'urgence établir un nouvel équilibre dans notre régime numérique. Nous devons définir à quelle quantité d'information nous nous connectons, quand et à quel moment. Quand devons-nous réduire nos apports, prendre le temps de les digérer et de les apprécier, voire décider de jeûner un peu ? À n'en pas douter, il y a d'ailleurs là une vraie opportunité d'affaires : se déconnecter, voilà le nouveau luxe.

Je crois que dans les toutes prochaines années, nos habitudes de consommation numérique vont évoluer du paradigme « plus, c'est mieux », typique de l'Internet 1.0 et de la vie déconnectée, au concept de « moins, c'est le mieux ». En nous attaquant à cet équilibre crucial entre l'ignorance et l'omniscience – et bien qu'aucun extrême ne soit désirable – nous pourrions vouloir nous inspirer d'Albert Einstein qui disait : « *Tout devrait être fait aussi simplement qu'il est possible, mais pas plus simplement.* » [153]

Chapitre 8
Précaution contre proaction

Le plus sûr – et néanmoins le plus prometteur – des futurs sera celui où nous accueillerons volontiers l'innovation, mais sans nous dissimuler les risques exponentiels qu'elle implique si nous abandonnons à d'autres la responsabilité de sa gestion.

La puissance de la technologie ne cessant de croître de manière exponentielle, je pense qu'il est primordial de définir un équilibre durable entre précaution et proaction. Se référer au principe de précaution signifie envisager de manière proactive ce qui pourrait arriver – autrement dit les conséquences possibles d'événements involontaires – avant de se lancer dans une recherche scientifique ou dans un développement technologique. Par contraste, l'approche proactive prend le parti d'avancer dans l'intérêt du progrès sans forcément avoir éclairci auparavant les ramifications et risques potentiels.

Devrions-nous réfréner les élans de la science, des inventeurs et des entrepreneurs dès lors que les inventions résultant de leur travail pourraient matériellement avoir des conséquences néfastes sur l'humanité ? Oui, absolument. Devrions-nous différer voire interdire les avancées scientifiques qui pourraient s'avérer majoritairement bénéfiques pour la société, mais qui nécessiteraient des règles garantissant une issue équilibrée ? Non, absolument pas. De toute façon, interdire de telles avancées ne serait probablement même pas possible.

La bonne réponse, bien sûr, résidera dans un équilibre sage et holistique entre ces deux pôles – un objectif réclamant de nous,

une fois encore, que nous devenions de meilleurs régisseurs de notre avenir.

Explorons plus en détails l'une et l'autre option.

Né à l'origine de considérations environnementales, le principe de précaution établit que ceux qui créent des innovations entrainant potentiellement des conséquences catastrophiques ne doivent pas être autorisés à continuer sans avoir prouvé que toute conséquence involontaire peut effectivement être maîtrisée. En d'autres termes, la charge de la preuve de l'innocuité d'une initiative est de la responsabilité de ceux qui souhaitent l'entreprendre.

Ce principe a été appliqué aux recherches sur l'ADN recombinant (la conférence Asilomar) et son interprétation a directement affecté le travail accompli sur le grand collisionneur de hadrons au CERN (Suisse), afin de répondre à l'inquiétude de voir ainsi accidentellement générer un trou noir. [154] [155] Comme dans le cas du grand collisionneur de hadrons, des précautions collectives doivent à l'évidence être prises quant aux développements technologiques, pour conjurer les risques d'innovations potentiellement désastreuses pour l'existence même de l'humanité. La Déclaration Wingspread (1999) résume ainsi le principe de précaution :

« *Lorsqu'une activité entraine des menaces pouvant aboutir à nuire à la santé humaine ou à l'environnement, des mesures de précaution doivent être prises même si les relations de cause à effet ne peuvent être scientifiquement établies. Dans un tel contexte, c'est au promoteur de cette activité, et non au public, d'assumer la charge de la preuve.* » [156]

La Déclaration de Rio a même présenté une clause encore plus forte : « Là où se manifestent des menaces de dommages sérieux ou irréversibles, l'absence de certitudes scientifiques avérées ne sera pas invoquée comme argument pour reporter des mesures appropriées, fussent-elles coûteuses. » [157]

J'estime que ces deux déclarations devraient toujours être prises en compte s'agissant d'Intelligence Artificielle (IA), d'intelligence des machines, de systèmes autonomes, d'édition du génome humain et de géo-ingénierie.

Par contraste, le principe de proaction avance que l'humanité a toujours inventé de la technologie, et ce faisant a toujours pris des risques. Par conséquent, nous ne devrions pas ajouter de restrictions excessives à ce que les gens peuvent ou ne peuvent pas inventer. En outre, ce principe stipule que nous devrions prendre en compte à la fois le coût de telles restrictions et celui des opportunités délaissées.

Le principe de proaction a été conçu par le philosophe transhumaniste Max More [158] et développé par la suite par le sociologue britannique Steve Fuller. [159] L'idée fondamentale du transhumanisme étant basée sur le concept de transcendance de notre biologie, autrement dit la possibilité de devenir au moins partiellement une machine, la proactivité désinhibée fait naturellement, sans surprise, partie du programme.

Un équilibre réfléchi et humaniste

Voilà comment je vois les choses : trop de précaution pourrait nous paralyser et du coup créer un cycle d'auto-censure qui s'amplifierait de lui-même. Proscrire la science de pointe, la technologie, l'ingénierie, les maths (STIM) et les inventions critiques aboutirait probablement à criminaliser ceux qui voudraient s'y engager. À l'évidence, il ne s'agit pas d'une bonne réponse au problème posé, ne serait-ce que parce que nous pourrions, par la science, faire des découvertes qu'il est de notre devoir humain d'accomplir, par exemple la possibilité de vaincre le cancer. Tout ce qui peut concourir à faire s'épanouir l'humanité nous oblige.

Néanmoins, une approche purement proactive ne serait pas souhaitable non plus, car la nature interdépendante, combinatoire et exponentielle des avancées technologiques dont nous faisons l'expérience aujourd'hui est tout simplement trop lourde

d'enjeux. La quasi-certitude que la technologie finisse, si nous nous conformons à la voie proactive énoncée aujourd'hui, par prendre le pas sur l'humanité, nous fait peur. De la même manière que trop de précaution finirait par étouffer le progrès et l'innovation, trop de proactivité libèrerait des forces puissantes et presque incontrôlables, qu'il est largement préférable de continuer à museler pour le moment.

Comme toujours, notre principal défi sera de trouver puis de maintenir un équilibre – entre la boîte de Pandore et la lampe d'Aladin.

Nous progressons actuellement sur un chemin exponentiel et combinatoire dans de nombreuses disciplines relevant des STIM. Bien des approches traditionnelles et prudentes s'avèreront inutiles, tout simplement parce que la vitesse du changement et la magnitude des conséquences involontaires potentielles se sont accrues de manière spectaculaire depuis que nous avons atteint le point de bascule de la courbe en 2016, en commençant à passer de 4 à 8 (et non de 4 à 5), accomplissant ainsi notre premier pas de géant. Les approches qui s'avéraient pertinentes lorsque nous passions de 0.01 à 0.02 ou même de 1 à 2 ne le seront probablement plus lorsque, de doublement en doublement, il sera question de passer successivement de 4 à 128 : les enjeux seront alors tellement plus grands, et les conséquences tellement plus difficiles à appréhender pour les esprits humain.

Imaginez les conséquences de s'être montrés trop proactifs en matière d'IA, de géo-ingénierie ou d'édition du génome humain. Imaginez ce que signifierait d'entrer dans une course aux armements avec des armes contrôlées par intelligence artificielle, capables de tuer sans aucune supervision humaine. Imaginez des états-voyous et des acteurs non-étatiques expérimentant le contrôle météo et provoquant des dommages atmosphériques irréversibles. Imaginez un labo de recherche dans tel ou tel pays pas si transparent, mettant au point une formule apte à programmer des super-humains.

Dans son livre *Notre invention ultime : l'intelligence artificielle et la fin de l'ère humaine*, l'auteur James Barrat résume bien ce dilemme :

« *Nous ne voulons pas qu'une IA puisse résoudre nos objectifs à court terme – s'il vous plaît épargnez-nous la famine – par des solutions nuisibles à long terme – en rôtissant chaque poulet sur terre – ou auxquelles nous aurions de bonnes raisons de nous opposer – en nous éliminant après notre prochain repas.* » [160]

L'enthousiasme technologique total et débridé est simplement trop lourd d'enjeux pour qu'on s'y engage inconsidérément sous prétexte que c'est inévitable, ou notre destin. À ce sujet, lire la déclaration originale du transhumaniste Max More en 2005 vaut la peine :

« *Le principe de précaution, quoique bien intentionné pour la plupart de ses partisans, rend les institutions décisionnaires naturellement enclines au statu quo, et reflète en réalité une vision réactionnaire et excessivement pessimiste du progrès technologique. Par contraste, le principe de proaction incite toutes les parties à prendre activement en compte toutes les conséquences d'une activité donnée – bonnes ou mauvaises –, tout en appliquant des mesures de précaution aux menaces réelles que nous affrontons.*

Bien que la précaution implique en elle-même d'utiliser la prévoyance afin d'anticiper et de se préparer à des menaces potentielles, l'argumentaire qui s'est agrégé autour d'elle menace le bien-être humain. Le principe de précaution a été sanctuarisé dans de nombreux traités et accords internationaux, rendant urgent de proposer un principe alternatif et de nouveaux critères. La nécessité du principe de proaction deviendra claire si nous comprenons les imperfections du principe de précaution. » [161]

D'une certaine manière, je ne peux pas être en désaccord avec la majeure partie des arguments de Max More, compte tenu notamment de mes expériences passées dans la Silicon Valley en tant qu'entrepreneur de l'Internet s'efforçant d'avancer à grands pas grâce à l'innovation. Mais, une fois encore, Max a écrit ceci en 2005 – soit près de dix ans avant que nous n'atteignions le point de bascule dans les technologies exponentielles. Ce qui, à l'époque, aurait pu sonner comme raisonnable quoique légèrement techno-centré, pourrait aujourd'hui conduire à de dangereuses décisions. Voulez-vous vraiment que votre avenir soit déterminé par des gouvernements opaques et irresponsables, par les dirigeants de la Silicon Valley, par des *venture-capitalists* avides ou par des organisations militaires comme l'Agence américaine pour les projets de recherche avancée de défense (DARPA) ?

Chapitre 9
Le bonheur au risque du hasard

Alors que la haute technologie sait simuler les sommets du plaisir hédoniste, comment nous y prendre pour protéger les formes plus approfondies du bonheur, celles qui impliquent empathie, compassion et pleine conscience ?

Bonheur : bonne fortune ou chance, dans la vie en général ou dans une circonstance particulière ; succès, prospérité.
Hasard : un événement heureux ; une coïncidence.
The Oxford English Dictionnary

Mais qu'est-ce que le bonheur ?

Tout au long de ce livre, j'avance que la recherche du bonheur humain maximum devrait être le projet prioritaire du progrès technologique. S'efforcer de parvenir au bonheur est une composante essentielle de l'état d'humain – qui nous réunit tous. Exactement de la même manière que nous avons une éthique (même si nous n'avons pas nécessairement une religion), la recherche du bonheur est un impératif universel qu'ont en partage tous les humains, quels que soient leur culture et leur système de croyance.

Nous sommes tous engagés dans une constante poursuite du bonheur tout au long de nos vies. Nos décisions quotidiennes sont mues par l'impulsion de créer des expériences agréables ou enrichissantes, que ce soit par la satisfaction d'un plaisir momentané, par l'attente d'une récompense ou d'un bénéfice à

long terme, ou par la recherche d'accomplissements plus élevés, qui dépassent les besoins élémentaires de nourriture ou d'abri.

Alors que nous faisons face à la convergence annoncée de l'homme et de la machine, je pense qu'il est essentiel que nous ne confondions pas la chance et le bonheur. La chance est accidentelle, alors que le bonheur repose sur l'établissement de bases judicieusement choisies.

Je pense fermement que nous devons absolument placer la question du bonheur et de l'épanouissement humains au centre de ce débat homme / machine. Quel serait le propos de la technologie, si ce n'était le développement de l'épanouissement humain ? Je pense quant à moi qu'il nous est en effet possible de façonner notre futur de manière telle que nous ne soyons pas simplement dépendants du hasard, mais que nous puissions créer les meilleures conditions possibles d'émergence du bonheur (nous y reviendrons plus en détail plus tard).

S'efforcer de définir le bonheur peut s'avérer une tâche trouble, car c'est un concept abstrait et subjectif. Voilà comment Wikipedia le définit :

« Le bonheur est un état durable de plénitude, de satisfaction ou de sérénité, état agréable équilibré de l'esprit et du corps, d'où la souffrance, le stress, l'inquiétude et le trouble sont absents. » [162]

Lorsque j'ai commencé à rechercher de quoi le bonheur était vraiment fait, je suis à plusieurs reprises tombé sur une distinction entre deux différents types de bonheur. Le premier, le bonheur hédoniste, est un état mental positif, en général temporaire, et souvent décrit avec les mots du plaisir. Il peut être fugace ou momentané, et nous conduit souvent à des habitudes. Par exemple, certains de nos plaisirs hédonistes peuvent nous conduire à des addictions comme la nourriture, l'alcool ou le tabac. Des réseaux sociaux comme Facebook ont souvent été

décrits comme des « pièges à plaisir », un mécanisme d'exhibition hédoniste générateur de plaisir.

Le second type de plaisir est connu sous le nom de plaisir eudémonique ou eudémonisme, une forme de bonheur et de contentement plus profond. Wikipedia décrit *eudaimonia* (du grec *eudaimonia*, « béatitude » ou bien-être) comme suit : « doctrine philosophique posant comme principe que le bonheur est le but de la vie humaine ». [163] « Épanouissement humain » est un autre synonyme d'eudaimonia et peut faire figure de terminologie mieux appropriée au propos de ce livre.

Quand j'étudiais la théologie luthérienne à Bonn au début des années 80 (ça vous surprend ?), j'étais profondément immergé dans les enseignements du philosophe grec antique Aristote. Et c'est à l'eudaimonia qu'il se référait il y a 2300 ans lorsqu'il écrivait que « le bonheur constitue le sens et le but de la vie, la finalité et le terme de l'existence humaine. » L'eudaimonia est bien sûr un concept central de la philosophie aristotélicienne, de même que les termes *arete* (vertu ou excellence) et *phronesis* (sagesse éthique ou empirique).

Eudaimonia, arete et *phronesis* – pardonnez-moi mon grec –, depuis lors, sont restés au nombre des objectifs constants de mon travail, et je pense qu'ils nous offrent des clés pour comprendre quel chemin l'humanité devrait emprunter alors qu'elle est embringuée – ou devrais-je dire blackboulée – dans le changement technologique exponentiel. En d'autres termes, nous sommes d'ores et déjà perdus dans un lieu où jamais encore l'humanité ne s'est rendue. Mais il existe en revanche des brins de sagesse ancienne (voir ci-dessus) auxquels nous pouvons nous raccrocher pour nous sortir du labyrinthe techno-centré dans lequel nous nous égarons de plus en plus.

Qu'est-ce qui nous rend heureux ?

Si l'épanouissement humain signifiait simplement une vie plus plaisante, un travail meilleur et plus efficace, davantage de profit et une croissance solidement entretenue par la technologie, alors

nous devrions à tout prix accepter que les machines et les algorithmes nous aident à atteindre ce but. Et, pour un moment seulement, alors que nous nous abandonnerions à l'inévitable spirale de l'hyper-efficience et de l'opulence que va certainement générer le capitalisme dévorant, il se pourrait en effet que cela fonctionne correctement.

PIB, PNB, IPV : d'honnêtes critères de bonheur ?

Gardons-nous de définir trop étroitement le terme « épanouir », surtout dans un sens trop économique ou financier, faute de quoi nous finirions par aboutir à des définitions dépassées comme PIB (produit intérieur brut) ou PNB (produit national brut), alors que nous ferions mieux de nous référer à des indices plus inclusifs comme le Bonheur national brut (BNB).

Le BNB est un terme initialement inventé dans les années 70 au Bhoutan – un pays que j'ai eu la chance de visiter juste avant que je n'achève ce livre. Il implique de mettre en œuvre, pour mesurer l'état d'un pays, une approche beaucoup plus large, holistique et écosystémique. Appliqué à la mesure du bonheur politique, le BNB se base sur les valeurs bouddhistes traditionnelles plutôt que sur les valeurs occidentales habituelles auxquelles le PIB ou le PNB font généralement référence – c'est-à-dire des indicateurs comme la croissance économique, l'investissement productif, le retour sur investissement ou l'emploi. Les quatre piliers de la philosophie du BNB reflètent de manière spectaculairement différente ce qui la sous-tend : développement durable, préservation et promotion des valeurs culturelles, conservation de l'environnement naturel et bonne gouvernance. [164] De la même manière, lorsqu'il est question d'évaluer nos décisions futures quant à la relation entre la technologie et l'humanité, je trouve que la notion de BNB fournit en parallèle une approche très intéressante, parce qu'elle place résolument le bonheur au centre de l'évaluation du progrès et des valeurs. Les facteurs économiques ne devraient pas faire de l'ombre aux questions liées au bonheur – un critère pourtant

évident – et l'efficacité ne devrait jamais être tenue pour plus importante que l'humanité (l'une de mes dix règles clés à la fin de ce livre).

Une autre manière de mesurer le succès des nations réside dans l'Indicateur de progrès véritable (IPV), qui évalue 26 variables liées aux progrès économiques, sociaux et environnementaux. [165] L'IPV est précieux car il prend en compte les externalités : les conséquences deviennent partie prenante de l'équation, ce qui est exactement ce que je propose quant au traitement des conséquences involontaires de la technologie. Ainsi, les indicateurs économiques de l'IPV incluent les inégalités et le coût du non-emploi ; de même, les indicateurs environnementaux devraient inclure le coût de la pollution, du changement climatique et des ressources énergétiques non-renouvelables ; tandis que les indicateurs sociaux devraient prendre en compte la valeur du travail à la maison, de l'enseignement supérieur et du volontariat.

Que se passerait-il si nous utilisions une combinaison de l'IPV et du BNB pour mettre en œuvre une mesure du progrès plus ethno-centrée ? C'est une question importante, car si nous continuons à mesurer des valeurs vaines, alors il est également plus que probable que nous continuions à faire des choses vaines. Ce serait une erreur cardinale à cette époque de progrès technologique exponentiel. Premièrement, les erreurs qui en résulteraient auraient des conséquences inattendues infiniment plus grandes, et deuxièmement agir de la sorte aboutirait une fois encore à conférer trop de puissance à la technologie et trop peu aux humains.

Si tout ce que nous mesurons sont les données brutes issues de telle ou telle action spécifique, comme le nombre de ventes réalisées par tel(le) employé(e), alors nos conclusions seront sérieusement faussées. Car en pratique, rien dans les facteurs humains, singuliers par définition, n'est si simple à mesurer – comme par exemple le nombre de relations établies avec des clients clés par cette personne, ou si elle ressent de la compassion

dans les sujets qu'elle traite ou les défis qu'elle relève. Plus nous prétendons que nos données (ainsi que l'intelligence artificielle qui les exploite) sont complètes au sens vraiment humain du terme et plus les conclusions du système seront erronées. Nous tendons à ignorer les androrithmes et à leur préférer les algorithmes parce que nous aimons les raccourcis et les simplifications.

Pouvoir mesurer à quel point la numérisation et l'automatisation contribuent à renforcer l'efficacité d'une entreprise ou d'un pays pourrait, sur le plan économique, enjoliver très sensiblement le tableau. Mais en revanche, mesurer le degré de bonheur de ses employés ou de ses citoyens au terme de ce même processus d'automatisation et de robotisation pourrait se traduire par une perspective sociale très différente.

En 1968, le sénateur américain Robert Kennedy stigmatisait déjà le PIB comme un étalon de mesure inapproprié, capable de « tout mesurer excepté ce qui rend la vie digne d'être vécue ». [166] À mes yeux, cela met en évidence un point critique : les algorithmes sont capables de mesurer ou même de stimuler n'importe quoi, excepté ce qui importe vraiment aux êtres humains. Cela étant dit, je ne cherche pas pour autant à déprécier ce que les algorithmes et la technologie en général sont capables de faire pour nous. Je pense simplement qu'il est important de maintenir la technologie à sa place, c'est-à-dire de l'impliquer quand c'est nécessaire, et de la tenir à distance lorsque c'est préjudiciable.

Échouer à définir ce que signifie l'épanouissement humain ne fera que renforcer les machines. Mon inquiétude, c'est que nous ne prenions conscience que tardivement d'avoir trop longtemps attendu pour définir correctement l'épanouissement humain. Nous avons fait notre affaire des plaisirs hédonistes parce que la plupart du temps, ils peuvent être manufacturés, organisés ou fournis par la technologie. Les réseaux sociaux en offrent un bel exemple : il nous est aisé de faire l'expérience d'être « likés » par les autres –

ce qui est, avouons-le, une forme d'hédonisme... un piège à plaisir numérique. Mais en revanche nous ne sommes probablement pas en mesure de ressentir le bonheur d'un contact humain personnel et approfondi (au sens où le définit le PERMA de Martin Seligman, un terme clé que j'exposerai ci-après). [167]

Peut-être ne comprendrons-nous seulement et véritablement la différence que lorsque chacun des traits qui font de nous des humains auront été soit remplacés soit rendus inutiles par une technologie niveleuse et hyper-efficiente, lorsque nous aurons oublié ou perdu le talent de réaliser quoi que ce soit par nous-mêmes. Ça n'est certes pas ce que j'espère, mais face à ces changements technologiques exponentiels, il me semble clair qu'il nous faudrait commencer à définir l'épanouissement comme le fait de se développer de manière saine. Autrement dit développer une vision plus holistique de notre avenir, une vision capable de dépasser les approches du bonheur fondamentalement mécanistes, réductionnistes et souvent hédonistes privilégiées par de si nombreux technologues.

Le psychologue Martin Seligman estime que le véritable bonheur ne procède pas uniquement de plaisirs externes et momentanés. Il a construit le modèle PERMA afin de résumer les résultats les plus importants de sa recherche en psychologie positive. [168] En l'occurrence, les humains semblent être plus heureux lorsqu'ils disposent de :

- Plaisir (nourriture savoureuse, bains chauds)
- Engagement (immersion dans une activité appréciée, même si elle est exigeante)
- Relations humaines (les liens sociaux se sont révélés des indicateurs de bonheur extrêmement fiables)
- Sens (en anglais *meaning,* c'est-à-dire le sentiment d'être partie prenante d'une quête ou de quelque chose de plus grand que soi)
- Accomplissement (avoir atteint des objectifs tangibles)

De fait, la technologie pourrait présenter une valeur significative comme support du Plaisir et de l'Accomplissement, et peut-être contribuer à l'Engagement. Par contraste, je ne crois pas que la technologie pourrait être d'une aide concrète dans la promotion des Relations humaines, ou pour construire du Sens. En fait, cela pourrait même être exactement le contraire, dans la mesure où la technologie peut s'avérer corrosive pour les relations humaines, par exemple lorsque nous persistons à nous cramponner à notre mobile durant un diner familial.

La technologie peut aussi brouiller les questions de sens (du fait d'une surcharge de données et d'une automatisation sans précaution), nous conduire de façon excessive à créer encore plus de bulles de filtrage (en ne nous nourrissant que de contenus présumés nous plaire) et ouvrir la porte à bien des manipulations médiatiques. Bien sûr, la technologie – en tant qu'outil et non en tant qu'objectif – est et restera universellement utile, mais seulement une fois que nous aurons davantage progressé sur l'échelle exponentielle – faute de quoi son utilisation excessive et la dépendance qu'elle crée pourraient bien nous être préjudiciables.

Je me demande souvent ce qui se produira une fois que les technologies exponentielles se seront véritablement enclenchées. Nos vies deviendront-elles plus hédonistes ou bien plus eudémonistes – davantage stimulées par l'impulsion du moment ou par des enjeux de sens plus profonds ? Tomberons-nous en pamoison pour des plaisirs toujours plus superficiels, des expériences dont les machines seront les moteurs et les médiateurs, ou nous efforcerons-nous d'atteindre à une forme de bonheur essentiellement humaine ?

La compassion, une vertu en prise directe avec le bonheur
Un facteur humain important à prendre en considération dans ce contexte est la compassion. Dans son livre de 2015 *Le Dalaï-lama lance un appel au monde : l'éthique compte davantage que la*

religion, le Dalaï-lama s'exprime sur la relation qui unit le bonheur et la compassion :

« *Si nous voulons être heureux nous-mêmes, nous devrions pratiquer la compassion, et si nous voulons que les autres soient heureux, alors nous devrions aussi pratiquer la compassion.* » [169]

La compassion – qu'on peut définir comme « le souci bienveillant envers les souffrances ou les malheurs d'autrui » – est l'une des choses les plus difficiles à saisir, et certainement l'une des plus difficiles à mettre en œuvre. La compassion est beaucoup plus ardue que l'intelligence ou l'agilité intellectuelle.

Pouvez-vous vous représenter un ordinateur, une application, un robot ou un logiciel doué de compassion ? Une machine qui ressent ce que vous ressentez, qui vibre à vos émotions et qui souffre quand vous souffrez ? Bien sûr, on peut prévoir la venue de machines capables de comprendre les émotions ou même de déchiffrer la compassion sur les visages humains et les attitudes corporelles. On peut aussi imaginer des machines en mesure de simuler les émotions humaines, simplement en nous copiant ou en apprenant de nos comportements, et dès lors sembler réellement ressentir des choses.

Néanmoins, la différence fondamentale est que les machines n'auront jamais la conscience d'être. Il ne leur pas possible d'être compatissantes, elles peuvent seulement espérer être en mesure de le simuler correctement. Voilà assurément une distinction critique qu'il nous faudra examiner dans tous ses détails face aux tsunamis technologiques qui s'apprêtent à déferler pour nous engloutir. Si nous persistions à confondre une simulation bien exécutée avec un véritable état d'être, à prendre une version algorithmique de la sentience pour une conscience véritable, alors nous ferions face à de sérieux problèmes. Cette confusion est également le défaut central du transhumanisme.

Selon moi, les machines vont devenir extrêmement performantes, rapides et bon marché pour simuler ou dupliquer

les traits humains, mais en revanche elles ne seront jamais vraiment humaines. Le véritable défi, pour nous, va être de résister à la tentation d'accepter ces simulations comme « satisfaisantes » et de leur permettre de remplacer les interactions fondamentalement humaines. Délaisser l'expérience eudémoniste véritablement humaine au profit des plaisirs hédonistes rapidement obtenus et partout disponibles procurés par les machines serait une folie pleine de danger.

Dans *Notre ultime invention : l'intelligence artificielle et la fin de l'ère humaine*, James Barrat écrit :

« *Un puissant système d'intelligence artificielle chargé d'assurer votre sécurité pourrait aisément aboutir à la décision de vous enfermer chez vous. Si vous réclamiez le bonheur, il pourrait vous rendre physiquement dépendant de lui, en stimulant sans cesse les centres de plaisir de votre cerveau. Si vous ne fournissiez pas à l'IA une très vaste bibliothèque de vos comportements préférés, et des moyens en béton pour vous assurer qu'elle sache déduire sans erreur quel comportement vous attendez d'elle, alors vous pourriez vous retrouver coincé avec ce qui se présente, agréable ou pas. Et dans la mesure où ce serait un système hautement complexe, vous pourriez ne jamais le comprendre suffisamment bien pour vous assurer que vous avez bien fait ce qu'il fallait.* » [170]

Le bonheur contre l'argent : expériences contre possessions

Les gens soulignent souvent que le bonheur basé sur les possessions matérielles ou la situation financière est somme toute d'un intérêt limité. Des recherches ont montré que dans les pays prétendument développés, le niveau général de bonheur augmente lorsque les gens gagnent davantage d'argent, mais seulement jusqu'à un certain point : différentes études suggèrent en effet que gagner au-delà de 50.000 / 75.000 US$ par an ne contribue pas à ajouter beaucoup de bonheur supplémentaire à la vie des gens. La corrélation entre le revenu et le bien-être, alors, décroît. [171]

Le bonheur ne peut pas s'acquérir ou s'acheter, il devrait par conséquent être impossible d'en emplir une application, un robot ou toute autre machine. Le témoignage de nos sens suggère que l'expérience vécue a un impact beaucoup plus durable que nos possessions sur notre niveau général de bonheur. [172] Les expériences vécues sont personnelles, contextuelles, opportunes et incarnées. Elles sont fondées sur ces qualités uniques qui nous rendent humains – nos androrithmes.

Ainsi que l'a noté le Dr. Janxin Leu, directeur des innovations produits chez HopeLab dans le blog du *Huffington Post* d'avril 2015 :

« *Des chercheurs de l'Université de Virginie, de l'Université de Colombie Britannique et de l'Université d'Harvard ont publié en 2011 une étude, après avoir examiné nombre de publications académiques en réponse à une apparente contradiction : lorsqu'on leur a demandé de faire le point sur leur vie, les personnes possédant plus d'argent ont indiqué se sentir franchement plus satisfaites de leur sort. Mais lorsqu'on leur a demandé dans quelle mesure ils étaient heureux sur le moment, les personnes ayant de l'argent étaient à peine différentes que celles qui en possédaient moins.* » [173]

Le bonheur humain est – ou devrait être – le but premier de la technologie

La technologie, un mot dérivé du grec *techne* (méthode, outil, compétence ou savoir-faire) et *logia* (connaissance, d'origine divine), a toujours été créée par les humains pour améliorer leur bien-être, mais aujourd'hui il semble probable que bientôt la technologie va être employée à améliorer les humains eux-mêmes.

Jusqu'à présent, nous étions habitués à créer de la technologie pour améliorer nos conditions d'existence de manière telle qu'il en résulte spontanément un bonheur plus probable et plus

prévalent. Par exemple Skype, GoogleTalk et toutes les applications de messagerie similaires nous permettent de nous connecter à quasiment n'importe qui, tout le temps et partout, et tout cela gratuitement. Aujourd'hui néanmoins, compte tenu du progrès technologique exponentiel et combinatoire, la technologie devient de plus en plus un but en soi. Et nous nous retrouvons à tenter d'obtenir davantage de « likes » sur Facebook, ou sommés de devoir constamment réagir à des notifications et des instructions, simplement parce que le système requiert notre attention.

Qu'en sera-t-il si l'outil devient le sens – ainsi que cela s'est déjà produit avec Facebook ? Qu'en sera-t-il si ces outils deviennent si irrésistibles et si commodes que nous les laisserons définir leurs propres objectifs ? Quand donc ces téléphones intelligents, écrans intelligents, montres intelligentes et lunettes de réalité virtuelle (VR) deviendront-ils eux-mêmes cognitifs, dépassant ainsi leur simple fonction d'outils ? Et qu'arrivera-t-il si nos cerveaux externes deviennent capables de se connecter directement à notre propre néocortex ?

La technologie n'a pas d'éthique – et vit dans une nébuleuse de nihilisme, un espace sans croyances

Même si la plupart d'entre nous sommes fans de technologie, il nous faut désormais admettre que celle-ci n'a pas la moindre considération (pour autant qu'elle en ait jamais eue) pour nos valeurs, nos croyances et notre éthique. Elle ne prendra en compte nos valeurs que comme de simples données permettant de comprendre notre comportement.

À l'avenir, les robots et assistants numériques intelligents (ANI) vont de plus en plus siphonner, lire et analyser des dizaines de millions de flux de données à mon sujet, et décortiquer chacune des miettes numériques que je vais laisser derrière moi. Néanmoins, quelle que soit la quantité de « données de Gerd » qu'ils seront en mesure de rassembler et d'analyser, ce n'est pas pour autant que logiciels et machines seront jamais à même de

comprendre réellement mes valeurs et mon éthique, tout simplement parce qu'ils seront incapables d'être humain de la même manière que je le suis. Il ne s'agira jamais que d'approximations, de simulations et de simplifications. Utiles, certes ; mais réelles, certainement pas.

Laissez-moi vous donner quelques exemples de défis éthiques que soulèvent les avancées technologiques.

Bien des savants atomistes n'ont pas envisagé la création de la bombe atomique lorsqu'ils ont commencé à travailler sur les défis scientifiques et mathématiques qu'elle sous-tendait. Einstein lui-même se considérait comme un pacifiste, tout en encourageant le gouvernement américain à construire la bombe avant qu'Hitler ne le fasse. Et comme que nous l'avons vu précédemment, J. Robert Oppenheimer, en général considéré comme le père de la bombe atomique, a regretté ses actions après Hiroshima et Nagasaki. [174] De fait, on peut donc affirmer que l'éthique du complexe militaire et politique au sein duquel ils évoluaient ont effectivement fait d'eux des contributeurs à la création d'armes de destruction massive.

L'Internet des objets (IdO) constitue un autre exemple très parlant : il est certain que la collecte, la connexion et la combinaison de vastes quantités de données issues de milliards d'objets connectés s'avèrera un grand bénéfice. Il se pourrait même que cela apporte des solutions potentielles à de nombreux défis globaux tels que le changement climatique et le suivi environnemental.

L'idée générale est qu'une fois tous nos objets devenus intelligents et connectés, nous serons en mesure de rendre de nombreux processus plus efficaces, de réduire les coûts et d'atteindre des résultats substantiels dans la protection de l'environnement. Mais bien qu'il s'agisse là d'idées intelligentes, on s'aperçoit aussi que les schémas actuels de mise en œuvre de l'IdO sont presque complètement dépourvus de considérations humaines, d'androrithmes et de préoccupations éthiques. Aucune visibilité sur la manière dont la confidentialité sera préservée au

sein de ce cerveau-global-dans-le-ciel, sur comment une surveillance totale pourra être évitée et sur qui sera tenu pour responsable de toutes ces nouvelles données. Aujourd'hui, on se focalise tout particulièrement sur les merveilles de l'efficacité et de l'hyper-connectivité, mais les conséquences involontaires et les externalités négatives de la technologie ne semblent être le souci de personne.

Dans le domaine de la santé, Peter Diamandis, expert dans la Silicon Valley de l'abondance exponentielle (et dont en général j'apprécie grandement le travail), évoque en termes positifs Human Longevity Inc., la nouvelle start-up qu'il a créée avec le pionnier de la génétique Craig Venter, ainsi que la manière dont elle va nous permettre de vivre plus longtemps – voire pour toujours. [175] Ce faisant, il semble pourtant largement ignorer la majeure partie des questions éthiques ou morales qui entourent le débat autour du vieillissement, de la longévité et de la mort.

Qui va pouvoir s'offrir ces traitements ? Est-ce que seuls les riches pourront vivre cent ans et plus ? Que signifierait devenir immortels ? La mort n'est-elle vraiment qu'une maladie, ainsi que l'affirme Diamandis, ou bien est-elle partie prenante, et à ce titre impossible à modifier, du fait d'être humain ? Les questions abondent, mais, à bien des égards comme dans les premiers temps de la recherche sur les armes nucléaires, nombre des technologues de la Silicon Valley semblent ne se soucier que d'avancer le plus vite possible, sans même un minimum de réflexion sur les problèmes que leurs innovations pourraient finir par provoquer.

« La mort est une grande tragédie... une perte profonde...
Je ne l'accepte pas... Je pense que les gens s'abusent eux-
mêmes lorsqu'ils affirment que mourir leur convient. »
Ray Kurzweil [176]

Le message-clé, ici, c'est que la technologie, comme l'argent, n'est ni bonne ni mauvaise. Elle existe simplement en tant que

moyen. Dans les années 1950, Octavio Paz, le grand poète mexicain, l'a bien résumé :

« Le nihilisme de la technologie réside non seulement dans le fait que c'est l'expression la plus parfaite de la volonté de puissance, mais également dans le fait qu'elle manque de sens. « Pourquoi ? » et « À quelle fin ? » sont des questions que la technologie ne se pose pas. » [177]

Je me demande d'ailleurs si le nihilisme des technologies exponentielles sera lui-même exponentiel ? Un millier de fois aussi nihiliste, et peut-être même aussi narcissique ? Deviendrons-nous finalement une espèce complètement dépourvue de conscience, de mystère, de spiritualité et d'âme simplement parce qu'il n'y aura plus de place pour nos androrithmes dans cet âge des machines annoncé ?

Deux choses me semblent réclamer un examen critique dans un tel contexte :

1. Une technologie vraiment désirable devrait toujours et avant tout être conçue dans la perspective de l'accroissement du bonheur humain et ne pas simplement résulter de la recherche de croissance et de profit, faute de quoi cette quête de croissance et de profit pourrait bien finir, d'ici peu, par nous transformer en machines nous-mêmes. Ce nouveau paradigme sera un changement majeur pour chaque entreprise et chaque organisation.

2. Les technologies porteuses de conséquences catastrophiques – comme la géo-ingénierie ou l'intelligence artificielle globale – devraient être encadrées et supervisées par ceux qui ont fait la preuve de leur sagesse pratique – ce que les anciens Grecs appelaient *phronesis*. La gérance de ces technologies ne devrait être abandonnée ni aux développeurs, ni aux grandes entreprises,

ni aux bureaucrates militaires, ni aux capital-risqueurs ni aux plates-formes Internet dominantes.

À quoi tous ces progrès technologiques se ramèneront-ils si nous ne nous épanouissons pas en tant qu'espèce, si nous ne sommes pas capables de réaliser quelque chose qui nous élève véritablement vers un nouvel état de bonheur ?

Confrontés à l'évaluation de la dernière vague de progrès en science, technologie, ingénierie et maths (STIM), nous devrions par conséquent toujours nous demander si telle ou telle innovation particulière est réellement en mesure d'améliorer le bien-être de la plupart de ceux qui sont impliqués dans sa réalisation.

Est-ce que des technologies plus rapides, moins chères et plus pratiques, davantage d'abondance, de consommation facilitée, de pouvoirs surhumains ou de profits économiques vont vraiment nous rendre heureux ? Des applications, robots et ANIs améliorés, de la réalité augmentée et de la réalité virtuelle plus puissantes, ou encore un accès instantané à un cerveau global via une nouvelle interface cerveau-ordinateur (ICO) signifieront-ils vraiment que nous, en tant qu'espèce comme en tant qu'individus, allons réellement nous épanouir ? Ou bien que ce seront d'abord ceux qui créeront, posséderont et proposeront ces outils et plates-formes qui rafleront les récompenses ?

Le bien-être humain devrait être l'objectif clé

Lorsqu'on en vient à discuter du futur de la technologie, il me semble que la notion de bien-être – le fait d'être dans un état de confort, de santé et de bonheur – est en train de devenir le mot-clé. Le bien-être implique une approche plus holistique, qui dépasse largement le fait de mesurer nos fonctions corporelles, notre puissance de calcul mental ou le nombre de synapses dans notre cerveau. Il exprime l'incarnation, le contexte, l'opportunité, la connectivité, les émotions, la spiritualité et un millier d'autres choses qu'il nous reste encore à expliquer ou même à comprendre. Le bien-être n'est pas algorithmique – il est

androrithmique, et fondé sur des notions complexes comme la confiance, la compassion, l'émotion et l'intuition.

La technologie est souvent très douée pour créer ce qu'on appelle des bons moments, comme le fait de pouvoir appeler un être aimé n'importe où et n'importe quand. Mais le bien-être, me semble-t-il, est quelque chose qui dépasse de beaucoup la simple facilitation technologique. Pour m'être moi-même immergé dans l'entreprenariat d'Internet et avoir tâté des start-ups liées à la musique numérique durant presque dix ans, je n'ai pris conscience qu'après la soudaine disparition de ma société .com, en 2002, en quoi un bien-être plus holistique est le produit de relations humaines, de sens, de projets et de contexte.

Le bonheur ne peut pas être automatisé !

La technologie peut-elle fabriquer du bonheur ?
Les technologies exponentielles telles que l'IA vont sans aucun doute tenter de créer les conditions favorables à l'accroissement du bonheur humain, ou même du bien-être. Et il ne fait aucun doute que d'aucuns chercheront activement à le fabriquer pour nous – ou, à tout le moins, à en produire une approximation numérique.

Nous entendons de plus en plus s'exprimer des arguments selon lesquels le bonheur pourrait être programmé, organisé ou orchestré par des technologies super intelligentes. L'argument-clé de ces penseurs techno-progressistes est que l'état de bonheur ne serait rien d'autre que le produit de la mise en œuvre des bons neurones, au bon moment et dans le bon ordre. Leur raisonnement repose que le fait que tout ceci n'est rien de plus que de la biologie, de la chimie et de la physique, autant de facteurs qui peuvent être compris, déchiffrés et copiés entièrement par des ordinateurs.

« Il faut s'attendre à une société de plus en plus dépendante des machines, tout en étant de moins en moins capable de les

fabriquer ou même de les utiliser efficacement. » Douglas Rushkoff : Programmer ou être programmé : dix commandements pour un âge numérique. [178]

Peut-être nous serait-il possible de créer un genre de machine à bonheur qui nous manipulerait, nous contrôlerait et nous programmerait, nous et notre environnement. Peut-être existe-t-il une app pour cela – ou peut-être nous en faudrait-il une ! Jetez donc un œil à www.happify.com et vous verrez comment l'idée d'organiser le bonheur a d'ores et déjà été marketée – un outil logiciel qui vous enseigne le bonheur ! On ne peut qu'imaginer de quelle manière cela tournera vers 2025 – une app qui se connectera directement à votre cerveau via une ICO ou un implant minuscule pour s'assurer que nous serons heureux en continu et – point décisif – que nous consommerons bien du bonheur en permanence !

Il me semble parfois que les entrepreneurs qui poursuivent de pareils exploits s'attendent à ce que les émotions humaines, les valeurs et les croyances fassent l'objet de progrès encore plus exponentiels via les STIM. Leurs raisons : une fois que nous serons suffisamment engagés dans cette voie, absolument tout pourra faire l'objet d'une programmation, y compris (vous l'aviez deviné) nous-mêmes. Alors, nous pourrons enfin nous débarrasser de nos contraintes biologiques et devenir des êtres vraiment universels – j'ai hâte !

Robots d'humeur et plaisirs technologiques

La technologie est déjà capable de créer, de programmer ou de manipuler des moments qui nous sont agréables (autrement dit un bonheur hédoniste) et ce *business* va certainement prospérer dans un proche avenir. C'est déjà le cas sur le fil d'actualité de Facebook, qui ne vous délivre que des éléments qui vous donnent le sentiment d'être épanoui et aimé. C'est en train de s'amorcer dans le e-commerce, avec des sites de vente en ligne qui emploient des hordes de neuro-scientifiques pour mettre au point

des réglages très fins offrant de nouveaux mécanismes numériques de satisfaction instantanée. Et c'est d'ores et déjà arrivé dans le secteur de la santé avec les nootropes (des drogues soi-disant intelligentes et des amplificateurs cognitifs) qui sont censés vous donner un coup de fouet sous la forme de capacités super-mentales.

Bientôt, le mouvement se poursuivra via des manipulations très élaborées de nos sens par l'entremise des conversations contrôlées de la voix et du geste (et non dactylographiées) que nous aurons avec nos assistants numériques omniprésents. Cela se produira également via des appareils de RA / RV comme Oculus Rift de Facebook, et au-delà de nouveaux types d'interface homme-ordinateur et d'implants neuronaux. Les ordinateurs vont se mettre à vouloir nous rendre heureux. À vouloir devenir nos amis. Et ils voudront qu'on les aime aussi. Sauf que cela n'aboutira qu'à aller plus mal (ou mieux, selon votre propre point de vue).

Un article d'Adam Piore de septembre 2015 dans le journal *Nautilus* met en lumière de quelle façon ces « bots d'humeur » pourraient fonctionner :

« *James J. Hughes, un sociologue, auteur et prospectiviste au Trinity College d'Hartford, envisage le jour pas si lointain où nous aurons démêlé les déterminants génétiques de neurotransmetteurs clés comme la sérotonine, la dopamine et l'ocytocine, et où nous serons en mesure de manipuler les gènes du bonheur – et si ce n'est pas le 5-HTTLPR lié au transport de la sérotonine, il s'agira de quelque chose de similaire –, avec un niveau de précision nanotechnologique combinant à la fois la robotique et la pharmacologie traditionnelle. Une fois ces « bots d'humeur » ingérés, il se déplaceront directement dans certaines zones spécifiques du cerveau et titilleront nos gènes en actionnant « manuellement » à la hausse ou à la baisse notre récepteur de* »

bonheur, influençant ainsi la manière dont nous ressentons les circonstances qui nous environnent.

« À mesure que les nanotechnologies deviendront de plus en plus précises, nous serons à même d'influencer les humeurs du commun d'entre nous de façon toujours plus subtile », explique Hughes, qui est par ailleurs directeur exécutif de l'Institut pour l'éthique et les technologies émergentes et auteur du livre de 2004 Citoyen cyborg : pourquoi les sociétés démocratiques doivent réagir à l'humain du futur revu et corrigé. [179]

J'ajouterais que la technologie numérique est déjà devenue assez bonne dans la fourniture de plaisirs hédonistes à ses utilisateurs. Pensez simplement aux apps, assistants personnels numériques et aux médias sociaux en général, dont le propos fondamental – se connecter aux autres – se ramène souvent à la quête d'une montée rapide de dopamine, issue des réponses de parfaits inconnus. D'une certaine manière, les réseaux sociaux sont déjà devenus des « générateurs de bonheur hédoniste » assez étonnants.

Mais bien sûr, la question clé reste de savoir ce que les avancées technologiques potentielles pourraient faire pour nourrir ou simplement encourager l'eudémonisme (c'est-à-dire le bonheur comme raison d'être de l'existence, comme projet de la vie humaine), soutenir notre élan vers un objectif noble, ou même pour découvrir le sens de la vie. Une mission qui me paraît impossible, tout simplement parce que la technologie ne s'interroge ni ne se soucie d'aucun objectif. Pourquoi d'ailleurs le devrait-elle ?

Reste par ailleurs la question de savoir si un tel bonheur eudémoniste peut être planifié, orchestré ou anticipé, numérique ou pas. Ce concept, le psychologue autrichien Viktor Frankl, fondateur de la logo-thérapie, l'a exploré dans son livre de 1946 *L'Homme dans sa quête de sens* :

« Le bonheur ne peut être poursuivi ; il doit être une résultante, et cela ne survient qu'en tant qu'effet indirect et involontaire d'un

investissement personnel dans une cause plus grande que soi, ou que produit dérivé de l'abandon de soi à autrui. Plus un homme s'efforce de démontrer sa puissance sexuelle, ou une femme sa capacité à éprouver l'orgasme, et moins ils seront en mesure de réussir. Le plaisir n'est, et doit le rester, qu'un effet indirect ou un produit dérivé ; il sera détruit ou gâché en proportion de la volonté d'en avoir fait un but en soi. » [180]

L'idée selon laquelle les plaisirs hédonistes sont les produits dérivés d'un plus grand épanouissement (l'eudémonisme) fait vraiment sens à mes yeux. D'où mon argument selon lequel nous devrions adopter la technologie – et en tirer plaisir –, mais ne pas devenir la technologie elle-même, car cela rendrait impossible l'expérience d'un véritable eudémonisme.

Faites attention à ce que vous souhaitez

Le débat autour du fait de savoir si nous devrions allonger spectaculairement la longévité humaine – et viser à mettre fin à la mort – est une belle illustration de la difficulté à déterminer si un progrès technologique en particulier pourrait se concrétiser par un plus grand épanouissement humain. Ce débat met également en relief l'un des plus grands dilemmes qu'il va peut-être nous falloir affronter bientôt : une chose donnée devrait-elle être faite sous prétexte qu'elle *pourrait* être faite ? Ou alors devrions-nous prendre en considération, au contraire, le fait de ne pas faire certaines choses, au motif qu'elles pourraient avoir des effets indirects négatifs sur l'épanouissement humain ?

Des technologies représentant des percées dans l'édition des gènes, comme CRISPR-Cas9, pourraient aboutir à mettre fin au cancer ou à la maladie d'Alzheimer, et en ce sens contribueraient clairement à notre bien-être collectif. Toutefois, une autre application possible de ce tour de magie scientifique serait aussi d'engendrer des bébés programmables, une longévité spectaculairement accrue ou même la fin de la mort pour l'humanité – mais sans doute uniquement pour la petite

proportion d'hommes possédant le niveau de ressources requises à cette fin ! Comment s'assurer que les avancées seront bien à 95% profitables à l'humanité, et ne seront pas cause de désordres sociaux, de terrorisme ou d'inégalités exponentielles ?

Dans la Silicon Valley, épicentre de la convergence humains-technologies, Peter Diamandis aime à dire que « la question est de savoir ce que les gens seront prêt à dépenser pour un bonus de 20, 30 ou 40 années supplémentaires de vie en bonne santé, ce qui est une immense opportunité. » [181] Ce commentaire met en exergue la philosophie de la Silicon Valley : tout y est question d'opportunités de *business*, même le bonheur humain.

Considérez par exemple l'essor de ce que l'auteur scientifique Amy Maxman a appelé, dans un article du magazine *Wired* de Juillet 2015, « The Genesis Engine » (littéralement « Le moteur de la genèse »), autrement dit le concept d'édition de l'ADN humain. [182] La première étape sera l'analyse de l'ADN de milliards d'individus afin d'identifier quels sont les gènes responsables de différentes affections et maladies. Il faudra, pour ce faire, une formidable puissance informatique ainsi que le soutien d'un large public. Deuxièmement, une fois qu'un gène aura été identifié comme le responsable de quelque chose d'aussi nuisible que le cancer par exemple (en supposant que cela soit aussi simple…), l'étape suivante consistera à trouver des manières de neutraliser ou de supprimer ce gène afin que la maladie ne puisse plus se développer. La troisième, dès lors, serait fondamentalement de programmer les gens exactement comme nous programmons des logiciels ou des applications aujourd'hui – en supprimant tous les mauvais *bugs* et en les enrichissant d'excellentes caractéristiques.

Cela vous apparaît-il comme un avenir désirable ? Bien des gens répondraient par un grand « Oui ! » à cette question, parce que cela paraitrait presque trop beau pour être vrai. Et même si notre esprit commencerait à hésiter devant ce que de tels exploits signifieraient dans un contexte élargi : qui pourrait s'offrir de tels traitements ? Qui règlementerait leur application ? Qui ouvrirait

tout grand les portes aux superhumains, mais les refermerait au nez des vieux humains naturels ? La possibilité de programmer nos gènes nous conduirait-elle, par inadvertance, sur le chemin de notre transformation progressive en machines ?

D'un côté, l'édition du génome humain à des fins de guérison des maladies se traduirait définitivement par un accroissement de notre bien-être et de notre bonheur ; mais à l'inverse, les mêmes avancées pourraient facilement entrainer guerres civiles et terrorisme. Imaginez simplement que seuls les super-riches puissent éviter les maladies fatales et vivre jusqu'à 150 ans, tandis que tous les autres se faneraient vers 90 ans ou même plus tôt – ou ne seraient même plus en mesure de s'offrir les soins médicaux de base. S'il y a jamais eu des raisons de recourir à l'agitation civile nourrie de pur désespoir, ne cherchez plus : les voilà. Comment pourrions-nous seulement concevoir d'offrir de telles possibilités sans évaluer au préalable leur impact humiliant, en termes éthiques et sociétaux ? Pourquoi faudrait-il que nous dépensions des milliers de milliards d'euros dans les STIM, mais que nous investissions tellement peu dans ce que j'appelle les enjeux CORE de l'humanité : créativité et compassion, originalité, réciprocité et responsabilité, et empathie ?

Un exemple positif

Il n'est pas nécessaire de rechercher des exemples aussi extrêmes pour trouver un argument irréfutable plaidant pour ou contre une expérience numérique bénéficiant de la médiation humaine. Prenez Wikipedia, une base de connaissance globale sans but lucratif : voilà un exemple positif de coup de pouce au bien-être collectif, administré par l'entremise de la technologie. La création de Wikipedia, à bien des égards, a nourri l'amélioration de la société humaine. À une époque où le savoir et l'information n'étaient pas aisément accessibles à chacun, Wikipedia en a ouvert l'accès à tous et en permanence – sans les coûts qu'auraient impliqué de payer dictionnaires à l'ancienne,

bibliothèques ou bases de données gouvernementales ou commerciales.

Il est largement admis que les utilisateurs de Wikipedia dans le monde entier en sont satisfaits et son co-fondateur, Jimmy Wales, est largement révéré pour avoir fait avancer le progrès collectif de la société grâce à cette innovation. En outre, les conséquences involontaires de Wikipedia, comme la disparition de la version imprimée de l'*Encyclopaedia Britannica*, peuvent être considérées comme négligeables.

Wikipedia, de ce fait, constitue un bon exemple de la manière dont la technologie peut stimuler le bien-être et l'épanouissement humains, quoique cela ne soit certainement pas sans défauts : ainsi, ma propre fiche en langue anglaise en a été supprimée en 2011, pour manque de notoriété. Par contraste, des innovations comme Tinder (une app de rencontre et de messagerie très populaire – juste au cas où vous n'auriez pas encore eu le plaisir de la découvrir), Google Maps ou Apple Watch ne contribuent pas au bien-être collectif de la même manière que Wikipedia l'a fait : même si elles sont sans doute utiles et même attachantes, elles ne sont que de simples expressions commerciales d'une approche « oui c'est possible » de nos modes de vie par la technologie. Utiles, sans aucun doute ; de nature à alimenter le bien-être général probablement pas, ou en tout cas pas au même niveau que Wikipedia.

Échanger le bonheur contre un hédonisme sous influence technologique ?

Imaginez que nous puissions aisément simuler le sentiment d'intimité obtenu avec un(e) partenaire sexuel(le) humain(e) en ayant recours à un robot sexuel attrayant, sophistiqué et piloté par une IA (et je confirme qu'il s'agit là d'une industrie en pleine croissance, au cas où vous vous poseriez la question). [183] Quelle qu'en soit la forme, avoir des relations sexuelles avec des robots est sans aucun doute une expérience éminemment hédoniste. On est d'ailleurs en droit de se demander si, du coup, nous serions

encore aussi intéressés qu'auparavant par la quête du vrai bonheur et d'une expérience sexuelle intégrale dans une relation interpersonnelle authentique et véritable, où il faudrait en réalité se battre pour que cela fonctionne bien. Ou bien deviendrions-nous si habitués à la disponibilité pour laquelle les robots sexuels sont conçus que nous en viendrions bientôt à adopter cette facilité d'usage ? Jusqu'à quel point cette attitude consumériste vis-à-vis du sexe s'avèrera-t-elle tentante ? Et, à l'inverse, qui sommes-nous après tout pour dénier aux gens le droit de profiter de ce qui leur plaît ?

Bien sûr, vous pourriez soutenir que nous serions encore capables de faire la différence – et en effet nous le serions. Mais dans quelle mesure nous sentirions-nous affectés, dans nos esprits mêmes, par un usage constant de robots sexuels ? Cela ne créerait-il pas de la confusion dans nos cerveaux jusqu'à distordre notre perception de la réalité – notre regard sur ce à quoi ressemble vraiment le monde réel ?

Des études menées sur des hommes regardant régulièrement de la pornographie ont montré qu'un tel recours intensif a un impact significatif sur le niveau de stimulation requis pour atteindre l'excitation sexuelle, ainsi que pour parvenir à l'orgasme. [184] Et maintenant, imaginez comment de telles perspectives pourraient être bouleversées par des robots sexuels, dont on peut être absolument certains qu'ils deviendront très intelligents, bon marché et incroyablement ressemblants à des humains – regardez donc quelques épisodes de la série d'AMC *Humans* pour mesurer jusqu'où cela pourrait aller. [185]

Cela signifie-t-il que nous devrions proscrire les robots sexuels parce qu'ils nous conduiraient à des pratiques inhumaines ? Pour ma part, j'estime que bannir les prochaines générations de robots humanoïdes n'aurait pas de conséquences néfastes, socialement et autre, mais bien sûr il est peu probable que cela entrave leur disponibilité. Voilà un exemple typique de la façon dont les avancées technologiques exponentielles (dans ce cas précis : peau artificielle, robotique et IA) pourraient nous conduire sur la voie

du bonheur hédoniste à une cadence toujours plus rapide, à moindre coût et avec une disponibilité généralisée.

Du coup, la question clé est la suivante : les technologies exponentielles vont-elle accroitre notre bien-être, et si tel est le cas, qui aura la responsabilité de s'assurer qu'elles ne dérapent pas, par inadvertance ou par dessein ? Qui décidera de ce qui est humain et de ce qui ne l'est pas, et jusqu'à quel point ne sommes-nous pas en train de franchir la frontière qui nous sépare, nous humains, des outils que nous avons créés ?

Telle est la tension, inhérente à la relation entre l'homme et la machine, que la technologie ne peut pas résoudre – même si à cet effet on pouvait finir par stimuler l'intégralité d'un cerveau humain et ses 100 milliards de neurones. La compassion et le bonheur, de même que la conscience, n'existent tout simplement pas en termes basiquement biologiques ou chimiques : il faut pour cela les interactions holistiques de tout ce qui est humain.

Il est peu probable que les machines ou les logiciels atteignent un jour ces états, même si, jusqu'à un certain point, ils s'améliorent rapidement dans leur capacité à les simuler. Il est clair par exemple que certains programmes informatiques peuvent déjà mesurer ou détecter la compassion en usant des techniques de reconnaissance faciale, et certains logiciels seraient probablement en mesure de simuler la compassion après avoir passé en revue des trilliards de variations d'expressions de visages et d'indicateurs linguistiques.

Les tentatives pour d'abord définir puis programmer des caractéristiques humaines comme la compassion, ou encore quelque chose d'aussi mystérieux que la conscience, relèvent apparemment d'un concept irréalisable et tiré par les cheveux, en tout cas dans un avenir prévisible. Mais une fois encore, le vrai danger ne serait-il pas qu'une simulation simplement convaincante puisse apparaître bien assez bonne comme cela aux yeux de la plupart d'entre nous ?

Je m'inquiète de plus en plus à l'idée que tôt ou tard, nous pourrions finalement accepter de nous contenter de simulations acceptables.

Remettre la technologie à sa place
Je crois fondamentalement que les ordinateurs, les programmes informatiques, les algorithmes et les robots ne seront probablement jamais en mesure de développer compassion ou empathie à la manière des humains. Robots et IAs sont des aides et des serviteurs, oui – mais certainement pas des maîtres.

Devrions-nous vraiment tenter d'utiliser des modèles mathématiques ou des intelligences mécaniques pour optimiser des résultats émotionnels ? Dans ce contexte de machines pensantes, devrions-nous vraiment tenter de déployer une meilleure technologie pour résoudre des problèmes politiques et sociaux – comme par exemple utiliser des techniques de surveillance dominatrices pour mettre fin au terrorisme ?

Les valeurs androrithmiques complexes doivent certes rester l'apanage des êtres humains, à la fois parce que nous sommes plus doués pour en extraire des expressions nuancées et parce qu'une implication directe dans ces problèmes constitue l'une des clés du développement de l'eudémonisme – un bonheur plus approfondi.

Je me demande souvent si un progrès technologique exponentiel pourrait générer une bonheur humain exponentiel, au-delà des 1% de personnes qui créent, possèdent et tirent parti de ces machines si brillamment miraculeuses. Est-ce un but vertueux que de construire une machine humaine parfaite capable de s'affranchir de tous ses défauts et insuffisances au point de finalement devenir dieu, quoique cela puisse vouloir dire ?

Je ne sais pas ce que vous en pensez, mais pour ma part ce n'est pas un monde que je m'efforcerais de faire advenir. Proposer de poursuivre dans cette voie, c'est comme de jouer notre avenir, prendre le risque d'empoisonner le puits dont userons nos enfants et les générations à venir.

Le bonheur ne peut pas être programmé dans des machines, automatisé ou vendu. Il ne peut pas être copié, codifié ou appris par cœur. Il doit émaner de nous, grandir parmi nous, entre nous, et la technologie n'est là que pour nous aider – en tant qu'outil. Nous sommes une espèce qui se sert de technologie, pas une espèce destinée à en être ou en devenir une.

Et pour en terminer avec ce sujet, pensez à ceci : le mot « bonheur » lui-même, en anglais, provient du mot viking, *happ*, utilisé pour dire « chance ». C'est en lien avec le concept d'*happenstance*, soit « par hasard ». Les apologues de la technologie peuvent professer qu'ils retranchent des vies humaines les éléments négatifs liés au hasard – et dont nous savons tous qu'ils sont légion, de la maladie à la pauvreté en passant par la mort elle-même. Néanmoins, ce faisant, il se peut aussi qu'ils altèrent systématiquement l'aptitude des êtres humains à faire l'expérience de niveaux de bonheur plus profonds, et qui ne dépendent pas de circonstances objectivement mesurables. Oui, par tous les moyens possibles, usons des outils de la technologie pour supprimer les risques les plus dangereux d'être humains sur la planète Terre. Mais en revanche, non, ne devenons pas les outils de nos propres outils, et n'abdiquons ni notre conscience versatile ni notre souverain libre arbitre pour une poignée de babioles et de frissons faciles, comme le firent un jour les natifs innocents de certain Nouveau Monde.

Chapitre 10
Étique numérique

*La technologie n'a pas d'éthique – et pourtant
c'est de l'éthique dont dépend l'humanité.*

Faisons un peu de mathématiques exponentielles. Si nous suivons le chemin que nous avons emprunté, dans huit à douze ans seulement – selon le point de départ à partir duquel on compte –, l'ensemble du progrès technologique va progresser du point de bascule actuel, de 4, à 128. Dans le même temps, la portée de nos valeurs éthiques va continuer à clopiner tant bien que mal sur une échelle de progrès linéaire, mesurée et finalement très humaine, de 4 à 5, ou 6, si nous avons de la chance. Autrement dit, elle ne s'améliorera qu'un petit peu, tandis que nous tâcherons de nous adapter à notre nouvel environnement.

Même si la loi de Moore finit par cesser de s'appliquer dans le domaine des circuits intégrés, bien des domaines de la technologie, des communications à large bande passante jusqu'à l'intelligence artificielle (IA) et à l'apprentissage profond, vont probablement encore continuer à se développer de manière exponentielle et avec des effets combinatoires – tous les changements se renforçant les uns les autres. [186]

Maintenant, zoomons un peu plus avant, de dix ans de plus, et il se pourrait bien que nous nous découvrions à 95% automatisés, hyperconnectés, virtualisés, ultra-efficients, mais aussi considérablement moins humains que nous ne l'aurions jamais cru aujourd'hui. Une société somnambule, qui marche dans son sommeil sur les boulevards exponentiels des méga-

changements (voir chapitre 3), une société qui ne fait aucune pause pour évaluer leur impact sur les valeurs, les croyances et l'éthique humaines ; une telle société, dirigée par des technologues, des capital-risqueurs, des intérêts financiers et militaires, est probablement sur le point de pénétrer dans un véritable âge de la machine.

Mais qu'entend-on par éthique ? En s'efforçant de dépasser la réponse évidente – déterminer de quelle manière on devrait vivre –, le mot grec *ethos* signifie coutume, habitude. [187] Aujourd'hui, nous employons le terme éthique comme un synonyme ou un raccourci des notions de morale, de valeurs, de principes, d'ambitions et de croyances. La première préoccupation de l'éthique est de se demander si quelque chose est juste ou pas dans une circonstance donnée. Ce qui vous apparaît approprié est le produit de votre éthique, et dans bien des cas il peut sembler difficile d'expliquer pourquoi quelque chose ne l'est pas. C'est clairement l'un des enjeux de la nécessité de s'entendre sur les règles éthiques élémentaires qui régiront l'âge exponentiel dans lequel nous nous apprêtons à entrer. Et c'est pourquoi un peu plus loin, je m'efforcerai de formuler certaines règles éthiques – des principes permettant d'encadrer le développement technologique.

> « *Aujourd'hui, le travail dont nous avons besoin est de savoir nous distinguer de nos machines. C'est, par exemple, de redécouvrir que toute connaissance est fondamentalement connaissance humaine, et que rien de ce qui mérite d'être qualifié d'idéal ne peut résulter d'un monde régi par l'ingénierie ; c'est en nous qu'il réside.* »
> Stephen Talbott [188]

Le bio-éthicien Larry Churchill suggère que « l'éthique, comprise comme la capacité d'examiner nos valeurs morales de façon critique et d'inspirer nos actions en fonction de ces valeurs, est une capacité humaine générique ». [189]

Dès lors, si l'éthique – examiner nos valeurs morales en termes critiques et orienter nos actions en conséquence – est de fait une capacité inhérente à l'humanité, ne devrions-nous pas a) ne jamais attendre des machines ou des ordinateurs que nous puissions les comprendre, et par conséquent nous méfier de leurs capacités croissantes d'auto-apprentissage, b) tenter d'encoder quelques notions d'éthique élémentaire dans les logiciels et d'apprendre à nos machines à les comprendre et à les respecter – autrement dit la question clé des « machines éthiques » ? [190] Voilà une question importante, pour laquelle nous allons rechercher des réponses ici.

Qu'adviendra-t-il de notre éthique si les machines deviennent capables d'auto-apprentissage ?

Les questions d'éthique surgissent vite parallèlement aux progrès exponentiels de la technologie. Par exemple en matière de voitures autonomes : vers qui la voiture devrait-elle se tourner si un accident s'avère totalement impossible à éviter ? Ou encore, dans le cas de robots domestiques, que devra faire le robot si le patient refuse de prendre son médicament ?

Lorsque les machines cesseront de suivre les indications de leurs arbres de décision préprogrammés pour commencer à apprendre par elles-mêmes, apprendront-elles également ces choses que même les humains trouvent difficile d'exprimer et de codifier ?

Les humains évitent les décisions rigides du type « si cette patiente a 35% de risques de se trouver confrontée à une affection dangereuse pour sa survie, alors il faut absolument qu'elle prenne tel traitement, même s'il faut pour cela employer la force ». Naturellement, les humains agissent de manière différente à différents moments, et il leur arrive de faire des erreurs. Accepterions-nous d'être soumis à de tels aléas de la part d'un robot, ou accepterions-nous qu'un robot exerce sur nous une telle contrainte ?

Dans sa nouvelle de 1942 *Runaround*, l'écrivain de science-fiction Isaac Asimov a défini les « Trois lois de la robotique », devenues tristement célèbres depuis lors :

1. *Un robot ne peut blesser un être humain ni, par son inaction, permettre qu'un humain soit blessé.*
2. *Un robot doit obéir aux ordres donnés par les êtres humains, sauf si de tels ordres entrent en conflit avec la première loi.*
3. *Un robot doit protéger sa propre existence tant que cette protection n'entre pas en conflit avec la première ou la deuxième lois.*

Ces lois sont-elles encore pertinentes aujourd'hui, et seraient-elles jetées à la poubelle avec des machines auto-apprenantes ? On peut imaginer un robot médical mis en situation de blesser des humains (même de façon marginale), pour peu qu'un autre humain à l'autorité supérieure (par exemple un médecin) lui enjoigne d'administrer un médicament de force. Dans un tel cas, comment notre robot saurait-il où commencer et où s'arrêter ? Un logiciel déciderait-il de verrouiller le réfrigérateur s'il nous faut respecter un strict régime alimentaire ? Nous couperait-il le téléphone et l'Internet pour nous empêcher de commander une pizza ? Surveillerait-il nos toilettes, à la recherche de traces de consommations inappropriées ?

Dans ce contexte, il apparaît clairement qu'aucune IA ne sera jamais véritablement intelligente si elle est dépourvue d'une sorte de module de gouvernance éthique, car alors il lui manquerait probablement les pièces du puzzle éthique que les humains, eux, prendraient en considération, ce qui la vouerait immanquablement à l'échec lorsque le besoin s'en ferait le plus sentir. Imaginez une IA pilotant votre véhicule autonome, mais incapable de déterminer dans quelles circonstances il serait ou pas acceptable de tuer un animal se trouvant sur la route.

Du coup, même si nous étions en situation de produire des robots intelligents en termes d'apprentissage et de prises de décision dynamique, il n'en reste pas moins qu'aujourd'hui, ils ne sont guère au-delà du point zéro en termes d'intelligence émotionnelle et sociale – deux termes qui sont en soi très difficiles à expliquer ou même à mesurer.

La question des machines apprenantes est l'une de celles qui me soucient le plus en termes éthiques. L'apprentissage profond est le domaine de l'intelligence artificielle qui a connu les investissements les plus importants depuis 2015 [191] et il est très probable que cela se poursuive dans les années à venir. Il n'y aura plus d'autre « hiver des IA », ni d'autre période où les investisseurs cesseront de miser sur ce secteur, de peur qu'on en surestime les promesses et que les résultats ne soient pas à la hauteur.

Imaginez simplement ce qui se passera si (ou quand) des machines infiniment puissantes et des superordinateurs seront en mesure d'apprendre à résoudre à peu près n'importe quel problème grâce à un immense flux de données en direct, c'est-à-dire sans avoir à répondre à des commandes ou à une programmation préalables. La victoire d'AlphaGo de Google DeepMind, dont nous avons parlé précédemment, est un exemple de premier choix de telles capacités d'apprentissage en action. [192] Avec l'apprentissage profond, des machines puissantes peuvent découvrir les règles, valeurs et principes sous-jacents, et de ce fait pourraient les comprendre et peut-être même les imiter. Et si cela était destiné à devenir le prochain grand phénomène de l'informatique (ainsi qu'IBM aime à le dire, de « l'informatique cognitive »), alors nous, simples humains, n'aurions plus la moindre possibilité d'évaluer si les recommandations de nos IAs seraient ou pas correctes, puisque les capacités de calcul des machines excèderaient de toute façon les nôtres dans des proportions spectaculaires. Voilà bien un problème vicieux : si nous inventons des machines dont les capacités dépassent les nôtres de plusieurs ordres de magnitude, avec des Q.I. de 50.000

et au-delà, comment saurons-nous si elles sont dignes de confiance ? Et qui sera en situation de les superviser ? Deviendront-elles sentientes à terme, d'une façon radicalement nouvelle ? Devrions-nous faire en sorte de leur inculquer un ensemble de paramètres éthiques humains désirables – et comment s'y prendre pour y parvenir ?

Dans son article « Une question de responsabilité » paru en 1987 dans le magazine *AI*, Mitchell Waldrop a écrit :

« *Une chose est manifeste... c'est que les machines intelligentes endosseront des valeurs, des hypothèses et des desseins, que leurs programmeurs aient voulu les en doter consciemment ou non. Ainsi, à mesure qu'ordinateurs et robots deviendront de plus en plus intelligents, il deviendra impératif que nous examinions soigneusement et explicitement ce que seront ces valeurs embarquées.* » [193]

Cette question présente encore plus d'acuité à mesure que nous entrons dans l'ère exponentielle, car il nous faut désormais définir ce que devra être le cadre éthique de l'ensemble des technologies exponentielles, dont l'IA, la géo-ingénierie, l'informatique cognitive et bien sûr, tout particulièrement, l'édition du génome humain. Ce qui inclut à la fois les notions éthiques programmées intentionnellement ou non à l'intérieur des machines par ceux qui les ont inventées ou fabriquées, mais également celles que ces machines auront pu apprendre d'elles-mêmes et enrichir au fil du temps.

Si Watson d'IBM est bien une machine pensante, de quelle manière va-t-elle prendre en compte les valeurs et paramètres humains subjectifs, ambigus ou non-dits, y compris entre les humains eux-mêmes ? Cette « éthique de la machine » sera-t-elle implantée par pré-programmation, ou sera-t-elle évolutive et adaptative, en utilisant les réseaux neuronaux d'apprentissage profond qui chercheront à imiter la façon dont le cerveau humain

acquiert de nouvelles informations ? Et si ces machines sont auto-apprenantes, comment les humains seront-ils en mesure de les vérifier, de les contrôler et de les modifier ? Comment ces systèmes répondront-ils aux myriades de permutations culturelles de l'éthique humaine ?

Les questions scientifiques les plus profondes au sujet de l'IA et de l'apprentissage profond, telles que la faisabilité technique du contrôle de telles intelligences émergentes, sont, pour l'heure, hors de portée de l'auteur de ce livre et de ce livre lui-même ; mais dans tous les cas, il est évident qu'une tâche abyssale nous attend. Et ainsi, dans un avenir très proche, il se peut que le métier d'expert en éthique numérique devienne un boulot aussi recherché que celui d'expert en *big data*. Peut-être cela sera-t-il un bon plan de carrière pour vos enfants ?

Et la religion, dans tout ça ?

Il est très important, également, de se souvenir que l'éthique diffère fondamentalement de la religion. Dans son livre très éclairant de 2011 *Au-delà de la religion*, le Dalaï-lama a remarqué que chacun possède une éthique, mais que certains ont seulement une religion. Et a appelé, de ce fait, à l'établissement d'une éthique laïque globale afin de guider nos décisions les plus fondamentales, comme celles qui concernent les armes autonomes dotées du pouvoir de tuer sans supervision humaine. [194]

La distinction éthique / religion doit absolument être maintenue lorsque nous en venons à discuter de sujets aussi brûlants que l'édition du génome humain ou l'augmentation non-biologique des humains. Je suggèrerais pour ma part que nous évitions autant que possible d'introduire la religion dans de tels débats, parce que les opinions religieuses sont loin d'être aussi homogènes et partagées que les valeurs éthiques élémentaires, et parce qu'elles sont souvent en opposition frontale avec les leçons de l'histoire et de l'expérience passée.

Arthur C. Clarke a mis en lumière cette distinction critique dans une interview de 1999 :

« *Aujourd'hui, les gens supposent que la religion et la moralité sont nécessairement liées. Pourtant, les fondements de la moralité sont vraiment très simples et ne nécessitent en rien le concours de la religion.* » [195]

Création d'un Conseil mondial d'éthique numérique : comment définir une éthique adaptée à l'âge exponentiel ?

J'aimerais traiter deux préoccupations majeures. Premièrement, tenter de définir ce que pourrait être un ensemble de règles éthiques globalement acceptables pour l'âge numérique exponentiel ; et deuxièmement tenter de définir ce qu'il nous faudrait faire pour nous assurer que le bien-être humain et les préoccupations éthiques restent effectivement en tête de notre agenda global, sans que la pensée machinique ne prenne le pas sur elles.

Il nous faut par conséquent définir un ensemble de règles éthiques numériques fondamentales – une éthique globale conçue pour l'Âge numérique : suffisamment ouverte pour que cela ne ralentisse pas le progrès et n'entrave pas l'innovation, et néanmoins suffisamment forte pour protéger notre humanité. Non pas une carte, mais une boussole, qui nous permette d'affronter un futur qui verra des technologies toujours plus puissantes commencer par renforcer puis augmenter l'humanité, mais finalement aussi, de plus en plus, la menacer.

À cette fin, je propose la création d'un Conseil mondial d'éthique numérique (CMEN), dont la tâche sera de définir ce que devraient être les règles de base et les valeurs universelles les plus élémentaires d'une société entièrement numérisée, spectaculairement différente de la nôtre.

Pour l'heure, nous nous sommes mis d'accord sur le fait qu'aucun état voyou ne devrait détenir de capacités nucléaires, même s'il est en mesure de le faire. Une situation complexe, bien

sûr, lourde de mensonges et de tromperies – et en mutation permanente –, néanmoins l'entente sur l'essentiel demeure, renforcée par le fait que toute option alternative implique de trop grands risques.

De la même manière, il nous faut désormais nous entendre sur les limites et la surveillance indépendante auquel nous souhaiterions soumettre l'étendue et le progrès de l'IA, du séquençage du génome et des autres technologies exponentielles.

Afin d'amorcer cette discussion, je propose ci-après un ensemble de suggestions, à titre d'essai. Je sais que c'est une tâche intimidante et, oui, il est peut-être même présomptueux de s'y essayer. Mais il faut bien commencer, alors, autant que ce soit moi qui m'y brûle le premier !

Pour soutenir le CMEN, il nous faut commencer par mettre au point un manifeste concis de l'éthique numérique, une sorte de traité global des droits humains exponentiels dans un monde toujours plus numérisé. Un tel manifeste, ainsi que le traité qui en découlerait, pourrait servir à encadrer et responsabiliser les entreprises qui inventent, fabriquent et vendent ces technologies (ainsi que leurs gouvernements). C'est primordial, dans la mesure où les implications du changement technologique exponentiel sur l'existence humaine ne peuvent plus être traitées comme de simples phénomènes périphériques, des effets secondaires sans conséquences immédiates pour ceux qui en sont la cause.

Le CMEN que j'envisage devrait compter dans ses rangs des individus avisés et bien informés issus de la société civile, du monde académique, des gouvernements, du monde des affaires et de celui des technologies, mais aussi des penseurs indépendants, des écrivains, des artistes et des leaders d'opinion (et l'auteur de ces lignes sera heureux de suivre le mouvement). Le Comité doit d'emblée être global, et devra à terme probablement être doté de pouvoirs similaires ou même supérieurs à ce que sont aujourd'hui ceux des Rapporteurs spéciaux des Nations unies sur les droits humains – en l'occurrence la capacité de surveiller, conseiller et rendre public abus et violations. [196]

Comme cela a été hélas le cas avec le développement durable, l'éthique fait souvent figure de dispositif cosmétique sur l'agenda, dont on peut se débarrasser vite fait dès lors que surgit quelque chose de plus important. C'est une approche fondamentalement viciée et très dangereuse au regard de la préservation de notre avenir à tous. Nous entrons dans une ère où des développements critiques vont survenir, graduellement puis soudainement, et nous ne disposerons tout simplement plus de la marge nécessaire pour reconsidérer nos options éthiques lorsqu'elles auront été irrémédiablement laminées par les machines pensantes. « *Wait and See* » signifie tout simplement abdication humaine.

Un nouveau calcul moral
Nous devons consacrer à l'éthique numérique autant de temps et de ressources que nous en avons consacrés aux technologies exponentielles. L'examen des conséquences involontaires des technologies exponentielles et la prévention des dommages potentiels causés à l'humanité – ce qui va bien plus loin qu'une simple inquiétude existentielle – exigent un niveau de soutien comparable à celui que nous avons apporté aux sciences responsables de ces changements. Le facteur humain nécessite autant de financement et de promotion de la science elle-même : il ne peut y avoir de STIM (science, technologie, ingénierie et mathématiques) qui n'aient leur CORE (créativité, originalité, réciprocité et empathie).

Dans son livre de 2015 *Machines of Loving Grace*, le reporter du *New York Times* John Markoff met en évidence la nécessité de ce nouveau calcul moral :

« *Les optimistes espèrent que les abus potentiels de nos systèmes informatiques seront minimisés si la mise en œuvre de l'intelligence artificielle, de l'ingénierie génétique et de la robotique reste focalisée sur l'humain plutôt que sur les algorithmes. Mais le bilan des industries technologiques ne porte*

pas trace de quoi que ce soit qui se réfère à l'édification morale. Il serait vraiment étonnant qu'une société de la Silicon Valley se prive d'une technologie lucrative pour des raisons éthiques. Aujourd'hui, toute décision de mise en œuvre technologique s'effectue très largement sur des critères de rentabilité et d'efficacité. Or ce dont on a besoin, c'est d'une nouvelle formule morale. » [197]

Cinq nouveaux droits humains pour l'Âge numérique

Voici cinq droits humains fondamentaux dont je suggère humblement l'intégration à un futur Manifeste de l'éthique numérique :

1. **Le droit de demeurer naturel, c'est-à-dire biologique**
   Nous devons conserver le choix d'exister dans un état non-augmenté. Nous devons conserver le droit d'être employés, d'utiliser les services publics, d'acheter des objets et de fonctionner en société sans être tenus de déployer de la technologie sur nous ou à l'intérieur de nos corps. La peur du « câblé ou viré » est d'ores et déjà un vrai sujet (quoique jugé inoffensif dans la plupart des cas) s'agissant des appareils mobiles et des médias sociaux. Et on peut aisément imaginer un avenir où nous pourrions être contraints, pour être employables, de porter des lunettes, des visières et des casques de réalité augmentée (RA) ou de réalité virtuelle (RV), ou bien, encore pire, que l'on nous présente l'utilisation ou l'implantation corporelle d'apps et de logiciels spécifiques comme une condition sine qua non à l'obtention d'un emploi. Dès lors, demeurer de simples humains ne serait plus suffisant – et ce n'est pas une perspective d'avenir désirable.

2. **Le droit d'être inefficaces, si cela permet de définir notre humanité fondamentale** – Nous devons avoir le choix de demeurer plus lents que la technologie. L'efficacité ne devrait pas être considérée comme plus importante que

l'humanité. Il pourrait bientôt devenir bien plus efficace et moins cher d'avoir recours à des diagnostics de santé numériques sur des plates-formes comme Scanadu que de voir un médecin à chaque fois que l'on est confronté à un enjeu médical. Je considère que ces technologies sont pour l'essentiel positives et qu'elles pourraient être l'une des clés permettant de faire baisser les coûts de santé. Néanmoins, cela signifie-t-il que nous devrions pénaliser les personnes choisissant de procéder autrement, ou contraindre à rentrer dans le rang ceux qui ne veulent pas que leurs données de santé se retrouvent dans le *cloud* ?

3. **Le droit à la déconnexion** – Nous devons préserver notre droit à interrompre la connectivité, à « rester dans l'ombre » sur le réseau, et à faire une pause dans nos communications, dans notre traçabilité et dans la surveillance dont nous faisons l'objet. On peut en effet s'attendre à ce que dans un proche avenir de nombreuses entreprises et employeurs fassent de l'hyperconnectivité une exigence par défaut. En tant qu'employé(e) ou conducteur(trice) sous contrat d'assurance, vous pourriez ainsi être pénalisé(e) pour vous être déconnecté(e) sans autorisation si vous-même ou votre véhicule ne pouviez plus être tracés sur le réseau. Être de notre propre gré techniquement déconnecté(e), à des moments que nous avons nous-mêmes choisis, est fondamentalement un droit important, car la déconnexion nous permet de nous recentrer sur notre environnement sans intermédiation et de vivre le moment présent. Elle nous permet également de réduire le risque d'obésité numérique (voir chapitre 7) et amoindrit la portée de la surveillance involontaire. Peut-être bien que la déconnexion est le luxe ultime – mais cela devrait surtout demeurer un droit élémentaire.

4. **Le droit à l'anonymat** – Dans ce monde hyperconnecté à venir, nous devrions conserver l'option de ne pas être identifiés et tracés, par exemple lorsque nous avons recours

à une application ou à une plate-forme numérique, ou encore lorsque nous postons des commentaires ou des critiques – à condition que cela soit inoffensif pour les autres ou que cela ne porte pas atteinte à autrui. Bien sûr, il subsistera des circonstances, évidentes, où compter sur un réel anonymat s'avèrera impossible et probablement déraisonnable, par exemple dans les transactions bancaires numérique. Néanmoins, il nous faudra nous assurer que des espaces protégés subsisteront, où le traçage ne sera ni nécessaire ni la norme, par exemple dans l'expression d'opinions politiques, dans l'échange de photos personnelles ou dans les consultations médicales. L'anonymat, le mystère, les hasards heureux et les erreurs sont des attributs humains cruciaux que nous ne devrions pas chercher à supprimer par des moyens technologiques.

5. **Le droit d'employer ou de faire appel à des humains plutôt qu'à des machines** – Nous ne devrions pas permettre que des entreprises ou des employeurs soient désavantagés s'ils choisissent d'employer des gens plutôt que des machines, même si cela s'avère plus coûteux et moins efficace. Au contraire, nous devrions leur prévoir des crédits d'impôts, et songer à des taxes d'automatisation pour les sociétés qui auraient massivement recours à des réductions d'effectifs en faveur des machines et des logiciels. Il faudrait que de tels impôts soient affectés au recyclage professionnel des victimes de licenciements pour cause technologique.

Il est important de noter que beaucoup de ces droits portent sur une importante question qui est au cœur de ce débat : quelle est la proportion de liberté que nous serions prêts à sacrifier afin d'être soit plus efficaces, soit plus protégés ? Il nous faut également nous demander ce que devrait être l'éthique de la sécurité, et de quelle manière la technologie sera mise à contribution sur ce sujet crucial.

15 commandements qu'il faut oser formuler

Par souci de faire avancer clairement le développement et l'intégration d'une éthique numérique globalement cohérente, voici quelques exemples spécifiques d'embûches technologiques qu'il nous faut éviter si nous voulons que l'humanité prévale. Je suis profondément conscient qu'en proposant de telles réflexions pour amorcer le débat, certains de ces commandements pourraient apparaître simplificateurs, idéalistes, irréalisables, utopiques, incomplets et sujets à controverse. C'est pourquoi je les présente humblement de manière simple, dans l'intention d'amorcer une discussion.

1. Nous n'attendrons pas des humains qu'ils se transforment eux-mêmes graduellement en technologie, pour la simple raison que cela satisferait aux besoins de la technologie ou des entreprises technologiques, ou que cela stimulerait la croissance.

2. Nous ne permettrons pas que les humains soient gouvernés ou dirigés par des technologies comme l'intelligence artificielle, l'Internet des objets ou la robotique.

3. Nous n'altérerons pas la nature humaine en programmant ou en fabricant de nouvelles créatures à l'aide de la technologie.

4. Nous n'augmenterons pas les êtres humains afin d'atteindre à des pouvoirs surnaturels qui supprimeraient la distinction entre l'homme et la machine.

5. Nous n'autoriserons pas les machines à s'améliorer d'elles-mêmes, et ainsi à s'affranchir du contrôle humain.

6. Nous ne chercherons pas à substituer à la confiance la surveillance de nos communications et de nos relations humaines pour la simple raison que la technologie la rendrait universellement possible.

7. Nous ne planifierons pas, ne justifierons pas et ne désirerons pas une surveillance totale sous prétexte que nous pourrions en ressentir le besoin.

8. Nous ne permettrons pas aux robots, aux machines, aux plates-formes ou autres technologies intelligentes de s'emparer des fonctions démocratiques essentielles de notre société, qui devront rester l'apanage des humains eux-mêmes.

9. Nous ne chercherons pas à restreindre ou remplacer la culture de l'expérience humaine véritable par des simulations algorithmiques, augmentées ou virtuelles.

10. Nous ne chercherons pas à minimiser les imperfections humaines simplement pour mieux nous accorder à la technologie..

11. Nous ne tenterons pas de supprimer les erreurs, le mystère, les accidents et le hasard en cherchant à les anticiper ou les éviter grâce à la technologie, et nous ne nous efforcerons pas de tout rendre explicite sous prétexte que la technologie pourrait nous en donner les moyens.

12. Nous ne créerons pas, ne développerons pas ou ne distribuerons pas une technologie quelconque dans l'intention de générer une addiction chez ses utilisateurs.

13. Nous n'attendrons pas des robots qu'ils prennent des décisions morales, et nous ne les équiperons pas de sorte qu'ils en viennent à contester nos décisions.

14. Nous n'exigerons pas ou ne stipulerons pas que les humains aussi puissent devenir exponentiels par nature.

15. Nous ne confondrons pas un algorithme efficace avec la vérité de la réalité humaine (« les logiciels trompent le monde ») et nous n'accorderons pas à la technologie une puissance indue au prétexte qu'elle génère des bénéfices économiques

Sur le sujet particulier du caractère devenu explicite de toute chose, les réseaux sociaux nous fournissent un enseignement précieux : ce qui auparavant relevait du non-dit – c'est-à-dire ce qu'on pouvait lire entre les lignes – est soudain devenu l'objet de toute l'attention, énoncé très clairement et amplifié par l'effet de

la pensée de groupe. Même si, par le passé, mon adhésion à tel groupe d'action citoyenne, telle organisation politique ou telle cause sociale pouvait être explicite, elle n'était pas pour autant largement accessible à tout un chacun. Mais maintenant que tout est connecté, chacun de mes commentaires peut être instantanément vu, examiné et consulté par tout le monde.

Nous ne devons pas rechercher l'efficacité plus que l'humanité
Les technologies exponentielles rendent rapidement tout ce qui nous entoure toujours plus efficace. Par voie de conséquence, tout désormais tend à devenir un service, tout est dans le *cloud*, tout est intelligent. Même le plus stupide des matériels sera doté de capteurs, contribuant ainsi à un tsunami généralisé de données qui, couplé à l'intelligence artificielle, pourrait solutionner à peu près n'importe quel problème. [198]

Tâchons d'imaginer à quoi pourrait ressembler un tel monde vers 2030. Lorsque littéralement tout sera tracé, mesuré et hyper-efficace, qu'arrivera-t-il aux choses qui ne pourront être quantifiées aussi aisément ? Que ferons-nous des émotions, de la surprise, de l'hésitation, de l'incertitude, de la contemplation, du mystère, des erreurs, des accidents, des hasards heureux et autres traits distinctifs humains ? Deviendront-ils indésirables parce qu'algorithmes et machines sont parfaits, programmés pour ne pas faire d'erreurs, fonctionnent 24 heures sur 24, 7 jours sur 7 et 365 jours par an, ne sont pas syndiqués et d'une manière générale font ce qu'on leur dit de faire (enfin, au moins cela sera-t-il le cas de la variété non-pensante…) ?

Le progrès technologique en constante progression voudra-t-il dire que les humains exprimant un trop grand nombre de ces traits non-déchiffrables par les machines seront considérés comme une perte de temps ou, pire, traités comme de simples grains de sable tombés la boite de vitesses de la Machine toute-puissante ?

Devrons-nous sans cesse adapter et modifier notre comportement, de manière à apparaître plus efficaces, ou du moins pouvoir le prétendre ? Est-ce que l'idée de l'efficience

totale s'imposera comme le grand égalisateur nous conduisant à nous comporter toujours plus uniformément ? L'obsession de la technologie, de son efficacité et de son uniformité absolues, nous conduira-t-elle finalement à rejeter l'acceptation tacite de l'inefficacité et des différences humaines ? Il me semble souvent que tel est bien le cas, même si cela prendra sans doute un peu plus longtemps ici en Europe – et encore plus longtemps en Suisse !

Si la recherche de l'efficacité la plus accomplie possible demeure une préoccupation prioritaire, alors la montée en flèche des performances de la machine dans l'âge exponentiel signifie probablement que nous humains n'aurons bientôt plus à nous investir dans quoi que ce soit. Passer, sur l'échelle de la technologie, d'un stade 4 à un stade 128 au cours de la prochaine décennie, ou peu s'en faut, suggère que bien des tâches pourront être accomplies 32 fois plus vite qu'aujourd'hui. Pouvez-vous vous imaginer la distribution, la banque et les transports devenir 32 fois plus efficaces qu'aujourd'hui ? Deviendront-ils également 32 fois moins chers, et si tel est le cas, quels en seront les effets sur notre économie ?

Il nous faudra être très prudents avant de prendre des décisions exclusivement inspirées par l'efficacité, car cela nous coutera certainement des emplois humains, amoindrira l'autorité humaine – à moins que cela n'incite les humains à s'automatiser, céder et finalement abdiquer (voir chapitre 4).

Dans bien des cas, nous pourrons être amenés à vivre avec ces insuffisances redoutées, et à accepter qu'elles fassent tout simplement partie de l'existence humaine, même si elles font obstacle à l'automatisation. L'autre option serait d'imposer l'efficacité sans pitié et de faire disparaître ceux qui ne s'y conforment pas : si vous insistez pour voir votre médecin en personne plutôt que de vous servir d'un appareil de diagnostic à distance, vous devrez payer une pénalité. Refuser de voir votre véhicule tracé en toute circonstance vous amènera à perdre la couverture de votre assurance. Ne pas accepter l'implantation

d'une puce dans votre corps signifiera que vous ne pourrez pas travailler pour telle entreprise.

Le secteur médical, en la matière, nous offre quelques précédents utiles pour ce qui est des débats encore à venir. Certains ont longtemps prétendu que les césariennes étaient plus efficaces que les naissances naturelles, et que par conséquent nous devrions tous renoncer à ce privilège – un cas très clair où la culture de l'efficience prend le pas sur l'humanité. [199] Compte tenu de la puissance exponentielle de la technologie, je pressens où cela pourrait nous emmener la prochaine fois à l'ectogénèse – la grossesse hors de l'utérus, les bébés nés en laboratoires.

Serait-il efficace de tracer votre voiture ou tout autre moyen de transport 100% du temps, sur chaque paramètre tel que vitesse, direction, accélération, température intérieure et qualité de l'air extérieure ? La réponse est oui. Cela s'inscrirait-il utilement dans une intention favorable à l'humain ? À bien des égards, la réponse est oui également : l'usage de véhicules autonomes et l'analyse des données de traçabilité pourrait aider à réduire significativement la pollution et mettre fin à la plupart des accidents. Cela dit, à bien d'autres égards, la traçabilité permanente serait également nuisible, car cela s'avèrerait l'outil de surveillance le plus parfait jamais inventé, qui nous forcerait constamment à agir de manière docile.

Il nous faut d'urgence poser la question si nous voulons vraiment remplacer nos sensibilités et capacités humaines innées par la promesse d'acquérir de parfaites fonctionnalités machines et graduellement éradiquer la signification même du fait d'être humains. Nous pourrions certes agir de façon ultra-efficace, mais en dernier ressort c'est nous-mêmes qu'ainsi nous volons.

Qu'en serait-il si seulement les 2% les plus riches avaient accès à de nouveaux traitements génétiques qui promettraient une extension spectaculaire de la longévité, pendant que tous les autres en seraient privés ? Verrions-nous alors se manifester encore plus de troubles civils et de terrorisme, en proportion d'inégalités toujours plus accrues directement issues d'avancées

technologiques exponentielles ? Imaginez simplement ce qui se passerait si de telles injections d'« ADN de la longévité » apparaissaient, mais que seuls les millionnaires pourraient s'offrir pour vivre jusqu'à 150 ans, tandis que tout un chacun continuerait à mourir plus ou moins comme d'habitude. Il me semble clair que nos paradigmes éthiques actuels, sous la pression du capitalisme ordinaire et des attentes des marchés, ne sont pas en mesure de répondre à de tels dilemmes.

La vie au-delà de l'algorithme

Alors, que pouvons-nous faire lorsque la technologie prend le contrôle là où elle ne le devrait pas ? Comment pouvons-nous nous protéger pour ne pas devenir de simples objets d'une hyper-efficacité d'origine robotique, nourrissant une IA géante qui en retour nous dicte nos vies en nous disant ce que nous n'avons plus le droit de faire ?

Nous devons nous demander si nos choix sont guidés par le désir de ne pas prêter le flanc aux machines, ou bien dans le but qu'ils soient positifs pour les utilisateurs humains – et nous devons poser cette question bien plus souvent que nous ne le faisons. Nous devons la poser lorsque nous votons de nouvelles lois, lorsque nous lançons un *business* et lorsque nous donnons notre argent à des entreprises technologiques. Voter avec nos portefeuilles est un outil puissant, dont les consommateurs ne se sont pas suffisamment servis en matière d'éthique numérique. Ironiquement d'ailleurs, avec la technologie, ce droit deviendra bien plus simple à exercer.

La question éthique, la question du but et du sens, doit venir avant la question de la faisabilité et du coût. Et si on pousse un peu plus loin la réflexion, la question primordiale en matière technologique ne sera pas de savoir si quelque chose peut être fait, mais pourquoi, quand, où et par qui.

Une autre réponse possible pourrait être de dire simplement non, de refuser plus souvent de participer, de rejeter technologies, processus, applications et logiciels qui ne sont pas clairement

conçus pour des usages humains, mais se contentent simplement d'amplifier le pouvoir des algorithmes. Peut-être devrions-nous concevoir un autocollant de mise en garde sanitaire, ou un timbre tel que ceux qu'on applique aujourd'hui sur les paquets de cigarettes, et qui nous indiquerait que tel programme, telle app ou tel appareil « est contraire à l'épanouissement du bonheur humain ».

Bien que l'efficacité et la recherche du profit soient parfois des objectifs qui en valent la peine, et en dernier ressort l'une des pierres angulaires du capitalisme, nous ne devrions pas nous appuyer sur la technologie pour promouvoir une croyance simplificatrice professant que seule l'efficacité est importante et méritante au regard des objectifs humains. Sur le long terme, la pensée machinique ne nous servira pas.

Chapitre 11
La Terre en 2030 : Paradis ou enfer?

Même si nombre des bouleversements annoncés sont bienvenus – comme le fait de travailler pour une passion plutôt que pour un salaire –, plusieurs des privilèges que nous tenions pour acquis – tels que la liberté de consommer ce que nous voulons ou celle d'exercer notre libre arbitre en matière de mœurs – pourraient devenir soit les vestiges d'un passé révolu soit l'apanage d'une poignée d'individus ultra riches et connectés.
Paradis ou enfer ?

Alors que j'écris ces lignes en 2016, nous avons d'ores et déjà atteint un point où une bonne partie de ce qui était considéré comme de la science-fiction s'est transformé en faits scientifiques avérés. Nous faisons déjà l'expérience de la science-fiction, y compris parfois ce qui s'avère être les effets indésirables des choix opérés par les générations précédentes : traductions automatiques, voitures pratiquement autonomes, nano-robots dans notre flux sanguin, intelligence artificielle capable de mener des cyber-guerres en notre nom et réfrigérateurs qui communiquent avec nos *smartphones* – lesquels, à leur tour, transmettent nos données à nos médecins.

Alors, zoomons ensemble jusqu'en 2030 afin de visualiser les avenirs vraisemblables d'un monde largement reconfiguré par le changement technologique exponentiel et voyons plus précisément à quoi pourraient ressembler quelques scénarios infernalisiaques. Je vous présente ci-dessous un calendrier de ces scénarios possibles, qui s'étend jusqu'à 2030.

2020 : hyper-connectivité et hyper-manipulation

Tout étant désormais en voie d'hyperconnection, les dix principaux cerveaux globaux – d'anciennes plates-formes Internet et entreprises médiatiques – se servent d'algorithmes pour évaluer et déterminer ce que je devrais voir, et de quelle manière.

En 2016, notre Facebook partagé et bien-aimé se servait d'algorithmes pour générer un flux d'informations correspondant parfaitement à mon profil, tout en s'assurant que je resterais engagé vis-à-vis de cette plate-forme le plus longtemps possible, en m'évitant d'être par trop exposé à des opinions divergentes ou à des messages négatifs.

Aujourd'hui, alors que six milliards de personnes sont en perpétuelle connexion à travers la planète, nous voyons tous des informations et des contenus différents, tout le temps. Nous interagissons avec ces plates-formes via la réalité augmentée (RA), la réalité virtuelle (RV) et les écrans holographiques, ou encore par l'entremise d'assistants numériques intelligents (ANI), de robots, d'apps passées de mode ou de ce qu'on appelait des sites internet. En 2020, les sites internet traditionnels déclinent aussi vite que les voitures à propulsion pétrole, puisque les IAs dans le *cloud* font tout le travail à notre place – sans avoir besoin pour cela d'interfaces graphiques séduisantes ou de designs futés.

Les éditeurs humains rendent également leur tablier, puisque les grandes bases de données, *clouds* intelligents et autres IA ont démontré qu'ils sont beaucoup plus efficaces, plus populaires – et pratiquement gratuits. En outre, ces systèmes ne s'opposent jamais à quoi que ce soit – ce qui permet aux publicitaires, aux marques et aux formations politiques de mieux en tirer parti et de dépenser leurs budgets marketing plus efficacement.

Les algorithmes prédictifs contribuent à prévenir le crime. En se servant des faisceaux de données publiquement disponibles des services de police, de la circulation routière, des travaux publics, de l'aide sociale et des départements de planification, les villes peuvent localiser les points sensibles. Elles sont alors en mesure

de croiser ces informations avec les données extraites des fils d'actualité, des e-mails, des activités sans fil et bien plus encore. L'intelligence artificielle peut ainsi analyser les données, découvrir de nouvelles corrélations et proposer des mesures à prendre pour prévenir le crime, telles que le renforcement des patrouilles de police, l'isolement des récidivistes ou les alertes de surveillance adressées aux contrevenants potentiels.

En 2020, le monde devient hyperconnecté, automatisé et uberisé – et tout le monde en bénéficie.

2022 : mon meilleur ami est dans le *cloud*

Des essaims d'ANI et de *bots* logiciels évoluent dans le *cloud*, prenant en charge bien des tâches routinières.

- Plus de recherches du meilleur restaurant ou du meilleur hôtel – nos *bots* de voyage s'en sont déjà occupé pour nous.
- Plus besoin d'aviser notre médecin de ce qui ne va pas – nos *bots* de santé l'ont déjà briefé – ou, plus probablement, ont déjà briefé son propre *bot*.
- Plus nécessaire d'anticiper de quelle manière se rendre d'un endroit à un autre – nos *bots* de transport ont déjà tout arrangé pour nous.
- Plus besoin de chercher pour quoi que ce soit – nos *bots* nous connaissent parfaitement, nous et nos désirs, et sont en mesure de le communiquer infiniment mieux que ce que nous pourrions exprimer en tapant des questions sur un clavier d'ordinateur. Chaque recherche, littéralement, a déjà été anticipée, et les réponses seront à notre disposition dès que nous en aurons besoin.

Mon ego numérique dans le *cloud* est devenu une véritable copie de moi-même, grâce à une combinaison d'outils rapides, peu onéreux et ultra-puissants, y compris les technologies mobiles du *cloud*, la personnalisation, la reconnaissance vocale et visuelle et

l'analyse des humeurs et des sentiments. Cet ego-là n'a pas encore de corps, mais lit mes données corporelles, tout le temps. Il n'éprouve pas de véritables sentiments, mais à coup sûr déchiffre les miens. Cette copie numérique de moi-même est désormais connue sous le nom de *HelloMe*.

HelloMe écoute, observe, me synchronise et m'imite ; au regard de mes données personnelles, il me connaît mieux que n'importe humain ne saurait le faire, et de loin. Mon ego numérique est connecté aux autres *bots* et IAs, qui sont devenus d'excellents compagnons. Si j'ai besoin d'informations, de recommandations ou de conversations, il me suffit, à moi ou à mon ANI, de le demander au *cloud* ; si je me sens un peu seul, il suffit de demander à *HelloMe* de me parler, exactement comme je le ferai avec un ami – mais sans s'encombrer de tout un fatras d'historiques, d'attachements et d'incompréhensions. Mes appareils mobiles sont intégrés à moi-même, sur et dans mon corps, et je profite de revêtements RA / VA sur mes lunettes, mes visières et mes lentilles de contact, en attendant de pouvoir très bientôt profiter d'implants neuronaux qui nous permettront de nous affranchir de toute forme d'interface externe, enfin !

Ce qu'Hello Barbie a été pour les jeunes enfants en 2015, *HelloMe* l'est pour nous aujourd'hui – une voix-dans-le-ciel intelligente, amicale et omniprésente, qui me comprend vraiment et rend ma vie tellement plus facile.

Avec le temps, j'ai même construit une relation personnelle avec *HelloMe*, que je considère désormais comme un ami cher. Et je suis impatient qu'*HelloMe* soit capable de reproduire les personnalités de personnes qui ne sont plus disponibles – par exemple des personnes décédées ou qui se sont placées hors de toute possibilité de connexion, comme cela s'est produit avec mon ex. Bientôt, *HelloMe* sera en mesure de communiquer exactement comme cette personne – en tout lieu et à toute heure –, transformant ainsi l'élaboration des relations humaines, tellement fastidieuse et chronophage, en une chose du passé.

Nous avons également ajouté un corps robotique à l'équation… Les personnes paralysées peuvent dorénavant se remettre à marcher à l'aide d'exosquelettes, à des coûts qui ne cessent de diminuer. On utilise des interfaces cerveau-ordinateur (ICO) pour piloter des avions et des porte-conteneurs géants. La possibilité de transformer nos pensées et notre activité cérébrale en déclencheurs informatiques modifie notre manière d'interagir avec les machines dans tous les domaines des affaires et de la culture. Nous sommes plus libres que jamais de contempler, créer, questionner et réfléchir.

Plutôt que d'absorber des médicaments pour réduire les pires effets d'affections comme l'hypercholestérolémie, l'hypertension artérielle ou le diabète, nous nous améliorons de plus en plus dans l'identification des éléments déclencheurs des maladies. Et nous commençons à employer les nanotechnologies, l'IA et la biologie du *cloud* pour nous attaquer à nos principaux problèmes de santé. Nous avons identifié les gènes qui pourraient commander la survenue de certains cancers. Une fois que nous saurons de quelle manière manipuler ces gènes sans danger, nous serons en voie de préparer l'éradication de ces maladies. Paradis, ou enfer ?

En 2022, mon ego numérique s'est installé dans le *cloud*, où il développe sa propre vie.

2024 : adieu à la vie privée et à l'anonymat

La technologie est devenue si rapide, si puissante et si envahissante qu'il n'est plus possible d'éviter d'être tracés, observés, enregistrés et surveillés – en toute circonstance. L'Internet des objets (IdO) a connecté nos voitures, nos maisons, nos appareils domestiques, nos parcs et nos villes, nos produits de grande consommation, nos traitements médicaux, nos médicaments et, bien sûr, nos gadgets et nos machines. L'Internet de Tout connecte nos esprits au réseau. Le concept naguère totalement futuriste d'un second néocortex – la connexion directe d'un cerveau externe au *cloud* – est en train de devenir lentement

réalité. La nouvelle frontière, pour les start-ups, c'est de développer et de fournir des publicités actives et des services de sauvegarde pour les réseaux neuronaux embarqués sur des machines qui finiront, via des ICOs, par pouvoir se connecter directement à nos propres néocortex.

Les appareils mobiles sont désormais presque entièrement contrôlés par la voix et le geste. Et la plupart des ordinateurs sont devenus invisibles – toujours là, toujours en observation, toujours à l'écoute, et toujours à notre disposition.

La connectivité est omniprésente : 90% du monde est connecté à très grande vitesse et à très bas prix. Plus rien ni plus personne n'est *offline*, jamais – à moins que vous ne puissiez vous offrir le luxe de vous déconnecter ou de visiter l'un des coins du monde encore hors-ligne, comme les Alpes suisses, devenues au nombre des destinations populaires pour vacances de « détox numérique ». Le *offline* est le nouveau luxe, aucun doute.

Le fait de se déconnecter ou de refuser le partage de données personnelles est socialement inacceptable et économiquement pénalisé. Les pénalités peuvent inclure une réduction très significative de l'accès à des services essentiels tels que la navigation, le transport et la mobilité, ou encore entrainer des primes élevées d'assurance et de couverture santé. Si vous ne fournissez pas vos données, on vous refuse le service. La vraie vie privée telle qu'on l'entendait avant l'ère Internet est désormais réservée aux très riches, car ils sont les seuls à pouvoir s'offrir l'usage des technologies qui orchestrent leurs vies numériques sans subir d'effet panoptique (tout ce qui survient sera observé). Les substituts numériques – des *bots* incarnés qui représentent des personnes réelles – font fureur, mais sont extrêmement couteux, sans parler de leur statut légal, souvent peu clair.

Soit vous êtes câblé, soit vous êtes viré. Dans la mesure où tout autour de nous est connecté, tracé et surveillé, il est devenu obligatoire d'être complètement câblé au travail. Et bien sûr, « au travail » ne désigne plus tel bureau dans tel bâtiment. Bien des personnes qui ont remis en question ce genre d'environnement de

travail sont désormais privées d'emploi, parce qu'elles étaient à la traîne en termes de ratios de productivité – lesquels sont, bien entendu, supervisés par un *bot*.

Aux yeux des employeurs, l'accroissement de l'efficacité au travail est irrésistible. La réalité augmentée, les appareils virtuels et les apps rendent désormais très facile de zoomer dans de grandes quantités de données ou de médias. Cet éventail d'outils permet une immersion profonde et multisensorielle dans des sujets complexes, qui auparavant nécessitaient d'avoir recours à des douzaines de personnes et à de nombreuses journées de travail. Tout se passe comme si notre cerveau était connecté à un second néocortex dans le *cloud*, nous donnant ainsi la possibilité d'accéder à un espace de performances neurales entièrement nouveau, qui transcende nos limitations antérieures.

Il n'y a plus de secrets, désormais. Tout ce que nous avons à faire, c'est de parler à une machine, partout et tout le temps, et elle trouvera les réponses pour nous – la plupart du temps gratuitement, quoique l'accès à certaines informations reste encore conditionné au paiement d'un droit élevé. L'anticipation et le profilage en affaires explosent, les outils d'exploitation de données de 2016 donnant l'impression, par comparaison, d'appartenir à l'âge de pierre. Les technologies de reconnaissance faciale sont si avancées qu'elles peuvent lire des milliers de visages en quelques fractions de seconde, archiver les expressions émotionnelles et créer des cartographies faciales complètes de tout ce qu'il nous est arrivé de ressentir, à tel endroit et tel moment.

Les cerveaux globaux élaborés par les quatorze grandes firmes et plates-formes technologiques dominantes collectent les données de six milliards d'utilisateurs connectés partout et en toutes circonstances. L'incroyable puissance de l'IA rassemble nos profils, et en déduit qui nous sommes et ce que nous nous apprêtons à faire. Une mine d'or pour les services de sécurité et de police, les gouvernements, et un turbocompresseur pour le marketing, la publicité et l'économie en général.

L'argent est devenu intégralement numérique, effaçant ainsi le dernier refuge de l'anonymat. Payer en liquide appartient désormais au passé – et d'ailleurs c'est la plupart du temps interdit. Chaque bonbon, boisson, ticket de bus ou rasade de whisky est noté dans les livres (ou plutôt dans le *cloud*), enregistré quelque part, partagé quelque part, signalé quelque part, et contribue à enrichir ce que les cerveaux globaux savent de vous. L'argent numérique a également rendu impossible de recevoir du liquide de quiconque – finis le travail au noir, les astuces sur les déductions fiscales et la triche sur votre déclaration d'impôt.

Les banques perdent d'énormes sources de revenus qui provenaient de leurs commissions scandaleuses sur les flux financiers, les transferts d'argent et leurs conseils d'investissements fumeux – mais maintenant, en revanche, elles gagnent à prendre position dans l'univers des données et des plates-formes. Désormais, il y a bien plus à vendre que de simples services financiers ; les données des consommateurs sont devenues la nouvelle unité de compte des institutions financières. Les données ne sont pas simplement le nouveau pétrole – maintenant les données sont aussi la nouvelle monnaie.

Le crime et les guerres se sont numérisés. Maintenant que tout et tout le monde est connecté, et que tout est source de données en temps réel, nous sommes devenus totalement dépendants de la connectivité. Tout ce qui est disruptif est considéré comme une agression contre « le système ». Les attaques sur les infrastructures technologiques, les accès non-autorisés à nos données et la manipulation des informations sont devenus une menace constante, et plus de 50% du budget militaire de chaque nation sont consacrés à la lutte contre les infractions à la sécurité, la cybercriminalité et les batailles numériques de toute nature. Le champ de bataille est numérique et les IAs sont les nouveaux soldats.

Bientôt, même le fait de penser ne sera plus considéré comme une activité privée. ICOs et implants peu couteux et simples

d'emploi commencent à voir le jour un peu partout, permettant des connexions directes vers ou à partir de nos cerveaux, donnant un prolongement à notre néocortex dans le *cloud*. Chaque pensée provoque une réaction physique dans nos esprits et dans nos corps, laquelle pourra très bientôt être enregistrée et au moins partiellement utilisée en matière de santé, de loisirs et de sécurité.

En 2024, nous sommes constamment connectés à des machines et elles deviennent de plus en plus performantes pour lire nos esprits.

2026 : l'automatisation généralisée et le Revenu Universel garanti

Fini le temps où les tâches de routine – accomplies par des cols bleus ou des cols blancs, manuelles ou intellectuelles – étaient effectuées par un humain. Les machines ont appris comment déchiffrer une langue, des images, des émotions et des croyances. Les machines peuvent également parler, écrire, dessiner et simuler des émotions humaines. Les machines ne peuvent pas être, mais elles peuvent penser. Des centaines de millions d'emplois sont transférés aux machines dans les centres d'appels, de maintenance, dans les services juridiques, de distribution, de production et dans la finance. La recherche et le développement sont également pris en charge par des machines. Nous avons vu les premiers exemples d'IA travaillant à des fonctions scientifiques il y a une dizaine d'années. Aux alentours de 2020, elles ont commencé à dépasser les scientifiques humains dans leur rapidité de découverte. Aujourd'hui, les robots assimilent de manière routinière des milliards de flux de données et mènent des expériences dans le *cloud*, appliquant des approches entièrement neuves à des défis scientifiques fondamentaux.

Les emplois purement humains se font de plus en plus rares, mais d'une manière générale, tout ce qui ne peut pas être numérisé, automatisé, virtualisé ou robotisé tend constamment à prendre de la valeur. Coupler des gens à des machines est devenu

la nouvelle norme – car dans bien des situations, une machine travaillant avec un humain surpasse encore n'importe quelle machine sans implication humaine.

Le revenu tend à se découpler du travail, et la rémunération ne dépend plus forcément du nombre d'heures travaillées. Être payé en fonction des résultats et de la performance émerge en tant que modèle dominant de rémunération. Et finalement, travailler moins devient une nouvelle norme (assurément un paradis aux yeux de beaucoup). Les coûts de beaucoup de produits et services de grande consommation comme les transports, le logement, les médias et les communications chutent de manière spectaculaire, parce que les machines effectuent le gros du travail, et qu'elles sont capables de produire la plupart des produits et services tellement moins cher. La seule chose qui continue à se renchérir, c'est de choisir de ne plus être tracé et surveillé en permanence.

La logique économique qui sous-tendait le fait de travailler pour vivre est en train de s'évaporer ; bien au contraire, nous commençons à choisir de travailler dans un but donné. Un revenu universel (RU) est d'ores et déjà en place dans douze pays, y compris la Suisse et la Finlande, et on s'attend en général à ce qu'il devienne un standard global dans les deux prochaines décennies, donnant le signal d'une nouvelle ère post-capitaliste.

Les machines accomplissant désormais tout le travail difficile, un nombre croissant de gens choisissent de faire ce dont ils ont envie, plutôt que de se cantonner à ce qui paie les factures. Le RU est devenu un facteur-clé du bonheur social, générant un nouvel essor des arts, des artisanats, de l'entreprenariat et de l'esprit public.

En 2026, l'automatisation est généralisée, le travail en déclin et les normes sociales sont en voie de réinvention.

2028 : le libre arbitre n'appartient qu'aux riches

Tout ce que nous faisons, disons, voyons et, de plus en plus, ressentons et pensons pouvant maintenant être tracé et mesuré,

l'importance du libre arbitre tend désormais à décroître, notre capacité ancestrale à prendre nos propres décisions sans pression extérieure se heurtant à l'obligation de composer. Il ne nous est plus possible de nous écarter aisément de ce que le système estime être le meilleur pour nous, tout simplement parce que tout est scruté. Tout est pensé pour rendre nos vies plus saines et plus responsables, pour amoindrir les coûts de santé et pour tendre vers une sécurité presque parfaite. Moyennant quoi nombre d'entre nous ne sont plus très sûrs de savoir s'il s'agit d'un paradis ou d'un enfer.

Nous ne contrôlons déjà plus notre propre régime alimentaire, parce que l'obésité et la surconsommation ont démontré, partout dans le monde, à quel point elles représentaient un fardeau majeur pour les systèmes de santé publique. Le sucre, le tabac, l'alcool et la caféine sont des substances strictement contrôlées. Chacun doit régulièrement se soumettre à des procédures de surveillance, qu'il s'agisse des intrants (la nourriture) ou de la production de déchets.

Les imprimantes 3D sont devenues il y a longtemps aussi bon marché que les imprimantes à jet d'encre, les coûts les plus importants étant ceux de l'encre et des matières premières les alimentant. Les imprimantes alimentaires utilisent dorénavant des ingrédients bios et sains pour produire des pizzas, des gâteaux, du pain et des desserts à volonté, ainsi que beaucoup d'autres possibilités avec des composants artificiels. La nourriture est devenue aussi abondante que l'information, la musique et la vidéo.

Cependant, notre liste d'achats reste déterminée par ce que nous sommes autorisés à consommer, en fonction de ce que disent nos données alimentaires dans le *cloud* dédié à la santé. Les réfrigérateurs ne nous donneront pas accès à leur compartiment alimentaire avant une certaine heure préréglée, et aucun restaurant ne nous servira de plats qui n'aient été préalablement approuvés par nos ANI.

En dernier ressort, c'est un gain pour tout le monde : les gens sont en meilleure santé, les gouvernements font des économies et les entreprises, en plein essor, de biens de grande consommation sont désormais en mesure de marketer des produits 100% personnalisés à l'attention de chaque consommateur individuel.

À moins bien sûr que vous ne disposiez de ressources illimitées pour tromper le système, pour acheter ou créer de fausses identités numériques, pour avoir accès à l'une de ces imprimantes alimentaires 3D vraiment hors de prix, ou pour vous approvisionner sur des marchés noirs alimentaires du *dark net* comme Milk Road – un successeur du site de marché noir Silk Road apparu au début du XXIe siècle.

De toute façon, comme nous le savons bien aujourd'hui, le libre arbitre a toujours été un truc très surfait !

En 2028, nos vies sont devenues tracées, guidées, organisées ; le libre arbitre et le libre choix sont du domaine exclusif des super-riches.

2030 : 90 est le nouveau 60

Aux alentours de 2030, technologie et pharmacie ont presque intégralement convergé. Les plus graves maladies du genre humain, dont le cancer, le diabète, les affections cardiaques et le SIDA sont en voie d'être vaincus par la bio-ingénierie avancée. Dorénavant, il est très rare que nous prenions des pilules pour combattre maladies et épidémies ; à la place, nous mobilisons de plus en plus la technologie et l'édition du génome pour observer, prévoir et prévenir l'occurrence des maladies.

Parce que nous avons analysé l'ADN de milliards d'humains connectés par l'entremise de la biologie du *cloud* et de l'informatique quantique, nous sommes désormais en mesure de déterminer avec une forte certitude quel gène précis est responsable du déclenchement de telle maladie. D'ici à cinq ans environ, nous serons capables de prévenir le cancer.

La longévité a explosé, et du même coup complètement bouleversé nos systèmes sociaux. La plupart d'entre nous étant désormais capables de vivre en très bonne santé jusqu'à 90 ans, et les robots et logiciels accomplissant pour nous la plupart des travaux pénibles, nous pouvons consacrer notre temps à aider les prochaines générations à comprendre le passé et découvrir le futur. Le RU ayant été institué par la plupart des villes et des nations, nous n'avons plus à nous soucier de nos retraites ou de gagner nos vies, comme nos pères et nos mères l'ont fait.

En 2030, la société est plus âgée, en meilleure santé, libérée du travail et en quête de sens.

Infernalisiaque – un chemin inévitable ?

Pourquoi le futur ne serait-il pas désirable ? Ces scénarios sont plausibles et pour le moins un peu conservateurs, si on les compare aux visions et aspirations techno-progressistes. La technologie a gagné sa guerre avec l'humanité, ce qui n'a d'ailleurs peut-être jamais été une guerre du tout. Quel besoin aurait-on de se préoccuper de valeurs humaines démodées et de hasards heureux, puisque les risques et les inconvénients d'être en vie sont en train d'être éradiqués à si vive allure ?

Avec une humanité finalement investie du contrôle de son propre avenir, qui donc aurait besoin de rêver d'un autre futur ?

Chapitre 12
Le temps de la décision

Il est temps de choisir votre camp.

Ce livre m'a été inspiré par les travaux de nombreuses personnes qui ont exprimé des préoccupations similaires et tout ce que je peux espérer, c'est que cela va contribuer à nourrir un débat mondial sur les buts et l'éthique de la technologie – ainsi que sur l'éthique de ceux qui la conçoivent et la diffusent.

De plus en plus, les humains et la technologie se chevauchent, interagissent ou même convergent – la façon dont vous en parlerez dépend de vos sentiments à ce sujet. Mais quoi qu'il en soit, ainsi que je l'ai indiqué dès le début de ce livre, voici ce qui ne fait aucun doute : je pense que l'humanité changera probablement davantage lors des vingt prochaines années qu'au cours des trois cent ans qui ont précédé.

La convergence homme-machine qui s'annonce se traduira par des victoires spectaculaires pour l'humanité, mais, simultanément, accroîtra les menaces envers elle. Il nous faut par conséquent devenir de bien meilleurs gestionnaires de nos inventions et de leurs conséquences, si nous voulons nous épanouir.

Oui, le progrès technologique paraît impossible à arrêter, car il est dans la nature humaine de conjecturer, de tester er de déployer notre *techne* – c'est-à-dire nos outils. À ceci près que nous avons finalement atteint le point où les standards et les politiques anthropocentrées, l'éthique numérique, les contrats sociaux et les accords globaux sur la manière d'humaniser ces technologies

exponentielles sont devenus aussi vitaux que les traités de non-prolifération nucléaire.

Dans un avenir très proche, la question ne sera plus de savoir si la technologie est en mesure d'accomplir ceci ou cela (car la réponse sera presque toujours oui), mais de savoir si elle le doit, et pourquoi.

Le danger est que si nous ne consacrons pas autant de temps et de ressources aux androrithmes (ces qualités qui nous rendent humains) que nous n'en consacrons aux algorithmes, non seulement la technologie finira par régner sur nos vies, mais en outre nous serons contraints, amenés ou convaincus de nous transformer nous-mêmes en technologie. Nous pourrions bien, alors, être devenus les « outils de nos outils ».

Quand je parle d'une technologie qui pourrait régner sur nos vies, je ne pense pas aux robots dominateurs de *Terminator Genisys*. [200] Mais je m'inquiète plutôt de ce que nous devenions totalement inutiles si nous en venions à être privés de technologie – autrement dit lents, incomplets, débiles, incompétents, paresseux et obèses.

Imaginez ce qui se passerait si nous continuions à dévaluer et éroder ces qualités éminemment humaines que sont l'intimité, le mystère, l'anonymat, les émotions, la spontanéité, la surprise, l'intuition, l'imagination, la spiritualité – tout cela pour pouvoir continuer à nous mesurer aux machines.

Si nous ne voulons pas devenir nous-mêmes de la technologie, si nous ne voulons pas être de plus en plus engloutis par le puissant vortex créé par les méga-changements, si nous voulons envers et contre tout rester « naturellement humains » en dépit des attraits considérables de ces technologies magiques, si nous voulons préserver ce qui nous rend réellement heureux et pas seulement ce qui nous fait fonctionner, alors il nous faut agir tant que nous sommes encore aux manettes. C'est le moment, maintenant.

Nous devons commencer à demander « pourquoi », puis « qui » et « quand », et pas seulement « si » et « comment ». Nous

devons nous poser la question des buts, et pas seulement des profits. Nous devons demander des comptes aux leaders industriels, tout particulièrement les technologues et les firmes qui les emploient. Nous devons tous les astreindre à adopter des démarches plus holistiques et à prendre en compte toutes les implications, les bonnes et les moins bonnes, de ce qu'ils proposent. Il nous faut également leur demander de reconnaître et traiter les conséquences inattendues de leurs décisions, et d'inclure ces externalités, quel que soit ce qu'ils créent, dans leurs stratégies d'affaires et leurs modèles économiques.

Les créateurs et les financiers de demain devront être tenus pour responsables de chacun de leurs actes – ainsi que nous-mêmes bien entendu, en tant qu'utilisateurs et consommateurs. Nous devons commencer à refuser notre clientèle aux entreprises qui ne nous semblent pas assez attentives à ces enjeux, et de même refuser de continuer à fournir nos contenus aux plates-formes qui cherchent à nous automatiser. Cessons d'être des contributeurs silencieux à la prééminence des machines pensantes, sous prétexte que nous serions forcément moins « appropriés ».

Si nous ne voulons pas finir avec ce que j'appelle le « remords d'Oppenheimer » – en référence au célèbre physicien J. Robert Oppenheimer, dont les découvertes ont contribué à faire de la bombe atomique une réalité, et qui par la suite a regretté ses actes et leurs conséquences –, alors nous devons nous engager en faveur du « camp humain » et placer l'humanité au-dessus de tout le reste.

À cet effet, je propose que nous tentions de définir les règles élémentaires de base de cet âge de la machine annoncé, règles qui détermineront quelles technologies seront les plus à même de promouvoir l'épanouissement humain, et donc encouragées, et lesquelles ne le seront pas. Il nous faut également apprendre à poser plus souvent les questions « quand, pourquoi et qui », de même qu'il nous faut réfléchir aux instances effectivement investies du contrôle de conformité à ces règles.

Il ne fait aucun doute que ce sera là une tâche énorme, et certainement lourde d'incertitudes quant au consensus global auquel nous pourrions parvenir, ne serait-ce que sur les règles les plus élémentaires s'appliquant à toute l'humanité.

Moyennant quoi, si nous avons à cœur de maîtriser les confrontations imminentes entre humains et machines décrites dans ce livre, nous aurons besoin d'une nouvelle forme de gouvernance globale, nourrie d'anticipations toujours plus affûtées. De règles de base à la fois incontournables et suffisamment flexibles pour ne pas inhiber le progrès. Intimidant ? Assurément. Impossible. Certainement pas. D'autres choix possibles ? Aucun.

Neuf principes à méditer

Afin d'alimenter le débat sur le meilleur chemin à emprunter, j'ai conçu neuf principes généraux. Ils s'efforcent de capter l'essentiel des arguments fondamentaux que j'ai présentés au fil des pages de ce livre – mais n'en restent pas moins un travail perfectible, loin d'être achevé ou définitif.

1. **Nous améliorer considérablement dans la compréhension de ce qu'est l'exponentialité et de ce qu'elle signifie pour le futur de l'humanité.** Nous devons apprendre à imaginer, puis à vivre avec les changements exponentiels et combinatoires. À court terme, se contenter « d'attendre et de voir » serait aussi stupide que de « faire sans réfléchir ». Il nous faut considérer « graduellement, puis soudainement » comme la nouvelle norme, et ne plus gâcher nos perspectives d'avenir alors qu'elles sont encore devant nous. Rappelons-nous aussi que notre futur est une matière en constante redéfinition et reconfiguration, et pas simplement quelque chose qui est destiné à advenir. Pour parvenir à reprendre la main, il nous faut être curieux et ouverts, nous immerger dans des scénarios potentiels, découvrir ce que pourrait vraiment être de vivre dans cet

avenir-là, nous mettre en relation avec des acteurs de ce même futur et améliorer notre conscience globale du Zeitgeist environnant. Supposons moins, découvrons davantage et débarrassons-nous de ces préjugés toxiques qui par le passé ont si bien fonctionné ! Prenons à bras le corps les progrès spectaculaires de la science, mais toujours dans le contexte du projet humain global. La technologie peut incarner l'enfer comme le paradis, ou les deux (#*hellven*), alors tâchons d'être à la fois proactifs et précautionneux, selon l'ampleur de ce qui est en jeu, où et quand.

2. **Nos défis les plus ardus génèrent souvent les plus incroyables opportunités (et vice versa).** Une bonne part de notre avenir dépendra de notre manière d'user de la technologie, dans une recherche d'équilibre délicate entre magie et maniaquerie – mais, espérons-le, sans basculer dans la névrose. Dans la mesure où, ainsi que le suggère William Gibson, la technologie est moralement neutre jusqu'à ce que nous la mettions en pratique, [201] atteindre ce point d'équilibre reposera davantage sur la concrétisation et la mise en œuvre des applications de la technologie que sur l'anticipation ou la réglementation des inventions elles-mêmes. Le futur n'est pas une question de oui ou non, mais plutôt de « ça dépend ». Je suis persuadé que si nous parvenions à faire entendre plus souvent des interrogations telles que « pourquoi ? » ou « pour quel usage ? », une approche plus mesurée de ces sujets émergerait.

3. **Il nous faut devenir de bien meilleurs gestionnaires de l'humanité.** Chaque responsable économique, chaque pionnier de la technologie et chaque haut fonctionnaire doit accepter de se sentir responsable de l'avenir de l'humanité, et agir en conséquence. Nos responsables civils et politiques doivent développer une compréhension profonde et une vision personnelle de la technologie au regard des attentes

de l'humanité et ainsi devenir les régisseurs de notre avenir commun. Dans tous les domaines de chaque secteur économique, nous allons avoir besoin de nouvelles formes d'hyper-collaboration et non d'hyper-compétition, de même que nous aurons besoin de mettre en œuvre une appréhension holistique de l'ensemble de ces domaines traditionnellement séparés.

4. **La technologie n'a pas d'éthique, mais une société sans éthique est condamnée.** Nous nous dirigeons vers un futur où littéralement tout ce qui nous entoure sera impacté par un tsunami d'avancées technologiques, et pourtant la manière dont nous nous représentons le monde, notre manière d'évaluer le bien et le mal, ou encore notre façon de décider d'utiliser ou pas telle ou telle technologie reste tributaire d'expériences passées, de grilles d'analyses anciennes et, pire que tout, d'un mode de pensée linéaire.

Notre éthique – et avec elle nombre de nos lois et règlements – reste fondée sur un monde qui progresse de façon linéaire et sur « ce qui fonctionnait » avant que nous n'atteignions le point de bascule sur la courbe exponentielle. Depuis qu'Internet est devenu un acteur significatif du commerce, nous nous sommes surtout concentrés sur l'exploitation de ses promesses économiques et commerciales. Mais en revanche nous n'avons pas suffisamment pris en considération son impact sur nos valeurs et notre éthique – une faiblesse devenue criante alors que nous entrons dans l'âge de l'intelligence artificielle (IA), de la robotique et de l'édition du génome humain.

Il y a eu récemment de plus en plus de discussions autour de l'idée de fabriquer des machines pensantes qui seraient en mesure de simuler l'éthique humaine. Bien que cela constitue un virage intéressant, je suis frappé de constater qu'il s'agit là d'un pas supplémentaire en direction d'un âge

généralisé de la machine et de la simulation – raison de plus, me semble-t-il, pour instituer un Conseil mondial d'éthique numérique. Alors que nous progressons vers la Singularité, et vers le point où les ordinateurs, organisés en réseau global géant, égaleront ou dépasseront les aptitudes et capacités du cerveau humain, il nous faut d'urgence établir un contexte éthique clair sur lequel la majorité d'entre nous pourra s'entendre. Ce n'est pas une tâche facile, mais elle est cruciale et il nous faut, malgré tout, nous y attaquer.

5. **Attention, vigilance : il est fréquent que les technologies exponentielles mutent rapidement de la magie à la névrose, d'où la nécessité de trouver un équilibre.** Si vous pensez que l'addiction à Internet, aux jeux et aux *smartphones*, ou que les pièges à plaisir des réseaux sociaux constituent déjà un sujet d'importance, alors attentez donc de voir se déployer tout ce qui nous attend ! Attendez donc de nous voir complètement immergés dans la technologie, au point de la voir pénétrer nos propres corps via la réalité virtuelle, les interfaces cerveau-ordinateur et les interfaces neurales.

Il n'y a littéralement pas de limites à ce que le progrès exponentiel pourrait rendre possible. D'où il résulte qu'il nous faut apprendre dès à présent à nous servir de la technologie de manière holistique et avec un respect accru pour les besoins et les manières de faire humains. Nous devons également rendre ceux qui inventent, fabriquent et commercialisent ces nouvelles solutions technologiques si attrayantes responsables des nouveaux écosystèmes qu'ils élaborent, et faire en sorte qu'ils nous fournissent des moyens effectifs d'en maîtriser ou d'en limiter les conséquences involontaires. Les fournisseurs de technologie doivent impérativement commencer à inclure les effets collatéraux dans leurs *business models* et contribuer à

l'élaboration de nouveaux contrats sociaux prenant en compte leurs effets toxiques.

6. **Nous devons enseigner à la fois les STIM et les CORE (Compassion, Originalité, Réciprocité et Empathie).** La technologie et l'humanité doivent l'une et l'autre figurer sur le C.V. – parce qu'au fond, science et philosophie font partie du même cursus. Toute société équilibrée sera demandeuse d'expertise dans les deux domaines – faute de quoi nous continuerons à faire pencher la balance en faveur de la pensée machinique.

De plus, une proportion de plus en plus importante de travaux scientifiques finira par être réalisée par des IA et des machines intelligentes ; c'est pourquoi il nous faut placer sur le devant de la scène le développement des talents et aptitudes exclusivement humains. La créativité, la compréhension, la négociation, le questionnement, les émotions, l'intuition et l'imagination seront encore plus importants qu'avant : tout ce qui ne pourra être numérisé, automatisé ou virtualisé deviendra extrêmement précieux.

7. **Il nous faut établir une distinction claire entre ce qui est réel et ce qui est copie ou simulation.** La connectivité totale, les machines pensantes, le *cloud* intelligent et l'informatique cognitive sont inévitablement à l'horizon de notre avenir, ce qui implique de ne surtout pas abandonner la distinction entre la simulation (les machines) et l'être (*dasein*), entre le calcul et la sentience, entre le genre machinique et le genre humain. Nous immerger dans un monde de simulations incroyables pourrait certes nous être très utile pour l'enseignement, les loisirs ou le travail, mais cela devrait-il pour autant devenir notre mode de vie en général ?

Ces technologies pourraient-elles devenir une sorte de drogue universelle dont nous serions perpétuellement avides

pour nous sentir complets ? Faudra-t-il établir des limites et des règles sur la quantité ou la profondeur technologique permises ? Et si la technologie cesse d'être ce que nous cherchons pour devenir *comment* nous cherchons, alors n'aurons-nous pas besoin d'être aidés pour continuer à opérer une distinction entre ces outils et nos véritables objectifs ? Construire des relations avec les humains doit impérativement rester plus important que construire des relations avec des machines. Embrassons la technologie, mais n'en devenons pas esclaves !

8. **Apprenons à demander Pourquoi et Qui, et pas seulement Si ou Comment.** Les décisions stratégiques futures sur le développement et le déploiement de la technologie devraient davantage relever du bon sens, du contexte, de l'objectif et de la pertinence que d'une simple évaluation de la faisabilité, des coûts, de l'échelle, des bénéfices et de la contribution à la croissance. La question du comment *doit* être remplacée par la question du pourquoi.

9. **Nous ne devrions pas laisser la Silicon Valley, ses technologues, ses militaires ou ses investisseurs être dépositaires du contrôle de la technologie au nom de l'humanité – et cela quel que soit le pays dont ils sont ressortissants.** Ceux qui financent, créent et vendent des technologies exponentielles ne seront probablement pas désireux de voir limiter leur puissance ou restreindre leurs applications potentielles. Ceux qui construiront des machines de guerre ne seront pas les mêmes que ceux qui se concentreront sur le bonheur humain. Ceux qui investissent dans les technologies disruptives pour générer des retours au centuple ne seront pas de ceux qui investiront dans l'élaboration de sociétés véritablement humaines pour le bénéfice du plus grand nombre. Ceux qui construisent ces

outils ont leur propre agenda, essentiellement lié au profit et au pouvoir – alors où interviennent, dans le processus de décision, les représentants des utilisateurs ?

L'évaluation des technologies exponentielles : sept questions essentielles à poser
Étant donné qu'une bonne partie de ce livre concerne la façon dont l'humanité pourrait sortir victorieuse de cette bataille imminente avec les technologies exponentielles, voici sept questions que j'estime essentiel de poser pour évaluer l'ampleur des changements radicaux en cours. J'ai bien conscience que dans bien des cas, la réponse correcte pourrait être « l'un et l'autre » ou encore « ça dépend ». Néanmoins, il me semble que le simple fait de prendre le temps de poser ces questions peut nous aider à comprendre plus clairement les compromis en question.

1. **Cette technologie est-elle en mesure de nous déshumaniser, incidemment ou à dessein ?** Cherchera-t-elle à remplacer par des algorithmes des interactions humaines importantes, qui ne devraient faire l'objet d'aucune intermédiation ? Procédera-t-elle à l'automatisation de fonctions exclusivement humaines, qui ne devraient vraiment pas l'être ? Cette technologie nous libère-t-elle de fardeaux non-nécessaires et non-essentiels, ou au contraire nous pousse-t-elle à faire l'impasse sur ce qui est fondamentalement humain ? Est-ce un vortex, ou un catalyseur ?

2. **Cette technologie contribuera-t-elle à faire progresser le véritable bonheur humain ?** Cela nous conduira-t-il à nous sentir plus heureux avec ce que nous possédons, à mieux atteindre l'*eudaemonia* et à une contribution personnelle plus harmonieuse ? Cela dépassera-t-il de loin la simple fourniture de plaisirs hédonistes ou bien s'agira-t-il essentiellement d'un outil hédoniste cherchant à nous

abuser sous les apparences d'un bonheur plus profond ?

3. **Cette technologie a-t-elle des effets secondaires involontaires et potentiellement désastreux ?** Nous fera-t-elle perdre collectivement notre autorité ou nous rendra-t-elle plus autonomes ? Aura-t-elle un impact significatif sur des écosystèmes cruciaux pour bien des gens et, si tel est le cas, fera-t-elle en sorte d'inclure la prise en compte de ces effets secondaires dans son schéma économique ?

4. **Cette technologie se confère-t-elle trop d'autorité à elle-même, ou encore à d'autres algorithmes, robots et machines ?** Ses utilisateurs seront-ils tentés, ce faisant, d'abdiquer leur propre autorité ? Nous sentirons-nous encouragés à lui déléguer nos capacités de réflexion ? Cette technologie sera-t-elle à notre service, ou se révélera-t-elle avant tout au service d'elle-même – autrement dit plus encline à prendre qu'à donner ?

5. **Cette technologie nous donnera-t-elle la possibilité de la transcender, c'est-à-dire de la dépasser, ou bien nous rendra-t-elle dépendants d'elle ?** Cette technologie placera-t-elle les humains dans un rôle subalterne, que ce soit par intention ou par accident ? Excédera-t-elle tellement nos propres aptitudes que nous serons amenés à suivre inconditionnellement ses conseils et ses décisions ?

6. **Les humains devront-ils matériellement se transformer ou être augmentés pour être effectivement capable de se servir de telle ou telle technologie ?** Cette technologie nous conduira-t-elle à améliorer nos corps et nos sens, ou bien agira-t-elle dans les limites existantes de ce que nous sommes ? Serons-nous contraints de nous améliorer et de nous augmenter si nous voulons accéder à des emplois, à l'éducation et à la santé ?

7. **Cette technologie sera-t-elle propriétaire ou en libre accès ?** Pourrons-nous nous en emparer pour l'aménager, ou bien sera-t-elle verrouillée ? Sera-t-elle accessible à tout un chacun, ou bien uniquement au 1% de super-nantis ? Accroîtra-t-elle les inégalités, ou bien contribuera-t-elle à les amoindrir ? Et comment serons-nous en mesure de connaître l'étendue de la richesse amassée par les fournisseurs dominants si la technologie peut contrôler notre accès à l'information ?

Êtes-vous dans l'équipe humaine ?

Lorsque j'ai, pour la première fois, entendu ce puissant meme de Douglas Rushkoff [202], j'ai aussitôt pensé que cela nous fournirait une excellente devise au fil de notre voyage en direction du futur.

Car voilà ce qu'« *être dans l'équipe humaine* » signifie pour moi :

- Placer notre épanouissement humain collectif au-dessus de toute autre préoccupation.
- Faire en sorte que les androrithmes, ces caractéristiques humaines telles que l'imagination, le hasard, les erreurs et les insuffisances, continuent à prévaloir, même si elles apparaissent inopportunes aux yeux de la technologie, ou incompatibles avec elle.
- Combattre toute prolifération des machines pensantes qui conduirait à remettre en question ce que nous représentons et ce dont nous avons besoin en tant qu'humains, sous prétexte que cela rendrait les choses plus faciles pour les technologies qui nous entourent.
- Ne pas succomber à la séduction qu'exerce la magie technologique, ne pas préférer la simulation de la réalité à la réalité elle-même, ne pas devenir dépendant(e) de la technologie.

- Ne pas préférer les relations avec des écrans et des machines aux relations que nous pouvons avoir avec nos semblables humains..

Ainsi que je l'ai indiqué en commençant ce livre, mon propos a été de mettre en relief les défis, d'enclencher le débat et de susciter des réponses argumentées. Et vous, que feriez-vous pour nourrir cet échange au sein de votre organisation, de votre communauté, de votre famille et de vos cercles d'amis ?

Pour ma part, je vais continuer à enquêter sur ce que signifie faire partie de l'équipe humaine, par le biais de mes activités de conférencier, consultant, auteur et réalisateur audiovisuel. N'hésitez pas à vous joindre à la discussion sur le site internet dédié à ce livre, www.techvshuman.com, et sur le micro-site www.onteamhuman.com.

Remerciements

Ce livre n'aurait pas vu le jour sans le soutien de toutes ces personnes formidables :

Ma chère épouse, **Angelica Feldmann**, qui a enduré avec amour et patience mon absence physique et/ou mentale au cours des 18 derniers mois. Mais aussi, ses critiques indispensables et son indéfectible soutien tout au long de la réalisation de cet ouvrage.

Jean Francois Cardella, producteur, directeur artistique, mon conseiller créatif et ami.

François Mazoudier, pour ses commentaires honnêtes et son amitié.

James McCabe, pour sa merveilleuse écriture de scénarios et ses corrections linguistiques.

Rohit Talwar, **Steve Wells** y **April Koury** — l'équipe de *Fast Future Publishing* pour leur compétence éditoriale et juridique pour transformer le manuscrit brut en un produit fini.

David Battino, pour le développement éditorial.

Maggie Langrick, pour ses modifications structurelles initiales et ses conseils avisés.

L'équipe de **Like.Digital** à Londres, pour la réalisation du site web www.techvshuman.com.

Benjamin Blust, mon *webmaster* et directeur technique.

Sur les épaules de géants

Ce livre s'inspire du travail de nombreux visionnaires: auteurs, écrivains, conférenciers, penseurs, personnalités, chefs d'entreprises et cinéastes. Merci à vous tous!

Voici la partie émergée de cet iceberg:

James Barrat	Andrew Keen
Yochai Benkler	Kevin Kelly
Nick Bostrom	Ray Kurzweil
Richard Branson	Jaron Lanier
David Brin	Larry Lessig
Erik Brynjoffson	John Markoff
Nicholas Carr	Andrew McAfee
Noam Chomsky	Elon Musk
Paulo Coelho	Thomas Piketty
El Dalái Lama	Jeremy Rifkin
Peter Diamandis	Charlie Rose
Philp K. Dick	Douglas Rushkoff
Cory Doctorow	Clay Shirky
Dave Eggers	Tiffany Shlain
John Elkington	Edward Snowden
William Gibson	Don Tapscott
Daniel Kahneman	

Ressources

Vous pouvez rejoindre la discussion sur la technologie contre l'humanité dans les réseaux sociaux, et consulter plus de contenu en anglais à travers:

Mises à jour régulières: www.techvshuman.com

Twitter: www.twitter.com/techvshuman

Plus d'information sur Gerd Leonhard et son oeuvre:

Site web en anglais : www.futuristgerd.com

Site web en alleman : www.gerdleonhard.de

Showreel de ses meilleures
présentations en 2017 : gerd.io/2017bestofgerd

Videos des memes clés de Gerd : www.humanity.digital

Twitter : www.twitter.com/gleonhard

LinkedIn : ch.linkedin.com/in/gleonhard

The Futures Agency : www.thefuturesagency.com

S'abonner à la newsletter : www.gerd.digital

Contact : books@thefuturesagency.com

Fast Future Publishing

Nous sommes une nouvelle génération d'éditeurs fondée par trois futuristes: Rohit Talwar, Steve Wells et April Koury. Notre but est de faire le point sur les dernières réflexions de futuristes établis ou émergents. Mais aussi de collecter le opinions de chercheurs clairvoyants et de penseurs du monde entier. Nous voulons partager ces idées et les rendre accessibles au grand public dans les plus brefs délais.

Notre série de livres FutureScapes est conçue pour aborder des thèmes d'actualité qui selon nous, propose des programmes pertinents pour les citoyens, les gouvernements, les entreprises et la société civile. *Technology vs. Humanity* est le deuxième livre de cette série.

Notre premier ouvrage, *The Future of Business*, comporte 60 chapitres concis. Il contient 566 pages de réflexion pointue émanant de 62 penseurs contemporains dans 21 pays différents sur quatre continents. Alors que les éditeurs traditionnels prendraient deux ans pour publier un tel ouvrage, nous l'avons fait en seulement 19 semaines!

Nous avons également créé un modèle commercial novateur qui contourne la plupart des pratiques traditionnelles de publication. Nous avons adopté une dynamique exponentielle à l'image de l'ère numérique afin de réformer le processus de publication, la distribution et le plan de partage des bénéfices.

Notre modèle d'édition garantit non seulement à nos auteurs mais également au noyau dur de l'équipe ainsi qu'aux partenaires associés à chaque ouvrage, un partage équitable des bénéfices. En outre, une partie de ces bénéfices est allouée à un fonds d'investissement pour financer les causes que nous soutenons. Pour *The Future of Business*, le fonds servira à alimenter des bourses d'études pour ceux qui souhaitent suivre des cours de

recherche prospective et de pratique. Pour *Technology vs. Humanity*, le fonds sera axé sur les initiatives visant à promouvoir le débat.

Nous espérons que notre histoire et notre approche de l'édition seront une source d'inspiration pour les entreprises qui évoluent dans l'ère numérique.

Au cours des prochaines années, Fast Future Publishing vise à publier le travail de futuristes inspirés. Nous invitons les futurs auteurs intéressés à compiler et à éditer des livres multi-contributeurs dans le cadre de la série FutureScapes.

Pour les commandes institutionnelles ou en gros de *Technology vs. Humanity* ou *The Future of Business*, ou pour un partenariat, ou pour soumettre une proposition de livre, ou pour discuter de la création d'un projet multi-contributeurs ou encore pour tout renseignement sur les possibilités de contrat à durée indéterminée ou opportunités de stage, vous pouvez nous joindre à *info@fastfuturepublishing.com*

Pour de plus amples informations: www.fastfuturepublishing.com

Références

1 Moore (s.f.). Consulté le août 2016 : http://www.mooreslaw.com/

2 Loizos, C. (2015). Elon Musk Says Tesla Cars Will Reach 620 Miles On A Single Charge "Within A Year Or Two," Be Fully Autonomous In "Three Years". Consulté le 1 août 2016 : https://techcrunch.com/2015/09/29/elon-musk-says-tesla-cars-will-reach-620-miles-on-a-single-charge-within-a-year-or-two-have-fully-autonomous-cars-in-three-years/

3 BMW i8 Review After 3 Months Behind The Wheel. (s.f.). Consulté le 1 août 2016 : http://insideevs.com/bmw-i8-review-3-months-behind-wheel/

4 Covert, J. (2016). *Tesla Stations in NYC on Verge of Outnumbering Gas Stations*. Consulté le 29 juin 2016 : http://nypost.com/2016/03/17/tesla-stations-in-nyc-on-verge-of-outnumbering-gas-stations

5 Hayden, E. (2014). *Technology: The $1,000 Genome*. Consulté le 29 juin 2016 : http://www.nature.com/news/technology-the-1-000-genome-1.14901

6 Raj, A. (2014). *Soon, It Will Cost Less to Sequence a Genome Than to Flush a Toilet — and That Will Change Medicine Forever*. Consulté le 29 juin 2016 : http://www.businessinsider.com/super-cheap-genome-sequencing-by-2020-2014-10

7 Vinge, V. (1993). *Vernor Vinge on the Singularity*. Consulté le 29 juin 2016 : http://mindstalk.net/vinge/vinge-sing.html

8 Webb, R. (2013). *The Economics of Star Trek*. Consulté le 29 juin 2016 : https://medium.com/@RickWebb/the-economics-of-star-trek-29bab88d50

9 *10 Nikola Tesla Quotes That Still Apply Today*. (s.f.). Consulté le 3 août 2016 : http://www.lifehack.org/305348/10-nikola-tesla-quotes-that-still-apply-today

10 Metz, C. (2015). *Soon, Gmail's AI Could Reply to Your Email for You*. Consulté le 29 juin 2016 : http://www.wired.com/2015/11/google-is-using-ai-to-create-automatic-replies-in-gmail

11 *Surrogates*. (2016). Wikipedia. Consulté le 29 juin 2016 : https://en.wikipedia.org/wiki/Surrogates

12 AMC Network Entertainment. (2016). *HUMANS*. Consulté le 29 juin 2016 : http://www.amc.com/shows/humans

[13] S, L. (2015). *The Economist explains: The End of Moore's Law*. Consulté le 29 juin 2016 : http://www.economist.com/blogs/economist-explains/2015/04/economist-explains-17

[14] Booth, B. (2016, 31 mai). Riding the Gene Editing Wave: Reflections on CRISPR/Cas9's Impressive Trajectory. [Weblog]. Consulté le 22 juillet 2016 : http://www.forbes.com/sites/brucebooth/2016/05/31/riding-the-gene-editing-wave-reflections-on-crisprs-impressive-trajectory

[15] Bostrom, N. (2014). *Superintelligence: Paths, Dangers, Strategies*. : Oxford University Press.

[16] Urban, T. (2015, 22 janvier). The Artificial Intelligence Revolution: Part 1. [Weblog]. Consulté le 2 juillet 2016 : http://waitbutwhy.com/2015/01/artificial-intelligence-revolution-1.html

[17] Yudkowsky, E. (c2016). *Quote by Eliezer Yudkowsky: "By far the greatest danger of Artificial Intell"*. Consulté le 13 de juillet 2016 : https://www.goodreads.com/quotes/1228197-by-far-the-greatest-danger-of-artificial-intelligence-is-that

[18] Diamandis, P. (2015, 26 janvier). Ray Kurzweil's Mind-Boggling Predictions for the Next 25 Years. [Weblog]. Consulté le 2 de juillet 2016 : http://singularityhub.com/2015/01/26/ray-kurzweils-mind-boggling-predictions-for-the-next-25-years

[19] Matyszczyk, C. (2015, 1 octobre). Google Exec: With Robots in Our Brains, We'll Be Godlike. [Weblog]. Consulté le 2 juillet 2016 : http://www.cnet.com/news/google-exec-with-robots-in-our-brains-well-be-godlike

[20] Hemingway, E. (1996). *The Sun Also Rises*. New York: Scribner.

[21] Diamandis, P. (c2016). Peter Diamandis. Consulté le 2 juillet 2016 : http://diamandis.com/human-longevity-inc

[22] Istvan, Z. (2013). *The Transhumanist Wager* : Futurity Imagine Media.

[23] Bailey, J. (2014, juillet). Enframing the Flesh: Heidegger, Transhumanism, and the Body as "Standing Reserve". [Weblog]. Consulté le 3 juillet 2016 :http://jetpress.org/v24/bailey.htm

[24] Brainmetrix. (c2016). *IQ Definition*. Consulté le 3 juillet 2016 - http://www.brainmetrix.com/iq-definition

[25] *Maslow's Hierarchy of Needs*. (2016). Wikipedia. Consulté le 3 juillet 2016 : https://en.wikipedia.org/wiki/Maslow's_hierarchy_of_needs

[26] Gibney, E. (2016, 27 janvier). Google AI Algorithm Masters Ancient Game of Go. [Weblog]. Consulté le 3 juillet 2016 : http://www.nature.com/news/google-ai-algorithm-masters-ancient-game-of-go-1.19234

27 Istvan, Z. (2014, 04 août). Artificial Wombs Are Coming, but the Controversy Is Already Here. [Weblog]. Consulté le 3 juillet 2016 : https://motherboard.vice.com/en_us/article/8qx8kk/artificial-wombs-are-coming-and-the-controversys-already-here

28 Izquotes. (c2016). *Iz Quotes*. Consulté le 3 juillet 2016 : http://izquotes.com/quote/70915

29 McMullan, T. (2015, 23 juillet). What Does the Panopticon Mean in the Age of Digital Surveillance? [Weblog]. Consulté le 3 juillet 2016 : https://www.theguardian.com/technology/2015/jul/23/panopticon-digital-surveillance-jeremy-bentham

30 *J Robert Oppenheimer.* (2016). Wikipedia. Consulté le 3 juillet 2016 : https://en.wikipedia.org/wiki/J._Robert_Oppenheimer

31 Barrat, J. (2013). *Our Final Invention: Artificial Intelligence and the End of the Human Era.* NY: Thomas Dunne Books/St Martin's Press.

32 *Techne.* (2016). Wikipedia. Consulté le 3 juillet 2016 : https://en.wikipedia.org/wiki/Techne

33 Kuskis, A. (2013, 1 avril). "We Shape Our Tools and Thereafter Our Tools Shape Us". [Weblog]. Consulté le 3 juillet 2016 : https://mcluhangalaxy.wordpress.com/2013/04/01/we-shape-our-tools-and-thereafter-our-tools-shape-us

34 Bailey, J. (2014, juillet). Enframing the Flesh: Heidegger, Transhumanism, and the Body as "Standing Reserve". [Weblog]. Consulté le 3 juillet 2016 : http://jetpress.org/v24/bailey.htm

35 Walton, A. (2015, 8 avril). New Study Links Facebook to Depression: But Now We Actually Understand Why. [Weblog]. Consulté le 3 juillet 2016 : http://www.forbes.com/sites/alicegwalton/2015/04/08/new-study-links-facebook-to-depression-but-now-we-actually-understand-why

36 *Being and Time.* (2016). Wikipedia. Consulté le 3 juillet 2016 : https://en.wikipedia.org/wiki/Being_and_Time

37 Gray, R. (2016, 12 février). Would You MARRY a Robot?. [Weblog]. Consulté le 5 juillet 2016 : http://www.dailymail.co.uk/sciencetech/article-3366228/Would-MARRY-robot-Artificial-intelligence-allow-people-lasting-love-machines-expert-claims.html

38 Santa Maria, C. (2016, 10 février). Inside the Factory Where the World's Most Realistic Sex Robots Are Being Built. [Weblog]. Consulté le 5 juillet 2016 : http://fusion.net/story/281661/real-future-episode-6-sex-bots

39 Watercutter, A. (2016, 21 janvier). The VR Company Helping Filmmakers Put You Inside Movies. [Weblog]. Consulté le 5 juillet 2016 : http://www.wired.com/2016/01/sundance-volumetric-vr-8i

40 McLuhan, M. (1994). *Understanding Media: The Extensions of Man*. USA: MIT Press.

41 Burton-Hill, C. (2016, 16 février). The Superhero of Artificial Intelligence: Can This Genius Keep It in Check?. [Weblog]. Consulté le 5 juillet 2016 : https://www.theguardian.com/technology/2016/feb/16/demis-hassabis-artificial-intelligence-deepmind-alphago

42 Lanier, J. (2010). *You Are Not a Gadget*. : Alfred A Knopf.

43 *Transhumanism*. (2016). Wikipedia. Consulté le 3 juillet 2016 : https://en.wikipedia.org/wiki/Transhumanism

44 Brand, S. (1968). *Whole Earth Catalog*. Consulté le 3 juillet 2016 - http://www.wholeearth.com/issue/1010/article/195/we.are.as.gods

45 *Descartes: An Intellectual Biography*. (s.f.). Consulté le 3 août 2016 : https://books.google.at/books?id=QVwDs_Ikad0C

46 Leonhard, G & Kusek, D. (2005). *The Future of Music: Manifesto for the Digital Music Revolution*. : Berklee Press.

47 Murphy, K. (2007, 03 juin). Life for a Man on the Run. [Weblog]. Consulté le 5 juillet 2016 : http://articles.latimes.com/2007/jun/03/entertainment/ca-mccartney3

48 Leonhard, G. (2010). *Friction Is Fiction: the Future of Content, Media and Business*. : Lulu.

49 Morozov, E. (2016, 30 janvier). Cheap Cab Ride? You Must Have Missed Uber's True Cost. [Weblog]. Consulté le 5 juillet 2016 : http://www.theguardian.com/commentisfree/2016/jan/31/cheap-cab-ride-uber-true-cost-google-wealth-taxation

50 Andreessen, M. (2011, 20 août). Why Software Is Eating The World. [Weblog]. Consulté le 3 juillet 2016 : https://www.wsj.com/articles/SB10001424053111903480904576512250915629460

51 Gartner. (2013, 12 novembre). Gartner Says by 2017 Your Smartphone Will Be Smarter Than You. [Weblog]. Consulté le 11 juillet 2016 : http://www.gartner.com/newsroom/id/2621915

52 Dick, P. (c2016). *Quote by Philip K Dick: "There will come a time when it isn't 'They're s"*. Consulté le 3 juillet 2016 : http://www.goodreads.com/quotes/42173-there-will-come-a-time-when-it-isn-t-they-re-spying

53 Cisco. (2016). *Cisco Visual Networking Index Predicts Near-Tripling of IP Traffic by 2020.* Consulté le 4 juillet 2016 : http://investor.cisco.com/investor-relations/news-and-events/news/news-details/2016/Cisco-Visual-Networking-Index-Predicts-Near-Tripling-of-IP-Traffic-by-2020/default.aspx

54 Khedekar, N. (2014). *Tech2.* Consulté le 3 juillet 2016 : http://tech.firstpost.com/news-analysis/now-upload-share-1-8-billion-photos-everyday-meeker-report-224688.html

55 Deloitte. (c2016). *Predictions 2016: Photo Sharing: Trillions and Rising.* Consulté le 5 juillet 2016 : https://www2.deloitte.com/global/en/pages/technology-media-and-telecommunications/articles/tmt-pred16-telecomm-photo-sharing-trillions-and-rising.html

56 Scanadu. (2016). *Scanadu | Home.* Consulté le 5 juillet 2016 : https://www.scanadu.com

57 Eggers, D. (2013). *The Circle.* : Knopf.

58 Leonhard, G. (2015, 21 avril). What Are These "Unicorn" Companies You Speak Of?. [Weblog]. Consulté le 3 juillet 2016 : http://thefuturesagency.com/2015/04/21/unicorn-companies-what-are-they-and-why-are-they-important

59 Foroohar, R. (2016, 15 juin). How the Gig Economy Could Save Capitalism. [Weblog]. Consulté le 5 juillet 2016 : http://time.com/4370834/sharing-economy-gig-capitalism

60 Gunawardene, N. (2003). *Sir Arthur C Clarke.* Consulté le 3 juillet 2016 : https://www.clarkefoundation.org/

61 McMillan, R. (2015, 25 février). Google's AI Is Now Smart Enough to Play Atari Like the Pros. [Weblog]. Consulté le 7 juillet 2016 : http://www.wired.com/2015/02/google-ai-plays-atari-like-pros

62 Metz, C. (2016, 27 janvier). In Major AI Breakthrough, Google System Secretly Beats Top Player at the Ancient Game of Go. [Weblog]. Consulté le 7 juillet 2016 : http://www.wired.com/2016/01/in-a-huge-breakthrough-googles-ai-beats-a-top-player-at-the-game-of-go

63 Swearingen, J. (2016, 7 mars). Why Deep Blue Beating Garry Kasparov Wasn't the Beginning of the End of the Human Race. [Weblog]. Consulté le 5 juillet 2016 : http://www.popularmechanics.com/technology/apps/a19790/what-deep-blue-beating-garry-kasparov-reveals-about-todays-artificial-intelligence-panic

64 Schwartz, K. (c2013). *FCW.* Consulté le 5 juillet 2016 : https://fcw.com/microsites/2011/cloud-computing-download/financial-benefits-of-cloud-computing-to-federal-agencies.aspx

65 Gillis, T. (2016, 02 février). The Future of Security: Isolation. [Weblog]. Consulté le 3 juillet 2016 : http://www.forbes.com/sites/tomgillis/2016/02/02/the-future-of-security-isolation

66 Duffy, S. (2014, 17 avril). What If Doctors Could Finally Prescribe Behavior Change? [Weblog]. Consulté le 3 juillet 2016 : http://www.forbes.com/sites/sciencebiz/2014/04/17/what-if-doctors-could-finally-prescribe-behavior-change

67 Pande, V. (2015). *When Software Eats Bio*. Consulté le 3 juillet 2016 : http://a16z.com/2015/11/18/bio-fund

68 Google. (2016). *Now Cards — the Google app*. Consulté le 5 juillet 2016 : https://www.google.com/search/about/learn-more/now

69 *Minority Report (film)*. (2016). Wikipedia. Consulté le 3 juillet 2016 : https://en.wikipedia.org/wiki/Minority_Report_(film)

70 The Economist. (2016, 23 juin). Print My Ride. [Weblog]. Consulté le 3 juillet 2016 : http://www.economist.com/news/business/21701182-mass-market-carmaker-starts-customising-vehicles-individually-print-my-ride

71 Bloy, M. (2005). *The Luddites 1811-1816*. Consulté le 10 juillet 2016 : http://www.victorianweb.org/history/riots/luddites.html

72 *Technological Unemployment*. (2016). Wikipedia. Consulté le 12 juillet 2016 https://en.wikipedia.org/wiki/Technological_unemployment

73 *Focus on Inequality and Growth* (Rep.). (2014). Consulté le 1 février 2016 : OECD website: https://www.oecd.org/social/Focus-Inequality-and-Growth-2014.pdf

74 Rotman, D. (2013, 12 juin). How Technology Is Destroying Jobs. Consulté le 31 juillet 2016 : https://www.technologyreview.com/s/515926/how-technology-is-destroying-jobs/

75 US Bureau of Labor Statistics. (2016). *Labor Productivity and Costs Home Page (LPC)*. Consulté le 10 juillet 2016 : http://www.bls.gov/lpc

76 Bernstein, A. (2015). The Great Decoupling: An Interview with Erik Brynjolfsson and Andrew McAfee. Consulté le 3 août 2016 : https://hbr.org/2015/06/the-great-decoupling

77 Peck, E. (2016, 19 janvier). The 62 Richest People on Earth Now Hold as Much Wealth as the Poorest 35 Billion. [Weblog]. Consulté le 15 juin 2016 : https://www.huffingtonpost.com/entry/global-wealthinequality_us_56991defe4b0ce4964242e09

[78] Oxford Martin School. (2013). *The Future of Employment: How Susceptible Are Jobs to Computerisation?*. Consulté le 10 juillet 2016 : http://www.oxfordmartin.ox.ac.uk/publications/view/1314

[79] Metz, C. (2016, 27 janvier). In Major AI Breakthrough, Google System Secretly Beats Top Player at the Ancient Game of Go. [Weblog]. Consulté le 10 juillet 2016 : http://www.wired.com/2016/01/in-a-huge-breakthrough-googles-ai-beats-a-top-player-at-the-game-of-go

[80] Armstrong, S. (2014). *Smarter Than Us: The Rise of Machine Intelligence* : Machine Intelligence Research Institute.

[81] Social Security Administration. (2010). *The Development of Social Security in America*. Consulté le 10 juillet 2016 : https://www.ssa.gov/policy/docs/ssb/v70n3/v70n3p1.html

[82] The New Atlantis. (c2016). *Stephen L Talbott — The New Atlantis*. Consulté le 10 juillet 2016 : http://www.thenewatlantis.com/authors/stephen-talbott

[83] Leonhard, G. (2015, 22 novembre). Is Hello Barbie Every Parent's Worst Nightmare? Great Debate. [Weblog]. Consulté le 10 juillet 2016 : http://www.futuristgerd.com/2015/11/22/is-hello-barbie-every-parents-worst-nightmare-great-debate

[84] Google. (2016). *Google News*. Consulté le 11 juillet 2016 : https://news.google.com

[85] Hern, A. (2016, 13 mai). Facebook's News Saga Reminds Us Humans Are Biased by Design. [Weblog]. Consulté le 15 juillet 2016 : https://www.theguardian.com/technology/2016/may/13/newsfeed-saga-unmasks-the-human-face-of-facebook

[86] Baidu. (2016). 百度新闻搜索——全球最大的中文新闻平台. Consulté le 15 juillet 2016 : http://news.baidu.com

[87] LaFrance, A. (2015, 29 avril). Facebook Is Eating the Internet. [Weblog]. Consulté le 10 juillet 2016 : http://www.theatlantic.com/technology/archive/2015/04/facebook-is-eating-the-internet/391766

[88] Warren, C. (2015, 30 juin). Apple Music First Look: It's All About Curation, Curation, Curation. [Weblog]. Consulté le 15 juillet 2016 : http://mashable.com/2015/06/30/apple-music-hands-on

[89] Brockman, J. (2014, 03 février). The Technium: A Conversation with Kevin Kelly. [Weblog]. Consulté le 10 juillet 2016 : https://www.edge.org/conversation/kevin_kelly-the-technium

[90] Quote Investigator. (2011). *Computers Are Useless They Can Only Give You Answers*. Consulté le 10 juillet 2016 : https://quoteinvestigator.com/2011/11/05/computers-useless/

[91] Kelly, K. (2010). *What Technology Wants*. : Viking.

[92] DeSouza, C. (2015). *Maya*. : Penguin India.

[93] Kahneman, D. (2011). *Thinking, Fast and Slow*. : Macmillan.

[94] Turkle, S. (c2016). *Sherry Turkle Quotes*. Consulté le 10 juillet 2016 : https://www.goodreads.com/author/quotes/153503.Sherry_Turkle

[95] Barrat, J. (2013). *Our Final Invention: Artificial Intelligence and the End of the Human Era*. New York: Thomas Dunne Books/St Martin's Press.

[96] The definition of automate. (s.f.). Consulté le 10 juillet 2016 : http://www.dictionary.com/browse/automate

[97] Wells, H. G. (2005). *The Time Machine*. London, England: Penguin Books.

[98] Schneier, B. (2016, 04 février). The Internet of Things Will Be the World's Biggest Robot. [Weblog]. Consulté le 11 juillet 2016 : https://www.schneier.com/blog/archives/2016/02/the_internet_of_1.html

[99] Ellen MacArthur Foundation. (c2015). *Circular Economy — UK, Europe, Asia, South America & USA*. Consulté le 11 juillet 2016 : https://www.ellenmacarthurfoundation.org/circular-economy

[100] Sophocles. (c2016). *Quote by Sophocles: "Nothing vast enters the life of mortals without"*. Consulté le 11 juillet 2016 : http://www.goodreads.com/quotes/1020409-nothing-vast-enters-the-life-of-mortals-without-a-curse

[101] Leonhard, G. (2015). *Automation, Machine Thinking and Unintended Consequences*. Consulté le 3 juillet 2016 : https://youtu.be/Gq8_xPjlssQ

[102] Asilomar Conference on Recombinant DNA. (s.f.). Consulté le 3 juillet 2016 : https://en.wikipedia.org/wiki/Asilomar_Conference_on_Recombinant_DNA

[103] Internet Live Stats. (2016). *Number of Internet Users (2016)*. Consulté le 11 juillet 2016 : http://www.internetlivestats.com/internet-users

[104] Clarke, A. (1964). *Profiles of the Future*: Bantam Books.

[105] Libelium. (2016). *Libelium — Connecting Sensors to the Cloud*. Consulté le 7 juillet 2016 : http://www.libelium.com

[106] Gonzales, A. (s.f.). *The Effects of Social Media Use on Mental and Physical Health* (Rep.). Consulté le 1 avril 2016 : Robert Wood Johnson Foundation website : http://www.med.upenn.edu/chbr/documents/AmyGonzales-PublicHealthandSocialMediaTalk.pdf

[107] De Querol, R. (2016, 25 janvier). Zygmunt Bauman: "Social Media Are a Trap". [Weblog]. Consulté le 7 juillet 2016 : http://elpais.com/elpais/2016/01/19/inenglish/1453208692_424660.html

[108] Long, D. (c2016). *Albert Einstein and the Atomic Bomb*. Consulté le 7 juillet 2016 : http://www.doug-long.com/einstein.htm

[109] Long, D. (c2016). *Albert Einstein and the Atomic Bomb*. Consulté le 7 juillet 2016 : http://www.doug-long.com/einstein.htm

[110] Clark, R. (2001). *Einstein: The Life and Times*: Avon.

[111] Einstein, A. (c2016). *Quote by Albert Einstein: "The human spirit must prevail over technology"*. Consulté le 7 juillet 2016 : http://www.goodreads.com/quotes/44156-the-human-spirit-must-prevail-over-technology

[112] Barrat, J. (2013). *Our Final Invention: Artificial Intelligence and the End of the Human Era*. New York: Thomas Dunne Books/St Martin's Press.

[113] Kurzweil, R. (c2016). *The Singularity is Near » Homepage*. Consulté le 7 juillet 2016 : http://singularity.com

[114] Quote Investigator. (2015). *With Great Power Comes Great Responsibility*. Consulté le 7 juillet 2016 : http://quoteinvestigator.com/2015/07/23/great-power

[115] Rushkoff, D. (2013). *Present Shock: When Everything Happens Now*: Current.

[116] McLuhan, M. (c2016). *Quote by Marshall McLuhan: "First we build the tools, then they build us"*. Consulté le 7 juillet 2016 : http://www.goodreads.com/quotes/484955-first-we-build-the-tools-then-they-build-us

[117] Tokmetzis, D. (2015, 23 février). Here's Why You Shouldn't Put Your Baby Photos Online. [Weblog]. Consulté le 7 juillet 2016 : https://medium.com/matter/beware-your-baby-s-face-is-online-and-on-sale-d33ae8cdaa9d

[118] Hu, E. (2013, 5 août). The Hackable Japanese Toilet Comes with an App to Track Poop. [Weblog]. Consulté le 6 juillet 2016 : http://www.npr.org/sections/alltechconsidered/2013/08/05/209208453/the-hackable-japanese-toilet-comes-with-an-app-to-track-poop

[119] Jones, B. (2015, 14 février). Is Cortana a Dangerous Step Towards Artificial Intelligence? [Weblog]. Consulté le 7 juillet 2016 : http://www.digitaltrends.com/computing/fear-cortana

[120] *Precobs*. (2016). Wikipedia. Consulté le 7 juillet 2016 : https://en.wikipedia.org/wiki/Precobs

[121] Gartner. (2013, 12 novembre). Gartner Says by 2017 Your Smartphone Will Be Smarter Than You. [Weblog]. Consulté le 11 juillet 2016 : http://www.gartner.com/newsroom/id/2621915

[122] Rushkoff, D. (2013). *Present Shock: When Everything Happens Now*: Current.

[123] NPR. (2013, 25 mars). In a World That's Always on, We Are Trapped in the "Present". [Weblog]. Consulté le 8 juillet 2016 : http://www.npr.org/2013/03/25/175056313/in-a-world-thats-always-on-we-are-trapped-in-the-present

[124] x.ai. (2016). *An AI Personal Assistant Who Schedules Meetings for You*. Consulté le 10 juillet 2016 : https://x.ai

[125] Green, C. (2015, 02 septembre). The World of Digital Assistants — Why Everyday AI Apps Will Make up the IoT. [Weblog]. Consulté le 10 juillet 2016 : http://www.information-age.com/industry/software/123460089/world-digital-assistants-why-everyday-ai-apps-will-make-iot

[126] Sorrel, C. (2016, 13 janvier). Stop Being A Loner, It'll Kill You. [Weblog]. Consulté le 10 juillet 2016 : http://www.fastcoexist.com/3055386/stop-being-a-loner-itll-kill-you

[127] *Digital globalization: The new era of global flows*. (2016, février). Consulté le 3 aout 2016 : http://www.mckinsey.com/business-functions/digital-mckinsey/our-insights/digital-globalization-the-new-era-of-global-flows

[128] Microsoft. (2016). *Microsoft HoloLens*. Consulté le 10 juillet 2016 : https://www.microsoft.com/microsoft-hololens

[129] Brien, D. (c2016). *Computers, the Internet, and the Abdication of Consciousness — an Interview with Stephen Talbott*. Consulté le 10 juillet 2016 http://natureinstitute.org/txt/st/jung.htm

[130] McKinsey & Company. (2010). *Why Governments Must Lead the Fight Against Obesity*. Consulté le 11 juillet 2016 : https://www.chefmarshallobrien.com/wp-content/uploads/2011/08/mckinsey-q-10-2010-why-gov-must-lead-the-fight-against-obesity.pdf

[131] Centers for Disease Control and Prevention. (2015). *Adult Obesity Facts*. Consulté le 11 juillet 2016 : http://www.cdc.gov/obesity/data/adult.html

[132] HAPI.com. (c2016). *Enjoy Your Food with HAPIfork*. Consulté le 11 juillet 2016 : http://www.hapi.com/products-hapifork.asp

[133] University of Rhode Island. (1997). *Food Additives*. Consulté le 11 juillet 2016 : http://web.uri.edu/foodsafety/food-additives

[134] Leonhard, G. (2014, 25 février). How Tech Is Creating Data "Cravability," to Make Us Digitally Obese. [Weblog]. Consulté le 11 juillet 2016 : http://www.fastcoexist.com/3026862/how-tech-is-creating-data-cravability-to-make-us-digitally-obese

[135] Rodale, M. (2013, 19 novembre). Food Addiction Is Real. [Weblog]. Consulté le 11 juillet 2016 : http://www.huffingtonpost.com/maria-rodale/food-addiction-is-real_b_3950373.html

[136] *List of Largest Internet Companies*. (2016). Wikipedia. Consulté le 15 juillet 2016 : https://en.wikipedia.org/wiki/List_of_largest_Internet_companies

[137] Transparency Market Research. (2015). Food Additives Market by Type (Flavors and Enhancers, Sweeteners, Enzymes, Colorants, Emulsifiers, Food Preservatives, Fat Replacers) and by Source (Natural and Artificial) — Global Industry Analysis, Size, Share, Growth, Trends, and Forecast 2015–2021. Consulté le 11 juillet 2016 : http://www.transparencymarketresearch.com/food-additives.html

[138] World Economic Forum. (c2016). *Digital Transformation of Industries*. Consulté le 11 juillet 2016 : http://reports.weforum.org/digital-transformation-of-industries/finding-the-true-north-of-value-to-industry-and-society

[139] Cornish, D. (2016, 12 avril). Korea's Internet Addicts. [Weblog]. Consulté le 11 juillet 2016 : http://www.sbs.com.au/news/dateline/story/koreas-internet-addicts

[140] Taleb, N. (c2016). *Quote by Nassim Nicholas Taleb: "The difference between technology and slavery"*. Consulté le 11 juillet 2016 : https://www.goodreads.com/quotes/610828-the-difference-between-technology-and-slavery-is-that-slaves-are

[141] Grothaus, J. (2014, 22 janvier). How Infinite Information Will Warp and Change Human Relationships. [Weblog]. Consulté le 11 juillet 2016 : http://www.fastcolabs.com/3025299/how-infinite-information-will-warp-and-change-human-relationships

[142] Vanian, J. (2016). More Smartwatches Were Shipped Worldwide Than Swiss Watches. Consulté le 3 août 2016 : http://fortune.com/2016/02/19/more-smartwatches-shipped-worldwide-swiss-watches/

[143] Katz, L. (2013, 08 mai). TweetPee: Huggies Sends a Tweet When Baby's Wet. [Weblog]. Consulté le 11 juillet 2016 : http://www.cnet.com/news/tweetpee-huggies-sends-a-tweet-when-babys-wet

[144] Internet Live Stats. (2016). *Twitter Usage Statistics*. Consulté le 11 juillet 2016 : http://www.internetlivestats.com/twitter-statistics

[145] Brouwer, B. (2015, 26 juillet). YouTube Now Gets over 400 Hours of Content Uploaded Every Minute. [Weblog]. Consulté le 11 juillet 2016 : http://www.tubefilter.com/2015/07/26/youtube-400-hours-content-every-minute

[146] Thornhill, T. (2012, 02 mars). Google Privacy Policy: "Search Giant Will Know More About You Than Your Partner". [Weblog]. Consulté le 11 juillet 2016 : http://www.dailymail.co.uk/sciencetech/article-2091508/Google-privacy-policy-Search-giant-know-partner.html

[147] Carr, N. (2011). *The Shallows: What the Internet Is Doing to Our Brains*: W W Norton.

[148] Carr, N. (2011). *The Shallows: What the Internet Is Doing to Our Brains*: W W Norton.

[149] Leonhard, G. (2010, 04 février). Attention Is the New Currency (and Data Is the New Oil). [Weblog]. Consulté le 11 juillet 2016 : http://www.futuristgerd.com/2010/02/04/attention-is-the-new-currency-and-data-is-the-new-oil

[150] Goodson, S. (2012, 05 mars). If You're Not Paying for It, You Become the Product. [Weblog]. Consulté le 15 juillet 2016 : http://www.forbes.com/sites/marketshare/2012/03/05/if-youre-not-paying-for-it-you-become-the-product

[151] Cisco. (c2016). *VNI Complete Forecast*. Consulté le 11 juillet 2016 (actualisation 2017) : https://www.cisco.com/c/en/us/solutions/service-provider/visual-networking-index-vni/vni-infographic.html

[152] Leonhard, G. (2013, 27 juin). The Coming Data Wars, the Rise of Digital Totalitarianism and Why Internet Users Need to Take a Stand — NOW. [Weblog]. Consulté le 11 juillet 2016 : http://www.futuristgerd.com/2013/06/27/the-coming-data-wars-the-threat-of-digital-totalitarism-and-why-internet-users-need-to-take-a-stand-now

[153] Quote Investigator. (2011, 13 mai). Everything Should Be Made as Simple as Possible, But Not Simpler. [Weblog]. Consulté le 11 juillet 2016 : http://quoteinvestigator.com/2011/05/13/einstein-simple

[154] Asilomar Conference on Recombinant DNA. (s.f.). Consulté le 3 août 2016: https://en.wikipedia.org/wiki/Asilomar_Conference_on_Recombinant_DNA

[155] Overbye, D. (2008). Asking a Judge to Save the World, and Maybe a Whole Lot More. Consulté le 3 août 2016 : http://www.nytimes.com/2008/03/29/science/29collider.html

[156] Campus Compact. (c2015). *Wingspread Declaration on the Civic Responsibilities of Research Universities.* Consulté le 10 juillet 2016 : http://compact.org/wingspread-declaration-on-the-civic-responsibilities-of-research-universities

[157] United Nations Environment Programme. (c2003). *Rio Declaration on Environment and Development.* Consulté le 11 juillet 2016 : https://www.un.org/documents/ga/conf151/aconf15126-1annex1.htm

[158] *Proactionary Principle.* (2016). Wikipedia. Consulté le 10 juillet 2016 : https://en.wikipedia.org/wiki/Proactionary_principle

[159] Fuller, S. (2013). *The Proactionary Imperative — Warwick University.* Consulté le 10 juillet 2016 : https://www.youtube.com/watch?v=A6J8y6K178c

[160] Barrat, J. (2013). *Our Final Invention: Artificial Intelligence and the End of the Human Era.* New York: Thomas Dunne Books/St Martin's Press.

[161] More, M. (2005). *The Proactionary Principle.* Consulté le 10 juillet 2016 : http://www.maxmore.com/proactionary.html

[162] *Happiness.* (2016). Wikipedia. Consulté le 3 juillet 2016 : https://en.wikipedia.org/wiki/Happiness

[163] *Eudaimonia.* (2016). Wikipedia. Consulté le 3 juillet 2016 : https://en.wikipedia.org/wiki/Eudaimonia

[164] *Gross National Happiness.* (2016). Wikipedia. Consulté le 3 juillet 2016 : https://en.wikipedia.org/wiki/Gross_National_Happiness

[165] *Genuine Progress Indicator.* (2016). Wikipedia. Consulté le 3 juillet 2016 : https://en.wikipedia.org/wiki/Genuine_progress_indicator

[166] JFKLibrary.org. (1968). *Robert F Kennedy Speeches — Remarks at the University of Kansas, March 18, 1968.* Consulté le 3 juillet 2016 : http://www.jfklibrary.org/Research/Research-Aids/Ready-Reference/RFK-Speeches/Remarks-of-Robert-F-Kennedy-at-the-University-of-Kansas-March-18-1968.aspx

[167] Seligman, M. (2012). *Flourish*: Atria Books.

[168] Seligman, M. (2012). *Flourish*: Atria Books.

[169] Lama, D. (2016). *An Appeal by the Dalai Lama to the World: Ethics Are More Important Than Religion*: Benevento.

[170] Barrat, J. (2013). *Our Final Invention: Artificial Intelligence and the End of the Human Era.* New York: Thomas Dunne Books/St Martin's Press.

171 Weissmann, J. (2015, 14 avril). This Study on Happiness Convinced a CEO to Pay All of His Employees at Least $70,000 a Year. [Weblog]. Consulté le 15 juillet 2016 : http://www.slate.com/blogs/moneybox/2015/04/14/money_and_happiness_when_does_an_extra_dollar_stop_making_us_more_content.html

172 Hamblin, J. (2014, 7 octobre). Buy Experiences, Not Things. [Weblog]. Consulté le 15 juillet 2016 : http://www.theatlantic.com/business/archive/2014/10/buy-experiences/381132

173 Leu, J. (2015, 24 avril). One Word Could Hold the Key to Health and Happiness. [Weblog]. Consulté le 3 juillet 2016 : http://www.huffingtonpost.com/hopelab/one-word-holds-the-key-to_b_7070638.html

174 *J Robert Oppenheimer.* (2016). Wikipedia. Consulté le 3 juillet 2016 : https://en.wikipedia.org/wiki/J._Robert_Oppenheimer

175 Diamandis, P. (2015, 21 juin). Data Mining Your Body. Consulté le 3 juillet 2016 : https://www.linkedin.com/pulse/data-mining-your-body-peter-diamandis

176 Kurzweil, R. (c2016). *Quote by Ray Kurzweil: "Death is a great tragedy...a profound loss...I don'"*. Consulté le 3 juillet 2016 : http://www.goodreads.com/quotes/410498-death-is-a-great-tragedy-a-profound-loss-i-don-t-accept-it-i

177 Paz, O. (1973). *Alternating Current*: Arcade Publishing.

178 Rushkoff, D. (2011). *Program or Be Programmed: Ten Commands for a Digital Age*: Soft Skull Press.

179 Piore, A. (2015, 17 septembre). What Technology Can't Change About Happiness. [Weblog]. Consulté le 3 juillet 2016 : http://nautil.us/issue/28/2050/what-technology-cant-change-about-happiness

180 Frankl, V. (1964). *Man's Search for Meaning*: Better Yourself Books.

181 Dashevsky, E. (2015, 6 février). Our Exciting, Weird, and Scary Future: Q&A With Peter Diamandis. [Weblog]. Consulté le 3 juillet 2016 : http://www.pcmag.com/article2/0,2817,2476315,00.asp

182 Maxmen, A. (2015, aout). Easy DNA Editing Will Remake the World Buckle Up. [Weblog]. Consulté le 3 juillet 2016 : http://www.wired.com/2015/07/crispr-dna-editing-2

183 Parsons, J. (2016, 6 janvier). Sex Robots Could Be "Biggest Trend of 2016" as More Lonely Humans Seek Mechanical Companions. [Weblog]. Consulté le 3 juillet 2016 : http://www.mirror.co.uk/news/world-news/sex-robots-could-biggest-trend-7127554

[184] Knapton, S. (2014, 29 mai). Watching Pornography Damages Men's Brains. [Weblog]. Consulté le 15 juillet 2016 : http://www.telegraph.co.uk/science/2016/03/14/watching-pornography-damages-mens-brains

[185] AMC Network Entertainment. (2016). *HUMANS.* Consulté le 29 juin 2016 : http://www.amc.com/shows/humans

[186] After Moore's law | Technology Quarterly. (2016). Consulté le 3 août 2016 : http://www.economist.com/technology-quarterly/2016-03-12/after-moores-law

[187] Dictionary.com. (c2016). *Ethos.* Consulté le 13 juillet 2016 : http://www.dictionary.com/browse/ethos

[188] Brien, S. (c2016). *Computers, the Internet, and the Abdication of Conscious- ness — an Interview with Stephen Talbott.* Consulté le 13 juillet 2016 : http://natureinstitute.org/txt/st/jung.htm

[189] *Ethics.* (2016). Wikipedia. Consulté le 13 juillet 2016 : https://en.wikipedia.org/wiki/Ethics

[190] *Machine Ethics.* (2016). Wikipedia. Consulté le 13 juillet 2016 : https://en.wikipedia.org/wiki/Machine_ethics

[191] CB Insights. (2016, 20 juin). Artificial Intelligence Explodes: New Deal Activity Record for AI Startups. [Weblog]. Consulté le 15 juillet 2016 : https://www.cbinsights.com/blog/artificial-intelligence-funding-trends

[192] Metz, C. (2016, 27 janvier). In Major AI Breakthrough, Google System Secretly Beats Top Player at the Ancient Game of Go. [Weblog]. Consulté le 10 juillet 2016 : http://www.wired.com/2016/01/in-a-huge-breakthrough-googles-ai-beats-a-top-player-at-the-game-of-go

[193] Waldrop, M. (1987, Spring). A Question of Responsibility. [Weblog]. Consulté le 13 juillet 2016 : http://www.aaai.org/ojs/index.php/aimagazine/article/view/572

[194] Dvorsky, G. (2013, 07 février). Dalai Lama Says We Need a "Global System of Secular Ethics". [Weblog]. Consulté le 13 juillet 2016 : http://io9.gizmodo.com/5982499/dalai-lama-says-we-need-a-global-system-of-secular-ethics

[195] Cherry, M. (1999). *God, Science, and Delusion: A Chat With Arthur C Clarke.* Consulté le 13 juillet 2016 : https://www.clarkefoundation.org/

[196] *United Nations Special Rapporteur.* (2016). Wikipedia. Consulté le 13 juillet 2016 : https://en.wikipedia.org/wiki/United_Nations_Special_Rapporteur

[197] Markoff, J. (2015, août). The Transhuman Condition. [Weblog]. Consulté le 13 juillet 2016 : https://harpers.org/archive/2015/08/the-transhuman-condition

[198] Burton-Hill, C. (2016, 16 février). The Superhero of Artificial Intelligence: Can This Genius Keep It in Check? [Weblog]. Consulté le 13 juillet 2016 : https://www.theguardian.com/technology/2016/feb/16/demis-hassabis-artificial-intelligence-deepmind-alphago

[199] Pietrangelo, A. (2015, 17 novembre). Cesarean Rates Are Finally Starting to Drop in the United States. [Weblog]. Consulté le 13 juillet 2016 : http://www.healthline.com/health-news/cesarean-rates-are-finally-starting-to-drop-in-the-united-states-111715

[200] *Terminator Genisys* [Película]. (2015). S. l.: Paramount Pictures.

[201] Josefsson, D. (c1995). *An Interview with William Gibson (by Dan Josefsson)*. Consulté le 3 juillet 2016 : http://josefsson.net/gibson

[202] Rushkoff, D. (c2016). *Douglas Rushkoff : Official Site*. Consulté le 13 juillet 2016 : http://www.rushkoff.com